DIVORCE

When It's the Only Answer

DIVORCE

When It's the Only Answer

TEXAS EDITION
Newly Revised and Expanded

Robin M. Green

The Ordinary Mortals Guide, Inc.
DALLAS, TEXAS

First printing 2005

ISBN: 0-9760526-3-6
LCCN: 2004096287

BEFORE DIVORCE
PROTECTING YOURSELF
THE DIVORCE CASE
DISPUTE RESOLUTION
CHILDREN IN DIVORCE
PROPERTY DIVISION

Table of Contents

Section IV: Settlement and Alternate Dispute Resolution

Section V: Children in Divorce

Section VI: Divorce Property Division

Preface

This is a book about choices. The information about divorce offered here is provided to help you make *decisions* about your divorce. This is not a book about divorce for divorce's sake. It is for those in the process of divorcing, contemplating a possible divorce, or attempting to aid a friend or family member with a divorce or bad marriage.

In divorce, you have the choice of either letting the divorce process take whatever direction it will or choosing to direct events as much as possible so that you are protected and benefitted. You must choose between being a victim of the system or of your spouse and taking charge of your life. Taking charge of your own life doesn't guarantee that everything will *always* come out the way you want it to, but it is more satisfying than just being a helpless victim. Victims, no matter how "good" their eventual results, are never happy.

Encouraging you to take control of the divorce process is not a sales pitch for divorce-as-the-easy-way-out. Divorce is *not* a simple, painless solution. Rather, divorce is sometimes the only realistic choice. The decisions you make in divorce, as in the rest of life, will not always be easy and clear-cut. If life were such that we could always choose the sane over the chaotic, we wouldn't need a lot of coaching about our decisions. Unfortunately, many of our decisions, particularly those made necessary by a crisis in the family, are decisions that, if it were possible, any right-thinking person would choose to avoid. But there comes a time when these hard decisions can no longer be avoided. Usually, it is these tough decisions, the murky choice of the proverbial lesser of two evils, that really count when it comes to making life better for our children and ourselves. One of my goals is to help you make these difficult decisions courageously and as intelligently as possible.

A divorce is not a "thing" or an object. Nor, contrary to popular belief, is it just a few pieces of paper down at the courthouse. What those "few pieces of paper" say can affect your well-being, health, and happiness for years to come. If your well-being is affected, it is likely that your children and any future spouse will also be affected. The view of divorce-as-a-document also fails to consider that you not only have considerable control over what the divorce decree says, but also over *how* the divorce decree gets written. For example, a child custody order contained in a divorce decree procured by sleight of hand is not as likely to ensure that your children get the love they need from *both* parents, as is a custody order agreed to after careful discussion. In the first instance, someone feels cheated. In the second, after discussion, the likelihood is everyone will feel partly responsible for the decision and help to carry it out.

Divorce is a process through which you change from the *legal status* of being married to the *legal status* of being single. While the basic concepts of the "divorce process" are fairly straightforward and easy to master, legal issues surrounding divorce can become quite complex and cannot always be described in simple terms. Divorce cuts across several fields of law. As well as being a law practice specialty in its own right, divorce often involves the law practice areas of litigation, property law, legal accounting, real estate, business law, taxation, tort law, and contract. Divorces may also involve dozens of other areas of law.

As daunting as the legal issues may be in a divorce, these are usually overshadowed by personal, non-legal issues. For most of us, divorce creates an emotional crisis that centers on confusion about self-identity, family relationships, religious commitments, philosophical ideals, community expectations, and economic realities. When leaving or being left by a spouse, it is these internal and mostly non-public issues that confound our heads, break our hearts, disturb our souls, and upset our stomachs. One of the ironies of "the divorce process" is that these underlying realities of love and hate, fear and loathing, friendship, loss, confusion, personal growth, honesty and deception, loyalty and betrayal that are the driving force behind marriage and divorce are seldom mentioned by name in law books and are often ignored by lawyers and judges handling divorces. Perhaps this is as it should be. Although society's experience with these matters of the heart has shaped our divorce laws and court system, no sane person wants the legislature or the courts to regulate our individual choices about our intellectual, emotional, and spiritual lives. History is replete with the failures of government attempts to control the human soul.

But, the "divorce system's" hands-off attitude toward things spiritual, emotional, and philosophical leaves the divorcing spouse with responsibility for *value judgments* and *life- affecting choices* that arise from the divorce process. If you are to make your own decisions and attempt, as much as possible, to control and shape your life during and after divorce, you must acquire at least a general understanding of the legal rules and regulations that control divorce, child custody, and division of community property. It is these legal rules that allow you to impress your values and ideals on the legal structures that will control aspects of your life, property, and relationships with your children after the divorce is over.

Therefore, *the primary goal of this book is to get you thinking* about your divorce, what you want and need from it, and how all this fits into the legal system. If you are to impose your personal values, goals, and ideals on the divorce process, you will need more than a cookie-cutter approach or one-size-fits-all divorce advice handed out on recipe cards. Such overly simplistic approaches often deprive divorcing spouses of the knowledge and control necessary to choosing the better alternatives available from the divorce system. Often days, weeks, months, or years later, when it's too late, a divorced spouse learns the consequences of not knowing or understanding rights, privileges, and opportunities that were given up at the time of divorce. If you pay a little attention and do some thinking now, before it's too late, this won't happen to you. Where simple rules apply, I set out the rules, give some examples or explanation, and move on. However, many of the problems of divorce are such that to attempt simplistic answers would be to indulge in quackery. Examples of complex problems that only you can answer include deciding whether or not to divorce, choosing a lawyer, deciding which parent should have custody of your children, deciding what property is most valuable to you, and deciding whether to try or to settle your case. In these areas of personal values and preference, my goal is to work through the problem in such a way as to aid you in thinking through options about your own case. This approach should get you thinking about issues in your own divorce and stimulate your discussions with your lawyer.

No single work on this complex subject can possibly cover every situation and eventuality. The purpose of this book is to help you get an overview of divorce so that you can better understand, identify, and deal with problems in your particular case. By attempting to give you an overview of the subject, I am often limited to covering subjects in a few sentences that could easily fill volumes. Though you need to be aware of this approach, you need not be alarmed by it. The old cliché says, "a little knowledge is a dangerous thing," but no knowledge at all is a disaster.

Despite what I have said about the personal nature of divorce, if you are looking for one of those books that tells you that you don't need a lawyer to get your divorce, you might as well put this one back on the shelf. A divorce may or may not be a serious legal matter. It is the legal equivalent of recurring chest pains in the medical field. Chest pains, standing alone, don't carry little red tags saying "serious" or "not serious." Chest pains may be a signal for serious problems with the heart, or they may be caused by simple indigestion. There is simply no way of knowing until thorough consideration is given by someone with adequate knowledge to make such judgments. This is precisely the position you are in when you are facing a divorce. You cannot know for sure what you have to lose or gain until you present your facts to someone able to ask the correct questions and make good judgments.

On the other hand, I do not subscribe to that school of thought that says you should turn over all of your problems and decisions to your lawyer. Many of the decisions about divorce are value judgments that have nothing to do with law and are none of your lawyer's business. Even the legal decisions of your case require that the law be applied to the particular facts. You know more about the facts of your case than anyone else—your lawyer included. So be as informed as you can. The more informed you become, the easier it is for your lawyer to represent you.

Many books on divorce attempt to give advice to divorcing spouses in all fifty states. The problem with this approach is that separate divorce laws are written for and by each state. While there are many similarities, there are also many differences of crucial importance. Although portions of this book, such as the general discussions about deciding whether or not to divorce, coping after separation, some of the general discussion about child custody, and the federal retirement laws, are applicable to divorces everywhere in the nation, most of the book is specific to Texas law and those divorcing in Texas. Although I wish to reach an audience beyond Texas, I believe it is more important and useful to give more specific and accurate information, even at the cost of reducing the size of the audience.

This book has been written out of my own experience in representing clients in divorce cases, in going through a divorce myself, and in over thirty-three years of handling a wide variety of lawsuits in many of the towns and cities across Texas. Having a personal perspective on divorce is helpful, because by its very nature, divorce does not lend itself to easy quotations from law books, footnotes from a psychology text, or answers given by the great philosophers. But, because this book is based on my experiences, it is necessarily limited and certainly does not encompass all situations. I urge you to check and compare it to your own experience and to the information you gain from others. In short, use all the information, experience, and wisdom you can get your hands on. I wish you the very best of everything in your endeavor.

How to Use This Book

Readers of the first two editions of this book often surprised and flattered me by saying, and sometimes showing me, that they had read straight through this book from beginning to end. If you want to read the whole book, I certainly don't want to discourage you, but that's not the way that I expect most readers to use this volume.

This book has been written in distinctive parts broken into chapters and topics so that you can choose those portions most applicable to your divorce. The Table of Contents allows you to focus quickly on topics that need your attention. Likewise, the book is indexed to particular divorce topics so that it may be used as a reference book as you progress through different phases of your case. Because it is designed to stimulate your thinking and to give you a general understanding of the subject, the index focuses on concepts. Because it is designed to give you an overview, there are no references to statutes or case citations to distract a reader from the focus on basic concepts.

Finally, this book is designed to be used in conjunction with the legal advice you receive from a lawyer. It should make you a more informed and intelligent consumer of the tailor-made advice that only an individual lawyer can give you about your individual case.

SECTION I

Before Divorce – First Things First

In this section:

Chapter 1

Should I Get a Divorce?

By all means marry. If you marry well, you will be happy. If you don't you will become a philosopher.

—Russian proverb

Decisions almost never come easily, and if you set out to write a list of the most difficult personal decisions, the decision of whether or not to get a divorce would be near the top.

Clients who come to me to talk about their marriage problems often say, "I never knew that divorce was so tough," or "I didn't know divorce hurt this much." Divorce is tough. But what these people are often struggling with is not actually divorce, but the question of whether or not to divorce. As painful as divorce is for most people, it is more painful to be caught in between, to be uncertain of just what to do about your marriage.

One reason a decision about getting a divorce is so difficult is because it is a decision that affects your identity. It is difficult to know who "I" am without first bumping up against other people in relationships. Often, one of the primary relationships from which we gain our identity is our marriage. A woman may identify herself as "John's wife," or a man may think of himself as "Mary's husband." For many people, it is an anchor point from which identity begins. A divorce shakes not only the economic and social ties you depend on, but it also brings your self-concept into question.

Frequently, we go from being someone's son or daughter to being someone's husband or wife. In these cases, it is the thought of divorce that causes us, for the first time, to identify ourselves without reference to a family.

Although this may not appear to be a big problem to someone on the outside, it can be a completely disorienting experience for someone going through it. It is the equivalent of taking a desert tribesman from the hot, perfectly flat desert, where he has spent every moment of his life of thirty years, and placing him in a distant village on the side of a mountain in the middle of a rain forest. Although some few may be able to make an instant adjustment to divorce, for most it is a shifting of the ground beneath. In simple terms, it is culture shock.

Not only the spouse and the marriage must be given up, but an important part of your own self-understanding is surrendered: the realization that "I" will not be able to think of myself in the same way. This helps explain the difficulty and pain of divorce even for those leaving the most destructive of marriages.

Difficult Decision – It Really Doesn't *Feel* Like This Is a Choice

Divorce is like surgery; it's not a goal that most of us set for ourselves. Usually, divorce is not what we want, nor is it "how we want it to be." It's not something we plan for or intentionally design. Mostly, we think of it as happening to someone else. But then, there it is. Sometimes it comes gradually, like a strange, slow-moving creature, working its way into our lives. In other cases, it's like a bolt-out-of-the-blue, sudden and unexpected.

So, if divorce is not wanted, why divorce? Why do we end up doing that which we never intended and would prefer to avoid? The answer is that divorce becomes the better of the bad alternatives. Divorce grows out of marriages that become intolerable and unlivable. The pain or disruption of the marriage is so great as to threaten the emotional, mental, or physical health of one of the spouses or the children.

This description of divorce-as-the-better-of-bad-alternatives seems so obvious and simple as to be laughable. But for spouses struggling with the decision of whether or not to divorce, there is usually nothing obvious or simple about it. This is because, from the perspective of a spouse in even the worst marriage, the view of the marriage is confusing, murky, and contradictory. Often, the person who is the source of the unbearable grief and pain is also the object of intense love. Even in the midst of unbelievable family disasters, there is confusion about who is at fault. Then, of course, there is the question that towers over all persons who have taken marriage vows, "Can it be fixed?" The central premise of marriage is the idea that you don't leave if it can be fixed. In short, your "gut" can be telling you that divorce is an absolute necessity at the same time that your head is telling you that no one in his or her right mind would ever leave such a "good" spouse. Or, vice versa.

Now, to this confusion, add the fact that intimate relationships often live and die by the most exquisitely subtle distinctions. One spouse's version of "undying love" can be perceived by the other as a manipulative, controlling "death choke." One spouse's view of selfishness can be viewed by the other spouse as an unwillingness to live one's life by the dictates of another. Even spouses who are being physically beaten often have doubts about whether or not they are themselves responsible. Emotionally abused spouses often believe that it is their own failures or bad conduct that are creating unhappiness in their marriages. In bad marriages, the old joke about "who's on first" and "what's on second" really applies. Intellectually, neither spouse has a clue about "who's on first." Emotionally, the spouses "know" that the marriage is "in the ditch." The dispute is solely about why things are going bad and whose fault it is.

Enter divorce. *Divorce is about drawing boundaries.* The divorce process starts drawing boundaries *before* all of the intellectual reasons for the divorce can be determined and, perhaps, *before* the spouses completely understand *why* they are divorcing. Irrational? Probably. But that's the point. Divorce is designed to provide space between parties who "can't make sense of what's going on" between themselves. Ironically, after separation, some spouses for the first time begin, intellectually, to sort out the crazy stuff. You hear them say things like, "All those years, deep down, I thought his drinking was my fault," or "Why couldn't I see that it was her unhappiness and not my imperfections that kept us from being intimate?" or "How could I have lived all those years with someone who was only married to me when we were together in public?" These statements and others like them may appear trivial to the casual observer, but to those who have struggled to try to understand why their marriages were so painful, these statements change the meaning of the words "divorce" and "separation." Like the word "surgery," these words take on a new meaning. Like a surgery that removes a disease or condition from one's body, a divorce or separation that relieves emotional or physical pain is not all bad, even if a person did not fully understand why it had to be done at the time he or she made the decision to do it.

What Are Your Choices?

In making a decision about divorce, the choices are limited. You can:

1. Stay married
2. Continue in a marriage of convenience (a marriage in name only)
3. Separate
4. Divorce

If your spouse has not already decided on a divorce (which is a basic assumption of this whole chapter), then usually each of these choices will be open to you to some degree. Although it is important to understand these options, simply knowing them will not help you make a good choice.

To make a good decision about your marriage or divorce, you must first look at your dreams, values, feelings, and thoughts. *After* you have worked out these internal things, then the external matters will be manageable.

Make Your Own Choice

The most important rule in this book:

You are the only person who can or should decide whether to initiate a divorce.

Many decisions involving your divorce can be made in whole or in part by someone else. But not this one. As the kids in the dugout say to the Little League batter, "You're the one!"

No matter how ill-prepared you feel or how little coaching you've had, no one on the sideline can swing the bat for you. And, in this case, not to decide is in effect to make a decision—not a very healthy or helpful decision, but a decision. It is a decision that says, "I'm afraid I'll make a mistake, so I'll decide—even before the ball is thrown—either not to swing or to swing at every pitch."

This is not to say that you must make the decision about your divorce instantly. On this one, you may step out of the batter's box for days, weeks, months, or even years. You may counsel, meditate, concentrate, take practice shots, change your mind, pray, read books on the subject, compare your plight with the soap operas, or stall (hoping your spouse will decide for you). In most cases, you can even call in sick. But finally, "You're still the one!"

If you get assistance from other sources to help you make the decision, you are on the right track. If you are shopping around for someone or something to make the decision for you, it is a virtual certainty that you are simply compounding your problem.

So what if you find someone who is willing to make the decision for you? Of course, the world is full of such people. Often they are parents. But before you let some lawyer give you a Gideon Bible and tell you to return to your spouse, or before some counselor reads from the *Playboy* philosopher and tells you that divorce is easy and it's where everybody ought to be, consider the following:

> The question of divorce is essentially the same as the question of marriage. If you didn't agonize over marriage in the same way you're agonizing over your divorce, it was because you didn't fully understand the implications. For most people, the implications of living together, living singly, living with someone they don't like, or living with someone who treats them badly, go right to the heart of their moment-by-moment existence. A conflict in your marriage is not unlike a conflict in your religion, politics, or vocation. A marital conflict, however, is usually more *intense* and more *continuous*. Hence, the price is usually higher.

If your father wants more than anything else for you to be a member of the Republican party, the cost of faking it as a Republican could be fairly modest. You only need to remember not to wear a Democratic lapel pin when you are with him and to leave out those hilarious anti-Republican jokes your friends are so fond of hearing after a couple of drinks. Above all, you need to remember to say "yes" to all of your father's leading questions at dinner parties and family gatherings. Really a modest price—considering his weak heart.

If, however, Daddy "couldn't stand to see one of his children divorced" or demands that "his little girl leave that bum," the cost of faking it could be substantial. The price of staying in the marriage to please Daddy could be fifteen lectures a day from your spouse regarding what a horrible person you are. Or, if you leave to satisfy Daddy, the price could be the loss of someone you care much about, but with whom you had some normal marital conflict. Depending on what you want out of life, the price for letting Daddy decide for you might be too high.

And if the price is too high, even considering poor Daddy with his heart condition, surely you aren't gong to sell out on the same terms to a lawyer, marriage counselor, family doctor, or snake oil salesman, who pretends that he or she knows what's best for your life!

There also is the "catch-22" to consider. Even if you let Daddy decide about your marriage or divorce for you, he really doesn't. You do. You decide to let him decide for you. You have to live with it. He doesn't. Remember, you're the only person who can decide. *"You're the one!"*

There Is No Magic Answer

Corollary to the most important rule in this book:

A checklist does not exist that will tell you whether or not to get a divorce.

If you read next month's "Can This Marriage Be Saved?" in the *Ladies' Home Journal* and the facts are exactly like those you're experiencing in your marriage, you still can't cop out on your decision and simply go along with what the magazine says.

Although certain signs and symptoms are extremely important in helping you make a decision about a divorce, they are not definitive. For example, if your spouse beats you, it must be obvious that this signals extraordinary problems for the marriage as well as danger to you personally. One would think that this would be a sure sign that a divorce must be filed immediately. Not so! One of the greatest shocks (and there are many) for lawyers beginning practice is to find that the woman who was beaten severely yesterday, and for whom the lawyer spent the night preparing a restraining order, now wants to return to her husband. And many of them stay married!

The opposite extreme is the woman who tells a friend that she is unhappy in her marriage but that her husband is "such a nice guy." Or the man admits he is thinking about a divorce but says his wife is "such a good woman." Now, common sense would tell you that no one in his right mind needs a divorce from a spouse who is a "really nice guy" or a "good woman." Right?

Wrong! Often one of the clearest signs that a marriage is over is when the words are uttered: "But he's such a nice guy" or "She's such a good woman." These statements often indicate problems that may lead to a breakup of a seemingly stable relationship.

I repeat: There is no clear sign or checklist that will tell you what you should do about your marriage.

Staying married (really married) is not one of those things in life that can be accomplished by just wishing it so. A real marriage, as distinguished from the marriage of convenience, is a relationship that is held together by some magic "goop" that you can't see, taste, or smell—like the sunflower that's in the sunflower seed.

It takes more than magic goop, however, to make a marriage. Just as the sunflower seed must have water, sunlight, and soil, the magic goop must have the addition of hard work, maturity, patience, courage, faith, and respect. But you can't do without the magic goop. It's like planting a rock, calling it a sunflower seed, treating it like a sunflower seed, and expecting it to grow. Call the magic goop what you will—love, mutual attraction, caring, commitment, respect, tolerance—it is absolutely necessary. Calling it "magic goop" is just another way of saying that it is mysterious, personal, and not subject to definition by science or law. Only you, by searching your own soul, examining your own heart, and using your own brain can make this decision about whether your marriage has what it takes to hold it together.

Even though we can't see, smell, taste, or hear this thing that makes a union a real marriage, we do know much about it. We know, for example, that it cannot be coerced or forced.

Love is a gift. If your spouse does not love you or care about you, you cannot get him or her to do so with a pickax or a crowbar. The same is true of you. If you don't love your spouse, you definitely cannot be tortured into doing so, nor can love be pulled out of you with a tractor. That's what you get for being human.

There is a myth around that love can be manufactured even if you don't have it. I have heard people say, "If you would just try, you could do it." To me, watching people trying to fall in love looks a lot like someone trying to push a rope. If it can be done at all, its only practical use is as a circus act. Practically, it just does not work. You *cannot* manufacture love. If you don't have it, you can't give it.

One more thing about magic goop: It can be killed off. You may be one of those people who started off legitimately and passionately loving your spouse, and now all of that love is gone. This usually happens for one of two reasons.

First, the outside pressures—money problems, vocational problems, interference from parents, and so forth—can sometimes be so great that the relationship is soon identified only with pain. Then there is no reward or pleasure for the magic goop. Second, the other spouse can kill off the love with shabby treatment—by never being happy with the partner's conduct or person.

This brings us to the question of whether love that has been killed off can be revived. This is a difficult question. The answer is uncertain, and the risks are great. Sometimes it is clear that what's gone is gone, and that's that. When former lovers hate each other so much that they can't stand to be in the same room together, at least it makes the answer to this question easier.

But if you're in between, it's difficult. If you don't feel any great love, but you still value the relationship for what it is, you probably need to examine how much scar tissue has grown over the wounds you have inflicted on each other. Sometimes, this psychological scar tissue has built up to the extent that it shuts out the good feelings right along with the bad. Some call this the "rubble factor." You must evaluate whether it is possible to remove the rubble from the site on which your relationship was built so that you can rebuild. Sometimes there's not even room for a tent amid the fallen stones of what was once a cathedral.

This is the reason that it is important NOT to file for divorce until you are *sure* that you cannot stay married. The divorce will just be that much more rubble in the way of your relationship. Filing a divorce for so-called "shock value" to try to help a marriage does *not* work.

There Is No Cure-All

Sometimes I think that here in America, the "lived-happily-ever-after" story somehow got out of control. It is almost as if a biologist traveling in some foreign land had discovered a beautiful butterfly. Wanting to share the beauty of these exquisite creatures, he brought a few back home. For a while, everyone simply kept a few around the house to admire. Over the decades, however, these butterflies multiplied until they were eating all of the pages out of the books and the crops from the fields, with hardly anyone noticing anything except their great beauty.

So it is with the "lived-happily-ever-after" stories. They are a beautiful part of life. Some of life *is* happiness. But we are eaten up with the idea that if we are successful in the pursuit of our goals, we will be happy ever after.

Some people make decisions about marriage and divorce thinking about gaining or losing happiness for the rest of their lives. Or, perhaps worse, they may believe that they are creating or destroying their spouse's, children's, parents', or lover's happiness by this *one* decision. Yes, you do have some responsibility for others, but responsibility taken to that extreme has the effect of depriving others of responsibility for their own lives.

There is no doubt a decision to marry or divorce is a momentous decision. But you must get it into perspective. Two swallows do not a summer make. Neither does one decision make or break your life. If you decide to stay married, you probably will need to affirm that decision on a daily basis. Rather than deciding the future success of your marriage in one fell swoop, you will have to make hundreds of little decisions every day that will determine, in large part, the health and happiness of you, your spouse, and your family. The same is true in deciding whether to divorce. Contrary to the way you may feel at the moment, you are not going to make or break your life by deciding to divorce your spouse, nor should you allow your self-importance to get out of hand, causing you to believe that your decisions can make your spouse happy or sad into eternity.

None of this is intended to understate the very serious nature of the decision you are facing. It *is* an awesome decision! But, whether you know it or not, you have been making awesome decisions that determine the very course of your life and those around you almost every day since childhood. These awesome decisions will go on being made every day that you are alive—divorced or married. To be sure, in every life there seem to be certain crucial junctures where life-or-death decisions are made. Whether or not to divorce is just such a decision.

In making these crucial decisions, isn't it healthier to realize that we already have been making the decisions a little bit every day? This is not the last decision of your life, even though it seems like it. You not only can change your life later, but as a healthy human being you obviously will continue to change thoughts, ambitions, opinions, and even your view of life. By one decision, you do not freeze your life into a pattern forever.

Make a Decision You Can Live With

If you must live with a decision, it is not as important for it to be right in terms of some academic philosophy as it is for it to be authentic or heartfelt from the view of conforming to your own values. The decision about your marriage or divorce is more likely to be a good one if you understand that it is *private and personal.*

You do not have to defend your choice in a college philosophy class. As a matter of fact, you don't even need to concern yourself with justifying it in court or in church or in a conference with your parents or spouse. Are you surprised that I say this? Then let me explain.

In almost every divorce there are two sets of reasons for the divorce: the public reasons and the real reasons. For example, Couple A gets a divorce. The rumor is that the cause was the wife's adultery. The real reason is that there was no affection between the couple. They hardly spoke. He refused to engage in even the slightest physical contact for the eighteen months prior to the couple's separation.

Couple B is said to be divorcing because the husband took an extra job that kept him away on weekends, so he never had time to spend with his family. The real reason is that both the husband and wife have said they each secretly thought on the night of their honeymoon that their marriage was a mistake. Each entered into the marriage because it was the accepted way of getting away from home. In addition, the wife literally cannot be in the same room for five minutes without, in some manner, telling her husband what an inferior person he is.

You must decide about your marriage based on the real reasons. Later, in court or in discussions with parents, you may have to deal with the public reasons—what someone else imagines or thinks.

If you can't stand her face, then you are entitled to that feeling, regardless of the fact that the public thinks she is a beauty queen. If you love him and are willing to walk across hot coals for him, regardless of the fact that everybody tells you that he is a complete S.O.B., you have the absolute right, and maybe even a duty to yourself, to walk across those coals.

Why emphasize the private nature of a decision about retaining or ending your marriage? It is because we are so conditioned to consider others in making decisions about our own lives. From childhood, we correctly learn that no sane person wants to be around someone who always must have his or her own way.

If you always demand to see the movie you want to see or take the trip you want to take, without regard for others, you may find yourself doing these things alone. As an adult, you have learned that you must consider the desires of the boss, your spouse, your customers, and friends, to name a few, in making your day-to-day decisions.

All of this consideration of others is healthy, until it comes down to the critical issues that involve the direction of our lives. If we allow someone to influence us in deciding about marriage, vocation, religion, or philosophy in the same easy way we are influenced about running an errand or taking the day off, then we are likely to find ourselves relegated, at best, to a meaningless life, or worse, to a life of anger and frustration.

Give Yourself a Break

I am amazed at how hard people are on themselves, especially people who are in difficult situations. This goes double for those struggling with the decision about divorce. *Trust yourself.* Have confidence that you will make the right decision to stay or leave in due time. If you haven't yet decided, your subconscious probably hasn't completed sending this problem through all of the convolutions of your brain.

I predict that when it's through cooking, you will know it. I also would guess that you have a good instinct for survival, that is, for doing what's good for you. If your survival instinct wasn't pretty good, you wouldn't have gotten this far. If your batting record hasn't been what you've wanted it to be (and whose has?), assume that you're going to improve it with this decision.

In less sophisticated days, it may have been assumed that difficult decisions could be made better by those with PhDs, MDs, and such. In more recent and rigorous times, we have learned that while those holding doctorates, medical degrees, and law degrees sometimes do make good decisions in their fields of specialization, they frequently lack something called "street sense."

In shorthand translation, this means that if you were to turn someone with a PhD in urban sociology out in the middle of a city slum, he or she would be lucky to get out alive, because academic training has not given this person the knowledge needed to survive on the street. So, when you are berating yourself about how badly you are making this decision, remember—you probably have more street sense about the street you live on than anybody else.

It may be a tough street. If we brought in a substitute from the bench with really heavy credentials to take your place in the game, the substitute might not play the position as well as you. The expert doesn't know your street; you do.

There are some very good reasons for the inertia that must be overcome in trying to make a final decision to divorce. It probably would be helpful for you to try to focus on some of your particular reasons for having difficulty. To get you started in this direction, here are a few items that seem to be frequent, if not universal, feelings people have while trying to adjust to divorce.

The Loss of Dreams

At the beginning of this chapter, I talked about the loss of self-identity that people going through a divorce experience. Very closely tied to this is the suffering that comes from having to give up your dreams and aspirations. Whether you realize it or not, you, as a healthy individual, are probably very attached to your goals, your dreams, and your aspirations. Giving up your dreams can be almost as difficult as giving up your children.

For most married people, dreams involve the spouse, children, and family living together in a marriage setting.

Like your children, your dreams are so close that they are almost a part of you. Giving up dreams is the emotional equivalent of pulling teeth without anesthesia. About the only painkiller I know for stopping the hurt and disappointment of lost dreams is the gradual development of new dreams. This is more easily said than done, and it always takes time. So while you're giving yourself a break, give yourself some time.

Guilt

I don't think it is possible to go through a divorce without having to deal with guilt. This is true even in the most sordid and unhealthy relationships. As children, we are taught that if we work hard, live clean and decent lives, and are honest, then good things will happen to us. So when bad things happen we naturally assume that we must have done something wrong.

Most of us do not look upon our own divorces, at least at first, as a good thing. Usually there is a tremendous sense of failure. If this is happening to us, we rationalize that we must have done something wrong or dishonest or that we've been lazy. For most, it is as if the decision to divorce is a gut decision based on some internal instinct, an instinct that our intellectual, religious, or philosophical concepts do not yet approve.

It takes time for our intellect to understand that there are some very good reasons why our guts made the decisions they did. Again, this is a big problem, and if your psyche is sending you messages that you need more time to deal with it, don't rush yourself.

Fear

People approaching divorce often have lots of fears. There are fears of loneliness, being alone, making mistakes, losing children, identity, and respect, not to mention fear of losing sex, and its opposite, the fear of promiscuity.

I will be last in line to tell you that there is nothing to fear. There is much in this life that is worth fearing. My perception of life is that the water is deep and the current is swift. But I have also noticed that irrational fears are one of the strongest undertows likely to pull us down. So we must constantly check our fears against reality to determine which are real and which are imagined. This can be done by giving yourself time to learn about and deal with these fears a little bit at a time, as if putting your toe in the water. For example, if you are afraid to leave your spouse because you are afraid of being alone, don't begin by taking a vacation by yourself in the middle of the desert or by going to a faraway city where you don't know anyone.

Instead, give yourself time and opportunity to learn. Begin talking to people who live alone or have lived alone. Make friends with people other than your spouse. Gradually allow yourself to understand that your spouse does not have a corner on the market for companionship or anything else. When you approach the problem in this manner, you will learn that being alone, as opposed to loneliness, is a part of life that sometimes is painful, but (surprise!) sometimes may even be pleasant. This is just an example. But you can think of ways to work through your fears rather than just being a victim.

There is one school of thought that says you teach people to swim by throwing them in the water with no warning or preparation. Life is such that you frequently will be exposed to the swim or drown situation. For example, if your spouse walks out at a moment's notice, you will have to deal with all of the fears instantaneously. Of course, you will probably do all right. But when you have options, don't be too hard on yourself just because you take the time you need to get over being scared. Dealing with fear more gradually and rationally, when there is time to do so, makes infinitely more sense.

Getting Divorced Alone or Together

In making a decision to divorce, it is necessary for you to be honest with yourself. The slightest consideration of this decision process reveals that without self-honesty you are bound to make a hollow decision no matter which direction you turn.

Now comes the question of whether you should be honest with your spouse. Should you tell your spouse about the divorce:

1. When it first occurs to you that marriage is not what you expected it to be.
2. When you have finally decided for certain that you want a divorce.
3. After you have emptied the bank account, sent the family jewels to Switzerland, and hired a moving company to take the furniture to a secret underground storage location in Colorado.
4. Never. Let him or her learn of the divorce only when the sheriff serves the "papers."

For couples who have had open and honest discussion of their marital problems, this question is not so difficult. Both spouses already know that divorce is possible or maybe even probable. In these cases, the discussion of divorce is only a short distance from the question of the marital problems.

But what about the case in which the mere mention of divorce produces physical violence or threats of physical violence? Here you may deserve the Congressional Medal of Honor if you attempt to be honest. Instead, you will get a blood transfusion and your head examined by some psychiatrist who surely will ask why you value honesty so much more than intelligence and physical well-being.

And what about the marriage in which, at the slightest hint of divorce, the non-income producing spouse and the children will immediately be cut off from food, clothing, and shelter? Here the reward for honesty may be watching your children go to sleep in the YMCA, while you wire your parents for money to hire a lawyer to straighten this mess out.

Finally, what about the spouse who promises that at the first hint of divorce, he or she will take the couple's three-year-old child and flee the jurisdiction? Be honest with this person and you may lose your child. Sure, they *usually* come back, but why take the risk?

If you find yourself married to any of these types or the many varieties that are akin to them, you need to do some *thinking* and *listening* before you do any *talking*. Instead of talking to your spouse, *first* talk to *carefully selected* and trusted friends. Talk with your counselor if you have one. By all means, talk with a lawyer *before* you act. Learn what your options are.

Often the planning that needs to be done is obvious. If physical violence is a problem, you may need to break the news over the phone or with other persons present.

If you are going to be starved out, the announcement may need to be delayed until you get a job. If assets are going to be hidden or wasted, then you must either take possession, get a restraining order, or face the loss of your share if you announce the divorce unprotected. And obviously, if your child is in danger of being hurt or abducted, then you must remove the child from your spouse's reach before you announce the divorce.

If you think this advice is harsh, then I suggest you realistically consider the alternatives. For instance, if you were counseling others about a similar situation, would you recommend that they put themselves into a situation in which they might be beaten up, have their property taken, or their children hurt? Of course not. You would suggest ways in which they could protect themselves. Do the same for yourself!

Consider the Risk

If the risk to yourself, your kids, and your property is an acceptable risk, then, by all means, it is better for everyone if your spouse knows that divorce is imminent. You probably know your spouse better than anyone else. *After* counseling with others regarding his or her responses, you probably are best able to judge the risk involved.

There are some good reasons for being frank with your spouse. The most obvious reason is that it allows him or her to begin making adjustments toward a life outside the marriage.

But there is a more important reason. Chances are, you put a lot of yourself into your marriage: your sweat, blood, tears, and hard work. If you leave it now in a destructive manner, that is to say by stomping on it or spitting on it, you are doing these things to something that is a part of you. You may be establishing a pattern of destroying your own handiwork or believing that, if you do something, it is bound to turn out badly. On the other hand, if you can leave your marriage with dignity and respect, you may send yourself a message that even your failures aren't so bad. The best way to lend dignity and respect to the end of your marriage is to be as honest with your spouse as he or she will allow you to be.

And there is an additional message to all of this.

If you are the one threatening physical violence or threatening to steal the children away and deprive them of your spouse's love; or if you are hiding property or emptying the bank account, not to protect it or survive economically but rather to deprive your spouse of his or her share, then take stock. You are telling yourself, as well as others, that the marriage that you had a part in making is not worth leaving in a dignified manner. Protecting yourself is one thing. Spitting on something you have created is quite another.

"Practical" Considerations Aren't Practical

You may have wondered why I have waited so long to talk about the practical aspects of making a decision to divorce. Up until this time, I have talked almost exclusively about the things that go on inside your head and heart—your feelings and emotions. I have done this because I believe that the most practical thing in the world to consider, when you are deciding something as serious as whether or not to divorce, is to decide what you really want. People who spend their time worrying about what they might or might not be able to do before they even decide what they want to do are fooling themselves. If you make statements like, "I can't get a divorce because I don't have any money to get my own apartment," or "I can't afford to stay married to this man because he doesn't make enough money," then you are playing games with yourself.

If, on the other hand, you say, "I have decided to divorce my spouse, but I am postponing moving out now because I do not yet have enough money to rent an apartment," then you are on the right track. People who talk in terms of what they cannot do are using so-called practical considerations to avoid taking responsibility for themselves and deciding what they really want to do.

Once you have made the decision that your marriage is over and there is not any realistic likelihood that it will be repaired, you can decide whether you want to continue in a marriage of convenience, separate, or divorce. Most couples who ultimately divorce live in a marriage of convenience for some time after they have decided that the real marriage is dead. Some do it for a matter of days or weeks. Others continue in such marriages for years.

Many men and women delay telling their spouse until the children get out of school or the spouse gets through with some crisis involving employment, or until they themselves finish another semester of college, or until they can get a job, or until after Christmas, or until somebody recovers from an illness, and so on.

Sometimes people stay in marriages that are destructive to their personalities without fully realizing the price they are paying. The emotional cost of supporting a bad marriage over long periods of time is staggering. Sure, it is important for children to have money to buy their lunches, to have their teeth fixed, and to have shoes, but it is also important for children to have a parent who has self-respect. Sometimes people who stay in marriages for long periods of time to make sure that their children are fed end up having their children emotionally damaged by watching destructive behavior go on between the parents.

In deciding to delay a divorce and continue a marriage of convenience, you are merely deciding that the benefits of the marriage, at least for the time being, outweigh the cost of leaving. This seems to me to be perfectly valid. The only caution I would inject is that, in weighing the costs versus benefits, you should certainly add in this emotional price you and your children may pay.

Legal Considerations in Delaying a Divorce

Texas law recognizes only two categories of marital status. You are either married or you are single. Once you become married, the only legal way to become single again is to be divorced. If you are unhappily married, distrustfully married, grudgingly married, separated, or abandoned, you are still married.

As you will see from the chapter on community property, when you are married, virtually all of your income is considered to be community property—meaning that your spouse has a share in the earned property. Accordingly, if you are married to a spouse who is not earning as much as you are, or not saving as much as you are, or is not as creative in finding investments as you are, by delaying your divorce, you are on a daily basis, increasing the amount of your estate that your spouse will share upon a divorce.

On the other hand, if you are married to someone who is making more money than you are, it may be to your economic advantage to delay the divorce and simply remain married or separated. This is, of course, assuming that your high-earning spouse is not involved in the process of hiding or wasting already accumulated marital assets.

When you read the material on child custody, you will see that the advantage in a child custody case can change from one spouse to the other over a period of time. Therefore, if you are in a good position to get custody of your children, you probably should consider going ahead with your divorce now, especially if you think you are likely to lose that advantage at a later time. On the other hand, if you feel like your position for custody may in fact improve, it obviously may be to your benefit to delay the divorce to a later time.

Even if you consider delaying your divorce for legal or tactical reasons, by all means go ahead and seek legal advice on the subject now. It would be regrettable to spend months, or even years, of your life attempting to gain an advantage that turned out to be an illusion. Also, you would do well to scrutinize closely the cost versus benefits in the way I mentioned in the previous section on practical considerations.

There is always risk in delaying a divorce for tactical purposes. Your spouse may also be making plans for a divorce. By delaying, your case may be filed in a court that is less desirable from your point of view. Your children may be taken out of state. Bank accounts and other property can be spent or wasted. If you move, you may be moving to a district where the courts are less sympathetic to your side of the case. Of course, these risks frequently can be minimized by keeping your eyes open and being aware of dangers.

A Healing Angel Can Help You Make Wise Decisions

A decision to divorce is linked to many other emotional, philosophical, and religious issues. These are personal value judgments tied to ethics, morality, religion, psychology, mental health, and, even life itself. This book is to help you reflect on these subjects. But, comprehensive and specific guidance on emotional issues comes from a trained counselor.

A psychiatrist, psychologist, licensed clinical social worker, licensed marriage counselor, or pastoral counselor is trained to help navigate the emotional storms of the soul. Also, many community organizations, churches, and synagogues have divorce support groups. *Don't be foolish! Use these resources!* Good decisions must include a healing component. Without healing, we are doomed to live emotionally crippled lives.

Things to Do When You Separate

Obviously, if you are rushing out the door to escape a beating or protect your children, forget about the following list. If, on the other hand, your situation allows you the time to think and plan, consider this "checklist."

1. *Copy documents.* Copy machines are plentiful and cheap. Paying a lawyer to obtain financial records is very expensive and time consuming. If you do not have needed information after the divorce is filed and/or your spouse becomes angry, you may be required to pay your lawyer to help you get information that your spouse refuses to turn over. If your spouse will control the records after separation, make copies before you separate. Things to copy include:
   - Recent paycheck and check stubs
   - Tax returns
   - Real estate instruments, deeds, and deeds of trust, if possible
   - Loan documents, promissory notes, financing statements, etc.
   - Financial statements
   - Certificates of deposits, savings passbooks, etc.
   - Stocks, bonds, statements from stockbrokers, etc.
   - Bank statements, checks, deposit slips on all accounts;
   - Checks or stubs showing income from trust, oil and gas production, sale of property, dividends, etc.
   - Employee benefit plans, retirement, profit sharing, pensions, etc.
   - Titles to cars, trailers, boats, motorcycles, airplanes, etc.
   - Statement of charge accounts, credit card accounts, house payments, payment books, and other records of debts
   - Insurance policies
   - Documents evidencing ownership interest in corporations, partnerships, trust, or businesses of any kind
   - Correspondence or emails related to businesses or personal matters
   - Any other items that seem to be related to the finances or marriage

2. *Protect keepsakes, heirlooms, collector's Items,photographs, etc.* Consider your spouse's personality. If it is likely that small items of relatively large economic or sentimental value may be damaged or hidden, take appropriate steps to protect these items. Photographs, scrapbooks, letters from parents and friends, special gifts from loved ones, and family treasures are all irreplaceable and, perhaps, priceless. Additionally, most of these items are small and easy to carry. If you're the one leaving, it's about a thousand times cheaper to move them to your parents' house than it is to pay a lawyer to go to court and get them for you. If there's only one copy of children's photographs or other items that are meaningful to both you and your spouse, consider getting duplicates made so that both of you can have one of everything. Not only is this the decent thing to do, it will save the cost of fighting over these objects and the cost of one or the other of you being angry over something special being lost.
3. *Ascertain whether or not any real estate is held only in your spouse's name.* If such realty is community property, or if payments for improvements have been made from community funds, these facts need to be promptly related to your lawyer. Upon the filing of divorce proceedings, your lawyer will probably file a *lis pendens* notice to prevent your spouse from selling the property without your knowledge.
4. *Do some thinking about joint bank accounts.* If possible, talk to your lawyer about this subject in advance. Circumstances vary so much that it is difficult to make hard and fast rules about this part of the transition from joint finances to individual accounts. Obviously, if your spouse is financially irresponsible, you have no choice. You must immediately establish your own separate account.

   If, on the other hand, your spouse is supporting you by continuing to deposit large sums in a joint account from which you pay joint bills and draw your living expenses, you may be hurting your own pocketbook to enter discussions about separate accounts. In deciding whether to "raid" the joint checking account, consider the following:

   a. If you are responsible for the day-to-day care of small children, you must have the funds to get them through the coming days. If it is likely that your spouse will cut you and the children off from your sole source of income, take the necessary funds to get you and the children through the coming days until a temporary order requiring him or her to pay temporary support can be entered, and the first payment can be received. This means every penny in the account, if necessary.

b. If you are suffering physical abuse or threats of physical abuse from your spouse, use whatever money you can get your hands on to get away. Rent an apartment, buy a plane ticket, hire a lawyer, etc. Money is not as important as your neck.

c. Try not to cause your spouse to write hot checks. If possible, notify your spouse that the funds are gone, before the spouse writes the checks.

d. If the funds in the account are not necessary for your survival, consider taking only half. If your spouse cannot be trusted with half the proceeds, and you must remove it all, be prepared to account for every penny.

5. *If you have young children, schools and day care centers should be notified that one of the parents has a new address and phone number.* As much information as possible should be given about the whereabouts of both parents. Since you are no longer living together, your child may have a needless wait of several hours if an accident or emergency keeps the one parent away and the school or day care center does not know how to reach the other parent to pick up the child. If the "other" parent is not accountable, this is definitely the time to get grandparents, uncles, aunts, friends, or other trustworthy adults "plugged in" so that they can be reached in emergencies or when there is just a plain old mix-up.

6. *Check your insurance coverage.*

a. Make sure that both you and your spouse have your names on the automobile insurance policy. Most standard Texas automobile policies cover the "named insured and members of household." Hence, a single name on the policy means that the other person is not covered when separation occurs. If your name is the single name on the policy, you are still not protected. Since your property could be taken to satisfy your spouse's torts, you must protect your spouse in order to protect yourself.

b. If your homeowner's insurance provides coverage for personal property, such as furniture, appliances, clothing, jewelry, etc., it is likely that this coverage will not protect the property taken by a spouse to a new residence.

c. If your spouse is the named beneficiary on your insurance, neither separation nor divorce will keep your spouse from receiving the payment upon your death. If this is not your desire, you must change the beneficiary. This may not be possible until after divorce.

7. *Protect your credit.* You are responsible for charges made by your spouse on joint credit accounts, whether or not you have knowledge that the charge is being made. Neither separation nor divorce will change this. If you desire to limit your liability in the future, you must notify each creditor that you will not pay for debts incurred by your spouse.

8. *Consider changing your will.* Your separation does not affect your spouse's right to inherit from you. When you divorce, any provisions in your will providing for your spouse to receive property from you will be disregarded. But, this is only when your divorce becomes final. Until then, your will is unchanged by law. Also, if you do not have a will, your spouse, by virtue of being the surviving parent, will probably gain control of any property that your minor children inherit from you.

9. *Establish separate credit.* If all of your joint credit accounts are carried in your spouse's name, you may not have the credit history necessary to obtain credit in your own name. The Equal Credit Opportunity Act gives you the right to have credit information in your own name from accounts used or held jointly with your spouse. Changing the credit history to your name does not guarantee that you will be able to get credit in your own name since other factors such as your income may also be considered; however, it might help.

Chapter 2

Coping after Separation

What is madness? To have erroneous perceptions and to reason correctly from them.

—Voltaire

The courage to be one's self is the courage to make one's self what one wants to be.

—Paul Tillich

So, it didn't work. You tried. God knows, you tried. But it's now one of those marriages that's just a statistic. Well, that's how you feel about it right now.

At least you don't have to worry anymore about whether things are going to work out or not. There's a certain relief in that. But now other problems are coming into focus on the horizon. New decisions must be made. And they will be tough ones.

Tough decisions ought to come at a time when you are at your best. This just makes sense. You don't play a quarterback in a big game when he has a broken leg. You don't compete in the beauty pageant still in your pajamas and with no makeup. Both quarterbacks and beauty queens are pampered for months so that on "D-day" everything will be just right.

You may have noticed that things don't work like this in your average human crisis. Frequently, tough, agonizing decisions could not come at a worse time. Often, you must play in the "big game" while running a high fever or compete in the "beauty pageant" after unclogging the sewer.

In a divorce, the rule of thumb that tough decisions come at tough times usually must be multiplied by ten. In divorce, there is an immediacy to making practical decisions, such as: How can I get a job? Where will I live? How can I feed my children? Who can I get to work on my car? How can I learn to cook fast enough to avoid starvation? At the same time, the ultimate questions of one's life—death, moral values, philosophy, reason for being, self-worth, guilt, fear, loneliness, confusion, and more—all appear on the scene.

This combination of practical decisions linked with personal confusion can sometimes make life tense. In fact, it makes most people feel desperate as hell. Life turns into a nightmare.

So, how do you cope when you're in the midst of this kind of crisis?

First, you pull off to the side of the road for a while. Look the situation over. At least do some emergency maintenance. Look at a map to see if you're going in the right direction. I know you're behind schedule and feel like you'll never get there on time. But you may be going in the wrong direction.

One of the tricks that desperation plays on the mind is to make you feel like there is less and less time to cover more and more miles. You must get this distortion of time under control. There is plenty of time. Operating in a time warp only makes the desperation worse. The more desperate the situation, the more important the need to pull off the road to determine what is real and what is fantasy.

Another trick that desperation plays is that it causes you to start looking for simple cure-all solutions—like finding the pot of gold at the end of the rainbow or being carried off by the knight on the white horse. When you're hurting, really hurting, you will try almost anything to end the pain. And there's the danger.

For everyone who is careful about offering specific suggestions, there are ten others who have simple cure-alls for your pain. Apparently, it is written someplace in the universe that when one of our species is suffering, that is the time to surround him or her with simple, hard-sell solutions. If, during your deepest depression, you suggest that you need help, you may be told to get religion, give up religion, get an extra job and throw yourself into your work, quit working, take up tennis, get massages regularly, get into sensory deprivation, sell Amway, see a psychiatrist, see a fortuneteller, move to a new town, don't move, find "someone else," take a vacation, take up yoga, become a marathon runner, and on and on *ad infinitum*.

Divorce Hurts

Although I don't have any simple solutions, I can give you some information.

First things first. Let's face it, divorce hurts. It is important to acknowledge this fact. It is also usually very difficult. Somehow, many of us equate admitting to being in pain with admitting failure or admitting to being a victim. Understandably, we see pain as being negative. Nobody likes it.

Therein lies the trap. To ignore pain is to be victimized by it. To ignore it is to have it control us, rather than giving ourselves a fair chance to work through it and learn from it and to become wiser. To ignore it is to turn a part of ourselves against ourselves without even knowing it.

To acknowledge your pain is to get over it faster. You get over it faster because it gives you a chance to see what you are hurting about. For this reason, it is helpful to come to an awareness of the components of the pain—that is, what is causing it.

Loss of Family

When you separate from your spouse, you separate from your family, especially if the spouse was the only person in the family. More than anyone else, the spouse usually represents the closeness, the habits, and the structure that come to represent family. And the spouse represents sharing—if there is a single word that describes the family, that word is "sharing." Families don't just share common names and economic resources, they share common experience. To give up the family is to give up the sharing.

This is one reason that it is still painful to leave a bad marriage. Even when experiences are painful, unhealthy, or self-inflicted, these things still amount to sharing. To give up a grudging, sordid, or painful relationship is still to give up what sharing there was.

Although there may be some few who would like to go off like Robinson Crusoe, most of us need other people around us, almost like we need air, water, and food. When circumstances in the family become so bad that we must leave, this still does not relieve our need for shared, close, intimate experience.

It is written that "it is more blessed to give than to receive." Where close, intimate, personal relationships are involved, the statement should read, "To give is to receive."

Separation, though a necessary and enriching part of life, cuts us off from the giving and taking, and thereby causes pain. One can only hope that it will enable us to share better later.

Everybody Hurts in One Way or Another

Now you will want to tell me about all of the people you know or have heard about who didn't hurt during their divorce, about people who left their spouses and went for a walk on the wild side of life, seemingly without a moment's pain.

Well, you can't put all of life in one punch bowl. Some people hurt so much and for so long during their marriage that there's not any feeling left when they separate. Some have money, a good vocation, a desire to be out of the marriage, and a great lover at the time they separate, so that they don't notice the hurt—until the lover leaves or they tire of the job. You also know from experience that many people hide their pain.

Of course, there are people who do not feel much at all, or at least do not feel as much as you happen to about your relationship. Consider yourself lucky not to be one of these people. Remember, you also were able to feel the love, the passion, and the excitement of the relationship. Would you trade these things to escape the pain?

I doubt it. The truth is that for healthy, normal people, there is something about tearing apart intimate, close commitments that involves the inner tearing of one's self. This is true of lost friendships and loves. But it is especially true of marriages.

The hurt of divorce is compounded by the fact that the pain is not shared. If a spouse, a parent, or a child dies, family and friends all know and understand how much pain is involved. A funeral is held, meals are fixed, flowers are sent, hands are held, and tears are shed—together. Similarly, if someone crushes a bone in a car accident, there is an understanding that it hurts. The sharing of the pain allows the person suffering the loss or injury to know that they are experiencing a common, authentic feeling that is appropriate for this time and place.

With the loss of a spouse, friends and family don't always understand the hurt, or if they do, most don't understand the awful extent of that hurt. This leaves the person experiencing the pain alone, unable to share the loss with anyone else.

How long will the hurt last? A day? A month? A year? No one can say. It depends on you. On how long the relationship lasted. On whether there are children. On how dependent you were on the relationship. All that can be said is that, in most cases, it will get better, gradually. There will be good days and bad days.

Losing Your Role

Maybe it would get better sooner if we were to spend a little time trying to understand what is happening.

Besides the fear of being lonely, the loss of love, and sadness about the breakup of the family, there are other, not so obvious things going on at the time of your separation and immediately thereafter.

Being lost is not always a matter of geography. If you place the king in jail and begin treating him like a criminal, you will confuse him more than you would if you take him to a remote location in the woods but continue to treat him like a king. Matt Dillon probably could adjust to a visit to Paris if you allow him to continue to be a real Wild West Marshal. If somehow you could require Matt to switch roles and become a fairy godmother, you probably would notice some psychotic behavior—even if he stayed home in Dodge City.

Like most of us, both the king and Matt Dillon must depend on the roles they play to know how to act. If the roles are changed, we often won't know how to act.

This is exactly what happens in a divorce: The roles get switched. One day you're Mr. Jones' wife; the next day you're on your own.

Like Marshal Dillon and the king, most of us are more dependent than we know on the structure and guidelines provided by our roles. The roles we play tell us what behavior is acceptable and what is not. We can continue our own behavior from yesterday or imitate others in similar roles. There is a good chance that we will be more than slightly disapproving of those who play roles different from our own.

All of this applies doubly to marriage, because marriage is one of the more rigid and structured roles in our society. The structure, rigidity, and formality of marriage is so much a part of the everyday life of most people involved in it that they think of it as a part of reality, just like the air they breathe or the water they drink. This feeling often makes divorce unthinkable. Often, they do not believe the divorce is happening until their spouses do not come home. Or a spouse will return to a home where there is overt mental cruelty or actual physical danger because the structure of the marriage is desperately needed for him or her to carry on daily life.

But for the person divorcing, the discovery that the structure of married life is missing is just the first blow in a fight that goes on for fifteen rounds. The next blow comes when the separated person finds that he or she doesn't know how to act. As a married person, he knew that he must act married. He knew that she cooked supper. She knew that he would take care of the car and the debts. More importantly, others always treated them as a couple. Even when the spouse was not there, friends and acquaintances treated them as if the invisible "other half" was lurking about someplace.

Divorce changes this—overnight! Some changes may be minor headaches, as when supper doesn't get cooked or the car doesn't start because it wasn't serviced. Some changes are gigantic, as when someone calls to ask for a date. Or, perhaps worse, when someone doesn't call.

To fit into the new role and expectations, the divorcing people must act or react differently—whether they want to or not. If they don't change acts, they will be assuming a role that is actually no longer theirs. All of this is the consequence of a natural resistance to changing the structure and roles that are comfortable to live with. This resistance to change is most obvious when a person who has been married for years, apparently without being attracted to anyone else, "falls in love" within a month of the separation. There is no doubt that this person is in love. The only question is whether he or she is in love with the new person or with the structure of marriage.

Changing acts is not easy. Years of training often have gone into learning the old role of husband or wife. When the car breaks down, the tendency is to wait for the husband to fix it. When he does not, then you continue to act like a mistreated wife—as though he were in the next room rather than a thousand miles away. When the house doesn't get cleaned, the clothes don't get washed, meals don't get cooked, many men respond like the neglected husband rather than the independent self-reliant man that their new role requires.

Becoming Aware of Your Controls

Even if you can't see the roles, they are there. These roles can't be changed easily because, over the years, to maintain the roles, you have built in *control.* You expected yourself to act like a husband or wife. Your parents expected it. Your friends, relatives, and acquaintances expected it. If you grew up around parents who were husband and wife, you probably already had deep expectations for yourself in the spouse role, even before you had one day of practice on your own.

When you started to step out of that role, your self-controls pulled you back. "My God, that's not what a wife would do!" "What would Mother think?" Or, "I would love to, but my wife wouldn't understand."

These sentences repeated over and over, out loud and silently to ourselves during long periods of marriage, have far greater impact than any brainwashing.

So, when you try to switch roles, you are likely to stumble a bit at first, cry at second, and want to give up at third. You run into failures.

Failure here wouldn't be so bad if you didn't already feel so bad about failing in your miserable marriage. Your marriage—one of the most important things in your life—and you failed! Now, to add insult to injury, you're continuing to fail at starting your new life after marriage.

Here the trap almost closes. Most people begin saying, "I've got to get hold of myself. I can't fall apart"—which in translation means—"I've got to add more *controls.*"

If we were going to make rules about conduct after separation, when times are hard, the first rule would proclaim: *Be careful about making rules for yourself.*

In difficult divorce situations, people almost always say in one way or another, "My life is out of control." In moderately difficult situations, the person may say in a very calm, controlled voice, "I just can't get it together." But, in more difficult circumstances, hands shake, eyes twitch, speech is nervous and rambling, or the person is depressed and dejected. The divorcing person describes his or her life, in so many words, as being confused, disoriented, or, in short, out of control.

The temptation for one listening and watching him or her spilling coffee on clothes and carpet is to say, "For God's sake, get control of yourself—get some discipline in your life." Usually, no advice could be worse. A closer look at these people usually reveals that they are already over-controlled. Often people in bad marriages have spent many years struggling to "make it work." When self-control has not been successful, they have added more self-control. When the rules they have laid down for their lives have not worked, they added more rules.

But this over-control is not always apparent on the surface, because control can never successfully hold everything in. Psychologists have known for years that whatever is in you is going to come out somehow. If you are frustrated and angry and you don't find some constructive way to rid yourself of these feelings, these feelings will work themselves out in ways that are less than helpful: angry outbursts at innocent loved ones or friends, loss of ability to concentrate on work, a heart attack, a car accident, depression, guilt, alcoholism, excessive eating, loss of sleep, and so forth.

The longer you avoid or defer getting your pain and problems out in the open, the bigger the explosion is likely to be. It is like a boil that is festering. The longer you wait to deal with it, the more you are going to have to deal with when it finally bursts. It's just a matter of time. The cruel irony of "control" is that the longer you use it to live your life, the more danger you run of losing control of your life.

"So," you say, "how do I go about solving my problems by easing off self-control? How will I ever get any work done? Won't I just go crazy? Won't I lose all of my morality and virtue? Who will feed my children? What will my parents think? Won't I spend my life in a bar and become sexually promiscuous?"

Well, maybe. But I doubt it. My guess is that you really do want to keep your job or some other job and feed your kids. But if you keep trying to feed your kids and do your job out of the bitter feeling that this is what you *ought* to do rather than what you *want* to do, it could be that, ultimately, you won't really care whether or not your kids are fed or your job gets done. If you should come to this point, or if you already have, you won't do your kids or your boss much good. Beating yourself over the head to get the job done is like working with the flu; the job gets harder every day, and there is at least a 50-50 chance that the flu will get you before you get the job done—especially if it's a big job.

Control Kills Joy

Control kills spontaneity. By the use of controls, you may be able to hold in the bad things for a while, but to do so you must also hold in the good things. If you force yourself to hold in your anger, you may avoid temper tantrums and other emotional outbursts, but you must also hold in your love for your children, your deepest and warmest feelings for your friends, and your ability to work and play.

There is something that you need to know about control. It's scary when the controls are lifted. This is because "bad" things usually are the first things out when controls are taken away. If you have been holding in and you decide to stop living your life with your hands squeezing your throat, the first words out of your lips are not likely to be the happy song of some hit musical. More likely the words may be a not-so-nice expression of some perfectly awful feelings that you have. All of this can be pretty scary even if you're the only one who hears your rage. It can be doubly disconcerting if you happen to vent your spleen on the wrong person—someone who is innocent or someone you cannot afford to offend, such as your employer, your divorce judge, or even someone who becomes the perfect witness for the other side in your divorce trial.

For example, a woman who has forced herself to live for years with a man who beats her probably is going to have a difficult time controlling her anger. She may scream at the wrong people, fear the wrong people, make bad decisions about her personal and financial life. Her anger and desperate need for affection may cause her to make such bad judgments that they will scare her into returning to her husband, where at least she knows to expect another beating.

Control Increases Desperation

Many men and women in bad marriages hold out for such a long time that by the time the decision to divorce is made, they literally are starved for affection. They have controlled this need to love and be loved, to touch and be touched, for so long that when the dam breaks they are likely to make bad decisions in an attempt to get the natural affection they need. They are like the man on the desert dying of thirst. His thirst will cause him to drink poisoned water. Or his desperate need will cause him to waste energy running at every mirage that appears, thinking it might quench his thirst.

The big secret about keeping over-control from disrupting or harming your life is to *make healthy, pleasurable choices*. Give yourself some of life's pleasures and treasures—*before* you become desperate. If you already are desperate, then you consciously need to choose some healthy ways to pamper yourself with some of the things you want and need—before you reach the point of doing something harmful to yourself and others.

Again, I return to the examples of anger and need for affection that are so common in people going through divorce. If you are angry, close the door, pretend that your spouse, your boss, or your parent is sitting in the chair and begin screaming at the "person." Sure, you're going to feel foolish. But you will feel better. Or call your best friend and tell him or her that you need to vent your frustrations on him or her. All of this is better than blowing up at your boss and getting fired, jumping on your child for nothing, or getting angry at someone who is really trying to help you.

If you need affection, the longer you wait to show your children affection, attempt to find friends, or make some rational choices about time for yourself, recreation, or even lovers, the more desperate you are going to be, and the more likely you are to make a desperate decision.

The point is, even though it is scary and even though you are going to make mistakes, you don't have to be a victim in taking the controls off any more than you have to be a victim by leaving them on. You can choose to be careful in making and enforcing rules for and against yourself. You can realize that even though your self-control helps you get what you want and need out of life, it can also be a block that absorbs tremendous amounts of your energy in struggling with yourself. You should not spend your energy in this way. There are enough real obstacles out there to absorb your energy.

And Now for the Magic Answer

As you probably have perceived by now, I am against magic cure-all answers. Life in general, and divorce in particular, are much too complex for simplistic solutions.

But here I must succumb. Where the pain, hurt, and confusion of a divorce are concerned, I do believe that there is a magic answer. Not a perfect answer, but one that is so superior to everything else that it must be used.

You must talk about your feelings. I have hinted at this earlier when I suggested that, if nothing else, you should talk to a chair or some other object. And this is better than *nothing*, better than just holding it in. But what you really need is to talk to a real, live human being. You need to share with another person. This sharing has the effect of breaking through the isolation and the loneliness that is so much a part of the pain of divorce.

But there is resistance to sharing one's "bad" feelings with another person. As children, we are taught that we are supposed to share candy bars, walks in the park, fun toys, and picnics. At the same time, we are taught that we are not to share our dirty underwear, our resentments, or our doubts about life. All of this is fine for arm's-length, business-as-usual relationships. But it tends to leave us pretty lonely during times dominated by dirty underwear, resentment, and doubt. It also probably means that our friends will get to know only some plastic facsimile of the person we really are.

There is an additional, important benefit that you get from sharing your feelings. You will find out that your problems and feelings are not unique. The pain you feel is shared by everyone who is alive. When you share your feelings with someone else, you may expect that he or she will be shocked at the grotesque condition of your life. If the person you talk with is open and honest, the response you get will be that they too have experienced these same feelings. Although we don't experience everything in the same way, we all experience broken dreams, disappointments, and confusion.

Yours is not the only marriage that failed always to be a walk in the high country with the delight of a beautiful scene at the end of every steep climb. *Every* relationship has times in its existence when it is a hot and thirsty walk on a dusty desert trail with nothing but the hope of a return to the high country. Yes, *every* marriage relationship, including those that don't end in divorce. Usually what you think is a sordid and unthinkable marriage, unique to only crazy people like you and your spouse, is really just a chunk of real life that other people have experienced too. While understanding that others share the pain will not end it, it will help you know that divine providence is not visiting a special blight on your house only.

But getting your feelings out in the open and breaking through loneliness, isolation, and paranoia are not the biggest payoffs that come from talking about what you feel. The biggest dividend comes from discovering what you really feel.

Finding Your Feelings

Remember, in the first chapter I told you that the most practical thing in the world is to decide what you really want. This is especially true at the time of divorce. Since divorce is a time of new beginnings, there is an opportunity to make decisions that will influence the direction of your life. To decide what you want or where you want to go, you must know where you are now. More than anything else, this means that you must know what you are *feeling*.

You might think that during a divorce, of all times, people would really know what they are feeling. It is a time when feelings are strong. There is hurt; there is pain; there is disappointment; often there is relief. Love, anger, guilt, a sense of failure are all present. But it does not follow that people are in contact with their feelings, just because the feelings are strong.

Because there are so many strong emotions, the overriding feeling is confusion. "Life simply doesn't make sense. Life is not like they said it would be. Or if they told me, I wasn't listening."

In addition, if you are the typical person going through a divorce, you have spent months trying to hold your marriage together. Frequently, during this period you have repressed your real feelings while you were trying to make the marriage work. Usually, this process of repression has involved considerable time spent on *how things ought to be* or how the spouse *should* behave or how life is *supposed* to be.

If there is a part of the divorce process that is equivalent to cancer in the human body, it is described in the little word "ought." People literally ruin their lives, destroy their health, waste their precious time, energy, and money in pursuit of what ought to be. "We still *ought* to be married. He still *ought* to love me. I still *ought* to love him. We *ought* to make my parents happy. We *ought* to stay together for the children."

Well, "ifs" and "buts" *ought* to be candy and nuts. But they just aren't. The only way to distinguish between what *is* in your life and what *ought* to be, is to say it out loud so that you can hear it, taste it, smell it, and beat on it if necessary. But, by all means, figure out the difference between what you really feel and what you think you ought to feel.

You cannot begin rebuilding your new life from where you *ought* to be. You aren't there. You are here with what you really feel—whatever that is.

"So," you may ask, "does this mean that I can't cure myself by holing up alone? Do I have to talk to other people about my feelings to survive a divorce?"

That is the crucial issue, the difference between survival and growth. Divorce is a time when new growth and awareness about life can come about. You have a choice. You may end up graduating from a divorce being more of a person than you were when it began. You can have more of you with which to live life, share with others, raise your kids, pay the rent. Or you can choose to hold it in, be bitter, shrivel, allow your roots to attach to only the hardest rocks on the steepest slopes. You'll probably survive. And if you do you'll be tough. But there won't be much of you to share with others or to live with yourself.

You might even end up smearing your bitterness a drop at a time over your future relationships. This is a tragedy, since it is much easier to dump this bitterness *intentionally* in some harmless place and get rid of it while saving only the nice things to give the people you care about.

I am not against your wallowing in your misery. There is an ancient piece of literature that, to paraphrase, says: For all things there is a season, a time for planting, a time for harvest. A time for loving. A time for parting. And the list goes on. To this list should be added that there is a time for wallowing in your misery. It just seems to be a part of life that has to be done. But for God's sake, *do it!* Don't just nibble around the edges. Wallowing in your misery is like anything else; it needs to be done with a certain style, flair, and above all, class. I don't know what this means for you except to say that friends and loved ones, somehow, have an instinctive ability to forgive almost any wallowing—except dragging it out so that it looks like it is going to take up your whole life.

The Dangers of Talk

Thus far I have focused on the positive aspects of talking about your feelings. But talking out your feelings is *not* a free shot. It can be hard work. There are several ways that our talking can be harmful:

1. You can focus on whose fault "it" is.
2. You can make a rule that you *must* talk.
3. You can fail to act on the things you say to yourself and become a self-defeat artist.
4. You can talk yourself into undertaking impossible tasks at impossible times.

These pitfalls must be avoided. Since there is more than meets the eye, we need to look at each in some detail.

Focusing on Fault

In talking about the pain of your divorce, you may be tempted to spend considerable time and energy focusing on whose fault it is that the marriage didn't work. Sometimes, this is necessary for a few weeks or maybe even months. You may really feel that your spouse is a bum who did you wrong. Or that she never told you the truth. If it makes you feel better when you're hurting, go ahead, call names. Tell the people you trust what an S.O.B. he is or what a bitch she is. Just because you don't say it doesn't mean that you don't think it or feel that it is so.

But remember, you need to be focusing on you, your feelings and your life. If you spend all of your time focusing on what he or she did to you, you don't have a chance to learn about your own feelings so that you can begin rebuilding your own life.

For some people, the bad spouse becomes an excuse for everything in their lives—all of their pain and failures, all of their losses and fears—the perfect excuse for everything that goes wrong. It doesn't take long to figure out that this is another way of avoiding living your own life.

If your divorce case becomes contested over the custody of children or the division of property, then it may be necessary for you to spend time, money, and energy in establishing just whose fault it was in poisoning the community well. This sometimes can be justified in a divorce because the very nature of the adversary system demands that decisions be based on fault or responsibility. Not to deal in these matters may mean that you will lose your children or property.

It is important, however, outside of preparing for trial, not to get carried away or to spend your life dwelling on faults. The reality of life is that the wells from which we draw our water sometimes become poisoned. And you can spend your whole life arguing over who poisoned a particular well. Often this debate is of mere academic significance. More often, and worse, it obscures the real issue: How are we going to get a new well dug?

There is a very important distinction between *fault* and *responsibility*. Often it is useful to decide who or what is responsible for an event. By doing so, we can better understand the causes of the event. By understanding our responsibility, we may be able to avoid the recurrence of the event, if it was unpleasant. Or we can cause it to occur again if it was pleasant. Or, if the responsibility belongs to someone else, then we can stop worrying about our own responsibility and move on to other things.

Fault, on the other hand, carries more pejorative connotations. Not only do we decide who or what caused the event to take place, we then go on to pass moral judgments on it. Passing moral judgment may be all right sometimes, but it takes a lot of energy that may be needed elsewhere.

When the decision for a divorce is made, the real issue becomes, *"How are the parties as individuals going to live the rest of their lives?"* Time spent rehashing the awful events of the last two years, five years, or twenty-five years of marriage wastes precious time, energy, and thought on matters that benefit no one.

Worse than squabbling over fault is faulting yourself—that is, passing heavy-handed moral judgment on your actions. This is not to say that you are not to take responsibility for your own life. To the contrary, personal responsibility means the difference between an anemic existence and a vital, full life. But faulting yourself, ironically and paradoxically, often leads to the avoidance of personal responsibility. The harsh moral judgment that is implicit in the word "fault" means that there is a need for a penance beyond one's control. Saying "I made a mistake" implies that I am responsible and can change my actions in the future. Saying "I was a bad boy" implies that I will be punished, that my future is beyond my control, out of my hands, and *not my responsibility* because of my nature.

There is an additional reason for avoiding heavy-handed self-judgment at the time of divorce. If there is a central theme to divorce, that theme is separation—separation from one's spouse, lover, family, and usually many friends and acquaintances who do not understand or approve. Harsh self-appraisals usually cause people to stand apart or isolate themselves from others that much more. You don't need this. There is already too much separation in your life.

But *not* faulting oneself is easier said than done. The overriding feeling of most people at the time of divorce is failure. "I have failed at something that was of major importance in my life. I have let myself and everyone close to me down." This sick feeling, gnawing in the pit of one's stomach, may recur for days on end at unexpected moments. It is difficult, indeed, to shake off once it attaches itself to your psyche.

Self-forgiveness may be the single most difficult thing in life. The Catholics have worked it out so that forgiveness must be dispensed by someone else—the priest. Although I am not a Catholic, I believe they may be sensible to require that forgiveness come from someone else. It may be that absolving our own failure, losses, and inadequacies is so difficult that we need to hear some other human being say, "It's all right—what's done is done—now you need to move on from the past and live in the present to build for the future."

If we must allocate responsibility, then we ought to realize that not all responsibility for failure of a marriage can be laid at the feet of the spouses. Our culture has extraordinary and unrealistic expectations for marriages. Marriage often is viewed as a panacea for solving every social, economic, physical, and emotional need in one's life. These expectations cannot be attributed to individuals alone. They are group expectations that are implicit in almost every social institution from the local church to nationwide advertising. Not infrequently, people marry as an escape. But upon entering the institution, the parties learn that it is extraordinarily complicated, with intricate convolutions that aren't apparent from viewing wedding pictures or even from sitting at the table listening to Mom and Dad discuss their problems.

Then, as if this weren't enough, the world around the institution of marriage has changed. There was a time when marriage was the main economic unit, not to mention the main unit of contact with other human beings. A couple might live on a farm miles from anyone else with only each other to ward off starvation and loneliness. Now many marriages exist in circumstances where both partners are working and hardly see each other. Often there is no common external purpose or goal for them to work toward together. Like people, institutions such as marriage need purpose and meaning to continue to be alive and vital.

So, is it any wonder that marriages die on the vine, even when the best of people are involved?

A Suggestion to Be Used for You – Not a Rule to Be Used against You

Before leaving the subject of feelings, there is something I must clarify: By saying that you should talk about your feelings, I am making a suggestion, not a rule. I am suggesting that you give yourself the *opportunity* to talk, not that you *force* yourself to talk and listen. If you can talk now, do so. If you can't, you may have to wait until you are ready.

You must have faith in yourself. You may have problems. You may have done something wrong, but you probably are doing much right—even if you can't talk. Each person has built-in experiences and instincts that equip him or her to handle individual pain better than anyone else. Therefore, I think that it is important to be very careful about handing out rules, regulations, harsh criticism, or demands to people when they are experiencing pain and struggle. The human body and spirit did not get to this point in evolution by being a slouchy, self-destroying mechanism. We must have faith that the healthy instincts will come through and that self-healing will do its work.

The Importance of Becoming an Actor

But just talking about your feelings is not enough. You must *listen* to what you say. And listening is not enough. The point of all of this talking and listening is for you to find out what you are feeling and thinking so that you will know what you *want* and where you want to go from here.

When I was in college, we spent time philosophizing about which was more important, "doing" or "being." Well, now I am certain that both of these things are the same. If you want to change your life and become a better, stronger, and wiser person, you must do so by *acting* on your aspirations to *be* that person. Talking about becoming is important, but it is just a beginning. The talk must be translated into concrete acts. If, on the other hand, you aspire to certain accomplishments for yourself, you must *decide* to become a different person to do these new things that you have never done.

We all know some academic type that can explain everything about his life from why his hair is curly to why his tenth marriage didn't work. This type is not much better than the chronic complainer who spends his whole life telling everyone who will listen how bad his life is. This is what *just* talking will get you. Be careful! It is very easy for your life to become just one big excuse.

Living, not just existing, is what life is all about. Marriage or no marriage, divorce or no divorce, life goes on. And you get to choose whether you want to participate in the direction it takes or just be swept along with the tide.

Set Realistic Goals

Many times after the shock of separation is over, there comes a shock from the assessment of damages. The people involved no longer have all of the resources of the family available. Some lose their homes. Others lose security and a meal ticket when the working spouse leaves. Others lose housekeepers, lovers, and counselors. Everybody loses habits, customs, and structures that were taken for granted.

The devastation of these losses often produces a desire to paint with a very broad brush. Those without homes set out to rebuild homes—overnight. Those who need jobs set out to get jobs—good jobs—right away. And those in need of love often set goals for finding Mr. or Ms. Wonderful by the end of the month. In short, people in their need to recoup try to build the Great Wall of China overnight.

There is nothing wrong with any of these goals. We all need goals and dreams. We all need homes, jobs, and lovers. Some of us even need to build the Great Wall or undertake some other project just as ambitious. But not in a week or a month and probably not in a year.

Let's be sensible. We are talking about starting over, often from a little above scratch. Some few may have the financial resources to go out and buy a house just like the one they had before and move in this week. Others may have instant avenues for new and exciting careers that they can step into overnight. Some few others may find the lover of their dreams waiting in the wings. But these occurrences are unusual and even when found aren't always what they seem to be.

For most of us mortals, the good things in life take time, especially after a divorce. And to ignore this is to set yourself up for a double whammy. You may think that the only way to cure the pain of your losses is to recoup everything overnight. But you will just demoralize yourself.

People who expect to find a lover in thirty days usually end the thirty days with the equally unrealistic assessment that, "I will never find a lover." People who expect to rebuild homes, with all the warmth, comfort, and good feeling of the old home in ten days usually end the ten days being demoralized by thinking that the task is an impossibility that should be abandoned. And those that give themselves two years to find happiness...

To be sure, most people who go through this unrealistic goal-setting process end up coming back with more realistic terms so that they can accomplish their dreams. But it is usually after periods of depression in which valuable time and energy are lost.

And, of course, these unrealistic goals may just be another way of excusing yourself from taking responsibility for your own life. *You* cannot move into the castle of your dreams and entertain the Knights of the Roundtable. You *can* clean up your apartment and have some friends over.

Divorce is a time for beginning again and for dreaming new dreams—big dreams. But it is also a time to force yourself to ground these dreams, large or small, by working on specifics one at a time. If your pain causes you to have trouble in bringing yourself back to the day-to-day problems of existence, use a pencil and paper to list specific little things that you must do. Force yourself to do one thing at a time.

One of the things that I have noticed about people who are in difficulty is that those who can deal with *specifics* usually begin to make positive progress. Those who can deal with one relevant fact at a time about their lawsuits are more likely to win than those who can tell their lawyer all about their lawsuit, how it ought to be tried, how it is going to come out, and what everyone they have talked to about it has said, but cannot bring themselves to deal with a single, relevant fact. Many people can tell you all about building a house, but never even get around to buying a set of blueprints. Those who can saw one board at a time or nail one nail at a time usually and eventually build a house.

Conclusion – Yes, Virginia, There Is a Santa Claus. It's Just Really Hard to Get to Know Him

And now we've come a good distance, talking mostly about what you want: about how figuring out what you want is the most practical thing in the world. We've covered the waterfront on the subjects of talking about your feelings, listening to yourself, and finally, working toward what you want.

But what is it that we're all working toward and trying to achieve? Well, you already know that nobody can tell anybody whether to be a butcher, a baker, or a candlestick maker. Such things are matters of individual preference and depend on opportunities involving time, place, and circumstance. I am also sure that you are painfully aware that the store shelves are full of books that at least imply that they will cure all your troubles and make you happy, such as *Eternal Happiness through a Salt-Free Diet.*

But there is a lesson on divorce that shows us an ideal to work toward while pursuing our individual choices of vocation, lifestyle, hobbies, and child rearing. We each need to be working toward being more independent, self-sufficient people who can stand on our own feet and live from the power of our own self-esteem.

I believe this is a lesson of divorce because most of us came out of marriages that had as their dominant features dependence on, and possessiveness of, one or both partners. As we are now painfully aware, these are not good features on which to build a relationship or live a life.

I am not advocating independence and self-sufficiency of a chauvinistic, narcissistic, or exclusive type. To the contrary. I am saying that we can only truly *share* ourselves, our personalities, our possessions, and our love with other people when we hold ourselves in high enough self-esteem to give these things without expecting an exact *quid pro quo* in return. If we cannot stand on our own feet, what we give to those around us is merely bait that we use to lure in those things we must have because we are so dependent. When we do this, we leave the blissful mount of intimacy and enter the rigorous field of politics.

When we can be independent and allow others close to us to be themselves without trying to possess them, we finally can offer those we care about an authentic, real person—not just a reflection of the desperation produced by the image on some billboard. Though some may be threatened by this independence and self-sufficiency, others will be attracted by your authenticity. They get to work or play with a real person. Your children get a real parent. Your lover gets a real lover and friend. And most important of all, you get you.

Chapter 3

Basic Divorce Concepts

It takes two to make a marriage a success and only one a failure.

—Herbert Samual

Because divorce is so commonly experienced by our families, friends, and acquaintances, you may already be familiar with most of the information in this short chapter. But, just in case you don't know some of the basic concepts concerning divorce, here are some terms and concepts you are likely to encounter when discussing the subject.

What Is a Divorce?

A divorce is a lawsuit to change the *status* of a relationship between two people from that of marriage to that of separate, single, unrelated people. The law requires that courts hearing divorces also deal with other ancillary issues such as property division, child custody, and child support.

A lawsuit carries the implication of strife, discord, and disagreement. But sometimes the parties to a lawsuit end up settling the case and agreeing to enter a court order reflecting that settlement.

This happens frequently in divorce. Sometimes, both spouses want a divorce, and there is no property or custody to dispute. At other times the parties reach an agreement as to how they want the property divided, who is to have custody of children, and how much support is to be paid. These cases are commonly called *uncontested divorces*.

If your divorce is uncontested, this means there is nothing to worry about at the final hearing. All of the decisions have been made ahead of time—before you arrive at the courthouse. Everyone knows how things are likely to come out. In the highly unlikely event that the judge does not go along with your settlement agreement, you will be allowed to go away and return on another day with a new settlement agreement or with preparation made for a contested hearing.

The lawsuit on an uncontested divorce is more like a short ritual than a lawsuit. The lawyer for the petitioner merely asks the petitioner a few simple questions. These questions are designed to prove the facts alleged in the Original Petition. The detail required in this testimony varies slightly from judge to judge, but usually an uncontested divorce hearing is over in five or ten minutes.

The term *uncontested divorce* is often used and has a variety of meanings. Seldom is a divorce completely uncontested. But even though couples usually have at least some differences or disputes, the majority of divorces, after discussion and negotiation, end up with *uncontested settlements*. On the other hand, some that begin as friendly, *uncontested* agreements end up as bitter battles.

So, when a lawyer advertises rates for uncontested divorces, or a friend tells you that you don't need to go to court because your case is uncontested, *beware!* You may get fooled by the term. Decisions need to be made on specific facts, and fees need to be set with specific understandings of who will do what, not based on a vague term.

Jurisdiction, Venue, and Residence

To maintain a divorce in Texas, *either* you or your spouse must have been a domiciliary of the state for the preceding six-month period and a resident of the county in which the suit is filed for the preceding ninety-day period. These periods are counted backward from the day the petition is *filed*.

The terms "domiciliary" and "resident" mean, roughly, that this is where you have been living. If you have been physically present in one place, the high probability is that this is where you are domiciled or have residency. College students and military personnel, however, *might* be away in school or in the service and have their residency "back home." You may take vacations or travel for a living and be gone from home without losing your domicile or residence, as these concepts also involve your intentions, as well as your physical presence and the location of your household goods.

After the petition has been filed, while the case is pending, you may move to some other location without having the court where your case is filed lose jurisdiction or venue. The critical period for residency purposes is *before* the case is *filed.*

Waiting Period

"A divorce shall not be granted until at least sixty days have elapsed since the day the suit was filed."

This law does not mean that your divorce *will* be granted on the sixtieth day after it is filed. That will depend on the judge's schedule, whether your case is contested, and other things. It means you cannot get a divorce in less than sixty days.

Grounds for Divorce

There was a time not too long ago when society would not grant divorce unless there was fault on the part of one person or the other. Marriage was seen as a contract that you could not escape unless you proved your spouse had done you wrong. As social values changed, it became a frequent occurrence for couples to stage fault on the part of one or the other so they could get out of hopeless marriages.

Now the law has changed. In addition to the fault grounds such as cruelty and adultery, a no-fault ground of divorce is available. This no-fault ground is referred to as *insupportability*. The statute reads:

> "On the petition of either party to a marriage, a divorce may be decreed without regard to fault if the marriage has become insupportable because of discord or conflict of personalities that destroys the legitimate ends of the marriage relationship and prevents any reasonable expectation of reconciliation."

This now means that any partner who does not want to be in a marriage can get out lawfully. The vast majority of all Texas divorces are granted on this no-fault ground.

Texas has also retained the fault grounds of cruelty, adultery, conviction of a felony, abandonment, living apart, and confinement in a mental hospital.

These fault grounds are virtually useless, except in cases where the court is being asked to make an unequal division of community property. Since judges are allowed to divide community property based on fault, in an aggravated situation where there is property involved, it might make sense to allege a fault ground if one exists. Alleging fault in a divorce involving a child custody dispute might be useful. However, judges usually are eager to hear all evidence that relates to the child, with or without fault pleadings.

Defenses

In earlier times when divorce had to be grounded on fault, courts allowed defenses to the divorce to be raised. For example, adultery was a defense to a divorce as well as a ground for it. A spouse could block a divorce by showing that the spouse who was asking for the divorce had committed adultery.

These defenses have now been pretty much abolished. The defense of *condonation* (it is assumed that having intercourse with a spouse *after* knowledge of the wrong alleged as a ground for the divorce constitutes forgiveness of the wrong) technically has been retained. It is hard to see how it would be useful, given the no-fault approach.

The fact is, anyone who wants a divorce can get it. The other spouse may be able to delay or stall, but ultimately a spouse committed to divorce is going to succeed.

Required Counseling

The judge has the authority to require the couple to counsel with any person chosen by the court. As a practical matter, very few spouses request court enforced counseling. Many judges will grant request for counseling on a limited basis. Few judges will insist on more than one or two sessions, if both persons do not agree to it. This is because judges know that counseling must be voluntary before there is much hope of success.

Appointed counselors are not allowed to testify in the divorce or in any other suit involving the couple or their children. Counselors are required to file a written report stating whether there is a reasonable expectation of reconciliation, and if so, whether further counseling would help.

Common-Law Marriages

If the marriage is a common-law marriage, does the couple need a divorce? Yes. A common-law marriage is a marriage entered into without benefit of a marriage ceremony or a marriage license. In Texas, these marriages are just as valid as ceremonial marriages. Texas now has a statute that recognizes informal marriages and defines an informal marriage in almost exactly the same terms as the courts have defined common-law marriages.

So, the term *informal marriage* can be used interchangeably with the term *common-law marriage.* In addition, the legislature has provided for the declaration and registration of informal marriages by completing a form provided by the clerk of each county.

Although such registration is not necessary to make an informal marriage valid, doing so removes the primary legal disadvantage of the informal marriage—proving its existence. *Just living together does not create a common-law or informal marriage.*

To create such a marriage you must have *all* of the following:

1. An agreement to marry. This agreement may be stated explicitly, or it may be implied from the circumstances and conduct surrounding your living together.
2. You must actually co-habitate. This means living together and doing all the things that husbands and wives do.
3. You must hold yourselves out publicly as husband and wife. There is no such thing as a secret common-law marriage. Someone else has to be aware of the arrangement for it to be valid.

The question most often asked about common-law marriages is, "How long do you have to live together to have a common-law marriage?" There is *no* time requirement. In theory, a common-law marriage can be formed in thirty seconds if all of the above requirements are met in that time period. This brings us back to the big problem with the informal marriage: proof. Obviously, it usually will be much easier to prove the existence of a marriage that has gone on thirty years than one that has existed thirty seconds. What does it take to prove the existence of a common-law marriage? There is no certain answer. It is a fact question, almost totally in the hands of the jury, if a jury is requested. In addition to the couple living together and calling themselves husband and wife, names on deeds, joint checking accounts, birth certificates of their children, and such, would all seem to be helpful. And, it should be noted, a person who already is married cannot enter into a valid common-law or informal marriage.

Do I Need an Annulment Instead of a Divorce?

It's possible, but not probable. To explain this we need to look at a little legal theory.

A marriage is a contract. A divorce is a suit to break the contract. On the other hand, an annulment is a suit that is brought to get the court to declare that the contract never existed.

So, you may ask, if the contract never existed, why do we have to go to court and have a judge say it didn't exist? Good question.

Some marriages are like this. These are marriages that are so repugnant to society that they are considered never to have existed. They are void. Examples of void marriages are marriages between brother and sister, parent and child, or during a marriage to someone else.

Since void marriages don't exist, it is not necessary to go to court to get rid of them. However, it is often desirable to file a lawsuit to get it *on record* that the marriage doesn't exist. Otherwise, the record of the marriage might be used against you. An example: In the event of death, a person whose marriage to the deceased was void because of a previous marriage, might still attempt to claim that he or she is the rightful heir.

These suits to set the record straight are called *Suits to Declare a Marriage Void.*

There are other marriages, less repugnant to society, that only become invalid if a court says that the marriage is invalid. These are called *voidable* marriages. Examples of voidable marriages: marriage by a person under the age of fourteen or by a person between the ages of fourteen and eighteen without parental consent; when one of the parties married under the influence of alcohol or drugs; marriages in which one of the other parties concealed impotency from the other; and marriages entered into because of fraud or duress.

A court will not grant annulments to such marriages if it appears that the person bringing the suit continued in the marriage after learning of the particular defect in the marriage contract. A divorce then will be necessary.

May I Change My Name in My Divorce?

Yes. The judge has the power, in his or her discretion, to change the name of either person in the final decree. Judges usually do so freely, with the exception that a few judges are reluctant for a mother who has gained custody of a child to change to a name different from that of the child.

How Soon May I Remarry after My Divorce?

To be granted a marriage license in Texas, you must swear that you have not divorced within the last thirty days.

Other states do not make this requirement, so that you might be able to travel to another state and be married sooner. If you're in that much of a hurry, I suggest that you at least take time to consult a good psychiatrist.

Divorce during Pregnancy

Can a divorce be granted if the wife is pregnant?

Probably not. All of the judges that I know are determined not to grant such divorces. Although I do not know of a statute that prohibits divorce during pregnancy, there are substantial practical problems. Before the child is born, it is difficult to assess the needs of the child. How much support is to be paid? Who should have custody?

Denial of Paternity

In the late 1700s, a rule known as Lord Mansfield's rule prevented the spouses from giving testimony that would bastardize a child. With some modifications this rule was retained in Texas until recently.

The rule has been changed. There is still a strong presumption that the husband is the father of any child conceived or born during the marriage. However, the father is entitled to deny paternity. To do so he must expressly deny that he is the parent in his pleading. A blood test must be ordered. The father who is making the denial probably will be forced to pay several hundred dollars for the blood test in order to get it. The results of the blood test are pretty much controlling. The father may still be required to pay temporary child support, pending the outcome of the blood test.

Failure to challenge paternity in the divorce precludes the father from later bringing a subsequent lawsuit to challenge paternity.

Effects of Remarriage to the Same Spouse

If you remarry the same spouse, the provisions of a divorce decree relating to custody of children are rendered ineffective and inoperative. The relationship between the parents and children is the same as it was before the divorce.

Remarriage to the same spouse does not affect the terms of the divorce decree regarding property division. Only property acquired after the new marriage will be considered community property.

Death of a Spouse

If your spouse dies before the divorce is granted, the effect virtually is as if the divorce had not been filed. The divorce proceeding is now moot, since both parties must be living for a divorce to be granted.

Death of an Ex-Spouse

If death occurs after a divorce, there is, of course, no legal relationship between the divorced parties. If the Managing Conservator of minor children dies, the surviving parent becomes the Managing Conservator. If the deceased former spouse has not rewritten his or her will since the divorce, the provisions giving property to an ex-spouse are disregarded, and the ex-spouse receives no property under the will.

Tape Recording and Eavesdropping

Betrayal of an intimate relationship is hard to swallow. Experiencing a betrayal or a perceived betrayal leaves us feeling vulnerable and angry. If you can't trust the things you were most certain about, how can you trust anything else? This causes us to look for ways to protect ourselves and/or to strike back at the betrayer. Sometimes this response to betrayal brings out the Agent 007 in our personalities. After all, what better way to get even than to expose the hypocrite publicly for who he or she really is? This, plus the advice of our most sympathetic and "knowledgeable" friends sometimes leads to a trip down to the electronic store to purchase a tape recorder, which will, no doubt, be used to trap the bad guy in the black hat and show him or her to be the scoundrel he or she really is. After all, tape recorders tell the truth, and truth is what justice is all about.

Don't do it! At least don't do it until you finish reading what I've go to say on the subject. Even then I hope you'll think really hard before you decide to use a tape recorder or engage in eavesdropping on your spouse.

First, let's talk about the legal problems. Unlike most of the discussions we are having in the pages of this book, violations of the *electronic wiretapping or eavesdropping laws* are criminal violations. You know, if you break this law "they" can come with handcuffs and put you in jail. And it's not just a state law. Both the Federal Government and the State of Texas have criminal laws prohibiting electronic eavesdropping. And make no mistake, if your tape recording is found to be a criminal violation, it will not be admitted in your divorce, and the fact that you have committed a crime will be held against you on such issues as child custody.

Now, what is *electronic eavesdropping*? The short answer is that it is electronically listening in on a private conversation to which you are not a party. In practical terms this means that you can legally tape-record conversations to which you are a party. Being a party means that you are one of the people talking or listening on the phone or to a personal conversation that is within earshot. In practical terms, this means that you can legally record all of your conversations between you and your spouse in person and on the phone. (I'm assuming your spouse is in Texas. Some other states absolutely forbid the tape recording of any phone conversation whether the recording party is a party to the conversation or not.) If, however, you decide to recordprivate conversations between your spouse and his or her lover, you have probably committed a felony. This means that you can't leave a tape recorder under the bed in which you suspect the conversation will take place, nor can you attach the tape recorder to the phone on which the two lovers discuss their daily plans right after you leave for work.

If you're the scorned lover or the parent whose child is being threatened by an irresponsible parent, I know how your mind works. You're already thinking ahead, wondering if you can legally record a telephone conversation if you are listening in on an extension phone. The answer is, you probably can, but don't do it. The courts have held that conversations are private only when there is *an expectation of privacy*. So, where at least one party to the conversation knows or should know that there is or may be an extension phone, there would seem to be no *expectation of privacy*. But Texas courts have taken a much harder line on this subject than the federal courts and the courts of other states that have similar laws. You simply can't count on prosecutors and judges to have a fine-tuned ear when it comes down to this kind of interpretation. Some courts may decide listening in on an extension is a felony.

I cannot tell you absolutely, categorically, *not* to use a tape recorder because, occasionally, I have seen tape records change the outcome of trials or cause favorable settlements. Much more often, however, I have seen tape recordings fall flat when they come into evidence or backfire on the party trying to use them.

The first practical problem with using a tape recorder is that it makes the party using it look sneaky. Looking sneaky can hurt credibility, and in courtrooms credibility is all there is. If you lose your credibility, you probably lose the case. The judge or jury may start to wonder, "If he or she is sneaky about this tape recording business, what else is he or she being sneaky about?" Of course, if the stuff on the tape recording is really good, the judge or jury is more likely to look upon the recording process as a necessity that could not be avoided to bring this important matter to the court's attention. If the recording is of questionable importance in the world of "he said, she said," then the loss of credibility usually outweighs any possible benefit.

The problem in making judgments about the potential benefits of the tape recording versus the potential loss of credibility is that the party making the recording usually sees it as "a gem" or "I got 'em now." This person hears the recording through the screen of all of the awful things his or her spouse did that led up to the conversation that was recorded. The fact-finder (judge or jury), on the other hand, was not present in bed or in the kitchen when all of the things leading up to the recording took place. This often leaves those listening in the courtroom perplexed as to why anyone wouldbother to record such a nasty conversation, or worse, they think the person making the recording is "a little over the top." Either way, this is not the attitude you want to be instilling in those who will make decisions about your property or children or both.

The second practical problem in making tape recordings is that the person making the recording often sounds at least as bad as the person on the tape. Often the person making the recording is trying to lead the other party into saying the awful things that he or she has said before or lead him or her into confessing again. This just doesn't work because the person doing the leading is doing all of the talking. So, a person who in a previous conversation has been vile, filthy, obnoxious, or threatening can now, in a later recorded conversation sound like a perfectly reasonable soul who is just being goaded or cross-examined by someone with nothing better to do. Of course, the spouse recording the conversation is still "hearing" all of the nasty conversations that occurred before and wondering why others don't understand.

Finally, no discussion of tape recording can avoid the issue of child abuse. Can a parent record a child's conversation with the other spouse or a third party if the parent suspects some sort of child abuse? The federal law and the law of some other states tends to say that a parent has this right. Texas currently has case law that strongly suggests that a parent has no such right in Texas and is committing a crime by recording a private conversation between the child and a third party. To my knowledge no Texas court has decided whether a parent has a right to listen in on an extension phone and record what is being heard. This is a difficult issue. Though it is a guess, I believe that Texas courts will develop a more mature, fact-specific approach to this issue. Parents definitely ought to have the right to monitor young children's contacts with third parties, including the other parent, if emotional or physical child abuse is realistically suspected. On the other hand, such monitoring should not be used as a pretext for interfering with a child's relationship with the other parent. Making such decisions will not be easy and one hopes that, except in the most extreme cases, the criminal law will not be seen as the tool for making such decisions. But, in all of your decisions on the subject, you ought to assume the worst and err on the side of caution. This is not an easy decision for a parent who believes his or her child is in jeopardy. Many parents will jump in boiling oil if they think it is necessary to do so in order to save their children.

So, even if you can tape-record legally, the best rule is: If you have any other reasonable alternative, don't use a tape recorder.

Chapter 4

Getting by Without a Lawyer: Bungee Jumping at the Courthouse

You know everybody is ignorant,
only on different subjects.

—Will Rogers

Hiring a lawyer is certainly not a magic answer that will solve all problems in divorce. A lawyer will be unable to give guarantees regarding the outcome of the case. But neither is there any magic in not hiring a lawyer. Beware of those who flippantly say you don't need a lawyer. If the legal system is anything, it is a big chunk of "real life." As in real life, the water is deep and the current is swift. To get through life or court you need all of the knowledge, tools, assistance, and power you can get. If, in the course of life, the trek takes you into court, you probably should use a lawyer.

While you don't need a lawyer for every decision in life, many unfair, unnecessary, and unfortunate things happen to people who are not represented or do not seek timely legal advice. It is difficult to describe adequately the sadness and regret that occurs when someone is told, "Your problem *would have been* extremely easy and inexpensive to solve had you dealt with it during the divorce."

If you are considering going through your divorce without hiring a lawyer, this chapter is my way of attempting to stimulate your thinking about what you are doing. It's an attempt to intellectually discuss *lawyers,* a subject which evokes strong emotional feelings in many people and causes some to make irrational decisions contrary to their own self-interest.

Is It Possible That I Don't Need a Lawyer?

Yes, it is possible that you don't need a lawyer. Those with "nothing left to lose" really don't have to worry much about legal representation. If you meet all of the following requirements, then you might avoid hiring a lawyer:

1. You don't own any property except clothing and personal effects with ordinary values. Make certain that you're not entitled to any retirement benefits, profit sharing plan, etc.
2. Your spouse owns no property that you intend to claim.
3. There are no community debts other than those you intend to pay, and you trust your spouse not to incur any debt while the divorce is pending.
4. You have no child by this spouse. Nor have you adopted any, and none are expected to be born. If you are a man, you must trust your wife not to get pregnant prior to the divorce.
5. Your spouse has hired a lawyer who is handling all of the paperwork.

If you fit into the above categories, then you probably don't need a lawyer. Nevertheless, if:

a. You plan to remarry; or
b. You are likely to inherit property; or
c. You have substantial earning capacity and are beginning to accumulate property; then I suggest that you obtain a certified copy of your divorce decree. Then, have a short conference with your lawyer to be sure that your divorce is in order and that you really are rid of your former spouse.

Do I Need a Lawyer?

There is a gray area where the use of a lawyer is desirable, but not absolutely necessary. For example, you say: "What if I have some property (a car), but I trust my spouse to have it awarded to me?" "Or, what if I have a child, but I trust my spouse (who is getting custody) to ask the court only for reasonable child support?"

These "what if" questions could go on forever. Eventually, you will have to decide what risk to take in doing without a lawyer. My personal prejudice is that, if your divorce involves children or significant property and you are my family member, my friend, or my client, I strongly recommend that you be represented by legal counsel. The entire American court system is built around the concept that every participant will look out for himself or herself and take care of his or her own interest. That's the reason it's called an *adversary system.*

No Rules Protect Unrepresented Parties

There is not a single rule in our laws or rules of practice that provides for any special accommodation or protection for a party who is not represented by a lawyer. There is, however, some case law that says that persons without lawyers are to be held to the same standards as those who are represented.

The Courthouse Plays "For Keeps"

When you're considering representing yourself, keep in mind that down at the courthouse they play for keeps. In the chapter on litigation, I discuss the "doctrine of finality," which is at the heart of our legal system. This seems to be a difficult concept for many people to understand. It's clear to everyone that if you bleed to death on the operating table, the operation can't successfully be repeated. Somehow these same people often think that if you are figuratively "bled to death" in the courtroom that you get "overs." Very seldom does this happen. The courthouse thinks it is on a divine mission every day and is reluctant to revisit today what it did yesterday.

Don't Mistake What You Could Have Done with Where You Are Now

Because lawyers do their work in public (unlike surgeons and plumbers), it is not unusual for people viewing what the lawyer is doing to think, "I could do that." Or, "If I hadn't married, I could have gone on. . . ." or "If I had training, I could do a better job than that guy."

If you think these thoughts, you are probably right. You probably could be a very good lawyer. But this is not the time or place to indulge in such fantasies. It is like learning to be a tightwire walker by beginning sixty feet up—without a net. Give yourself a break! Even Superman must have done some low, slow practice flights before going public.

Playing Tennis in Moving Water

Before undertaking your own representation, you need to understand that few legal rules, especially those relating to courtroom procedure, are written in bedrock. It is not possible to handle a lawsuit competently by simply memorizing the rules that seem to apply to each stage. As the facts of a case unfold, the rules that apply shift. For example, a conversation or written document that is objectionable as hearsay in one instance, may be admissible into evidence when it is offered for another purpose. Likewise, what is relevant can shift form moment to moment as the issues of a case change. Some judges construe the rules of pleading very strictly, not allowing evidence except on matters that have been pled. Others are quite liberal in "finding" pleadings or even allowing amendments to pleadings. These are just examples to show that law is fluid rather than solid. In other words, a part of the "game" is that the net and the out-of-bounds lines sometimes move in strange and surreal patterns.

Someone Is Being Paid to Trip You Up

Lawyers are in one of the very few professions in which someone else is paid to make their working conditions adverse and their work difficult. If you undertake your own representation, it may be that your day in court will be sunny, that the judge will greet you with a smile and spend every moment trying to please you. But don't be surprised if your spouse has hired some lawyer to whom the judge listens and who has numerous reasons why your spouse should receive many benefits and you should receive many liabilities. Of course, this will seem really unfair. But, it's the way the court system works.

A Fool for a Lawyer

You should also consider the old cliché among lawyers that "he who represents himself has a fool for a client." I can think of a couple of exceptions to this rule, but by and large it is true. Most good lawyers hire another lawyer if they become a party to a lawsuit.

Divorce Lawyers Are Plentiful

In trying to decide whether to represent yourself or hire a lawyer, consider that divorce lawyers are plentiful. Getting professional help on any problem is made more difficult by the uniqueness of the problem. For example, if you own an antique exotic foreign car with a fuel injection system, getting professional help to fix it may be more difficult than if you own a Ford. It's not that the Ford is any less complex. It's just that more people are familiar with how to fix it. Fortunately, for those seeking help in ordinary, run-of-the-mill divorces, these cases are very much mainstream legal problems. There are lots of not-too-complex divorces and lots of lawyers who are able to handle them adequately and economically. This helps the quality and price of the legal services. From a purely economic point of view, it is probably cheaper to hire a lawyer than it is to spend the time trying to learn enough to protect yourself.

Examining Your "Mind-Set" about Lawyers

You're exactly right. I don't have a clue about what you, the individual reader, is thinking. But, I fear that there are certain "mind-sets" or preconceived ideas about lawyers that blind some to the benefits available from having legal representation. For this reason, I want to examine, quickly, some of the reasons that people give for not wanting to employ a lawyer. If after considering this reasoning, you still don't want to use a lawyer, you will have only lost a few minutes, and perhaps, your own reasons for proceeding without a lawyer will be all the more clear.

Lawyers cost more than they are worth.

No doubt, lawyers are expensive. But so is almost everything else in this society, especially anything that has to do with personal services. The relative cost of goods and services is a subject that every one of us either consciously or unconsciously considers almost every day of our lives as we spend our money and purchase the necessities of life.

Let me suggest that, for many, the hardest part of spending money to employ a lawyer is the fact that they are spending money on an *intangible*, something they can't hold in their hands, see, taste, or keep under lock and key. If you buy a new car, you can drive it, park it in the driveway, and show it off to the neighbors. If you buy groceries, clothes, or take a vacation, you can feel, see, taste, and experience your purchase. This is usually not so when you pay money to spend time with your lawyer. Usually, it is not altogether clear just what you are spending your money for.

This lack of a tangible, easy-to-see, and easy-to-define product is not a reason for depriving yourself of the protection provided by having adequate legal representation. Rather, this is the time to do some thinking about the values and assumptions of concreteness instilled by advertising that seems to say, "it's not real unless it's concrete." Of course, beginning to think about such things is dangerous. Before you know it, you may be reconsidering just what *intangibles* cause you to make such incredible monthly payments on that new car that spends most of its time in the parking lot and drives almost exactly like the one you had before that was already paid for.

A lawyer will deprive me of control of my case.

To the contrary, a lawyer should give you more control over your case and your destiny. Remember, the lawyer will work for you, not vice versa. If your lawyer doesn't behave as you want, you can fire him or her and find one who understands that his or her duty is to you and your case.

Real lack of control comes from participating in an adversary system that assumes you will have representation when you don't. Without a lawyer, there is absolutely no one on your side watching out for your good. The judge is prohibited by law from taking sides.

Lawyers are all no good. You can't trust any of them.

Of course, some think this is true of all humanity. But, in fact, lawyers are like the rest of the human race. Some are good, and some are not to be trusted. Although lawyers seem to have a corner on the current stereotype market, the same could be said of every group of people on earth. If the lawyers you know seem to fit the negative stereotype, perhaps it's time for you to meet some different lawyers. You owe it to yourself not to make life's important decisions based on stereotypes and generalizations that paint entire segments of humanity with one brush.

Lawyers don't do anything I can't do for myself.

I believe that one of the legal profession's "public relations" problems arises in large measure because many people do not understand what lawyers do. Before attempting your divorce without a lawyer, you might want to read the next chapter on "Hiring a Lawyer." Understanding what you are getting for your money might make it easier for you to write the check to hire the lawyer. Or, if you decide to represent yourself, at least, it will give you a better idea of what you are undertaking.

Chapter 5

Hiring a Lawyer: What Smart Shoppers Need to Know

I'll not rest until everyone sees that it is a shame to be a lawyer.

—Adolph Hitler

If you were employing a carpenter to build a house, it might be helpful if you had some idea of how you want the house to look and how you intended to use it. Your chances of actually getting the house you want will improve if you have at least some idea about how houses are built, what carpenters do, how electricians and plumbers work, and the types of materials that are usually used in building the house you want.

Now that you are about to employ a lawyer, you need to understand what a lawyer can and cannot do for you. Although some in our society routinely use lawyers and understand their power, use, and function, many have not really thought about what lawyers do.

Be Informed or Be a Victim

I wish that I could report that all clients have a positive experience with their lawyers. Unfortunately, as a practicing lawyer, I am exposed to many people who have had a bad experience with a prior lawyer. There are a variety of reasons for this. A few lawyers are obviously awful human beings with whom no one should have to deal. Some have a really bad "bedside manner." Sometimes the reason for the dissatisfaction is the client. Some clients are just impossible to please and would not be pleased even by a saint.

But this problem is more complicated than bad lawyers and unreasonable clients.

Sometimes divorce clients are unhappy with their chosen lawyers because they were unsophisticated and passive shoppers. These passive shoppers, apparently, choose lawyers while on "autopilot," having little or no idea of what they are looking for in a lawyer or what a lawyer will or can do for them. Many of these unsophisticated shoppers, it seems, find lawyers who are also on "autopilot." The client doesn't ask about anything, and the lawyer doesn't tell them anything because they don't ask, until one day when the client figures out that they're unhappy with the direction things are going. In short, these unhappy people didn't understand that hiring *and* using a lawyer is a participation sport. If you sit on the sidelines mentally, you just get potluck and, in an adversary system, potluck is usually not good.

Another set of divorce clients ends up unhappy because they got precisely the kind of lawyer they "asked for." These unhappy souls are usually people who hired a lawyer when they were extremely angry, frightened, or hurt. The sole factor considered in the selection of their lawyers was whether the chosen lawyer would be good at striking out, hitting back, or getting even with their spouse. To put it bluntly, these people were looking for a lawyer with a personality disorder, and that is what they got: a "loose cannon," a "mad dog," or a "time bomb." When they were hiring this personality type, it never occurred to them that they would have a great deal more contact with this unpleasant person than their spouse would.

This chapter is intended to give you an overview of what lawyers do and to get you started thinking about the kind of person you might want to represent you.

Dump the Simplistic View

Many people view the law office as a sort of stationery store in which the lawyer draws documents. These people think that they are purchasing documents. While the preparation of documents is important, it is the least important of the services that your lawyer has to offer. If you use your lawyer only for this purpose, you are paying a high price even if you go to the most cut-rate guy in town. More importantly, you are missing the real benefits that a lawyer can provide to help you succeed in your divorce.

You Are the Captain of the Ship

Lawyers are consultants, not dictators. No, this does not mean that you should micro-manage your case, telling your lawyer what pleadings to file, what evidence to present, what phone calls to make, and when and how to schedule hearings. It also does not mean that your lawyer will agree with you or give you only the advice that you want to hear. But it does mean that you are in control of the overall direction of your case, whether or not you will accept a settlement, make a settlement offer, go to trial, agree to fight for custody or give up custody of your child, and anything else that has to do with the ultimate outcome of your case.

The central concept is that lawyers represent clients. No, I'm not trying to insult your intelligence. I really want you to think about this. Sometimes, it's in the most *seemingly* obvious things that we get the horse hitched up to the wrong end of the cart. In a society that operates on profit, we occasionally lose sight of who the customer is. *Some* salespersons at car dealerships have the mistaken belief that automobiles and those who buy them exist for the benefit of the dealership and the people who sell cars. This same attitude can be detected occasionally among those who sell insurance, groceries, hamburgers, undergarments, and those who treat the sick and take care of the dead. This tendency to confuse the person who is to provide the service with the person who is supposed to receive the benefit is sometimes strong enough to motivate unnecessary surgery. Think about this. One human being will cut on another just to get paid.

The legal profession is not exempt from this confusion of the servant with the one who is to be served. In our ranks are those who act as if God made clients so that lawyers can have lawsuits. As in other trades and professions, often lawyers are unconscious of having lost sight of the customer. Like everyone who is absorbed in his or her work, lawyers become accustomed to going through the same routines and having the rent and the payroll due at the same time every month. This, of course, is a part of the lawyer's or the law firm's absolute reality. A lawyer must do the work and get paid for it or find some other line of work.

But, I will not let the legal profession off the hook by saying that the only lawyers who have lost sight of the customer are those who have done so unconsciously. In the legal profession, as in every trade or profession, are those whose only goal is to make the sale. This make-the-sale-at-any-cost is done in a variety of ways. The legal profession has a reputation for "creating needless litigation." But needless litigation, though widely condemned by the general public, is but a small part of the real problem. There are lawyers who never litigate who are geniuses at charging for ridiculous and needless services. A common abuse arises in legitimate cases in which one of the lawyers insists that even the simplest issues be handled in the most complex and difficult manner. This is done in a variety of ways, but it always has as its central theme an unwillingness to be reasonable, which is often accompanied by rudeness and condescension—you know, the very things your mother told you were the best way to start a fight over nothing.

Lawyers providing unnecessary or counterproductive services do not do so in a vacuum. For such lawyers to exist, there must be clients who are at least susceptible to being sold such "services." In fact, believe it or not, there are many clients who demand lawyers willing to be unreasonable and rude, thereby creating costly and needless expense for themselves and their opponent. You probably have better things to do in life than waste your time and money playing these games. But this is only half the picture. Your spouse may seek a lawyer who will provide the drama that is missing from his or her life. If your spouse chooses this approach, you and your lawyer may have little choice but to respond to an opposition that desires to do everything the difficult and expensive way.

You, on the other hand, can make sure that your divorce is not "lawyer-driven" and that the services that are being performed on your behalf are undertaken because you need them and not because it is financially beneficial to your lawyer. You can do this by remembering that.

- Your lawyer works for you and not vice versa; you hired him or her, and you have an absolute right to fire him or her at any time for any reason.
- *Decisions in your case should be fact-driven* and not based on your lawyers ego needs, his or her self-image, or demonstrations of loyalty to you or of his or her aggressive nature.
- Your lawyer has a *fiduciary duty* to you; this is the highest duty recognized by American law; among other things, it means that your lawyer must always place your interest above his or hers and be scrupulously honest about every aspect of your case.
- You always have the right to ask *why* something is being done; if there is not a good reason for doing it, then maybe it doesn't need to be done; just because you *can* do something to your opponent doesn't necessarily mean that you should do it.
- Although procedural decisions should largely be made by your lawyer with your informed consent, you are in control of the ultimate issues and decisions about what is and is not valuable in your life and your lawsuit.
- Both you and your lawyer should be involved in a cost-benefit analysis of the various aspects of your case; while some things may be required for the defense or prosecution of your case, others may be optional.
- A huge part of your lawyer's job is to tell you things you may not want to hear; if your lawyer is always agreeing with you rather than suggesting that you consider your options or examine your approach, you might want to check your wallet.
- You must have a general idea of what your lawyer's function is in order to evaluate his or her activities and obtain the result you desire; most of the rest of this chapter is devoted to discussing that subject.

The Lawyer as Diagnostician

Among a lawyer's most important functions is *diagnosis.* Obviously, all divorces are a lot alike, but each case has issues that make it different from other cases. There has never been a divorce case just like yours, with the same people, the same facts, and the same judge or jury. An issue that a lawyer sees in your case may be of little or no consequence, or it may be of monumental importance.

One thing is for certain: Legal issues are not always obvious. Subtle differences in facts can completely change the outcome of a case. The essence of diagnostic training in law school and for bar examinations is "issue identification." If a law student cannot identify the "legal issues" that result from subtle changes in a fact scenario, that student will probably not ever become a lawyer. In law practice issue identification is even more difficult than in law school because cogent facts are frequently mixed and intermingled with layers of other facts and emotional issues that have little or nothing to do with the case. Moreover, practicing lawyers must also identify cultural issues, community values, and political issues that may affect a case as much or more than the "legal issues" taught in law school.

Finally, in an adversary system in which your opponent is raising new issues and changing strategies, a lawyer attempting to diagnose or analyze a case is shooting at a moving target. It is more like a chess game in which you can't make a decision until you consider your opponent's last move and the moves that he or she is likely to make after your next moves. This is particularly true in divorce and child custody cases because the actual facts of the case can and do change as the case proceeds.

Good legal analysis not only results in better outcomes for cases, it also results in savings of time and money. Your lawyer's clear analysis, indicating that a settlement offer is reasonable or that there are few benefits likely to result from the pursuit of a particular theory or strategy, allows you to end the legal process more quickly. This can save precious resources needed to start a new life or take care of children.

In a world that demands action and admires action heroes and macho decision makers, *good diagnostic procedures and legal analysis are often the first things to be thrown overboard.* Because clients can't see the lawyer's brain when he or she is thinking about the case, many clients are reluctant to pay for something so vague and intangible. This, of course, causes lawyers to search for "billable events." Like doctors and dentists, who long ago learned to bill for "procedures," lawyers have learned that it's easier to get paid if you "do something." Not only must they do something, it must be something tangible and identifiable. So, like doctors who have learned that they can't get paid for *not* prescribing pills or for *not* doing procedures, lawyers have learned to file pleadings, have conferences, set hearings, appear in court, and a zillion other things that are sometimes necessary but are not something you would do if the mission can be accomplished without jumping through these hoops. Besides, all of these activities are easier than thinking about the case precisely because they require little or no thought.

Yes, I can understand why you're reluctant to pay your lawyer just to think about your case. You are right to be suspicious. Many of our action heroes have learned that they can add heft to their billable hours by adding in charges for periods of "legal analysis" when they are really thinking about their golf game or planning this season's big charity event. But, I believe you can figure out who really cares enough about you and your case, not to mention about being a good lawyer, so that you won't be fooled for long by those who are supposed to be finding ways to help you out of your troubles.

In short, you must respect yourself and your case enough to demand that the attorney representing you provides the real thing: careful and thoughtful consideration of your case. I can almost guarantee you that you're going to pay for these services whether you actually receive them or not. You might as well dump the phoneys and find a lawyer who will shoot straight with you and give you the real stuff: his or her brain power. But keep in mind that it takes heart and soul to motivate the brain.

The Lawyer as Advocate

I believe advocacy is an attitude. Some people seem to be born with it, others have to develop it, and some never get it. Advocacy is an attitude of loyalty and a willingness to struggle. Sometimes it's loyalty to what's fair and right. At other times it's loyalty to another human being who is in need of protection. Advocacy is not limited to lawyers or the legal profession. You see it even in children on the playground who will intervene, sometimes at their own peril, to stop a bully from beating up a smaller child. Advocacy is commonly found in parents who will do all manner of things to protect their children. Good doctors advocate that their patients stop smoking. A teacher who goes the extra mile to make sure the slow learner knows how to read is definitely an advocate.

By the very nature of what lawyers do, advocacy is a must. A good legal advocate is not the person who brags and huffs and puffs and puts on a big show; rather, it's the lawyer who privately and internally commits himself or herself to the idea that nobody is going to run over his or her client. Sometimes it means going toe-to-toe like everyone sees on television and thinks that is the way real lawyers do it. But, more often than not, to be an advocate means coming in early and staying late to get out a restraining order or making the extra phone call to make sure that something really is going to happen or checking a document twice to make sure that the client really is protected or even discouraging an angry client determined to go to court from doing so. Yes, it's mostly boring stuff that nobody sees, but it makes a difference. As an old lawyer told me when I was a new lawyer, "To be a good lawyer you usually don't need to be a hero, but *every day and always* you must struggle to protect your client." That lawyer was a real advocate.

It's difficult to think of a more important role for a lawyer than as *advocate*. After all, the American court system is referred to as *an adversary system*. This ought to be a sufficient hint that you probably are going to be in trouble if you show up with someone who is not going to fight for you. The right to be represented by a lawyer is so important that in criminal cases it is guaranteed by the United States Constitution. Many years ago, in my early practice as a prosecutor and criminal defense lawyer, I became convinced that there is only one thing worse than not having a lawyer; that is having a lawyer who will not or cannot fight for you. The very essence of lawyering is fighting for and protecting the client's interest.

Even if, at the time you hire a lawyer, you don't think your case is going to court, by the very act of retaining a lawyer, you should be buying an insurance policy insuring that, if push comes to shove, your interest will be protected. The importance of having a lawyer who is capable of trying your case cannot be overemphasized, because the bottom line in our legal system is a trial in the courtroom. As is stated elsewhere in this book, most sane people want to avoid trials, if possible. But, because avoiding a trial is not always possible, if you don't have a lawyer who is capable of trying your case, you're placing yourself in the awkward position of running a bluff.

Moreover, you misunderstand the legal system if you think your lawyer acts as advocate only when you are in the courtroom. Clients come to lawyers because they are vulnerable right then, not just months later when their case comes to trial. A good lawyer acts as advocate for his or her client from the moment the lawyer is hired. When you are represented by a lawyer, you are negotiating from a prepared and informed position. You are putting everyone on notice that you are taking responsibility for yourself and your own business and that you demand to be treated with adequate respect, honesty, and fairness. There is an expression among lawyers that the best way to settle your case and avoid a trial is to prepare for trial. Therefore, *the first step in attempting to avoid a trial is to hire a lawyer who is capable of trying your case.*

There seems to be a widespread misunderstanding of what is meant by *advocacy* or by a lawyer "fighting for a client." Some clients seem to think they have to choose between a lawyer with the temperament of a half-blind, raging bull on one hand or a Milquetoast, timid, do-nothing lawyer on the other. This harmful misconception can become a self-fulfilling prophecy. By choosing such lawyers, clients can unwittingly create unnecessary litigation and expense on the one hand or an unfair, one-sided settlement against themselves on the other. Good lawyers know that *divorces, like other lawsuits, are fact-driven. The lawyering required should depend on the facts of the case, the behavior of the opposing party, the court you are in, and what you really want out of your divorce.* A lawyer is neither a good advocate nor acting in your best interest if he or she starts or continues unnecessary wars. Likewise, you are not being well served by a lawyer who encourages you to accept an unfair or lopsided settlement just because he or she is not trained or prepared to try your case.

Being a good advocate does not mean "egging you on" to try your lawsuit or encouraging you to take unreasonable positions. A huge part of advocacy is advising and encouraging the client to avoid risk. Just as your doctor's job is to *advocate* that you stop smoking, follow a heathy diet, and use your medications properly, your lawyer's job is to be your *advocate* by advising you to make the most sensible decision available.

Frankly, good advocacy often has little to do with confrontation of the opponent. A perfect example of this is the drafting of your divorce decree. Attention to even small details in the decree can make a big difference in child custody and property issues. Often, the opposing lawyer or spouse is not much concerned with the details in the final decree. By paying attention to how the details of the decree may affect you, your lawyer is acting as your advocate and protecting your interest.

Another misconception is that to be a good advocate a lawyer must be rude or unkind. One need only spend time around the very best trial lawyers to know this is not true. Some of the best trial lawyers are kind and considerate as they introduce devastating facts before the judge or jury. As these lawyers make scorching arguments, they do so in a way that causes judges and juries to appreciate the politeness as well as the strong argument being presented. Yes, there is a time to go toe-to-toe, to raise the voice, and to refuse to be pushed aside. But, day-to-day, gratuitous rudeness or unkindness should never be mistaken for good advocacy. More often than not, rudeness and unkindness are counter-productive.

Advocacy seems to be a product that sells. Since lawyers, like practitioners of all other trades and professions, must sell their wares, there is always a lot of talk about "fighting for clients," "aggressive representation," "ruthless pursuit of the client's rights," or being "one of the state's premier trial firms." This self-advertising language is used by those who know that you will be reading it or hearing it at a time in your life when you are frightened, desperate, angry, or all of the above. When you hear this kind of self-praise, stop and take a deep breath. Remember, the one with the most convincing stories about how he was the best quarterback was usually not the same fellow who could really throw the football. You might want to look at other aspects of a lawyer's personality to try and determine whether this person really has the character and brains to be there for you in the tough times when you will really need the help.

Finally, it's worth saying again that, even as your advocate who is obligated to fight for you, your lawyer still works for you. You are in ultimate control of the positions your lawyer takes on your behalf, what you demand from your opponent, what you are willing to give up, and whether your lawsuit is to be tried or settled. If your lawyer does not agree with your assessment, the things you are asking for, and the things you are willing to concede to the other side, he or she has an obligation to tell you of his or her disagreement and to give you advice consistent with that position. But ultimately, your lawyer must follow your instructions on all these matters. After all, it's your case.

In short, to be a good advocate, a lawyer must be passionate, care about the client, and be committed to his or her own profession. But, being passionate, caring, and committed does not require overly dramatic displays or checking one's brain at the door.

The Lawyer as Diplomat

Some lawyers never miss an opportunity to start an unnecessary war. These lawyers take pride in their belligerent, antisocial conduct and the extra fees that such behavior produces. Worse yet, some clients are pleased with this conduct, believing that this is "what lawyers are supposed to do." The really bad news is that it only takes one of these lawyers to start a war or, at least, create a lot of needless expense.

Fortunately, most lawyers would not dream of starting a needless war or an unnecessary battle. For some, it's a matter of conscience; for others, it's just common sense. Their necessary-wars-only approach has nothing to do with being passive or unwilling to protect their clients. Many are excellent trial lawyers who routinely pursue their clients' rights in court. Most don't think of themselves as high-minded or missionaries. They simply take their profession seriously. To them the court system is a sacred and necessary tool for social justice and stability. It is not a game for their amusement, and their clients' lives are not to be toyed with or needlessly put at risk. They pride themselves in charging only for work that needs to be done.

Lawyers who want to avoid unnecessary wars must be diplomats. They probably don't think of themselves as diplomats, but that is what they are, and many are very good at it. Their diplomatic techniques come right out of kindergarten and are regularly used by civilized and decent people everywhere. Here are some examples of how you might save time, money, perspiration, and wear and tear if you were the lawyer running your divorce:

- First, ask politely, even if your client is absolutely entitled to whatever is being requested. If your opponent refuses, there still will be plenty of time to make shrill demands and, ultimately, force the offending party to comply.
- A telephone call to inquire whether or not your opponent will agree is much easier and cheaper than preparation of lengthy pleadings, scheduling one or more hearings, preparing witnesses, appearing at one or more hearings, and waiting for the judge to reply. If your opponent says "no" to the telephone call, there will still be time for fun and games at the courthouse.
- When your opponent calls asking for something to which he or she is entitled and will ultimately get anyway, consider agreeing to provide it rather than forcing a judge to order compliance with your opponent's request. This will save the time required to prepare the pleadings and schedule hearings. It also might garner future concessions from your opponent or favorable rulings from a judge who now believes that you're reasonable because you requested only necessary and reasonable things from the court.
- Tell the truth. Most people understand that they can't rely on anything said by someone who didn't tell the truth the first time. Don't promise something that can't be delivered. Don't promise something that won't be done.
- Don't threaten, interrupt, belittle, or ignore those who are just trying to converse about difficult subjects. Remember, talk is cheap and fighting, even in court, is very expensive. If a lawyer must threaten people for no reason, perhaps a career as a professional wrestler would be more suitable.
- Don't act as if you and your client are better than those on the other side. Don't call them names, be condescending, arrogant, rude, boast-

ful, etc. All of these things may temporarily titillate and thrill a shriveled ego, but they also tend to make the opposition relish any and all opportunities to make life difficult for you. Again, this creates needless expense.

It is likely that these common-sense rules of civil behavior, commonly practiced by a majority of lawyers around the state, save clients many millions of dollars in legal fees and cost every year. When your lawyer uses this common-sense, low-key approach, it is not a sign of weakness. Rather it is in your best interest. Lawyers who use diplomacy frequently obtain better results through agreements than could have been obtained in court. This is because the kid everyone likes is the one more likely to get the extra cookie.

But make no mistake, *diplomacy is not a solution for every case.* While it takes only one to make war, *it takes both parties to make peace.* In other words, even if you're willing to be reasonable, your opponent can veto the diplomatic process. Therefore, if your levelheaded and reasonable lawyer tells you that all of the suggestions that I have made above won't work in your case, at least not yet, you need to listen. When you have a lawyer or a party as an opponent who wants to fight and is not interested in reasonable discussion, attempts at diplomacy are a waste of time and money. Your lawyer will tell you why he or she thinks it's not a good idea to attempt to negotiate in these cases.

A classic example of a lawyer who would not negotiate is a lawyer against whom I regularly handled cases years ago. When I was hired in a case in which this lawyer represented the opposing side, I soon learned it was of no avail to make calls or attempt any kind of discussion with this lawyer. He would not return phone calls, respond to correspondence, or enter negotiations in any other way. The only choice was, depending on the circumstance, to set a hearing on a temporary matter or set the case for the final trial. After the hearing or trial began, at some point, this lawyer's client would be called as a witness and testify until a recess was requested by my opposing counsel. During that recess, after the judge left the bench, the opposing lawyer would tell his client, in front of me, my client, God, and everybody else present, that he or she (the client) was a horrible witness. Then, with little or no fanfare, we two lawyers and our clients would go into the hallway outside the courtroom and settle the case, usually on terms that were worse for the opposing client than could have been obtained before the hearing or trial. Over the years, I watched this scenario play itself out a dozen or more times. Of course, most lawyers unwilling to negotiate don't follow such a crude and senseless process as I have described. But, many, many lawyers and/or clients will begin divorces with the attitude that they are going to have their way about everything and, therefore, that discussions are unnecessary. As discussed in Chapter 11, this reluctance to be reasonable lasts until the client gets a few bills from the lawyers, loses a temporary hearing or two, and is actually required to answer difficult and embarrassing questions at his or her deposition. By then, their lawyer is satisfied with the fee that has been earned for all of this needless work, and the client has decided that lawsuits and divorce are not as much fun as he or she had imagined. It is at this point that both sides can finally discuss settlement and, often, the case can be settled in the way that it should have been settled months or years earlier.

Finally, there is the common scenario of diplomacy and negotiations breaking down. Frequently, reasonable parties and attorneys begin divorce cases by attempting to negotiate a settlement only to learn that the parties cannot agree on a final settlement. At this point, diplomacy and negotiations break down, and the parties agree that the case will have to be tried. Usually, but not always, the silver lining to this kind of negotiation impasse is the fact that negotiations and reasonable discussions between the parties have narrowed the issues so that a trial can be limited to the real differences between the parties, thereby shortening the process and saving time, money, and human relations.

The Lawyer as Counselor

The first sentence in this book says, "This is a book about choices." This theme continues on every page with my urging you to make the deliberate decisions necessary to control your own destiny. But the right to make a decision is meaningless without an adequate understanding of its consequences. Not knowing that one branch of the road leads one off a high cliff is essentially the same as not even noticing that you passed a fork in the road. If you go off the cliff, the result is the same whether or not you actually saw that you had a choice of which road to take.

The purely logical observer, having just landed from the planet Mars, would quite rationally assume that the acquisition of the knowledge and information necessary to make sound decisions would be easy. After all, the world is full of knowledge and information. You can get vast stores of knowledge from roadmaps, guidebooks, checklists, how-to books, talkradio, and lots of friends and family who seem to have quick, simple answers to everything. But, as it turns out, there is a lot more to life than just logic, and knowledge and information are useless without the *insight* and understanding necessary to apply them to your own problems.

Consulting with a lawyer is your best opportunity to gain the knowledge, wisdom, and insight necessary to make good decisions in your divorce. Lawyers are trained to recognize legal issues. The very nature of *law practice* is the attempt to focus this legal training on the solution of specific legal problems for specific clients. Many lawyers do a pretty good job of solving these problems. Some lawyers, who did just fine in law school, never get the hang of applying legal knowledge to a specific client. None of us is perfect, and only the egomaniacs among us are always happy with their own results.

Because the outcome of every single divorce, even those that "don't go to court," is shaped by the courthouse and the legal system, someone working outside of that system is at a distinct disadvantage in giving advice about decisions needed to navigate that system. Courts and the legal system are realities that cannot be escaped even by those who choose to spend all of their energy focusing on "the system's" shortcomings.

It must be obvious by now that this book was written to provide people like you with knowledge and insight to aid you in obtaining your divorce. In fact, I wrote the first edition of this book because I realized that lawyers don't always have the time to answer questions, and many clients cannot afford all of the consultation and counseling needed to get through some divorces. Of course, reading this book is consistent with my use-everything-you-can-get-your-hands-on philosophy. But, no book, no matter how good, can focus legal knowledge and insight on *your specific problems*. Additionally, as I have said, in divorces as in all lawsuits, identifying legal issues and adjusting your response is a moving target because the facts change, and your opponent changes strategy, sometime from moment to moment. Only a real live lawyer interacting with you and your case can provide you with play-by-play action and help you make decisions needed to avoid the icebergs that might punch a hole in your divorce boat.

Generalist or Specialist – Looking Past the Labels

As you seek a lawyer to represent you in your divorce, should you hire a lawyer with broad and extensive experience in a variety of areas of law practice or a lawyer with experience *only* in divorce? My answer is, unless you have a very simple divorce, *you want a lawyer with both* broad experience *and* adequate knowledge of divorce. This may appear at first blush to be a contradictory statement, but it's not. There are adequate numbers of lawyers all over the state who have both broad, extensive experience in legal practice as a whole *and* also know plenty about divorce. Frankly, these are the lawyers you're looking for, and you should be very suspicious of anyone who tells you that your lawyer does not need one or the other of these qualifications.

The reason you must be so vigilant on this issue is because Texas has no system of internship or apprenticeship for lawyers. A lawyer can—and some do—leave law school, take the bar examination, and go directly into law practice without any supervision, restriction, or limitation on the kinds of cases that can be handled. Even if a lawyer goes to work for an experienced lawyer or law firm, there is no assurance that he or she will be exposed to anything outside of a very limited area of practice.

You may assume that a few years in practice will take care of any lack of experience. This may be true. The problem is elucidated by the old joke that inquires, "Do you have twenty years of experience, or do you have one year of experience twenty times?" This may not be such a serious question for lawyers working on corporate tax issues. Perhaps all they need to know about law or life can be found in tax codes. The same might be said for dozens of other areas of law, but probably not about divorce. Divorce has a way of cutting a broad swath across law and life. One divorce may consist only of child custody, expert witnesses, rules of evidence and court rules and procedure, and questions about trial strategy. The next divorce may be totally dominated by questions of corporate ownership, governance, and finance. Most divorces have several combinations of trial, child custody, and property ownership questions intermingled with huge doses of human emotion and psychology. These issues require a lawyer with broad and comprehensive experience in a variety of areas of law practice.

My emphasis on the need for broad, comprehensive legal knowledge is not intended to minimize the need for specialized knowledge about divorce. Neither is it calculated to demean those who dedicate themselves to maintaining knowledge of family law and divorce. I consider myself to be a member of this group. But acquiring and maintaining the narrow band of knowledge represented by the Texas Family Code is relatively easier to achieve than the more comprehensive knowledge and experience a lawyer acquires by handling a wide variety of complex and difficult cases over time.

Texas lawyers practicing in a particular legal area for a requisite period of time may apply for a certification as a specialist in the particular field, such as family law, taxation, civil trial law, criminal law, bankruptcy law, and several other areas of practice. The certification process requires a written examination, extensive documentation of experience, and recommendations of other lawyers and judges who can vouch for the applicant's experience in the area of practice in which certification is sought. In short, the certification process is nothing to be sneezed at. Many lawyers cannot meet the experience requirements for a particular area of practice. Some might not be able to pass the test for a given area. Many who could meet the experience requirements and pass the test simply do not want to go through the extensive application and vetting process.

Because I am board certified as a civil trial lawyer by the Texas Board of Legal Specialization, you might assume that, if I were hiring or recommending a trial lawyer or a lawyer to try a civil lawsuit, that I would recommend only board certified civil trial lawyers. Not so. Yes, there are many board certified civil trial lawyers that I would recommend, but there are others who have this certification who I would be careful to never recommend to anyone. More importantly, if I limited myself only to board certified civil trial lawyers, I would be excluding some of the best trial lawyers in the state. In fact, some of the best trial lawyers and divorce lawyers I know are so busily and successfully trying lawsuits that the last thing on their mind is worrying about getting a certification.

Yes, some of the best divorce lawyers in the state are board certified family law specialists, but many are not certified as a specialist in this area. If you limit yourself to the label of board certified family lawyer, you will deprive yourself not only of some of the best divorce lawyers in the state, but also the best trial lawyers, the best business, real estate, and transactional lawyers, the best corporate or trust lawyers. Depending on the kind of divorce you have, lawyers in some of these other areas of specialization may have more critical and relevant knowledge than someone who knows only "family law."

So, as with the rest of the advice in this book, we again discover that it's dangerous to rely on simple labels to try to solve difficult problems. Instead, you have to keep your eyes and ears open, pay attention, use your lifetime of training and judgment, and *think*. If you do those things, you'll end up with a lawyer who will do you a good job.

Some Lawyer Types to Avoid

Avoid the kamikaze lawyer.

We all want lawyers who will fight for us. Lawyers pride themselves on fighting for their clients. Lawyering is, after all, not a profession for timid souls or persons with thin skin.

Should you encounter a lawyer who makes speeches about or implies how he will win your case at all cost; that he will crash and burn for you if necessary; will lie, cheat, steal, or trick the other side or the court, then you need to find another lawyer.

Think about it. The legal system, in general, and lawyers, in particular, belong to a network. It is a community of people who handle the same kind of business day after day, year after year. To handle the large volume of cases that must be handled, lawyers and judges must rely on what they are told by each other, even when they are on opposite sides.

Some things are considered appropriate; others are not. Lawyers expect each other to throw hard punches. But most lawyers and judges will only allow one unprotected punch below the belt before they start returning in kind or stop doing business. Your lawyer is allowed to disagree strenuously on your behalf. He is not allowed to say one thing and do another. Your lawyer is expected to present your case in the very best light and not reveal weaknesses in evidence. On the other hand, if he gets caught misrepresenting facts, it will not only adversely affect your case, it will adversely affect his credibility with the lawyers and judges in the community. It is a fine line, but it is taken very seriously by those working regularly in the courthouse.

In short, all of the kamikazes have already crashed; some of them just don't know it yet. If your lawyer is willing to use unscrupulous methods in your case, he probably has done so for someone else before now. Seldom do you find a judge who smiles at this sort of thing. Even less often do you find judges or lawyers with short memories concerning things like being hit from behind.

Hence, when you hire a lawyer who does business like this, you get all of his liabilities as well as the benefits. Usually the costs vastly outweighs the benefits.

Avoid the lawyer who claims to have "special knowledge" or "insider contacts."

Remember, since judges are lawyers, all lawyers went to law school with judges and have friends who are judges. Usually both lawyers in a lawsuit know the judge and, if they don't at the beginning of the case, both lawyers will certainly have a "relationship" with the judge by the end of the case. Therefore, if a lawyer says or implies that he or she is the lawyer for you because he or she has a "special" relationship with the judge, run away to some other lawyer as fast as you can. Many times lawyers are happy with the judge and glad to be in the court in which the case is filed because the particular judge will listen to both sides or because they feel that they know how to communicate with this particular judge. But, these are advantages that are not unique to one lawyer, and this is a far cry from "having a judge in my pocket." Statements of this type from a lawyer are unethical, inappropriate, and potentially illegal. In my experience, when a lawyer *tells or implies to a client* that he or she has "insider" connections, the client is the one who frequently gets left holding the bag.

Avoid the lawyer who is certain about everything and has no doubts.

George Armstrong Custer was the general who commanded the army against the Indians at the battle of Little Big Horn. Although Custer himself was killed in that battle, his spirit is still alive in the form of those who have personalities just like his. Their motto should be "often wrong, but never in doubt." The reason these always-certain personalities get along so well as judges, doctors, lawyers, and business executives is because society is organized so that someone else has to suffer the consequences for their mistakes. For example, if a judge gives a child to an abusive parent, the child's life may be ruined, whereas the "infallible" judge never thinks of the case again. (At least Custer was among those who died for his mistakes.) *Nothing*, or at least not much of anything, on this earth is for certain. If your lawyer won't even discuss risk, probabilities, and possibilities, you might want to consider a second opinion or selecting a different general to lead your troops.

Avoid the lawyer who is cynical or condescending.

Of course, as with the rest of the human race, lawyers don't come right out and say, "Oh, by the way, I'm cynical and condescending." Additionally, some of the "best" sales people are the ones who are the most cynical. Because these people are cynical about you and your problems, they can and will say whatever needs to be said to sell you and keep you sold. But, if you listen closely, usually you can detect when someone thinks you and your problems are beneath him or her. If you get these signals, it's time to look elsewhere for your legal help. You need someone who is genuinely committed to your legal representation. This is not possible for a person who sees himself or herself above it all.

Avoid the lawyer who is "emotionally involved" with you.

A lawyer who is "in love" with you is no better than the cynical lawyer who does not care about you at all. You probably know by now that we do not make good judgments about or for people with whom we have close attachments. A certain amount of "surgical objectivity" is required of your lawyer. Yes, your lawyer needs to understand your pain. But, if you require him or her also to become your confessor, admirer, close friend, and confidant, you will have lost the objective view needed in your lawyer.

Avoid the captured lawyer.

You need honest, objective advice. This is difficult to get from someone you "own." If a lawyer reports to you in your company chain of command, has your father or uncle as his or her best client, or cannot tell you "no" because he or she is married to your sister or brother, this lawyer is not in a position to tell you things you don't want to hear. Perhaps, just as importantly, you won't listen to what this lawyer says when it doesn't agree with what you want to hear. This "trapped" lawyer is not the person you need. Your slave cannot give you good legal advice.

Avoid reliance on so-called listings or "top ratings."

Earlier in this chapter we discussed board certifications awarded by the Texas Board of Legal Specialization. As I stated, a board certification has its limitations and does not provide nearly all of the information needed to select a lawyer. But, board certification is the real thing in the sense that it is based on objective standards. It really does require a lawyer to pass a formidable examination, meet a certain level of experience, and have confidential recommendations made by other lawyers who have observed the lawyer in practice. Many other listings and ratings of lawyers do not have objective standards—unless you consider a beauty-pageant-like selection process to be objective. Many of these "top listings" have more to do with advertising than with actual qualifications. Some lawyers even campaign for these listings by requesting their friends to vote for them. No doubt some of the lawyers chosen for these special honors and "outstanding" lists are good lawyers. But, you should not make your choice based on a listing in "Who's Who Among

Great Divorce Lawyers" or "Best Lawyers In The Birdville Metropolitan Area" or "*The Classy Lawyer Magazine*'s Best Lawyers In Texas" or any lawyer's claim to be "A-rated" in anything or anywhere. The questions you need to ask yourself are, "How would *The Classy Lawyer Magazine* know who is best?" and "What are the politics of getting on this list?" Of course, to answer these questions, you would need a degree in sociology and the investigative budget of a metropolitan newspaper. So, instead, why not spend your time and energy interviewing lawyers and making your choice of who will represent you based on information that is readily available from meeting, questioning, and checking out a few lawyers?

Avoid lawyers who make exaggerated claims or tell you that they don't lose cases.

Unfortunately, Perry Mason made a big impact on the public's concept of what lawyers do. If any physician talked in terms of never having lost a patient, any thinking person would know that he hadn't treated very many patients or that the patients he had treated were not very seriously ill. In any event, he is not practicing medicine, but rather is taking an ego trip.

Lawyers are in precisely the same position. If you open a law office, cases are going to walk through the front door that are terminal. The people with these cases often need help worse than anyone else. If the lawyer is really doing his job, the issue becomes how to mitigate damages or reduce punishment, rather than worrying about winning or losing.

It is unethical for a lawyer to make promises about the outcome of your case. Good lawyers are very careful to tell you that they are merely making predictions. Many things are fairly certain at the courthouse. But when you start hearing the guarantees about outcome, it is time to get it in writing (preferably backed up by a bonding company) or leave.

Avoid loud mouths.

In every city there seems to be some lawyer who is a name-dropper and wants everyone in every restaurant to know that he or she is the busiest attorney in town and represents all the important people. I have even know some lawyers to play this game on television or in the newspapers. If a lawyer tells you about his or her other important clients, this is not the lawyer for you unless you enjoy having your life and secrets scattered about.

Be suspicious of more-for-less claims.

Our court system operates on the free enterprise system. This means that if you want to be heard in court and have your rights protected, you must pay legal fees and expenses. The philosophical problems with this approach to justice are obvious and could be discussed at length. On your way to court is not the time to get involved in such discussion. It is a reality that you must accept if you are going to survive your divorce.

The point is, economic rules apply. Fortunately for you, since the supply of lawyers is large, the price of competition is great. Although there are lawyers who gouge on the price, I trust you will look out for those. But also watch out for the lawyer who says he or she can provide greater services for lower prices than anyone else. In a competitive market, things don't work this way. And since legal services are not tangible items, it is safe to bet that he or she who promises more for less may really be giving less.

Since you write the check to the lawyer, you may be tempted to see the lawyer as only an economic predator in the jungle of the free enterprise legal system. Remember, the lawyer also is one of the hunted in this jungle. His cost for library, secretaries, space, and other costly necessities is much the same as that of every other lawyer. Hence, when a lawyer promises you more for less, he or she is either dumb, malicious, or is charging someone else extra, to provide charming, deserving people like you with charity—just the way the grocer charges some people double for beans so you can have yours free.

Be suspicious of a lack of experience.

Good lawyers, like fine wine, are not made overnight. In law practice, as in everything else, experience is important. This is not to say that a lawyer with twenty-years experience is better than one with two-years experience. The contrary is sometimes true. Experience varies. One lawyer who has been in practice for only one year may have tried more cases than another who has practiced for ten years.

A debate has been going on for years about which is more important, theoretical knowledge as it is gained in school or practical experience as it is gained on the job. Those engaging in this argument usually overlook the obvious answer: both.

The legal profession has not yet bit the bullet and faced the fact that a formal internship or apprenticeship is needed after law school. The profession has been able to avoid this because practically every lawyer, sooner or later, gets this experience informally. But, unless your divorce is exceedingly simple, you do not need to be represented by someone who is just out of law school and getting this experience at your expense, without the supervision of a more experienced lawyer.

Don't make the perfect the enemy of the good.

No, all lawyers are not equally competent. But, words like "competent," "smart," "powerful," and "articulate" must always be qualified. If some lawyer is said to be competent, the question must be asked, "Competent to do what?" The law is so vast and the skills required for different aspects of law practice so broad that no one can be competent to do everything. A lawyer who is a good tax lawyer may or may not be a good trial lawyer. The best trial lawyer in town before a jury may have previously offended the judge in your case and be very ineffective in that court. The most brilliant legal scholar in town may be totally disinterested in your case and give it only passing care and interest.

The looking-for-a-savior mentality is not helpful in choosing a lawyer. Lawyers, politicians, doctors, and others sometimes try to sell themselves by playing the role of the benign super-protector. The truth is that the perfect quarterback does not exist and never did, except in the minds of those who attended the game only on the day when their quarterback could do no wrong.

When you hire a "good lawyer," you will be hiring a real person, someone with strengths and weaknesses. Not infrequently, the lawyer's strong points will also be his or her weaknesses. For example: If your lawyer is a passionate advocate on your behalf, he or she may not be as coldly objective about your case as is needed. Or, if the lawyer possesses an incredible objectivity, it may be that he or she will lack the passion to fight for your cause when it is difficult or discouraging. A lawyer who is an extremely competent trial technician may ruin a settlement because aggressive behavior in his or her personality blocks the perspective needed to see the advantages in a settlement. There are strength-weakness trade-offs in every personality, although they are more apparent in some than in others. The recognition of these strength-weakness trade-offs will allow you to recognize that you need an attorney with balance and humanity, rather than some imaginary super-lawyer.

Be careful about lawyers who are too easy to hire in complex cases.

Most of us are more comfortable in less formal relationships. Stiff relationships tend to "put us off" or make us suspicious. But, the important things in life require a little formality. If you find a lawyer who is very casual about taking you on as a client, this lawyer may be very casual about the way your case is handled. This may be all right for a very simple case, and it works for many lawyers who operate high-volume, clinic-type practices that cater to very simple divorces. However, a lawyer who undertakes a complex case in a casual manner very likely won't be able to follow through on the commitments necessary to meet the challenges in such a case.

Most lawyers who are serious about what they do will be concerned about whether you have the financial, emotional, and mental resources necessary to follow through in your divorce. Clients who can't afford legal fees have the potential of literally putting a lawyer out of business. The court system, landlords, employees, and software companies, to name just a few, require lawyers to make payments to stay in the game. Likewise, most lawyers have experienced a client's unanswered phone in the days leading up to a hearing or trial. Having a client who doesn't show up either mentally or physically is no fun.

If your lawyer does not *clearly* tell you what the agreement is between the two of you, that should be your cue to ask yourself whether this lawyer is really taking your representation seriously. Those who rent expensive equipment or make agreements involving substantial money do not do so without firm understandings. In all except the simplest cases, undertaking your representation is just such a substantial undertaking.

Some people are alarmed if a lawyer or other professional presents them with an engagement letter or a contract of employment. A cause for greater alarm should be if you are not presented with such a contract or engagement letter. True, many of the terms of this agreement will limit and define what the lawyer will do for you. But, this written agreement tells you exactly what you are contracting for, what your obligations are, what your lawyer is obligated to do for you, and what you can expect.

Likewise, you should not be pressured into quickly signing a contract for employment or an engagement letter. Although most lawyers have standard agreements that they routinely use with clients, this may be your only time ever to hire a lawyer on a substantial matter. Therefore, the contract between you and the lawyer should not be treated as something that you must quickly sign "as is." This is just another way for a lawyer to treat you and your case as another run-of-the-mill matter. Lawyers who take their relationships with their clients seriously want the client to understand and actually agree with any hiring agreement that is signed. These lawyers will not object to your taking the agreement and considering it over hours or days and discussing it again before signing it. Undertaking the representation of a client is a serious matter that deserves serious consideration. You need to make sure that this is your lawyer's attitude toward you and your case.

Be careful about "flat-fee" or "fixed-fee" contracts in complex matters.

The problem for lawyers in divorce cases or other complex litigation is that the lawyer has very limited control. No lawyer can know how long a lawsuit is going to take or what issues will arise. Therefore, if a lawyer agrees to take your contested divorce case on a so-called "flatfee," you should be very suspicious. You may think that you are "cutting a good deal" and that the lawyer will be forced to take the risk for anything that goes wrong in the case. My experience in watching lawyers who operate in this manner suggests to me that the more likely scenario is that at some point your "flat-fee" lawyer will just stop working on your case.

An hourly rate can be very high and painful for clients, but it is usually the best and fairest alternative. The only alternative for lawyers who are unwilling to be put out of business or simply breach an agreement with a flat-fee client, is to set flat or fixed fees so outrageously high that they will cover all contingencies.

Contingent fees in which the attorney takes a percentage of the recovery are properly frowned upon in divorce cases. This is because the recovery of at least a portion of the community property is a virtual certainty. Perhaps contingent fees should be reserved as a rare last resort in cases in which a spouse is going to lose his or her interest in property unless unaffordable representation is obtained.

Find an attorney who you believe will be honest and fair with you in charging hourly rate fees.

Think hard about whether you want an attorney who does not carry malpractice insurance.

I cannot say that I would not hire an attorney who does not carry malpractice insurance. This is because I know a few very good attorneys who, after thinking about it, have decided that they will not have malpractice coverage. Because I am personally acquainted with other outstanding attributes that each of these lawyers has, I would, without hesitation, engage one of these lawyers to represent me. But, I must hasten to add that, for lawyers I don't know, whether or not they have malpractice insurance would be an important factor in my deciding whether to hire them.

Does having malpractice insurance make someone a better lawyer? Absolutely not. Does having malpractice insurance mean that a client has a better guarantee of getting a good result from a lawyer? Again, absolutely not. Most decisions made by lawyers are "judgment calls" in which the lawyer is allowed to use his or her best judgment without incurring any malpractice liability regardless of whether the decision turns out to be prudent in hindsight. But, I believe that having malpractice insurance indicates that the insured lawyer has an attitude of responsibility toward the client. This may not always be true, because some lawyers have malpractice insurance to protect their wealth. Most lawyers, like most Americans, however, are probably "judgment proof." That is, the assets they own are all in exempt property such as homes, retirement plans, automobiles, insurance policies, etc. When these lawyers make the rather large sacrifice of purchasing malpractice insurance, a part of the reason may be for their own financial protection, but there is also another element that has to do with seeing to it that clients are protected if someone in the office drops the ball. Also, it seems to me that many lawyers who don't carry malpractice insurance are also the ones who cut corners in other ways, including their own access to legal materials, the quality and quantity of staff used to service clients, continuing legal education, etc. Of course, all of these other things are extremely difficult to quantify. But, that's the beauty of malpractice insurance. It's an objective question that can be answered with an objective answer. Either a lawyer does or does not have it and, if so, can tell you the limits of liability.

Use your own judgment. If you go into the average lawyer's office and ask about malpractice insurance, you may be shown the door or you may be labeled as a "troublemaker." But it really is a fair question for any lawyer. It is also a question that should be asked of the State Bar of Texas. Why aren't all lawyers required to have malpractice insurance of some kind?

Chapter 6

Locating a Lawyer

Discourage litigation. Persuade your neighbors to compromise whenever you can. As a peacemaker the lawyer has superior opportunity of being a good man. There will still be business enough.

—Abraham Lincoln

There is a very important rule concerning hiring a lawyer. *Don't equate locating a lawyer with choosing a lawyer!* Obviously, if you don't know any lawyers, you must go through a process of learning some lawyer's name, street address, approximate age, national origin, whether he or she appears smart or dumb, whether she smiles all the time or looks like she has just lost her mother. By just meeting the lawyer, you are going to learn additional items such as whether he is cross-eyed or her nose runs all the time. But, just because you met the lawyer and learned all of these things does not mean that you have to marry the poor devil. You are a client, not a social worker. You are trying to find someone to help you! You can get up and walk out. You can shop around. You can say, "I'm not ready to hire a lawyer yet, I just want to hire a few minutes of your time."

After reading the last chapter about what lawyers do and how they work and *after thinking about what you want in the way of a lawyer*, you should be able to use this location process to find one or more lawyers who fit the description of what you're looking for.

How do you locate a lawyer?

There are five ways that I know:

1. You know or meet a lawyer
2. Reputation or asking someone
3. Advertising
4. Russian roulette with the phone book
5. Calling a lawyer referral service

These are methods of *locating* a lawyer. I am not implying that you must meet "x" number of lawyers before you make a choice. If you are absolutely satisfied with the first lawyer you locate (as you very well may be), then you may want to choose that lawyer to represent you. If, however, you have the slightest doubt, why not look further before you make a choice?

If you already know a lawyer in whom you have confidence to either represent you, or refer you to another lawyer, you really have already made a choice. This is fine, as you will see when we get down to the discussion of making choices.

Reputation

Bar associations are fond of saying lawyers don't need to advertise because lawyers get their business by reputation. Reputation is a word that has a nice solid sound—like "you can rely on it." The implication is that people will hear about and recognize good products. It's a great theory, especially when spoken with some authority by a distinguished gentleman in a $900 suit behind a walnut desk. But I fear that reputation is often as susceptible to manipulation by packaging and marketing as it is by the quality of the product. Another word for reputation might be gossip. This is not to say that all reputations are inaccurate or should not be relied upon. To the contrary, we rightly make many of our day-to-day decisions based on hearsay, gossip, and opinion. All of this is just to say that reputation has limited use in choosing a lawyer. A lawyer who wears a pinstripe suit, appears at the right cocktail parties, and has a pleasant personality can have a fine reputation in circles, while a lawyer who spends all of his time in the library and wears white socks might be viewed as a nerd by the same group.

Of course, some of the validity of reputation or gossip can be discerned by considering the source. For example, a lawyer is probably a better source of an opinion about another lawyer's ability than your hairdresser.

Advertising

Advertising is a good locator, but choice should be based wholly on other factors.

Advertising has been hailed by its supporters as the answer to the lack of adequate legal representation available to the public at large. Although it probably is a step in the right direction, it certainly isn't a cure-all in choosing a lawyer. It probably is less reliable than reputation.

Lawyers are now advertising free initial consultation. Take them up on it! Go in and see what he or she has to say for himself or herself. Then go away and consider if this is who you really want to represent you. Make them stick by the "free" part of the ad.

The Internet has been hailed as the answer to everything. Make no mistake, the Internet is advertising. The large media companies that have traditionally supplied lawyers with library and software are marketing Internet listings and websites to lawyers. Lawyers, along with everyone else in business, are spending heavily so that you can search them out on the Internet. That's fine, but you must still see it for what it is: advertising.

Russian Roulette

Taking a chance by just picking a name out of the phone book or off of the Internet also gives you good odds of getting an adequate lawyer. But you should attempt to exercise choice and increase your odds and chances for success.

Lawyer Referral Services

This is just a narrower form of Russian roulette, since most referral services allow any lawyer who desires to have his or her name included on a list to do so. Of course, lawyers listed as specialists give you the assurance of getting someone who, at least, has had enough interest in the subject to get additional training.

SECTION II

Protecting Yourself

In this section:

Chapter 7

Protecting Yourself from Your Spouse: Physically, Emotionally, and Financially

Selfish is not living as one wishes to live, it is asking others to live as one wishes to live.

—Oscar Wilde

Many dangers are relatively easy to avoid if you know the danger is there and take reasonable steps to avoid it. Often, we are hurt by the *unexpected*—the thing that "comes from out-of-nowhere." After we are "wiped out" by one of these out-of-nowhere events, we look back and say, "If I had paid even the slightest attention, I would have seen it coming." But of course, by then, it's too late.

That's what this chapter is about—getting you to think through the ways you might be harmed by your soon-to-be-ex-spouse. This information is not intended to warn of a "spook behind every bush." In fact, my intent is just the opposite—to call your attention to the very specific fact that your prior relationship with your spouse may make you vulnerable to being harmed by him or her.

In many divorces restraining orders and injunctions are totally unnecessary. Many divorcing spouses, from beginning to end, sincerely bend over backward to protect and care for their divorcing partner. If your spouse is putting money in the bank account, insisting that you and the children take the best car and remain in the nice big house near the school, or doing other similarly positive things, don't bite the hand that's helping you. But, at the same time, don't doze off at the wheel.

Sincerity is not always easy to judge. There are more "good guys" in divorces than the press would lead you to believe; however, there is also an adequate supply of smooth and sophisticated manipulators angling to take advantage of their power over the partners they are divorcing. These spouses use their partners' love, trust, loyalty, pity, or even their sense of fair play, to hurt, betray, manipulate, or cheat them. Often a spouse is victimized precisely because he or she feels safe or comfortable with the spouse; or perhaps more accurately, he or she feels comfortable with the *relationship* with the spouse. In other cases the spouse is victimized because he or she feels helpless or trapped because of a continuing co-dependancy or other pathological attachment to his or her partner. The point is, you must not feel *safe* in your dealings with your spouse. And, even if you don't feel *safe* in the conventional sense, you must understand intellectually that your relationship makes you vulnerable to manipulation that can harm you.

So, let's "do the inventory" on your spouse and, perhaps more importantly, your relationship with him or her. Use the next few pages to stimulate your brain and help you think about your own situation—just in case you may have missed something and before it's too late to do any thing about it.

Do Not Expect Other People to Protect You If You Won't Protect Yourself

Your community is built around many institutions and individuals who will help protect you from violence, manipulation, and abuse. The police, the courts, neighbors, your lawyer, your family, and friends will all help you avoid getting hurt or cheated. However, if you expect other people to protect you when you don't *use your own head* to protect your own body, mind, and soul, then you will make fools out of those trying to help you and get yourself hurt to boot. If you don't take care of yourself, then who can? Or more to the point, who should?

Getting Your Brain in the Game – Why Now Is the Time to Re-Evaluate Risk

Divorces don't just fall out of the sky. With rare exceptions, divorces are not filed unless there is something *wrong—really wrong*! And spouses who divorce for trivial reasons—without something being *really wrong*—are sometimes the most psychopathic and dangerous to deal with. So, if a divorce is a reality in your life, you owe it to yourself to re-evaluate your relationship with your spouse realistically and objectively in light of the fact that:

1. We are now getting a divorce.
2. That means there is something *really wrong.*
3. I may not yet fully understand *what* is wrong.
4. If I wait for future events to educate me about *what is really wrong,* it may be too late to prevent me from being badly hurt or damaged.

In other words, if you attempt to go through your divorce believing intellectually and emotionally that you are dealing with the "man or woman I married," you could be setting yourself up to be badly hurt. By hurt, I mean physical injury or being tricked out of children or property.

Avoiding Pivotal Moments of Divorce Disaster

Divorces are often filed based on shock or fatigue. In other words, *divorces usually arise out of intensity of feeling and not out of clarity of thought.* The filing spouse acts out of a feeling that *something* is so wrong that it demands this huge, previously unthinkable step of dissolving the marriage. This intensity-over-clarity factor is usually doubly true for a spouse receiving notice that his or her marital partner has just filed for divorce. For many, divorce produces feelings of *intense confusion.* The world is "turned upside down." Some experience only *intense relief.*

It is common knowledge that divorcing spouses often focus strong negative feelings on the other spouse. Anger, hatred, bitterness, resentment, hostility, betrayal, or revulsion are intense feelings commonly thought to dominate the divorcing spouse's psyche. But, contrary to popular belief, these strong emotions usually don't end up as neatly wrapped bombs carefully aimed at the other spouse. In many divorcing spouses, these strong feelings are mixed with a huge dose of guilt, self-doubt, depression, self-loathing, fear, loneliness, shame, confusion, denial, and, yes, even love or pity for the soon-to-be-former-spouse. So, in most divorcing spouses, *not only is there lack of clarity in thought, there is lack of clarity in feeling.* This means that in moments of highest stress, the dominant controlling factor is the overwhelming blur of *intense, mixed feelings*. In short, these powerful, mixed feelings are the kind of "bomb" that may hurt the spouse carrying it rather than the intended target.

So here's the emotional picture of most of us going through divorce: (1) the other spouse figures heavily into our *hugely intense and mixed feelings*; and, (2) our relationship with our spouse is the central stage upon which most of our experiences, habits, feeling, and interactions of the past few years have played out. Given these factors, guess who is likely to be at the center of a *pivotal moment* when we are overwrought, distressed, or temporarily crazed? Our spouse!

And how do these *pivotal moments of divorce disaster* play out? Often, because the human race is, by and large, exceedingly lucky, nothing really bad happens. But it can. Those who routinely deal with divorce have stories of bizarre irrational incidents that sometimes border on being unbelievable. Some examples of *pivotal moments of divorce disaster*:

- A spouse agrees to give custody of the children to the other parent who has had little or nothing to do with their day-to-day care.
- A spouse may agree to move back in with a physically violent spouse. Or have "just one meeting" with a homicidal spouse.
- A contract is signed so a drug addict can sell the house. This, of course, was done as a good faith gesture to show the drug addict that his or her spouse was being supportive.
- Money, often the only money, is turned over to a spendthrift.
- We make love "one last time" only to learn that "we're pregnant."

- A spouse's "confession" to irrelevant feelings turns a heretofore uncontested case into an all-out war.
- A spouse is persuaded that he or she doesn't need a lawyer and that he or she should agree to give his or her spouse all or most of the marital assets.

This is a short list of examples of how you, too, can be victimized during your divorce.

Lawyers are bewildered by this kind of conduct. When clients engage in such conduct, lawyers say "I only represent idiots." Psychologists, who are better trained in these matters, talk of psychotic behavior. And this is probably right. But it misses the point.

People living under extremely stressful conditions suffering intense, mixed-up emotions can and do make intelligent decisions. But doing so usually requires thinking things through *before* the disaster occurs. When we give ourselves the opportunity to work through, intellectually, the dynamics of our own feelings about our soon-to-be-former spouse, we give the "higher functions" of our cerebral cortex the ability to take control away from our "reptilian brain." This usually allows most relatively normal people to avoid the catastrophes that can arise from dealings with a divorcing spouse. If you are in this position, it is important to begin the process of *thinking through it* right this moment.

The Three-Minute List of Ways Your Spouse Can Harm You

Let's take three minutes to think about ways you can be harmed by your spouse. For many, nothing on the following list will apply. It will confirm that there is little to worry about. Others, who are confronting overt hostility from a spouse, won't need any list to remind them that they are under threat. But, if something on this list vaguely sounds or feels like something you have heard or something you recognize in your divorce, pay attention! Using your head for just a few moments may cause you to see a blip on your radar screen that saves you a lot of grief.

Ways your spouse can hurt you:

- Physical Violence. If you have been physically assaulted or if your spouse has threatened physical assault, you must take this seriously. You must realize that it is not your fault. Nothing justifies this conduct. The next chapter describes ways to protect yourself from physical violence.
- Physical or sexual abuse of your children. Whether you like it or not, if your spouse is abusing your child, that is also a threat aimed directly at you. This is because the child welfare authorities will hold you responsible for any abuse to your children that you did not report. This may cause your children to be taken away from you. You cannot cover for your spouse on any physical or sexual abuse of your child without losing your child.
- Emotional Abuse. Most abuse in marriage is mental or emotional. Filing a divorce usually does not automatically stop this wonderful activity. The real danger to you arises when your spouse uses this technique to persuade you to give up rights to children or property. Emotional abuse can also drain your mental and emotional resources, the very things you need to live life and be happy. If you continue to be affected by this kind of conduct from your spouse, consider going to a trained counselor, such as a psychologist or social worker.
- Persuading you not to participate in the divorce process. Failing to defend yourself in the divorce court means that you can lose everything; this includes your children. You can even lose your separate property to which your spouse has no legal rights. Much of the rest of this book has to do with defending yourself in a divorce.
- Persuading you to sign a settlement agreement that you don't understand or that has not been carefully thought through by you and your lawyer.
- Persuading you to make "side deals" that aren't revealed to the court or included in the divorce decree. These "deals" are not enforceable. This is a good way to lose whatever the "deal" is supposed to represent, whether that is rights to your children, your property, or portions of your power over your life. Everything about these "side deals" is triply true if your spouse is insisting that the agreement must be made right now and there is no time to think about it and

wait and consult your attorney. Don't sign agreements, deeds, promissory notes, titles to motor vehicles, checks, or anything else under these circumstances.

- Persuading you not to hire a lawyer. If there are special reasons to use only one lawyer, let it be your lawyer. Why should you be the one to do without legal advice? If one lawyer is representing you both as an *intermediary*, turn to the chapter on "Hiring a Lawyer" and read the section on intermediaries.
- Using the court system to harass you. Everyone has the right to defend himself or herself in court and prosecute his or her lawsuit to the full extent of the law. But, some divorcing spouses go far beyond what is necessary to prosecute or defend their cases and use the court system for pure harassment. Unfortunately, there are lawyers who specialize in this kind of conduct. They file unnecessary motions, take unnecessary depositions, and convert basically uncontested matters into unnecessary formal hearing and proceedings. There is not a lot you can do about this kind of conduct, except to use your own legal resources wisely. This kind of conduct often backfires on the spouse attempting to use it. Remember, the offending spouse is having to pay his or her lawyer for all of this unnecessary work. Many lawyers willing to engage in this kind of conduct are not even loyal to their own clients. Some lawyers infamous for needless churning of the file and harassment are also known to dump their clients routinely after the money to pay fees runs out. Also, a few good judges are willing to pay attention to this kind of conduct and require the offending party to pay the other party's attorney fees and cost for having to defend against harassing or needless conduct.
- Attempting to turn your children against you. Make no mistake, this kind of conduct is aimed right at your heart. If you are experiencing it, you know it can be one of the most painful and distressing things in life. Read the section on "Parental Alienation Syndrome" in the chapter on child custody.
- Interference with the rearing of your children. There is a type of parent who, though absolutely incapable of parenting, makes it his or her lifelong crusade to ensure that no one, including the other

parent, teachers, scout leaders, coaches, other relatives, the police department, or anyone else will have any opportunity to help the child grow up. As you might imagine, this type of person frequently also can't get along with their spouse, so they end up divorced. If you happen to have a child with this type of parent and care about your child's well-being, you can look forward to many years of battle in which you will be a primary target. You will need to keep good records and educate the divorce court about how this spouse does business, so you should get started now.

These are but a few of the many ways that you can be harmed by your spouse. Again, I urge you to use this brief and incomplete list to think through the ways that you might be harmed by your spouse and ways that you might prepare mentally to avoid or minimize the harm.

Psychological Protection

Even if your spouse isn't violent, manipulative, or otherwise dangerous to you, a divorce requires some rather severe shifting of psychological attitudes toward your spouse. No matter how bad your marriage has been, you probably still have feelings of loyalty and responsibility toward your mate. You have just been in a relationship where openness, honesty, and forthrightness were necessary to intimacy and success in your marriage.

But if you continue to tell your spouse about your feelings or your desires, you probably are setting yourself up to have these things used against you. Refusal to continue sharing your feelings with your spouse is not deception. There is now a good part of your new life that is none of your marriage partner's business. It is like telling the auctioneer how much you are willing to spend for an item. If you do, you shouldn't be surprised when the bidding stops at just the amount you mentioned. Your spouse was formerly your partner in bidding at the auction. Now, no matter how painful it is, your spouse is in a different position with different interests to protect. You are now separate bidders at the auction, often bidding on the same things.

This doesn't mean that you can't ask him the location of the "magic" plug he always used to unstop the sewer or solicit from her the forgotten name of the good baby-sitter. While such exchanges of information are not critical to survival, they do make life more pleasant and add a touch of civility and class to the not-too-easy ritual of separation. But there are two things you must not do. Do not depend on your spouse for advice about your divorce. Do not use your spouse as a counselor by continuing to share hopes, dreams, aspirations, or angers with him or her. For these things you must turn to old friends, new relationships, your lawyer, a psychologist, a psychiatrist, your family, or the newspaper boy. But do not turn to your spouse.

Even assuming good intentions on everybody's part, taking advice and counseling from your spouse, at this point can still get you hurt accidentally. No matter how well intended the friendship and trust between you, the words belie the fact that *you are separating.* Sooner or later the words and the actions must come together. And if you're beyond getting the marriage back together, it is the words that will have to change. Start now, before you do more damage to your already bent psyche.

Who knows, maybe you and your spouse will end up friends—later. (Miracles do happen!) But not now. Now is the time for pulling back, learning to be separate.

Chapter 8

Protecting Yourself from Violence

Barbarism is the absence of standards to which appeal can be made.

—Jose Ortega y Gasset

All cruelty springs from weakness.

—Seneca

If your spouse physically abuses you, you must protect yourself. In some cases, separation and filing for divorce do not always stop the physical violence or threats of violence.

If physical violence is even a possibility with your soon-to-be former spouse, there are some rules you must follow to protect yourself.

If you are in the midst of a violent episode when you read this (if, for example, you are afraid your spouse will show up any minute and beat you up), don't wait to read this chapter and think things out philosophically, just call the police. The police can work with you to keep you out of harm's way. They can put you in contact with a protective shelter organization so that you and your children can be kept safely hidden from your spouse until other steps can be taken to ensure your safety. Of course, the very next step you should take is to contact a lawyer and begin legal proceeding leading to protective orders, restraining orders, and/or injunction.

You Must Be Consistent

It is not unusual for spouses who are violent to be very inconsistent in their conduct. One day they may be "nice" and sweet, bending over backward to show respect and regard for you. The next day the physical violence or threats of violence return to the scene. If you join in this manipulative game, you must expect that you are increasing the probabilities of being hurt.

Once you are convinced that physical abuse is a part of your spouse's response, you must draw some realistic lines and maintain them constantly. You must get away and stay away. You must draw an imaginary line at your curb or your front door and let it be understood that your spouse is not to cross that line, even when he or she is nice. Although this may seem absurd at the moment, and your spouse may even try to use it to get sympathy from onlookers, it might keep you from being beaten on another day when he or she is not nice and no one else is looking. If you allow the violent person to come in and sit on your chair or at your table, the probability increases that you are going to experience the same violence or threats of violence when the two of you are alone. *Hence, the easiest way to avoid violence is to make sure that the two of you are never alone again.*

It might be uncomfortable for you and the kids to sleep on pallets at your sister's house while you are having the divorce papers served on him or her, but it is more comfortable than being beaten up. Having a friend walk you to your car after work might not always be convenient, but good friends don't mind.

Know where your police or sheriff department's twenty-four hour operations entrance is. If your spouse tries to pull you off the road in your car, drive very calmly, within the speed limit, to that entrance. If you cannot safely exit the car and enter the station before your spouse arrives, then begin honking the horn. If you cannot make it to the police station, you need to have in mind some other all-night facility where people are located. Go there. Create whatever scene is necessary to attract attention and call the police.

If your spouse is one of the really crazy kind that might beat you up even with other people around, then you have two alternatives:Have someone around who is bigger, stronger, or meaner than he or she (if that's even possible) or *hide*. Yes, you heard me correctly, hide. If he or she can't find you, he or she can't hurt you. Have the divorce papers served at a time when you can leave town until the temporary hearing is held. Although this is not the way you would want to be treated or to treat someone if you had a reasonable choice, your choice is either to risk injury or do it this way. That decision ought to be easy. See the topic on *protective shelters* below.

Another thing about hiding. If your spouse is really dangerous, this is the only alternative. Restraining orders are effective against the vast majority of abusers. But, every year across the state, spouses who are supposedly being protected by restraining orders are killed or badly injured by seriously crazy spouses who often also kill themselves.

Call the Police

Do call the police—every time your space (home or workplace) is trespassed. Once you make it clear that you are afraid of the spouse and do not want him or her around, do not fail to report intentional entrances into your places. By all means be as calm and reasonable as possible in describing to the police the trespass committed by your spouse. Remember that other people don't always tell the truth when making such reports, so don't be surprised if the police are skeptical.

If you file criminal charges for assault or trespass, do not withdraw them or fail to cooperate in their prosecution. If you do, you will find the police and prosecutor less than sympathetic the next time you complain. No matter how much you feel sorry for your spouse, you must protect yourself by letting these public officials know that you will cooperate with them in protecting yourself.

Police departments have become very sensitive to domestic violence complaints. Police have always been willing to respond to domestic violence calls, but in the past, the tendency was to write a report and not take any action or make an arrest. This is no longer true. Now, it is likely that someone will be arrested. Nevertheless, there are still times and places when officers are reluctant to step into a dispute between husband and wife.

If you had difficulty in getting the police to respond to your calls for help by taking affirmative action when you were suffering violence during the marriage, keep in mind that the police will probably be more responsive to your complaints now that you are separated. This is not to justify the physical abuse that you received while married. The law forbids anybody to beat on anybody else—married or not. But police and prosecutors sometimes become demoralized and feel helpless in trying to referee domestic violence. They know that if they stop it on one occasion, it will flare up again in a day, a week, or a month after the complaining party has refused to press charges. Hence, do not fail to call for help just because you could not get help before. Remember, police departments keep records of such complaints. You should also write down the name of the officer investigating your complaint, in case the record cannot be found. Later, if police and prosecutors become convinced that your spouse is a chronic offender, they are more likely to prosecute more vigorously.

Use Go-Betweens

Use third-party places to exchange custody of the children for visitation. In very serious cases, you might want to consider arrangements for the children to be let off and picked up at their grandmother's house or at a close friend's. If this is handled right, the kids will think nothing of it; it will be just another trip to Grandma's or to the cousin's house. This might keep you from having to play the guard dog at the front door while the kids are present.

Use the Phone

All the discussions about child visitation or exchanges of property should be conducted over the telephone. Because your lives have been entwined for years, discussions must sometimes be held between spouses parting ways. If, however, violence is a possibility, then these discussions can and should be held over the phone. Here you should use your best and most controlled personality. Not one ugly word! And if your spouse becomes verbally abusive, tell him or her as politely as possible that you are going to hang up—and do so.

Get a Cell Phone

No, I don't work for the phone company. And, yes, I do agree that many people who have cell phones don't need them. But, if your spouse is of the violent variety who is intent on catching you at a vulnerable, helpless moment, such as when you are in the car alone, a cell phone can be a wonderful defense. It might save your life or keep you from being injured. If your spouse knows you have a cell phone, it may even keep him or her from coming around or waiting for you after work.

Use Court Orders

If violence is likely, there is no excuse for failure to have court-ordered protection after a divorce is filed. If your spouse has used violence against you or threatened violence, the divorce should include a restraining order or injunction. A statute makes the violation of such an order a criminal offense. It is a Class B misdemeanor, and conviction may be punished with up to six months in jail. It is no longer necessary to prove that you were beaten. If the court order says that your spouse is not to come around your home or workplace, then his or her very presence there is a crime. If he or she is present when the police officer arrives, then he or she will be committing a crime in the presence of the officer. This means that he or she can be arrested on the spot without a warrant. If he or she has already left the premises, then if the officers believe your statement that your spouse was present, a complaint will be filed. A warrant will then be issued for his or her arrest.

If you are protected by a court order, your lawyer will probably provide you with a copy of the statute. Of course, *it is desirable for you to have a certified copy of the court order in your possession.* This will save you time and give you added protection.

In the unlikely event that you cannot get assistance from the law enforcement officials, then you can still fall back on the restraining order. The stages are:

1. Your lawyer asks the court to grant a restraining order.
2. If the court grants the request, then it becomes effective on your spouse when it is served on him by the sheriff.

3. Within ten days (or sooner, if your spouse makes a request to the court), a hearing is held to decide if the temporary restraining order is to be continued in effect. If the court continues the restraining order, it is now called a "temporary injunction."
4. If your spouse violates either the temporary restraining order or the injunction by doing injury to you, or coming around you, then your lawyer must file another motion asking that he be held in contempt.
5. Your spouse must be served with the motion for contempt and given notice of the date of the hearing.
6. At the hearing, your spouse is given opportunity to "show cause" why the court should not find him in contempt.
7. If the court thinks that its order was intentionally violated, then your spouse might be placed in jail.

An additional discussion of temporary orders is found in Chapter 10.

Shelters

Most metropolitan areas in Texas now have housing facilities for spouses and children who are threatened with physical violence by a spouse, significant other, or a parent. Of course, these shelters have social workers or trained staff to counsel and assist persons dealing with family violence. These institutions go under different names in different communities. Some local organizations are referred to as Women's Protective Service, Family Crisis Center, Domestic Violence Prevention, or similar names. The shelter nearest you can be located by calling the National Domestic Violence Hotline 1-800-799-SAFE (7233). Or a list of local organizations and their phone numbers can be found at the website for the Texas Council on Family Violence at www.tcfv.org. Different local organizations provide these services in their own way using a variety of approaches, all designed to provide protection from a violent partner or parent.

SECTION III

The Divorce Case – Basic Procedures

In this section:

Chapter 9

Beginning Your Divorce: Filing a Lawsuit

Everyone has a will to win,
but very few have a will to prepare to win.

—Vince Lombardi

As far as the courts are concerned, a divorce is a lawsuit—nothing more, nothing less. Like any other lawsuit, divorce can involve disputes over money or property, disputes over children, questions about tort or contract. In a divorce, however, the court is being asked to change the status of the parties. As far as the law is concerned, the parties are now married. The divorce suit asks that the *status* be changed, so that in the future the law will consider them as separate, unmarried individuals.

In Texas, the person who initiates the divorce is called the *petitioner*. In other lawsuits in Texas and in other jurisdictions, sometimes the initiator is referred to as the *plaintiff* or the *complainant*. These words sometimes are used interchangeably, and lawyers will know to whom you are referring no matter which one of the words you use. The person against whom the lawsuit is brought in a Texas divorce case is referred to as the *respondent*. However, this person may sometimes be called the *defendant*.

It is a basic rule of our legal system that all parties to lawsuits have the right and opportunity to defend against the things that are being said against them. For this ideal to become a reality, both parties must know what the other side is saying against them, that is, whether they are being charged with breach of contract, stealing the other person's mule, or doing physical harm to the other man's wife.

If one party is not told what the other party is claiming ahead of time, there will be no way to prepare evidence and defend against it. Therefore, lawsuits are conducted by written pleadings. It might be helpful to think of these pleadings as something akin to letters written to the court, telling the court why it should or should not grant judgment for or against a particular party.

In a Texas divorce case, the lawsuit is initiated by a pleading referred to as the *Original Petition. When people say they have* "filed for divorce," *what they actually mean is that an* Original Petition *was filed in the courthouse and a filing fee was paid.* A divorce petition will contain such formalities as names, addresses, and ages of the petitioner and the respondent. It must ask that a divorce be granted and must set out the petitioner's request for custody orders for the children, division of the property, requests for child support, and injunctive relief.

The respondent then replies to the court by a document referred to as the *Original Answer*. In the Original Answer, the respondent (other spouse) may state that the court does not have jurisdiction or that the lawsuit is filed in the wrong county. Texas is a jurisdiction that does not require a response to everything in the Original Petition, but allows the respondent to put everything into issue by denying, generally, everything that the petitioner has alleged. The respondent is also allowed to ask for anything that the petitioner could ask for in a lawsuit. This is done by filing a *counterclaim* in addition to the Original Answer.

Of course, as time goes on, events may cause the parties to want to add to their lawsuits or to drop some complaint they had, or they simply may discover that they have forgotten something that they wish to allege against the other party. They are allowed to do this by *amending* their pleadings, which then are referred to as "*First Amended Original Petition*" (or fourth or fifth), or "*Third Amended Original Answer.*" In addition, if parties do not wish to change their entire answer, they may simply supplement a pleading by filing a "*First Supplemental Answer*" or "*First Supplemental Petition.*" Supplemental pleadings have the disadvantage of not having *all* of the pleadings in one document, since a supplemental answer or petition does not replace the previous documents as does an amended pleading. Pleadings sometimes are referred to also as "*motions,*" such as *Motion to Compel, Motion to Modify*, or *Motion for Summary Judgment.*

There are some strenuous limitations on pleadings in Texas divorce cases. In earlier times, pleadings sometimes were used as a way of slandering the other party. For example, a bitter wife might allege as grounds for the divorce that the husband had committed adultery and set out in detail the names of the persons with whom he allegedly had sex and the details of the sex act. Or an alienated husband might allege physical cruelty and set out in detail just how the wife had abused him and the kids over a number of years.

Texas courts now properly frown on this sort of pleading activity. The law now provides that such allegations are to be stricken from the court records upon motion of the slandered spouse. For the most part, Texas divorce pleadings follow very standard language, merely reciting that one of the grounds for divorce is adultery or mental cruelty. This has had the effect of standardizing divorce pleadings. In divorce cases, unlike other kinds of lawsuit in which pleadings often contain detailed fact descriptions, pleadings are "forms" that use key words to raise particular issues, claims, or defenses.

If the party who is being complained against wants to know in more detail the specific facts of such allegations, then he or she must use "discovery" (to be described very shortly) to determine the exact facts and allegations.

Although the general rules of pleadings are very simple, in trial they can become a life or death matter. Certain elements of pleading are very technical and can keep you from being able to raise a defense or assert a complaint or ground for relief in court. For example, if you do not raise a plea to the jurisdiction of the court or the plea of venue (that you're being sued in the wrong county) at the beginning of your initial pleadings and in the proper way, you very likely will be giving up all such complaints. Another example is something called Affirmative Defenses. There are certain defenses that must be pled affirmatively and cannot be raised by a general denial. These are matters best left to your lawyer's experience.

Getting Everybody in Court

Everybody knows a lawsuit involves a dispute between at least two people. Therefore, the mere filing of a petition at the courthouse by one person will not get the lawsuit underway. There must be a way to bring in the other person or persons with whom there is the disagreement so that they can participate in the lawsuit. Just as there are invitations to a party, there are invitations to a lawsuit. In Texas, the invitation to the lawsuit is called a *citation*. A citation is a document that has the plaintiff's original petition attached to it and says:

> "You are hereby commanded to appear before the Honorable District Court of Sunshine County, Texas, at the courthouse of said county in Sunshine, Texas, by filing a written answer, at or before 10:00 A.M. of the Monday next after the expiration of 20 days after the date of service of this citation, to plaintiff's petition filed in the court on the 2nd day of September, 2006..."

Of course, the citation also contains the names of the parties, the number of the case, and the court that will hear the case. In some cases, such as when a temporary hearing is to be held, orders are attached to the citation ordering that a hearing is to be held earlier.

In other jurisdictions, the citation might be referred to as a "summons" or "legal process." In Texas, it is almost uniformly called a citation.

The citation must be personally delivered to the respondent by a sheriff, other law officer, or a person authorized by court order or by registered or certified mail, return receipt requested. Under circumstances where a defendant or respondent is difficult to serve or hiding from the law officer, courts are authorized to direct process to be served in some other manner reasonably calculated to provide the person with notice.

Since I am saying the citation is like an invitation, you may be wondering whether you are required to show up. If you receive an invitation to a party, of course, you don't have to go. It's sort of like that with the citation. If you don't go to court, no one will arrest you nor will your name be placed on any blacklist. There is a difference, however. Instead of just having the party without you in the case of the citation, they go ahead and have court without you and pretend that you are there. Because you do not appear, the court assumes that you have nothing to say in your behalf. The other side is usually given whatever it is they are requesting from the court. In addition, if you show up later, it is very unlikely that the judge is going to want to have another party for you, since he or she already has spent his time and the taxpayers' money having a party that was designed for you in the first place.

All of this is referred to as the *doctrine of finality*. There is a strong public policy that once the trial has been held, the case is over—forever. Speeches are often made emphasizing our right to a day in court. That means just what it says: one day and one day only.

As you might imagine, the requirement of the citation or invitation to court is not a mere formality. It goes to the very essence of our entire legal system. Before a court takes any action, our philosophy of government requires that the parties who are to be acted against have notice that such action is contemplated. And this notice is not just a hollow motion to be carried out nonchalantly. It is given for a purpose. That purpose is so that the persons who might be affected by the court's orders will have an opportunity to be heard. This opportunity to be heard is also to be given in a meaningful fashion. It is not to be delivered to the parties as they are dragged before the court. It must be given far enough in advance so that they will have time to make preparations, hire a lawyer, track down evidence, and think through what they want to say to the court and to the other party. So if you should receive a citation telling you to be in court, you are to take it seriously. To ignore it is to run the risk of losing all of your rights, property, and children. It is one of the most important documents that you will ever hold in your hands, so far as deciding the direction of your own life.

This should also cause you to be more understanding when you are the moving or initiating party. When you want something to be done, you must allow the other person involved in the lawsuit adequate time to receive, consider, and respond to your demands. This is true not only in the beginning of your lawsuit, but throughout its course when you are adding new demands or making changes in your positions.

Waiver of Citation

Sometimes the respondent to a divorce is just ready to "get it over with." In such cases Texas courts allow the respondent to file a document called a Waiver of Citation with the clerk of the court, stating that he or she waives service of citation. This may be invoked to avoid the embarrassment and the trauma that may arise when the sheriff appears on the front doorstep. This document must be completed very precisely. It must be sworn to. It must not be dated or sworn to before the original petition is filed with the clerk. In essence, it allows the petitioner to take the divorce on whatever terms he or she so desires. The judge of a particular court may use some discretion and restraint in controlling the terms of judgment in this situation. However, you can't count on it. As you can see, the Waiver of Citation can be a very dangerous instrument.

Warning: Don't *sign a waiver in your divorce case if you have either kids or property. See the topic "Do I Need a Lawyer?" in the Chapter 4.*

When Both Sides Have Lawyers

Service of citation can also be avoided if the non-suing party (respondent) agrees to file a written answer. When the respondent has already retained an attorney or intends to do so very soon, the cost of serving a citation can usually be avoided if the petitioner's lawyer will contact the respondent's lawyer. Usually the two lawyers can agree that the respondent's lawyer will be mailed a copy of the petition and that the respondent's lawyer will file a written answer within a reasonable period of time. Where it is possible to do this, I strenuously recommend that this procedure be followed. Having citations served on the other party creates more hard feelings and anger in a divorce case than perhaps any other single event. Therefore, avoidance of having the sheriff serve the citation saves attorney's fees, time, and loss of work from extra emotional stress.

Of course, you do not absolutely have to have a lawyer to file a written answer. In some circumstances, filing an answer on your own may be far more desirable than signing a waiver of citation prepared by your spouse's lawyer. This is because if you file a written answer on your own, at least you will be given notice of the hearing. With a waiver of citation, you may not even know when the hearing takes place. Often, a general denial is adequate as an answer. WARNING: However, filing the general denial does present substantial risk. You may waive your rights to plea a privilege, a plea to the jurisdiction, affirmative defenses, and grounds of recovery, which the general denial will not raise.

The Case of the Missing Spouse

If your spouse cannot be located for service of citation, this does not mean that you cannot get a divorce. Under such circumstances the court allows citation by publication. This means that the citation can be published in the newspaper, on the theory that your spouse can read it and have notice that the divorce is taking place. Avoid this if possible. It costs more money. The cost of publishing the ad in the newspaper is added to your court costs. And you must pay court costs for the spouse. The court hires an attorney *ad litem* to assure that citation by publication is necessary and not just a concocted means of keeping the absent spouse from having actual notice of the hearing. Citation by publication has the additional disadvantage of being unable to obtain personal jurisdiction over the absent spouse for child support or money judgments under this kind of citation.

For couples who do not have either children or property, Texas law provides a sensible manner of citation by publication. The notice is merely placed on the courthouse "door" (bulletin board).

Personal Appearance

Citation may also be avoided by having the non-suing spouse (respondent) simply appear in person in court. The personal appearance gives the court jurisdiction over the respondent. If you are the petitioner, this really is not a satisfactory method for either you or your lawyer. This means that on the day of the hearing, you and your lawyer must go to the courthouse and wait to see if your spouse will arrive. My experience is that people who will not file an answer, hire a lawyer, or sign a waiver, frequently are also not reliable enough to show up at the courthouse. Instead of waiting to see if these people will show up for the divorce, I recommend that they be served with citation, except in the most unusual circumstances.

Court Communications after All Parties Have "Appeared"

After all parties to the divorce have appeared in court, they still must be kept informed of everything that is happening in the case. This is accomplished by rules that require parties to send the other party copies of every motion or pleading filed in court. This is accomplished by requiring each attorney or party who is not represented by an attorney to attach a *certificate of service* to each document filed with the court certifying that a copy of the document was sent to the other party and the date and manner it was served.

Another aspect of communications during a lawsuit is that no party is allowed to talk with the judge about the *substance* of the case without the other party present. Such one-sided, one-party communications with the court about the case are called *ex parte* communications and are strictly prohibited. But, as usual, it's not this simple. For the legal system to operate, parties must contact the court, the court's secretary, or the court coordinator to schedule hearings, discuss the length of time required for a hearing, obtain the court's signature on orders setting hearings or on orders pertaining to matters on which the court has already ruled. Obviously, to do this they must contact the judge either directly or indirectly. So, the line between what is "procedural" and thus proper to discuss *ex parte* with the court and what is "substantive" and thus improper to discuss without the opponent present is not always clear or exact. The vast majority of judges handle this very well. There is a small minority of judges who don't seem to get it when it comes to cutting off conversations that move into discussing the facts of a particular case.

Associate Judges

In the more metropolitan areas of the state, the number of divorce cases have outstripped the ability of the government to furnish judges to hear these cases. The legislature has responded by giving judges the authority to appoint associate judges to hear cases. If your divorce is being heard in a metropolitan area, it is likely that the temporary hearing in your case will be heard by an associate judge.

These associate judges are in essence "assistant judges" that can do almost everything the judge can do except, theoretically, make final decisions. The associate judge can only report findings of fact and recommend to the judge what decision should be made.

After the associate judge makes his or her findings and recommendations, either party has the right to ask for a hearing before the judge that referred the case to the associate judge if such a hearing is requested within three days after receiving notice of the associate judge's findings. At this hearing all evidence must be presented again before the judge since it is a new trial (trial *de novo*) on the issues appealed.

This appeal to the judge may not be all it seems. At the same time the judge is hearing evidence, he or she will have the findings and recommendations of the associate judge in front of him or her. Since most judges do not want to encourage appeals, because this would defeat the very purpose of having associate judges, there is a strong tendency to back the associate judge by making a decision consistent with his or her findings.

Getting Your Uncontested Case Set for Hearing

If you and your spouse agree on all aspects of your divorce, you will sign an agreed divorce decree, and your case will be referred to as *uncontested.* As a general rule, after the sixty-day waiting period has passed, it is easy to have uncontested divorces heard. In many counties they are heard as "walk-ins," or there is a weekly docket call designated for such cases to be heard. This means that usually, though not always, your uncontested case can be heard and concluded in a week or two.

Getting Your Contested Case Set for Trial

Perhaps no single item in the divorce process produces more frustration, misunderstanding, and anger than the problem of getting the contested case set for trial. This is especially true since almost everyone who is going through a divorce has at least one friend who was able to get his or her divorce within a day or a week after requesting that it be heard. Further, the friend of the frustrated litigant cannot understand why all divorces can't be handled in such an easy and sensible manner.

The difference between divorce cases is like the difference between night and day. The case that was set immediately for hearing was an uncontested divorce in which *both* parties had everything settled and wanted to get it over with. A contested case is a totally different matter. A contested case is nothing more than a lawsuit, which must be set on the court's trial docket along with other cases to be tried.

So how do you get your contested divorce case set for trial? The case is set on the court's *docket,* which is a list of cases set for trial. It is impossible to tell you how the court that is hearing your divorce case will handle its docket. Texas judges are allowed much discretion in deciding how they will handle their own dockets. There is no general across-the-state rule as to how a judge must compile the list of cases that are to be heard in his or her court. This may seem ridiculous to you when you are having difficulty in getting your case to trial. However, when you consider that the state is made up of 254 counties, some with only a few people spread over several hundred square miles and some with large metropolitan populations, you can see why it is impossible to formulate one set of rules for handling and setting cases for the whole state.

Many Texas courts have *local rules* that require the use of *scheduling orders.* A *Scheduling Order* is an order entered by the court, usually after agreement and consultation with the attorneys, establishing deadlines for all of the events leading up to the trial of the case *and* setting a date when the case will be tried.

Your lawyer can give you a general summary of what the rules for setting cases are in the court in which your case is to be tried. It is certain that your lawyer will have a thorough understanding of these rules, since he or she must work in these courts on a daily basis.

Chapter 10

Asking the Court for Help at the Beginning of the Case: Temporary Orders for Custody, Support, and Protection

Diplomacy is the art of saying "Nice doggie" until you can find a rock.

—Will Rogers

Temporary Hearings

Everybody knows that divorces, especially the more complicated variety, don't happen overnight. By law, a Texas divorce can't be granted in less than sixty days, and everyone knows that most divorces take much longer than that, many lasting for several months and some lasting a year or more. So what do you do if you can't wait that long for help from the court? What if you need child support right now? What if there is a heated dispute between you and your spouse over who will have custody of the children and where they will live? Perhaps your spouse has undertaken a systematic program of spending or hiding all of the community property.

The answer to all of these problems is to ask the divorce court for a *Temporary Hearing* at the beginning of your case, immediately upon the filing of the divorce. Divorce courts expect this because you are not alone. A significant percentage of the divorces filed request the court to enter temporary orders. Some divorce cases even include *Temporary Restraining Orders* that are issued by the court even before the spouse being served with divorce has been served with the citation or, perhaps, even has knowledge of the case.

Temporary Hearings in most divorce courts are typically heard within days of the divorce being filed. Sometimes and in some courts, scheduling a hearing is more difficult, so that it may take a couple of weeks.

The time allotted for *Temporary Hearings* is very limited, usually a couple of hours or less. The court will definitely not be interested in your life story since the subject matter covered is limited only to those "housekeeping" matters that will ensure that life will remain on an even keel during the pendency of the divorce. In legal language this means maintaining the *status quo*, keeping things as they are by protecting children and property, and making sure that support is paid so that everyone can live while the case is pending. Even in more complex and unusual cases in which a court might allocate several days for a *Temporary Hearing*, the subject will still be restricted only to those items that must be dealt with to keep things as they are while the divorce is pending.

In the case of temporary custody and control over children, do not think that the court's goal of maintaining the *status quo* will keep the court from taking the custody from a parent who is not taking proper care of the children. At *Temporary Hearings* that involve children, the court will be interested "in the best interest" and best welfare of the children.

Temporary Orders – How They Usually Come into Being

There are two kinds of court orders: temporary and final. The final orders are sometimes referred to as *permanent court orders* or *final judgment* or *decree of divorce. Temporary orders* are also referred to as *interlocutory orders*. The final order is entered after the court has had opportunity to hear all of the evidence and to have a full trial.

When it is not possible or desirable to wait until a full-blown trial can be had to enter a court order, courts enter interlocutory orders. If your divorce involves a heated dispute over child custody, it is highly probable that after a temporary hearing, the court will enter a *Temporary Order* saying where the children will live while the divorce is pending, who will pay child support while the case is pending, and how much that temporary child support will be.

Of course, divorcing couples often are able to agree on these *temporary matters*. Such agreements sometimes make temporary orders unnecessary, or if one of the parties to the divorce believes that temporary orders are necessary, agreement between the parties allows them or their lawyers to sign, present to the court, and have entered *Agreed Temporary Orders*. But, when the parties can't agree on where and with whom the children will live and who will pay child support in what amounts, it is still necessary for these matters to be resolved. Therefore, a *temporary hearing* will be held in which evidence will be heard and issues of how life will be lived during the pendency of the divorce will be resolved by the court.

But temporary orders are not limited to issues of child custody and child support. For example, if a divorce involves a dispute over a racehorse, it may be necessary for the court to order the person who has possession of the racehorse not to sell the horse. If a jury trial or final hearing before the court cannot be had for several days, weeks, or months, and if the judge does not order the spouse who has possession of the horse not to sell the horse, there may not be anything to fight over at the final hearing, as the horse may already have been sold. Of course, if the horse were sold, the judge could award to the non-possessing party money from the sale of the horse, if the court found that such was appropriate for property division. But since racehorses are unique creatures, and since the horse might turn out to be the separate property of the non-possessing spouse or the spouse who possessed the horse might spend the money from the sale of the horse, the court might enter a temporary order to make sure that the horse is available at the time of trial of the final divorce case. Remember: The racehorse is just an example. Temporary orders are available to protect all of the couple's property while the divorce is pending.

You may ask yourself why temporary orders cannot be avoided by simply holding the final hearing immediately and having the judge decide the case once and for all. I have already mentioned that juries cannot always be brought in immediately. In addition, the parties must be given time to prepare their cases by gathering evidence, securing witnesses, planning strategy. Also, temporary orders do not require the kind of decisions that final orders do. For example, in the case of the racehorse, it may be very difficult and require a very long trial to decide the true ownership of the horse or how the horse fits into the overall division of community property. On the other hand, it is easier for a judge to see that if there is a legitimate dispute, the horse should not be sold, or if it must be sold the money should be held in escrow pending the final divorce.

We have already mentioned the additional Texas requirement of the 60-day waiting period before a divorce can be granted. Since the 60-day waiting period is a constant reality in Texas divorces, it is necessary to make use of temporary orders during this period of time, if there is a dispute that cannot wait until final hearing.

Judges can enter temporary orders involving matters of:

1. Child custody and visitation
2. Child support
3. Spousal support
4. Ordering either or both of the parties not to sell or waste community property
5. Ordering either or both of the parties not to come around each other, either at home or at work or any other place they might be
6. Ordering either or both of the parties not to do physical harm to the other
7. Ordering either or both of the parties not to interfere with the house, car, or that which is in the possession of the other party
8. Ordering payment of interim attorney's fees

Neither the law nor any court requires that temporary orders be entered in a Texas divorce. They are optional. If you do not need such orders, you may simply file the divorce suit, then wait at least sixty days before going into court to have your hearing, and at that time, have only final orders entered involving your divorce, custody of children, support, and divisions of community property. In many cases, it is preferable that the divorce be handled this way. Often, couples can agree as to how things are going to be handled in the interim period and thereby avoid the necessity of having the court enter temporary orders.

Notice: Be very clear, however, that if you do not have temporary orders entered after the filing of your divorce, the rights of both parties to the divorce are the same as they were before the filing of the lawsuit. Both parties have equal rights to all children. The management of the community property remains the same. Both parties have a right to come in or about the home in which they have been living. In short, even though a divorce has been filed, if no temporary orders are entered, as far as the law is concerned, you are still married, with all the rights and liabilities of a married person.

Sometimes judges enter temporary orders before giving the other side the opportunity to be heard. For example, a judge might enter an order to restrain a husband from doing physical violence to a wife. Or one of the spouses might be enjoined from removing a child from the jurisdiction of the court. It is obvious that if a court always waited to have a hearing on such matters, the beating might already have taken place, or the child might already have been removed by the time the hearing comes about. There are, however, very severe limits placed on such orders entered without giving the person against whom the order is issued an opportunity to be heard. First, any order entered without opportunity to be heard is effective for only fourteen days from the date it is signed by the judge. And any person who is subjected to such an order without a hearing can demand a hearing within two days of the time that such order is served on him or her. In other words, such orders issued without hearing are to be used only until such time as a hearing can be held, and the law requires that such a hearing be held very quickly. In addition, until a hearing is held, a spouse cannot be ordered out of the house, ordered to pay child support, deprived of custody of children, prevented from operating a business, or prevented from using money for living expenses. In other words, temporary orders entered against a party before he or she has opportunity to be heard are limited to those minimal things needed to preserve the status quo, such as not doing bodily violence, not running off with the children, and not hiding or selling community property.

Court orders that are entered *without hearing* are usually referred to as *Restraining Orders*. For example, they restrain the party against whom they are issued from threatening, harassing, or assaulting the other party, interfering with the custody of a minor child of the parties, selling or disposing of community property, etc. If these same orders are entered after a hearing, they are generally referred to as an *Injunction*. So for all practical purposes, an *injunction* and a *restraining order* are the same thing. Even if temporary orders are necessary, it is preferable, when possible, to use the injunction only. This avoids having the person restrained without affording him an opportunity to be heard. This leaves a better taste in everybody's mouth.

Unlike the final judgment or order, the temporary order is not "written in stone." Thirty days after a "final" order is entered (if no appeal is taken or motion for new trial is made), and except for certain enforcement and clarification powers, even the trial judge who enters a final judgment loses power (jurisdiction) to change or modify it (although corrections can be made under certain circumstances). On the other hand, the trial judge usually retains complete control over the temporary orders. The judge is free to change, dissolve, or increase a temporary order if it is necessary.

Temporary Orders, unlike final orders, judgments, or decrees, are usually not *appealable* to higher courts. There are a few exceptions to this rule, but the exceptions don't often arise in divorce cases. For this reason, what the trial court says in the temporary orders is pretty much what you get. Of course, the trial court retains the power to modify its own temporary orders, but courts are usually reluctant to do so unless facts or circumstances change after their initial ruling.

Parachuting in behind Enemy Lines – The Temporary Hearing for Custody

If you have a hearing on temporary custody or child support, there are some things you need to know:

1. Because these hearings are set quickly, you may not have much time to prepare for the hearing. Although a few days' notice might not sound like a short time to you, around a law office with other emergencies scheduled, it can mean that lawyers and clients are thrown into hearings with little time to meet and prepare.
2. The time allowed for the hearing will be very short. This means that you may have only minutes to explain to the judge why you are the person who should be allowed to designate the child's residence during the pendency of the case and why you should receive child support. You can do this, but you cannot do this and tell your life story in detail.
3. This hearing may be the critical event. Because divorces often are pending for many months and occasionally for a year or more, the person who has custody will often be able to establish a "track record" that a court will be reluctant to change when the divorce is finally heard.
4. You need to know facts and events of your child's life by heart. These include: birthdays, baptisms, hospitalizations, names of teachers, doctors, friends, day care arrangements, baby books, eating habits, where the child has lived and when, and any other significant events in the child's life.
5. You need to know the basic concepts of the Standard Visitation Order used by Texas courts. A general discussion of this procedure is found in Chapter 19 on Child Custody. You need to understand and be able to explain why you and your spouse have not been able to work out an agreement regarding the temporary custody of your child.
6. If you have been the primary care provider for your child, you need to be able to discuss the facts of that care with the court. If you have not been the primary care provider for your child, you

need to have exceedingly good reasons as to why you should be put in that position.

7. Read the checklist found under "Preparing to Testify" on page 177.
8. If you have critical witnesses who can testify about critical events that should affect the court's decision about temporary custody, find out about their availability in the coming days and discuss this with your lawyer.
9. Finally, when you talk with your lawyer about preparation for the temporary hearing, be prepared to modify everything I have told you in this checklist. That's why you have a lawyer who knows about the specific facts of your case.

Chapter 11

Discovery: Obtaining the Information You Need to Settle or Try Your Case

Knowledge is power.

—Proverb

Information and knowledge are the thermonuclear weapons of our time.

—Thomas A. Stewart

So now, after a divorce has been filed, your spouse still has all of the records of the family business, banking, and finances, and he or she won't turn this information over to you or your lawyer. Moreover, although your children are living with you while the divorce is pending, your spouse is working diligently to gather evidence that will be used at the divorce to try to persuade the court to name him or her as the parent with the right to designate the children's primary residence. You have learned that he or she has hired so-called experts, such as psychologists, who, you suspect, will testify that you are not a fit parent to have custody of the children. Again, your spouse refuses to tell you anything about the evidence that he or she is gathering for this "sneak attack" custody case.

Luckily for you, the court system has been dealing with people like your spouse for a long time. Your spouse is not the inventor of this game of "Hide the Ball." The court system is ready for your spouse. This chapter is a summary of the ways your lawyer can obtain the needed information from your spouse. The process of getting this information from your spouse is referred to as *Discovery.*

This whole chapter is predicated on the assumption that your spouse has information that you need and cannot obtain without using the legal process. The checklist after Chapter 1 lists several items, such as tax returns and bank statement, that you should obtain copies of when separating. If, perchance, you have other ways of obtaining the information you need without resorting to legal process, by all means do so. If your accountant is as loyal and friendly to you as to your spouse, ask him or her for financial records. You may get them. I had a case in which the spouse's secretary provided her boss's spouse with all of the financial records just because she wanted the spouse to get a fair shake. (A sense of justice is a wonderful thing.)

First, You Ask Nicely

The bad news about discovery is that it can be very expensive. For this reason, if possible, you should avoid an all-out "discovery war." Although your spouse "won't cooperate or give you any of the information you need," he or she may change his or her little mind. Lawyers who prefer to "play the game straight up" rather than just run up the bill, routinely have heart-to-heart discussions with stubborn clients just like your spouse, explaining that, in the end, the court is going to require that this information be provided. It is likely that your spouse's lawyer will also explain that "discovery wars" are very expensive for everyone, even the person who starts the war by refusing to cooperate in sharing information or the person who makes ridiculous demands for unreasonable amounts of information. Of course, your spouse may hire the kind of lawyer who loves to start discovery wars so that he or she can run up the bill. Although this is not a happy event, keep in mind that very soon your spouse will be getting some very hefty bills for legal work related to fighting over information to which both sides are rightfully entitled. Regrettably, you'll be getting some statements for legal fees also, at least until your spouse wakes up and smells the coffee.

The bright side of *discovery* in many divorce cases is that, because disclosure can be compelled, couples voluntarily exchange all necessary information. Just the availability of the discovery devices makes their use unnecessary. Both sides know a discovery war will be costly, so they ask themselves, "If the other side is going to get the information anyway, why not just go ahead and give it to them?"

This is not to say that "friendly discovery" is cheap or pain free. It still takes lots of time to exchange and analyze information. Even the agreements to avoid discovery wars require thoughtful, detailed attention. Understanding and organizing information that is obtained in preparation for trials or settlement usually can't be avoided. But, when the parties cooperate, the cost is a fraction of what it would be if everyone spends days or weeks attending hearings on Motions to Compel, Motions for Protective Orders, and such.

For the reasons just discussed, good lawyers usually at some point pick up the phone and talk with their opponents about cooperating on the exchange of information. Often, this results in lowering hostilities and saving wear and tear as well as costly legal services. On the other hand, if your lawyer knows that the other side is being represented by a lawyer or a firm that has a reputation for just "running the clock" and refusing to be reasonable, he or she is probably not going to waste the time and money to make the call. When these kinds of lawyers are involved, it's a waste of time to "first, ask nicely." Just crank up the word processor and begin the war.

Unfortunately, this may mean a bitter, bloody battle in which both sides are sworn to refuse to give anything that is not absolutely required. This forces lawyers on both sides to dot all the *i's* and cross all the *t's*. As I said earlier, even in such cases, the dotting of the *i's* and crossing of the *t's* often becomes unnecessary after both sides have had the pleasure of receiving bills from their lawyers.

What Is Discovery?

Discovery is a generic term used formally and officially in the Texas Rules of Civil Procedure and also informally by lawyers and others in general conversation. It is a shorthand reference to those methods used in a divorce or other lawsuits to obtain information, documents, and other potential evidence from the opposing party. Formal *discovery* comes into play after a lawsuit is filed. Compliance with *discovery requests* or *demands* is not optional. Failure to comply can result in sanctions, which may include money fines, the exclusion of evidence in the trial, and even the dismissal of a party's claims or defenses.

Discovery includes several different, separate, and distinct legal mechanisms:

- The Oral Deposition
- The Deposition by Written Questions
- Request for Disclosure
- Written Interrogatories
- Requests for Admissions
- Request for Production of Documents
- Request to Inspect Items or Premises
- Motions for Inventory of Assets and Debts

These different types of discovery mechanisms or procedures may be used individually or in conjunction with one or more of the others. In very simple uncontested divorces, it may be unnecessary to use any of these methods.

The Scope of Discovery: What You Can Get

You may have seen a lawyer in a courtroom stand and say, "Your honor, we object because that information it not relevant." While that may be a perfectly good objection in the courtroom, it would not be a good objection in any pretrial discovery. That is because the scope of discovery is not limited to what is relevant. In pretrial discovery, parties are entitled to discover *anything that is relevant or that might be calculated to lead to the discovery of anything that might be admissible in evidence.* As you can see, this is a pretty broad road to drive on.

However, there are other limitations. For example, there are privileges such as the attorney-client privilege, which can be invoked so that information does not have to be disclosed. The rules governing discovery are complex, but may arise in conversations with your lawyer from time-to-time.

An Overview of Discovery

Pleading, you'll remember, is the method for parties to set out their demands, claims, and defenses for the benefit of each other and the court. If, however, you look at the pleadings, you will see that they are only the barest outline of what the other side is demanding. For example, in a divorce case, your spouse may ask for the child support by pleading that he or she is entitled to reasonable child support. Or the pleadings may allege that during the marriage, the parties have acquired community property, and upon hearing, the court should make a reasonable division of this property.

For you to be able to proceed in court, you may need to know specific facts that the pleadings don't tell you. For example, if you don't know how much money your spouse makes, you won't know how much child support he or she can afford to pay. Often the wife doesn't know the full extent and value of the community property, if the husband has been the one to operate the business over the years. So to make decisions about the tactics that should be pursued in the handling of the case and to be able to prove facts that are in your spouse's hands or in someone else's hands, you may need to have information ahead of time. Discovery allows each of the parties to a lawsuit to ask each other questions ahead of time. It also allows testimony and information to be gathered from third-party witnesses before the trial.

Unlike most of our rules of court, discovery is a relatively modern innovation. In the adversary system as it existed in England and in the early United States, a trial was a game of surprises. It was very much like a chess game that was run by very formal and rigid rules, with neither side knowing what evidence the other side was going to present in court. Because everything was done in court, the parties could only guess what evidence the other side possessed. Surprises were the rule of the day. It was out of this system that legendary heroes such as Perry Mason came into being.

In the twentieth century, this system of trial-by-ambush came into disfavor. Although everyone realized that the system was more fun for lawyers and more exciting for onlookers, someone finally figured out that trial-by-ambush was not a good way of finding out the truth, which is what trials are supposed to be all about.

Accordingly, the system of discovery has gradually developed so that everyone can know what everyone else is going to do ahead of time. This is not to say that every item of evidence is discoverable. Nor is it to say that it is desirable to spend the time and money to find out every conceivable piece of evidence that the other side has in every case. If, however, you have questions about matters that go to the heart of your case, discovery is a tool that is available to find out such information.

Just because discovery is available, however, does not mean that you should force your lawyer into using it. Discovery does not always make sense in every case. First, it is terribly expensive and time consuming. A rule of discovery that appears very simple when you are reading it or having it described to you can, and often does, become drawn out, confused, and complex in its application. Second, as your lawyer is already aware, discovery is a double-edged sword. By asking questions of your spouse or demanding that your spouse dig up information, you may be forcing your spouse into preparing a better case against you. Often, parties come into court unable to prove matters that are crucial to their side of the case. If this is the case with your spouse, you may be hurting yourself by helping your spouse get ready for trial.

Sworn Inventories

The court can require your spouse to file a written inventory in which he or she is required to swear to a list of all of the items owned by the community (assets) along with an appraisal of the cost of each item. Such an inventory would also include a list of all outstanding debts owed by your spouse individually and the community jointly.

This device is very useful when the opposing spouse has been the sole manager or primary manager of a small business or farm owned by the community or has managed the finances of the marriage. If the spouse leaves out pertinent items in the inventory, he or she runs the risk that other discovery will uncover them and that such discoveries will be brought to the attention of the judge. Judges usually frown severely on such matters.

I put this discovery device at the top of the list because in many divorces it will produce the biggest bang for the buck. Your lawyer can quickly and cheaply prepare a Motion for a Sworn Inventory, requesting the court to order your spouse to list all community and separate property and provide a value for each item. Courts readily grant such motions and order that sworn inventories be provided. Perhaps even more often, opposing lawyers will agree to the entry of an order providing for a sworn inventory without the necessity of a hearing. This is because they know the court is going to require the inventory anyway. Of course, if you request your spouse to provide a sworn inventory, don't be surprised when you, too, are required to provide such a document.

Depositions

Deposition is a method whereby testimony can be given by witnesses ahead of time, just as if it were being given in court at the trial. Witnesses can be compelled to appear for deposition (subpoenaed), just as they can be compelled to appear in court. They can also be compelled to bring documents and records to a deposition (*subpoena duces tecum*), just as they can be compelled to bring such documents to court.

Although the deposition can be taken at the courthouse in a courtroom, frequently it takes place in one of the lawyer's offices or in a neutral conference room. When the need arises, it can be had in a hospital room or in the home of one of the witnesses or at any other location that is suitable and convenient to the parties.

At a typical deposition, the lawyers for both sides will be present, along with the witness, a court reporter, the parties to the divorce, and, sometimes, a videographer making a videotape transcript of the testimony. The court reporter swears the witness to tell the truth in the same way that the witness would be sworn in court. The lawyer for the side that is taking the deposition will then begin asking questions of the witness, to which the witness responds with answers just as would be done in court.

If your lawyer is taking the deposition of a witness, it may or may not be necessary for you to be present. If the witness is testifying to things that you know about, your lawyer probably will want you to be present so that you can tell him or her whether the witness is telling the truth.

Depositions are used to establish what an opposing party or hostile witness is going to testify to at trial. Lawyers refer to this as "tying down" witnesses. If witnesses have sworn to a deposition, it is more difficult for them to change their story in court. If they do, the deposition can be used to impeach the testimony in court by showing the prior inconsistent statement.

Depositions also are used to preserve the testimony of persons who cannot or will not attend court. If a witness is in ill health and unable to go to court, frequently his or her deposition will be taken and the deposition read in court. This is also true of persons who are in such ill health that it is likely they will not live to testify in court.

In addition, there is a limit on the distance a witness can be required to travel to attend court. In a civil lawsuit in Texas, the parties are allowed to subpoena people within a 150-mile radius of the courthouse. This means that if the witness is more than 150 miles from the courthouse and will not voluntarily attend the trial, then it is necessary to take their deposition. The lawyer who desires the testimony will simply arrange to take the person's deposition at a location at or near where the witness resides. If necessary, the witness can be subpoenaed to attend the deposition at that location. The deposition will then be transcribed and can be read in court or shown by video as if the witness were present and testifying.

There are still other witnesses who are willing to testify but become very hostile at the idea of having to miss work or other activities to attend the trial. The use of depositions can keep these witnesses on friendly terms, when for all practical purposes, they would be useless in a trial because of anger over having to be there.

Depositions can also be used to uncover unknown facts. For example, if your spouse always has been the one to manage the family business and finances, and you have no such knowledge of these matters, a deposition may be a way for your lawyer to learn what is at stake in the divorce. At the deposition, your lawyer can ask such things as the whereabouts and numbers of checking accounts, saving accounts, stock brokerage accounts, real estate investments, sources and amounts of income, cost of business expenses, and other assets. In this way, your spouse may be forced to talk about things that he or she has never been willing to talk about or divulge to you.

Taking the deposition of an opposing party or hostile witness has great advantages over other forms of discovery. *The witness is forced to answer the question on his or her own, in the presence of you and your lawyer, without having an answer prepared by a lawyer, accountant, or fortuneteller.* In other forms of discovery, answers are, more often than not, prepared for parties by these professionals. This is why, in a push-shove situation, many lawyers believe the deposition to be far and away the best discovery device available.

Depositions have the disadvantage of being expensive. It is not unusual for the cost for the court reporter to take testimony and to prepare a transcript to be one hundred dollars per hour or more. Paying for video transcription is also expensive. There are ways to economize by making your own voice recording or video transcription. However, the cost associated with the inconvenience and awkwardness usually ends up absorbing any savings.

Depositions also have the disadvantage of leaving out the passion, conviction, and earnestness that are often the most important elements in live testimony given in court. After taking down the testimony in shorthand, the court reporter later will type it or have it typed into written form. Therefore, when the deposition is read to the judge or jury, it is a reading of only the words that come off a cold printed page, rather than from the heart of a convinced individual. To some extent, showing a videotape of the deposition can overcome the lack of non-verbal cues that we all rely on in judging the credibility of a speaker.

It is worth pointing out that the cold, passionless printed form of a deposition can also be an advantage. If your lawyer is having to depend upon a witness who does not make a very good impression or appears unsure or dishonest, it may be that the cold words of the deposition will be more desirable than the presence of the person in court. Remember: All disadvantages are sometimes advantages.

Request for Disclosure

A *Request for Disclosure* is a standard procedure in which a standard form can be used to get basic information that may be used in a trial. Although the Request for Disclosure is designed for other types of civil lawsuits, it can also be useful in a divorce case. When a Request for Disclosure is made, the party on whom it is served must provide the requesting party the following information within 30 days:

a. The correct names of the parties to the lawsuit
b. The name, address, and telephone number of any potential parties
c. The legal theories and, in general, the factual basis of the responding party's claims or defenses
d. The amount and any method of calculating economic damages
e. The name, address, and telephone number of persons having knowledge of relevant facts, and a brief statement of each identified person's connection with the case
f. For any testifying expert:
    1. the expert's name, address, and telephone number
    2. the subject matter on which the expert will testify
    3. the general substance of the expert's mental impressions and opinions
    4. if the expert is retained by, employed by, or otherwise subject to the control of the responding party
        A. all documents, tangible things, reports, models, or data compilations that have been provided to, reviewed by, or prepared by or for the expert in anticipation of the expert's testimony
        B. the expert's current resume and bibliography
g. Any indemnity and insuring agreements
h. Any settlement agreements

i. Any witness statements
j. (Other items not likely to be applicable in a divorce case)

The Request for Disclosure is an easy and relatively inexpensive way to obtain basic information that may be important in a divorce case involving child custody or complex property division issues. A pleading that can be prepared in a few minutes that will obtain the names of "all persons with knowledge of relevant facts" is worth consideration anytime. Keep in mind that when you send it, you're probably going to get one back, and it takes a lot more time to answer it than to send it.

Written Interrogatories

Written Interrogatories are nothing more than questions that one side in a lawsuit sends to the other side to be answered. Unlike depositions, written interrogatories can be asked only of a party to the lawsuit. In asking written interrogatories, it is important to understand that the other side's lawyer will help answer the questions.

Written interrogatories should be reserved for questions that are not subject to interpretation, such as: "List the banks, account numbers, and amounts of all checking accounts in which you have any ownership interest." If you ask such questions as, "Why did you cause the breakup of this marriage?" you are going to get back a barrage of useless garbage. This means that interrogatories are of limited use in your divorce case.

Request for Admissions

Another discovery device is something known as the *Request for Admissions.* This is a device whereby the courts allow you to send statements of the facts of the case to your spouse. He or she must admit or deny the truth of each statement within a given period of time. The advantage of this device is to let you know what is going to be agreed to in court and what you must spend time proving.

For example, if you send a request for admissions to your spouse stating that "for the five years immediately preceding the filing of this divorce, your salary has exceeded $150,000 per year," you can force your spouse to answer this statement by either admitting it or denying it. If he or she admits it, then you have established it for all purposes and need spend no more time and energy in trying to prove it. If it is denied, you know that you must subpoena records of income, banking accounts, expenditures, and whatever else might be necessary to prove that he or she has made more than $150,000 per year in this period.

Once again, it is important to note that the request for admissions can be used only against a party to the lawsuit. It is not an appropriate method for gaining testimony from third parties.

Request for Production of Documents

It very well may be that your spouse has some or all of the records indicating income, production of business, or cost of supporting the family. This information may be necessary for you to prove your case in court or to decide how much property and money you are entitled to on settlement or how much child support you are entitled to or must pay.

The Texas courts have a procedure called *Request for Production of Documents*. If, for example, your wife has in her possession all of the joint income tax returns that you as a couple have filed for the last five years and will not turn these returns or copies of them over to you, you may file with the court a request that she produce them for your use in preparing your lawsuit. If she refuses to produce the copies, it is highly likely that the judge will make her regret her failure to comply.

Request for Inspection

If your spouse has in his or her possession items of personal property that you need to inspect or have appraised or photographed, you can request that such items be produced for inspection, examination, appraisal, or analysis. The same is true of real property or buildings. If your spouse has such property under his or her exclusive control, such requests allow inspection or appraisal so that photographs can be taken and measurements made.

Deposition upon Written Questions

Besides the oral deposition in which your lawyer appears and asks questions orally, there is a form of deposition in which your lawyer can prepare written questions to be asked of a witness. The list of questions is prepared along with a pleading asking for the *deposition by written questions*. The other side is given a period of time in which to prepare written questions to go along with the taking of the deposition. These questions are forwarded to a court reporter who then schedules an appointment with the witness or, if necessary, subpoenas the witness and asks the witness the written questions, taking down the answers given by the witness.

This method of taking depositions is desirable only when the lawyer knows the witness will give straightforward answers or when the issues are very narrow. This method also is desirable when a witness is located far away and the lawyer cannot spend the time and money to travel to that location to take the deposition.

Motions to Compel

Just because discovery requests are sent does not mean that they will be answered. Sometimes discovery is not answered just because the party to whom the request is made is living in stubborn defiance or denial. On other occasions there is a legitimate reason for not turning over the discovery because the information being requested is *privileged* or not remotely connected with anything to do with the case. Of course, few litigants or lawyers are so stupid as to defy the court outright. So, even if refusal to comply with discovery request is completely unjustified, a creative lawyer will think of some way to disguise the refusal as a legitimate objection.

Regardless of whether the denial of a discovery request is justified or not, the first step for the party requesting the information is to file a Motion to Compel. This is the device that brings the discovery dispute before the court. At the hearing on the Motion to Compel, the court can then decide whether the refusal of discovery is justified. If the court finds that the withholding of the requested information is not justified, the refusing party will be ordered to produce the information and will probably be required to pay the other side's attorney fees for bringing the Motion to Compel. Likewise, if the court finds that the Motion to Compel was not reasonable, the discovery will be denied, and the party that brought the motion may be required to pay the other side's attorney fees for resisting the motion.

Discovery Sanction

Refusal to provide discovery is not without risk. When a party fails to comply with a discovery request, the court has a variety of sanctions that can be applied. These range from requiring the payment of attorney fees all the way to excluding evidence at trial or depriving a party of the right to present his or her case or defense. Of course, the court's response must be calibrated and appropriate to the level of defiance or dishonestly displayed by the party.

Protective Orders

Discovery is not all positive. Since it is very costly, it is possible that one party to a lawsuit will use it to abuse the other party. For example, a party can propound a list of interrogatories that are lengthy and difficult to answer. In taking depositions, parties can and sometimes do ask questions that have no possible relationship to the lawsuit and are calculated simply to harass or embarrass the party to whom the questions are directed. For such circumstances the courts have provided that protective orders can be issued to protect parties from such abuses.

Parties who desire such protective orders may file a *Motion for a Protective Order* with the court, setting out the reason that protection is needed. The judge then will decide whether such a protective order should be granted.

Before asking for such a protective order, it is important to understand that the latitude a party is allowed in discovery is fairly broad. The test for deciding whether a particular item is discoverable is not whether the item is relevant and could be introduced in court. Rather, the test is whether the item could lead to something relevant. This gives the parties fairly broad latitude in using discovery to hunt for evidence and search out facts that might be related to the party's financial dealings and conduct.

Hiring Detectives

If your divorce case is anywhere near the average divorce case, you won't need to hire a detective. I would go a step further and say that, unless you absolutely must, you should avoid hiring a detective or investigator. Am I prejudiced against the use of detectives? Probably. Yes, I have used investigators in divorces and other cases. I will, in all likelihood, use investigators in my cases in the future. But, it needs to be the right case, and the vast majority of divorce cases are not the right case for an investigator. Here are my objections.

There are some very good private investigators. But many private investigators have spent too many years watching too much television and seeing way too many movies. Too many times the investigator follows the wrong car, watches the wrong house, or goes through the wrong garbage. I have taken depositions and been in courtrooms in which the other party was able to make the private investigator *and* the person for whom the investigator was working look like the keystone cops. In other words, the inept actions of the investigator destroyed the credibility of the person for whom he or she was supposed to be working.

If you are thinking of hiring an investigator, *please* discuss it with your lawyer before doing so. If an investigator is a must, your lawyer is probably the person with the best information about whom to hire.

Another disadvantage of investigators is cost. Even if an investigator is successful, it is often only after hours and hours of waiting and watching. This means that even with low hourly rates, the cost can be substantial.

In short, use investigators only if you have to. When possible, rely on copy machines, your own snapshots or videos, neighbors, friends, family, teachers, and others who will make much more credible witnesses than someone who is on your payroll and will be expected to testify favorably for you.

Chapter 12

The Trial of Your Contested Divorce Case

Always do right. This will gratify some people, and astonish the rest.

—Mark Twain

The courtroom is the bottom line of *bargaining*. One of the things you and your spouse are bargaining over is whether you will go to court.

If, then, you are too fearful about the courtroom, you may be inclined to settle too cheaply. If, on the other hand, you do not understand that the trial of a lawsuit is an expensive and somewhat uncertain undertaking, you may not accept a bargain that is many times better than a trial.

All of which is to say that you need a *balanced view* of the courtroom. This can come only from knowing what to expect. This chapter is a brief summary of courtroom procedure to give you that overview. Be very clear that this outline is only part of the reality of trials. Courtrooms are paradoxes. On the one hand, what goes on there is extremely simple and straightforward. Then again, trials can become complex mind-bogglers that resemble *Alice in Wonderland*. To calm nervous clients, I often tell them to relax—that the courtroom is like any other room—four walls, a ceiling, and a floor. The people there, the judges, jurors, and lawyers, are the same people you might meet on the street.

All of this is true. But if you go into a courtroom at the right moment, you may observe a scene so absurd that it could only be described by a Kafka novel or a Dali painting. If, in these moments of chaos, a legal scholar were describing what was happening, he would surely say that it was nonsense. An objective psychiatrist would tell you that all of the participants were schizophrenics involved in a mass delusion. If you ask the lawyers involved about the judge, in public, they would say he was mistaken; in private, of course, they would say what they really mean: The old so-and-so is crazy. These assessments, right or wrong, overlook the fact that this is just the nature of the trial beast. After several hundred years of trying to improve trials, the beast is still not completely housebroken.

Absurdity is present in the courtroom, but it is important to keep it in perspective. It is the exception and not the rule. Going to court is like taking a trip on one of the early airlines in the 1930s. Usually the trip was safe and predictable. Often you had to fly a little off course to go around thunderstorms. Sometimes you were forced to turn back, wait, and finally take a different route. The pilots of these early airplanes described flying as "hours and hours of boredom, punctuated occasionally by brief moments of stark raving terror."

The stark raving terror part is probably a little strong for the courtroom, since people don't die in the crashes that take place in court. But the point is the same: The courtroom is a place where events are almost under human control and are *almost* predictable.

The analogy can be pushed a little further. In flying, the most carefully maintained airplanes and the best trained pilots have less likelihood of crashing. In court, if you are honest, forthright, have done your homework, and are taking a *reasonable* position, you increase the likelihood that you will be able to stand clear when and if the roof falls in. If you are *unreasonable*, boisterous, demanding, and enjoy going out on a limb, you are increasing the odds against you for disaster.

Mastering Your Own Emotions about the Courtroom

No, it's not just you. *Everyone* is afraid of the courtroom. That is, all sane people feel fear when it comes to thinking about going to court. It's the nature of the beast. Bad things happen in court. People are sent to prison or have their property taken away from them. People who go to court only because they have devastating injuries are sometimes turned away with nothing. In divorce cases parents are forced to risk losing custody of their children, and many spouses are faced with the possible loss of all, or a portion of all, of the property they own on this earth. And, it's not just the parties to lawsuits who fear the courtroom. A significant percentage of lawyers will tell you that they just won't go there. Many other lawyers, who won't admit it, tremble at the very idea of ending up in a courtroom trying a case. Even those of us who regularly try cases never completely get over the worry that things won't turn out as well as we had hoped for our clients who must submit their fate to a judge or a jury.

But litigants and lawyers are not the only ones who feel this fear of trials. Prospective jurors often say that they are very nervous about serving on a jury. Jurors fear making a mistake in deciding about other people's lives and property. Even some judges need to cover up their fear and discomfort of God-only-knows-what by being grumpy and disagreeable. Witnesses who speak clearly about events when questioned in their living rooms suddenly become unavailable and lose their memories when actually requested to testify. No, you are not alone in your dread of the courtroom.

So, you ask, "Why would anyone take his or her case to court if everyone is so fearful of going there?" The answer is that people go there because they feel that they have no choice. That's the reason you may end up trying your divorce case. If your spouse tries to deprive you of your children or of property that is rightfully yours, then your choice is either to submit to your spouse's unfair or ridiculous demands or go to court. This is why you need to deal with your fear of going to court—so that your spouse will not be in a position to take unfair advantage of you.

The fact that you are aware of your fear of the courtroom is a very good thing. Many of the most devastating events that take place in courtrooms happen to people who have been living in denial. These people stroll blithely into the courtroom with an absolute belief that their own pet thoughts and theories are synonymous with reality. Sometimes it's a client and a lawyer who have both become attached to some pet theories of how the universe operates. More often it's simply a client who has been ignoring his or her lawyer and others for months while they begged him or her to reconsider offers to settle. Because, unlike you, this person has no doubts, he or she has no fears. Courts frequently deal harshly with these misguided souls. See, fears and doubts are good. None of us can live without them.

People in denial are probably afraid—so afraid that they are unwilling or unable to bring their fear to a conscious level. That's what you've got to do: You must become aware of your fear and deal with it on a conscious and intellectual level rather than allow it to eat at you unconsciously and emotionally. This will allow you to put your fear to good use. You and your lawyer will be motivated to work hard planning how your case will be handled if push comes to shove. At the same time, you will be reasonable about the positions you take and your willingness to settle. Your fear will cause you to factor in a reasonable value for the risks you are taking by trying your case. Then, if you find yourself sitting in a courtroom, you will know that you are there only because your opponent forced the matter to trial. If this is the case, you will realize that you really don't have that much to lose. If your property or your children are going to be unfairly or unreasonably taken from you, wouldn't you rather it be done by a judge or jury rather than by just caving into your spouse's crazy demands?

There is another positive aspect to your fear of a trial, and that is the fact that your spouse is having to go through the very same experience of fear of the courtroom. If you have lived with a bully for years who has always been able to run roughshod over you, mastering your fear of a trial will finally put you on equal footing. This equality will come at a time when you are struggling for the rights and resources necessary to begin a new life.

There are some really wonderful things about courtrooms. They are very public. Everyone, even the weak, is given an opportunity to tell his or her story, and the person who shouts loudest is frequently the person who does *not* win. These wonderful facts should help quiet your fears if you have been subjected to life with a bully. Someone has just changed the rules, and this is bound to make the average bully all the more uncomfortable about his or her upcoming day in court.

Trials Are about Credibility

We've all been told that trials are all about finding out the truth. This is probably a satisfactory description for school children or citizens who are casual observers of the process. But if you're a party to a lawsuit who may end up in court, you're probably looking for a deeper understanding of "what is really going on here." You may be asking yourself, "What do I need to know to make sense of this proceeding I'm about to go through?" That is not only an excellent question; it's the correct question.

Trials are about credibility. The essence of what the parties are struggling over is *who is credible and who is not.* If the fact-finder, be it judge or jury, does not believe what you are saying, it is very unlikely that you will receive much help when it is time for a decision to be made. The question of credibility does not just pertain to the party. Because the lawyer is arguing on the client's behalf, the lawyer must guard against losing credibility. Likewise, should a party call a witness or present a document that is questionable, these too can destroy a court's willingness to believe what is being said by or on behalf of a party.

Yes, cases are lost because a party tells a weak story that is just not credible to the court or jury. But, just as often, cases are lost because someone tells a story that is just a little too good or just a little overstated, giving the opponent the opportunity on cross-examination to raise questions about the party's credibility. Lawyers worry, not only about a witness making exaggerated claims in testimony, but also about their own statements to the court or jury. Most lawyers have experienced or observed the negative effects of making a statement or promise to a judge or jury that cannot be delivered in the form of evidence. Trials turn on just such seemingly unimportant events because they raise questions in the mind of the court or jury about the lawyer's credibility. "If he or she is exaggerating or misrepresenting this point, what else could be wrong with the client's case?"

We human beings judge credibility from many things besides the substance of what is being said. Tone of voice, gestures, hesitation at the wrong moment, insensitivity, over-dramatization, inappropriate anger, lack of sympathy, rudeness, ingratitude, irresponsibility, impoliteness, and dozens of other quirks in behavior can destroy one's credibility. It's all about nuance. This is why trial lawyers say, "A picture is worth a thousand words, and one gesture can be worth a thousand pictures."

If all of this does not cause you to be humble at the prospect of having someone sit in judgment on you and your life, you might want to check your grip on reality. As it turns out, however, humility and trust are a big part of what it takes to present your case to a judge or jury. You must make the best presentation you can with the attitude that, at some point, you will "offer it all up and turn it over to the judge or jury to decide." It's this genuine humility and trust that allow a judge or jury to see you as human. Humanity is a part of authenticity. Authenticity probably has a lot to do with credibility. In other words, credibility comes from working hard to control, as much as you can, the presentation of your case, but also at some point willingly handing control over to the fact-finder, be it judge or jury. Yes, with the help of a good lawyer who understands the process, you can credibly present yourself and your case in court! Isn't that, essentially, what you have to do in the rest of your life?

Preparation for Trial

It used to be that a lawyer could announce "ready for trial" if he or she had the witnesses and documents available to prove his or her side of the case. Practically, this meant that if the case was not too terribly complicated, much of the preparation could be done at the last minute. A last-minute witness could be interviewed the night before the trial and called in to testify the very next morning. A document that had been overlooked until just before trial could simply be marked with an exhibit number and introduced into evidence.

All of this has changed with modern rules of discovery. If the other party has requested information about witnesses, documents, and other evidence that are to be used in the trial, this information must be transmitted to the adverse party well in advance of the trial or it cannot be used. *As a practical matter, this means that, if your divorce is complex and contested, you and your lawyer must be ready for trial at least thirty days before the case is set for trial.* The Texas rules of court require that most discovery material and answers be transmitted to the opposing party more than thirty days before the trial. In other words, if your spouse's lawyer has requested the names of witnesses and you fail to properly provide the name of a crucial witness more than thirty days before trial, you probably won't be allowed to call that witness. The same is true should you fail to provide copies of a document you wish to introduce in evidence.

For a litigant or lawyer who is not prepared, denial of admissibility of critical evidence can be brutal. It can work hardships even on well prepared parties who have properly done all their homework well in advance. Witnesses and documents, after all, do sometimes show up the day before the trial or during the trial. Sometimes courts make exceptions and allow the use of this last-minute evidence that could not have been discovered in advance, but admissibility is not a certainty.

The reason for this policy requiring evidence to be turned over to the opposition well in advance of trial is to avoid the old, historic trial-by-ambush. Modern trial lawyers frequently point out that trial-by-ambush has been replaced by discovery-by-ambush. That is to say, much discovery is now sent to the opposing party in the hopes that a failure to "jump through all of the hoops" in filing discovery answers will mean that a party will not be able to get crucial testimony or documents into evidence. The real result usually is that the opposing party responds in kind, sending a correspondingly difficult-to-answer set of discovery back to the original sending party. Hence, when the case is set for trial there is a "balance of terror" with both attorneys concerned about whether all of the hyper-technical *i's* have been dotted and *t's* crossed. This concern is lessened to the extent that a lawyer has spent much of the client's money paying either the lawyer or the paralegals to double- and triple-check discovery technicalities. Money is usually spent on Motions for Protective Orders and hearings before the court to make certain that the other side's overlybroad discovery is not going to be used as a device to exclude legitimate evidence at trial.

In short, much of the "trial" of your case must take place weeks or months before you get to the actual trial, or it's too late.

Judges

In Texas, as in other states, it is the function of the judge to preside over the trial and to decide questions of law. Questions of facts are reserved for the jury. If neither of the parties wants a jury trial, then the judge decides questions of both law and facts. In a trial, whether the driver turned the car to the left or not is a fact question. Whether or not the law required or allowed the driver to turn to the left is a law question.

The "catch-22" of Texas divorce is that the fair division of community property is considered to be a question of law within the exclusive power of the judge to decide. And the judge is given broad discretion in making this decision (subject to some limitations that can be imposed by having the jury find facts regarding fault, value of the property, character of property, etc.). In other words, trial judges have broad discretion, and the appellate courts don't usually overrule the trial judge's decision.

To help your lawyer negotiate and try your case, you must have a realistic understanding of the judge, both as an individual and as a public official. It is unhelpful to have a stereotypical view of your judge either in idealistic or cynical terms. You need to see him or her as a person who will respond in a particular way to particular events.

There are four outstanding things that need to be said about Texas trial judges in relation to divorce cases:

Judges Have Limited Time

Most judges are very busy and have a heavy caseload. The ones that aren't really busy and overworked think they are. For your purposes, as a party to a divorce suit, the effect is the same. Assume that your case will get very limited time. Pick and choose those issues that are really important to you. *Do not force your lawyer to fight over the salt and pepper shakers or the toothpick holder.* This will turn off both the really busy judge and the pseudo-busy judge. Your lawyer may decide as a tactical matter to ask for the Avon bottles anyway, but give him or her some slack in making this kind of decision.

Texas Judges Must Stand for Election

This means that to stay on the bench and keep their job, judges must be politicians. They should not be criticized for this as it is we, the public, who have set the system up in this manner. As a party to a divorce suit, you must realize that if you place yourself on the wrong side of public opinion, you will make it very difficult for the judge to help you. For example, in a small town where the population is very much against marijuana and alcohol, you will make it very difficult for the judge to show sympathy for you if you are frequently seen having wild pot and beer parties. Or if you live in a big city where the populous is up in arms over pollution, and you are president of one of the biggest polluting companies in town, don't be surprised to see your spouse on television leading the antipollution forces at the same time the sheriff rings the doorbell with your divorce papers. Your spouse's lawyer understands that the judge must run for election.

Your Judge Will Be Normal

Your judge will have at least the requisite number of prejudices and strong opinions it takes to be a human being. If you or I were on the bench, the same would be true. Just as with us ordinary mortals, the nature of these prejudices varies a good deal from judge to judge. When and if you learn what your judge's prejudices are, don't try to change them or convince the judge that he or she is mistaken. You would be surprised how many missionaries there are in the world. The lawsuit has nothing to do with the correctness of the judge's opinion about life. The important consideration for you is whether you are going to come out of court with the things you need to survive and prosper. Accordingly, you must steer your way around the dangerous and rocky shores of your judge's strong opinions. Your lawyer will be of great help in doing this. In fact, he or she probably will be able to do it so well it will look easy.

All of these things assume that your judge will be normal. The *vast majority* of District Judges in Texas are normal and will make normal decisions about your case. It is naive to suppose, however, that judges are unlike the rest of the population. Among judges there is a small percentage whose personalities do not fit into the range of normal behavior. Judges, like other human beings, can be sadistic, have sexual hatreds, be paranoid or schizophrenic, senile, or infantile. On a lesser scale, there are judges who have never had children, have never run a business, have never had to earn a living, have never been without money, have never lived on your side of the tracks, or, in fact, have just never experienced a multitude of the problems or situations that they may be having to make decisions about. This presents an abnormal lack of experience that can produce absurd results.

The problem with these unusual judges is magnified in two ways. First, since these judges are public officials having to live in a fish bowl, they must continuously suppress their particular problem, even to the point of denying it to themselves. Second, the public and the judicial system absolutely refuse to acknowledge that this sort of problem even exists. The saving grace is that your lawyer will probably know about these extreme problems with particular judges. The chances are very high that he or she will be able to steer you around the potential disasters that might be created by presenting the *wrong case in the wrong way to the wrong judge.*

Your Judge Hears Cases Very Much Like Yours on a Frequent Basis

If you had to hear large numbers of domestic relations cases, you would soon come to believe that only the names and faces change. The facts are very much the same. This causes some judges to be jaded and insensitive. More often it causes judges to be realistic. Judges soon come to realize that many of the events that occur in a marriage are subtle. Accordingly, judges usually don't want to hear testimony about who did wrong unless the event is clear, strong, and socially unacceptable in the particular community.

Jury

In Texas, all parties to civil lawsuits, including divorces, have the right to a jury trial simply by making a request for a jury and paying a jury fee. In the District Court, it is a twelve-person jury, with the vote of at least ten of the twelve persons being necessary for a verdict.

In cases where a jury is requested, the jury has exclusive right and responsibility to decide all questions of fact. These questions of fact are presented to the jury by the judge, along with instructions as to the law they are to follow in making their decision. The jury is not asked to decide who will win or lose the case but is limited to deciding one fact question at a time. A sample question for a jury might read:

> Do you find from a preponderance of the evidence that it is in the best interest for the child of this marriage, that the Petitioner or the Respondent be appointed Managing Conservator?
>
> Answer: ("Petitioner" or "Respondent")

It is not at all unusual for ten to twenty questions of this nature to be submitted to a jury in one case. After the jury answers such questions, then the judge applies the law to such answers and finalizes the ruling of the court in the form of a decree of judgment.

Juries can play an especially important role in Texas divorce cases in the area of child custody. In Texas, the question of child custody is considered almost a pure fact question within the exclusive power of the jury to decide.

Texas law considers the fair decision of community property to be a question of law for the judge to decide. Parties still have a right to have a jury decide the fact question of which property is "community" and which property is "separate" and the value of the property. In addition, judges are required to justify community property division based on facts of the case. Fault in the breakup of the marriage is one of the facts that the judge may consider. Fault can be determined by a jury. Thus, by determining fault, juries can indirectly play a role in property division.

Of the tens of thousands of divorces granted every year in Texas, only a handful of these cases are decided by juries. But, this fact can be misleading. First, the vast majority of divorce cases are largely uncontested or end up being settled after negotiations. This means that neither judges nor juries make a real decision in these cases. Judges merely approve the settlement. Second, there are a number of cases that are settled because one spouse has requested a jury trial and the other spouse is simply unwilling to face the exposure of his or her conduct to a jury. Also, parties are sometimes unable or unwilling to commit the resources necessary to try their cases to juries. For these reasons, juries probably play a larger behind-the-scenes role in Texas divorce cases than might appear at first blush.

A significant percentage of lawyers in Texas have never tried a jury trial. There is an even higher percentage who have very limited experience with juries and are committed to never trying jury cases. For this reason, lawyer psychology standing alone can play a huge role in the settlement of cases in which the other party has demanded a jury.

Picking a Jury (*Voir Dire* Examination)

If either you or your spouse elects to have a trial by jury, it becomes necessary to choose a jury to hear the case. The selection of the jury is a combination of random chance mixed with a certain amount of selection and input by each of the parties to the lawsuit. It works this way. The names of prospective jurors are selected at random from a list of qualified jurors in the county. If it is a large county, several hundred people may be told to report to a central jury room or jury pool. In divorces and other civil cases, usually about thirty to thirty-five persons are sent to each courtroom in which a jury trial will be conducted. Upon arrival at the courtroom to which they have been assigned, prospective jurors are seated in numerical order so they can be asked questions by the attorneys. Jurors are first asked questions by the petitioner's attorney and then by the respondent's lawyer.

Each of the lawyers may spend anywhere from just a few minutes to several hours examining the jury on their backgrounds, outlooks on life, experiences, prejudices, and service on prior juries. Lawyers may ask questions of the jury panel as a whole or of individual members. This process of asking the jurors questions and choosing a jury is referred to as the *voir dire* examination. The method used varies greatly from lawyer to lawyer, and most lawyers vary the kind of *voir dire* examination used, somewhat, from case to case.

If, during the questioning, it becomes apparent that a particular potential juror is disqualified, it is likely that one of the lawyers will ask that the juror be excused. Such disqualification comes about when it appears that a particular juror is so prejudiced toward one side and against the other, or is so prejudiced by one of the issues in the case, that it would be impossible for this person to be a fair and impartial juror. After giving both sides an opportunity to question the juror about his prejudices or partialities, the judge may be convinced that the juror should be excused. Excusing a juror in this manner is called a *challenge for cause.*

After both sides have had an adequate opportunity to question the potential jurors and all challenges for cause are made, the judge will, typically, give the jury a ten-to-twenty minute recess. It is during this short recess that the lawyers choose the jury. In a civil case, each side is given six *strikes* or *cuts*, meaning that they are allowed to strike off the names of six persons whom they would *least* like to have on the jury. These strikes or cuts technically are called *peremptory challenges.*

After each lawyer makes these cuts, the jury list for each side is handed to the clerk. The clerk selects the first twelve names that are left on the list, excluding those removed for cause or by peremptory challenges. These twelve people are the jury to hear the case.

The selection of the jury is one of the most difficult things a lawyer does. During the *voir dire* examination, the lawyer must:

1. Make a speech
2. Become acquainted with and know considerable amounts of information about thirty-five people
3. Explain basic legal facts so that they can be understood by the average housewife, carpenter, or candlestick maker
4. Keep the other lawyer off his back, at a time when the other lawyer may decide to create as many problems as possible
5. Try not to upset the judge or bore the prospective jurors, when the judge obviously is more interested in getting the case over with, than in who wins or loses.

During this time, the lawyer does not need the added problems of a client who wishes to have a therapy session. Nor does he or she need a lecture on who should or who should not be allowed to sit on juries in general and in this case, in particular. Your lawyer will tell you what role he or she wishes you to play in the *voir dire* examination. It is probable that you will be asked to take notes and give brief comments about outstanding events and personalities that you may notice.

It is my experience that the parties to a lawsuit are of very limited help to a lawyer in choosing a jury. This is because there is so much going on in the courtroom (for example, interaction of forty personalities at one time) that the average person simply has his or her senses overloaded. This means that if you are able to detect a couple of hostile looks or favorable responses from the jury panel, you will have been more than average help to your lawyer. Do not be upset, however, if your lawyer does not dwell upon your responses in picking a jury. The lawyer is trying to sort out, literally, hundreds of answers, gestures, innuendos, and implications that he or she has seen in the short time that the *voir dire* has lasted. You will do yourself harm by insisting that he or she give extra attention to you at this time.

The Rule

There are thousands of rules of procedure and evidence that affect the conduct of cases in Texas courts. Of these rules, only one of them is referred to as *The Rule*.

Before the beginning of evidence in most cases, the judge will ask, "Does either side wish to invoke the rule?" By this question, the judge is asking whether the attorneys wish to have the witnesses excluded from the courtroom so they cannot hear the testimony as it is being given. If either side desires that the rule be invoked, the judge will swear all the witnesses present and instruct them that they are to remain outside the courtroom during the testimony and that they are not to discuss the case with anyone except the lawyers for both sides.

Of course, the parties to the litigation (you and your spouse) are excluded from the rule and are allowed to remain in the courtroom. On other occasions, the court may except other persons from the rule, such as expert witnesses, who are needed by the attorneys to aid in litigation. Lawyers sometimes use the rule to exclude persons from the courtroom whom they do not want present and whom they never intend to call as witnesses.

If the rule is broken, it is very likely that the witness involved will not be allowed to testify.

The Order of Proceedings at Trial

The order in which evidence is presented in a case is the same, regardless of whether the case is being tried before a judge or before a jury, except that in a jury trial several hours will be spent selecting the jury before the trial itself begins. The plaintiff or petitioner begins the trial. At the outset, the attorney for the petitioner has the option of making an opening statement. If the petitioner's attorney makes such an opening statement, the respondent's attorney has the option of going ahead and making his or her opening statement at this point. Occasionally, attorneys simply choose to begin presenting evidence without making an opening statement.

Next, the petitioner begins presenting his or her evidence in the form of witnesses, depositions, documentary evidence, and such. The attorney for the petitioner may begin by putting the petitioner on the witness stand to lay the basic groundwork for the case. It is not unusual for the petitioner's attorney to call the respondent as the very first witness. This has the advantage of forcing the respondent to tell his or her story without ever having had anyone else testify. After the petitioner has presented all of his or her evidence, the attorney for the petitioner announces to the court that the petitioner *rests*.

At this point, the respondent begins putting on his or her case. The respondent's attorney has the option of making an opening statement if an opening statement was not made earlier. Evidence is presented in the very same order and way that it was presented by the petitioner, that is, testimony, depositions, documentary evidence, and so forth. In fact, the respondent may call on some of the very same witnesses that presented all of the evidence that he or she desires to present or is able to produce. Then, when he or she is finished, the attorney for the respondent announces to the court that the respondent *rests*.

The petitioner now has the opportunity to present evidence to rebut the evidence that the respondent just presented. After this process is completed, the attorney for the petitioner will announce to the court that the petitioner closes.

If the trial is before a jury, typically, at this point, it is necessary to recess for a period of time ranging from a few minutes to a few hours. This recess is necessary so that the court's written instructions (*court's charge*) and questions for the jury can be prepared in writing. Usually the judge and lawyers have done considerable work on the court's charge before this time. However, even if this is the case, adequate time must be allowed so that each side will have an opportunity to request that additional items be included in the court's charge or to object to items that already have been included. After the court's charge to the jury is prepared, then the argument to the jury takes place.

The closing arguments are in the same order, whether they are made to a judge or a jury. The parties usually are given a limited period of time in which to make their closing arguments. First, the petitioner argues, usually for about one-half of the time allowed by the court. The respondent then makes his closing arguments. The petitioner then concludes with the final portion of his or her closing argument.

After the closing arguments are concluded, if it is a jury trial, the jury retires to deliberate the case. In a divorce case in Texas, as in other civil cases, at least ten members of the jury must agree on all the issues that the court requires them to answer, and it must be the same ten.

If the trial is before the judge, the judge may either announce his decision immediately after both parties conclude their arguments or announce that the case is being taken under deliberation and that a decision will be made later. Judges usually decide divorce cases immediately.

If a judge is trying the case without a jury, although the order of presentation of the case describe above is still used, it is usually less formal than in a jury trial. Because a jury does not have to wait, the court and the attorneys may agree to change the order somewhat. Of course, this depends on the judge's temperament as well as both attorneys' willingness to be flexible.

Presentation of Testimony

Witnesses testify by giving either testimony under *direct examination* or testimony under *cross-examination.* "Direct examination" is distinguished from "cross-examination" primarily by the fact that a lawyer conducting "cross-examination" can ask leading questions, whereas a lawyer conducting direct examinations cannot. A leading question is a question that calls for or suggests a particular answer. For example, a lawyer cross-examining a witness might ask, "Isn't it true that the fence was black?" A lawyer directly examining a witness would be required to ask, "What color was the fence?"

Direct examination is required on witnesses who are "friendly." Cross-examination is allowed on witnesses who are hostile. So, when your lawyer calls you to testify, he or she will not be allowed to ask you "leading questions." By contrast, when you are cross-examined by your spouse's lawyer, you should expect that most of the questions put to you will be leading questions. When a lawyer calls a witness to testify, it is presumed that the witness is a "friendly" witness and thus not subject to cross-examination by leading questions. There are exceptions, of course. Should your lawyer call your spouse as a witness, it will be obvious to all that your spouse is a hostile witness simply because he or she is the adverse party. If your lawyer calls one of your spouse's parents or one of his or her friends, your lawyer may ask the judge to allow this witness to be cross-examined as a "hostile" witness.

Perhaps because of television, many people believe that trials turn on cross-examination. It is true that cross-examination can be of critical importance in pointing up inconsistencies or demonstrating problems with a witness's testimony. But good old direct testimony is the workhorse that brings home the bacon in most trials. This is because direct examination is the place where you and your other witnesses get to tell your version of your story. Likewise, the opposing party and his or her witnesses get to tell their version of the story when the opposing lawyer has them on direct examination. If one side or the other does not do a good job of telling its version of the story, it usually does not take much cross-examination to defeat that side of the case. Poor stories stick out like a sore thumb, even in the courthouse. On the other hand, lawyers cringe when they hear their clients on direct examination telling stories that "are too good to be true." The too-good-to-be-true story does not work well because, in just a few minutes, the witness telling the story is going to have to go through cross-examination and answer questions about some of the details of his or her story.

Contrary to popular belief, doing a good direct examination is usually more difficult than cross-examining a witness. Issues in trials involve real life, and it is usually not easy to compress a chunk of real life into a few minutes of clear, direct, easily understood, and compelling testimony. The witness needs to have a cozy chat with the judge or jury to explain information that might help resolve the case. But this "cozy chat" must be in question-and-answer form. The witness, who usually feels uncomfortable with the process, may not be able to understand what the lawyer is asking in these open-ended, non-leading questions. In short, direct examination requires teamwork between the witness and the lawyer, and often the two are obviously not on the same team or, at least, not marching to the beat of the same drummer. This awkwardness has a high potential for destroying good testimony that the witness could easily communicate to a friend dropping by the house for a chat. It's not easy, but it's the lawyer's job during direct examination to put the witness in the state of mind that will allow him or her to tell their story just as if they were sitting at home at the kitchen table.

Cross-examination, on the other hand, requires only that the lawyer know the facts of the case and the theories on which it is being tried. If a lawyer is knowledgeable about the subject matter on which a witness is testifying, there is a high probability that the lawyer can ask the best questions that can be asked. Contrary to popular belief, this does not mean that the witness will fall to his or her knees and finally tell the truth. Of course, knowledge of the facts of a case usually cannot be acquired overnight. But, as previously discussed, your lawyer has been learning about your case since the moment you walked through the door to hire him or her. Often, your lawyer will have taken the deposition of a witness just for the purpose of preparing cross-examination. All of this should provide you with good odds that witnesses will be adequately cross-examined in your divorce trial.

You and your lawyer should plan and discuss your direct examination ahead of time. The amount of time for preparation of the client's testimony varies from client to client and from case to case. In some cases, preparing a client to testify may only take a few minutes. Often it can take hours. However long it takes, it needs to be approached deliberately and thoughtfully. You would never make a speech without spending at least some time deciding what you are going to say and how your are going to say it. Although you have your lawyer's questions to lead you through your testimony in a way that you would not in a speech, preparation is still needed.

The Rules of Evidence

In deciding what will be admitted into evidence in your divorce case, the judge follows the Rules of Evidence. This is a comprehensive set of rules interpreted by many volumes of case law, which has been handed down on its various aspects. A lawyer who does not believe that a particular document or portion of testimony or even the entire testimony of a witness is admissible at the trial can object to its admission into evidence. If the objection is valid, based on the rules of evidence, then the document or testimony will be excluded. Although the rules are very detailed and complex, courts are given considerable leeway in deciding whether much evidence will be admitted. Keep in mind that even in trials in which few objections are made, there is a silent drama taking place in the minds of the lawyers about what evidence is admissible and what should be objected to.

Verdict

The answer the jury gives to the questions is called the *verdict*. The verdict should not be confused with a ruling of the court, a judgment, a court order, or a decree. The verdict is simply an answer to the fact questions involved in the case or at least some of the fact questions. For the verdict to be translated into a ruling of the court, the judge must put the fact decisions found in the jury verdict together with the legal rulings that he makes. It is then that the judge enters the order of the court, the *decree*, or *judgment*, whichever you want to call it.

Both appellate courts and trial courts are very reluctant to contradict or set aside jury verdicts. This is why juries can play such an important role, especially in child custody cases.

The Divorce Decree – The Object That Everyone Is Aiming For

In a divorce case, the final written order of the court usually is called the *divorce decree*. In other civil cases, this final written order is referred to as the *judgment*. Frequently, the judge makes an oral pronouncement from the bench stating his or her ruling to the attorneys and parties to the lawsuit. Although this oral pronouncement constitutes the court's ruling, it is necessary for it to be reduced to writing so that it can be referred back to over the following days, months, and years. Once it's reduced to writing, if it's not appealed or changed during the thirty days after it is signed, the decree is pretty much "set in concrete" and becomes the "law of the land" as to all things that were or should have been a part of that divorce case.

The divorce decree is the document that ends your divorce case and tells you what rights you have with regard to your children, child support, and all of the property that was accumulated during your marriage. This means that it's also the document that may take away some of your rights. This one document is what everyone was struggling over and arguing about during the divorce. Whatever the judge writes into this document determines the rights and treatment of the spouses after the case is over.

Although in contested cases judges are the ones who decide what will be in the decree and the ones who sign the decrees, in Texas it's the common practice for the court to assign one of the lawyers the job of drafting the decree. Usually, but not always, the court will instruct that the opposing lawyer be allowed to review the document for "form," that is, to determine whether it actually reflects what the judge ruled from the bench.

In many cases, the judge does not need to make a decision about the custody of the children, the amount of child support, or who gets what property. This is because the parties have already settled the case and entered into an agreement as to what will be contained in the divorce decree. Although technically the court still has an absolute right to veto any settlement between the divorcing spouses, courts are overwhelmingly inclined to approve any settlement agreement that is reasonable or nearly reasonable. This is because the courts have enough problems deciding those cases that don't settle. When cases settle, the court is usually presented with a *proposed* agreed divorce decree that is signed by both spouses and each of their attorneys, indicating that the case is settled on the terms contained in the document being presented. After hearing the basic evidence outlining why a divorce should be granted and the terms on which it is being settled, the judge signs the agreed decree. This gives the agreed divorce decree the same force and effect as all other judgments and court orders. With the sweep of the court's pen, what was just a contract between the parties takes on the full force of a court order. This gives it the full authority of the court and state authority.

Sometimes divorcing couples enter into agreements that settle the case before they even reach the courthouse, with all of the language of the proposed decree worked out in advance. But, agreements to settle cases often arise in the midst of a trial. When this happens it is important to have the lawyer and client double-checking the communications between themselves to make certain that all the terms, conditions, and understandings are actually being read into the court reporter's record and that these items get translated into the written decree that will be prepared for the court's signature. And, as always, a proposed divorce decree that is being submitted for a court's signature should be checked and rechecked by the lawyer, the lawyer's staff, and the client. This is not a document to read by lightly skimming over it.

Appeal

Texas divorce cases may be appealed to the Court of Appeals. There are several of these courts in the state. After the case is heard by a Court of Appeals, the case may be appealed to the Texas Supreme Court in Austin.

WARNING: An appeal generally is not a way to win a divorce case in Texas. Even if the trial court's ruling is grossly unfair, there is still a high probability that an appeal will not be successful. You must rely on a lawyer who has a thorough understanding of the facts of a particular case, if you are contemplating an appeal.

Texas courts make two kinds of decisions: fact decisions and law decisions. Fact decisions cannot be appealed. It is only if the judge has made a mistake in a ruling on the law that the case can be successfully reversed on appeal. If there is *no evidence* or *insufficient evidence* to support a fact-finding, then this becomes a question of law that can be appealed. Example: If the fact-finder has found that "the fence is black," there must be *some* evidence to support this conclusion. Furthermore, this does not mean that all bad decisions about law questions can be successfully appealed. Trial courts are given broad discretion on many so-called questions of law. This means that the judge has broad discretion.

The outstanding example of this in Texas is the division of the community property. The decision regarding the division of community property is a question of law. You can't have a jury make this decision even if you want them to do so. Now, if the judge should make a division that is unfair, you would assume that you could successfully appeal. But you probably can't, unless it is a serious mistake. This is one of those areas where the judge has broad discretion.

Still, don't underestimate the importance of the appellate process in Texas divorce cases. The fact that the process is available keeps judges within the guidelines set out by the law. Because there is the possibility of an appeal, the judge is careful to follow the rules. But within the legal guidelines, there is much slack (i.e., discretion). There is much that appellate courts leave to judges and juries. Hence, we must often rely on the fancy footwork of persuasion, rather than upon the crude force of a threat to appeal.

Also, you can take consolation in the fact that however uncertain, inconsistent, and irrational the legal system is, the other side (your spouse) has to play the same game, by the same rules, and take the same chances. That helps a little, doesn't it?

Preparing to Testify

Your lawyer will have specific suggestions and instructions to help you in preparing to testify. These instructions will be based on your specific personality, your specific case, the kind of hearing, and the temperament of other parties involved, particularly the judge. Nevertheless, here are a few rules that will serve you well. Your lawyer will probably give you written instructions that are similar to these.

1. Except in unusual circumstances, conform to the question-and-answer system of giving evidence. You may have seen a movie in which the hero takes the witness stand and explains everything to everyone's awe and amazement. This technique is successful only in the movies. The judge in your case will insist that you not make a speech.
2. Only answer the question that you have been asked. Do not attempt to make a speech about something that has not been asked. This will draw objections. It will offend the judge. It may offend the jury.
3. Do not attempt to answer a question until you are absolutely sure that you understand what is being asked. If the question is unclear or ambiguous, ask that it be repeated. If you still don't understand, continue to say so. Do not use this to try to avoid answering a clear question.
4. When being cross-examined by the other side, do not volunteer information. You are not answering a friend's questions. Use the shortest answers consistent with accuracy. If a question can accurately be answered with a "yes" or "no," this is usually the answer that should be given. Your attorney will have the opportunity to fill in gaps by asking you questions at a later time.
5. On the other hand, do not be badgered into giving an answer that is not accurate. Remember: The opposition can ask leading questions–that is, questions that call for a particular answer. Do not agree with opposing counsel just for the sake of politeness. For example, if opposing counsel insists that a question can be answered with a "yes" or "no," but you do not agree, do not give in. Firmly but politely stick to your position.
6. If you do not know the answer to a question just say, "I don't know." You are not expected to know everything.

7. Do not allow yourself to be rushed. If need be, think about the question before answering.
8. Do not force the opposing counsel to "dig" an obvious, but painful or embarrassing fact out of you. Some things are black and white. Is this your fourth marriage? Were you convicted of drunk driving? Do you have an illegitimate child? Did you flunk out of college? If you hedge on your answer to this kind of question, you only make matters worse. Be smart. Tell it like it is. Of course, there may be mitigating circumstances. Don't try to explain now. Let your lawyer bring up the items in due course.
9. Do not admit your worst thoughts. Only you know what is in your head—your thoughts, feelings, intentions, etc. All normal people of reasonable intelligence have had *bad* thoughts, such as murder, suicide, theft, lust, etc. Keep in mind when testifying that thoughts and emotions are usually *mixed*. While you are testifying is not the time to have a therapy session and disclose all of your bad feelings. Temper your answers with the qualifications and reservations that are absolutely necessary to give a true picture of the human mind.
10. Leave yourself running room on amounts of money, dates, times, addresses, physical dimensions, etc. Use words like "approximately," "I think, but I'm not absolutely sure," "more or less, etc." If you have records giving exact figures, offer to consult those records.
11. Do not try to memorize your answers. If you have kept notes or diaries of events or have given a deposition, by all means consult these to refresh your memory. Do not, however, try to testify in exactly the same words.
12. When any lawyer makes an objection, stop speaking immediately.
13. Unless your lawyer indicates otherwise by making an objection, you must answer all questions. Do not say, "Do I have to answer that?"
14. Be polite. Show your good manners. This does not mean that you are to give in or be pushed around. Be firm. But make up your mind that, if necessary (and it usually is), you will disagree without being disagreeable. Remember: To lose your temper is to increase the odds of losing your case.
15. Do not expect every question to be a trick question. There are just not that many trick questions. By looking for the hook in everything, you will appear to be calculating or dishonest.

16. Dress neatly, but conservatively. If you err, do so slightly on the formal side rather than the informal.
17. If it is a jury trial, jurors will be watching you as much as they are listening to you. Hence, you are giving testimony every moment you are in the courthouse—not just while seated on the witness stand. Jurors will be as curious about you as you are about them. You are giving evidence at the counsel table, in the hallway, at the concession stand, and in the bathroom. Be polite. Be human. *Never be condescending.*
18. Never appear bored or indifferent. Show everyone that you are taking the case seriously.
19. If you make a mistake because you are nervous, apologize and say you are nervous. This will help you relax.
20. Use conversational tones. Talk in the same manner that you would to family, friends, or persons on the street. Speak up. Most courtrooms are large. Many have poor acoustics. Do not put your hand over your mouth. Recognize that it is your responsibility to communicate your side of the case in a manner that can be reasonably understood.
21. Do not argue with the other side's lawyer. Do not ask the other lawyer questions, except to clarify questions. If the lawyer is rude or unkind, do not respond in kind. Continue to be polite while firmly resisting and disagreeing. The judge or jury will reward you for your politeness.
22. Opposing lawyers sometimes ask you if your lawyer told you what to say in your testimony. Your answer should be that you discussed the testimony you would give and your lawyer told you to tell the truth.

Sometimes opposing lawyers ask, "Who did you talk to about your case or the testimony you gave here today?" The implication and tone of the question suggest that there is something wrong with talking to your lawyer or anybody else about the case. There is nothing wrong with your having talked to other people about your case. Just answer the question.

Depositions

Some special rules apply to deposition testimony.

1. Since the other lawyer is sizing you up to see how you will perform in court, all of the foregoing rules apply. If your deposition testimony is good, this may improve your bargaining position.

2. Most smart lawyers are very polite to witnesses at depositions. Do not worry about being browbeaten by your spouse's lawyer.
3. Let your lawyer do the fighting. Since there is no judge present to rule on evidence or make other rulings, depositions can develop a "free-for-all" atmosphere. A small minority of lawyers use this absence of the judge to try to intimidate the other side. Your lawyer may ignore this, or if it gets out of hand, decide to "push back." Let your lawyer make this decision.
4. You and your lawyer have great control of the deposition's pace and schedule. Since there is no judge or jury, you may decide when you need a drink of water, to use the bathroom, to take a break, to talk with your lawyer. Of course, this gives you great freedom in working with your lawyer. The other side may try to limit this by having the court reporter note the lengths of breaks or conferences. This usually is not a problem.

SECTION IV

Settlement and Alternate Dispute Resolution

DISPUTE RESOLUTION

In this section:

Chapter 13

Bargaining with Your Spouse

The most powerful words in negotiations:
Your Honor, We're ready for trial.

—Old lawyer saying

There are two ways to get what you want from your divorce. You may go to court and ask the judge to award you the property and terms you want. Or you may get your spouse to agree to give you what you want.

DISPUTE RESOLUTION

Obviously, if you have a choice, settlement is better than a trial. Trials are expensive, time-consuming, and risky. Nevertheless, you cannot rule out the possibility of a trial in your divorce. Your spouse may be so unreasonable as to give you no choice.

But a trial is a last resort. It is for you what war is for the defense of the country. First, you use all diplomatic channels to resolve your differences. If the other person then continues to invade your territory, you can go to court, knowing that you did everything possible to avoid the risk and expense of a trial.

A negotiated settlement does not mean that someone must lose. Frequently, both parties come out better in an agreed settlement than they would if they had gone to trial. This is because they know infinitely more about their business than does the judge. Even if a judge singles out your case and gives it extra time (which isn't going to happen), there is no way that the judge can know as much in a few minutes, hours, or even days about your wants, dreams, aspirations, abilities, and so forth, as you do. After all, you and your spouse probably have had years to learn about the value of your property and to consider its potential use and merit.

At a trial, the judge may give you one-half of a business that you really don't believe is worth anything, when all along you really wanted the house. Or, you may be given the stove and your spouse given the refrigerator, at a time when your aunt has died and left you a good stove, but you don't know how on God's green earth you will find a refrigerator. It happens.

In most divorces the risk is not just that the judge will take away most of one spouse's property and give it to the other. Although this is definitely a risk, an additional danger is that the property you have will be shuffled in such a way that neither person can maximize the use of what they get.

The message is clear: Unless you don't have any children or property or your spouse is already giving you everything you want, you must negotiate to get what you want and need, to survive a divorce and live your life afterward.

Settle It at Any Cost

Substantial numbers of divorces are settled with lopsided property settlements: That is, one spouse gets substantially more property than the other. Such settlements usually are not based on facts that are likely to cause a judge to divide the community property unevenly. Rather, these settlements come about because one spouse decides to give up. "Just get it over with," the client says. "Give him whatever he wants." At the divorce bargaining table, these words tell even the dumbest spouse that he or she has just been dealt another ace.

In divorce language this translates into: "Okay, then just give me the house, car, child, or all of the above, and I will tell my lawyer to get it over with."

Sometimes the "get it over with" psychology is justified. More often, it is an invitation for disaster to walk right through the door. This approach fails to consider that the new life that is symbolized by the divorce has many of the same requirements for survival as the world of marriage.

If there was great financial difficulty in your marriage, financial trouble probably is going to continue, at least for a while, after the divorce. If you felt lonely and unloved in the marriage, it is likely that it will take some time after the divorce for you to overcome these feelings. The point is that the way you get your divorce can greatly increase or lessen the pain of adjustment to the new life.

All of this comes more clearly into focus when you consider that somebody in your marriage (if you are typical of most couples) is going to begin the new single life without a can opener, a bed, a stereo, a dining table, or perhaps even a car or a home. The consequences of doing without or trying to replace one or two of these items may be totally insignificant. On the other hand, the loss of all these items adds up to economic disaster and can create culture shock over and above such things as divorce and loss of children.

The most dangerous aspect of this "settle-it-at-any-cost" mentality is that the effects are not always immediately apparent. Everyone comes out of the courtroom relieved. It is only in later years, after eating many beans, talking to many unhappy and mean creditors, and being unable to send your children to the dentist, that an awareness of the mistake comes about.

The compound nature of this tragedy is only understood if you keep in mind that I am talking about something that need never happen. I am not discussing poverty divorces, where the resources simply don't exist. I am talking about people who give away what is rightfully theirs.

Why would anyone do this—just give away their property? As I have said earlier, it is not unusual, and there are probably many reasons. However, if you are one of those get-it-over-at-any-price people, it is fairly safe to bet that: (1) you feel guilty and pity your spouse; (2) you can't stand your spouse's face, personality, or anything else about him or her, and you don't want to have anything else to do with him or her; (3) you have a lover who you think will solve all of your problems; or (4) your spouse is blackmailing you by saying that if you don't settle, he or she will tell the judge, your mother, or your friends about your affair, that you use marijuana, that you drink beer, etc.

Giving in because of these problems will not only jeopardize your property and make life more difficult for you, it probably won't get you what you think you are trading for.

First, if you feel guilty and pity your spouse, there is a good chance that this is one of the root causes of your divorce. Chances are that within a few months you will understand, intellectually, what you now know in your guts: He or she uses your feelings of pity and guilt to manipulate you.

By "giving in" you are not only continuing in the rut that you have been in, but may be allowing yourself to be manipulated into a settlement in which you will be forced to listen to the Poor Pitiful Me act for a couple of more years. Watch out! This kind is tricky. It may help to understand that you are not helping him or her by giving in. You are just delaying your spouse from taking responsibility for his or her own life.

Second, if you can't stand your spouse, let your lawyer do the talking. Make a hard and fast rule that you simply will not talk with him or her. Here again, a poor settlement may mean that you will not be given the power over your property that you need to avoid your spouse in the future.

Third, if you have a lover, face the fact that your new relationship has a better chance if you are able to stand on your own feet financially and emotionally. A part of what you bring to this new relationship must come from your marriage that is just ending. If you walk away from assets that you need to live, it follows that you and your new lover will have to come up with these assets from your own sweat and blood. While this may not make your new lover love you any less, it probably won't make him or her love you any more.

Fourth, if you give in to being blackmailed, this is like being bluffed out of your chips before the cards are even drawn. Often people giving in for this reason don't even tell their lawyer. This is not only stupid; it is arrogant! What is a really wild and embarrassing story to you is probably fairly routine to your lawyer. Tell your lawyer about your spouse's threat. Handling cheap threats is usually the easy part of a lawyer's job. There is a good chance that your lawyer will tell you that the threat is meaningless because the judge in your case doesn't pay attention to this kind of evidence.

Or, if it is a serious threat, your lawyer will know how to minimize it. Chances are, if it is really damaging, your spouse has done you a big favor by telling you ahead of time. Now you can prepare to meet it. If you are being threatened by something really serious, talking with your lawyer will allow you to weigh the risk and make a more rational decision. Even in this circumstance it is usually not necessary to give up completely. If you don't spook, you probably can cut your losses very substantially.

If your spouse is threatening to tell a friend, your mother or father, your child, or the preacher, face the fact that bargaining with this kind of mentality simply is not possible. He or she is going to tell no matter what you do. Again, talk to your lawyer. Consider using a confrontational approach to this sort of blackmail. Tell your spouse that you can't stop him or her, that it will not really hurt you as much as the person who is being told, and that you are prepared to live with your actions.

If you then believe that he or she is really going to tell your mother, consider telling her yourself. Here, rely heavily on your own instincts. Usually a bare outline of events is more desirable than all of the gruesome details. Upon telling your mother that you had an affair with the postman, there is a 50-50 chance that she will say either that she considered it herself and should have done it years ago or that she wonders why you are telling her since she already knew anyway.

If, on the other hand, you come from a family that is extremely straight with heavy-handed consciences, consider not saying anything. There is a 90% chance that they will refuse to believe your spouse anyway.

Shifting from Intimacy

In divorce, the need to be less than forthright and candid with the bargaining opposition presents some special problems. In the process of buying a car or selling a house, most people don't feel compelled to reveal their doubts, fears, motives, or regrets. Most would feel awkward or ridiculous to make such revelations under these circumstances. Dealing with a spouse is a different matter. In marriage, the goal is intimacy. This requires honesty beyond the minimum standard of truth about the facts only. Hence, spouses often feel that they are being dishonest if they don't continue to give their mate advice, counseling, and openness. This sometimes works. More often, in a divorce there comes a time when one spouse starts using this honesty in a manipulative fashion. Honesty depends on the nature of the relationship as well as truthfulness. If you live along a dead-end road, honesty does not require that you rush out the front door to warn every traveler that they are in for many miles of needless travel to get nowhere. To do so would be to become the village fool. On the other hand, if you see your spouse, a friend, or a child trudging such a hopeless dead-end path, then your standard of honesty may require you to make all reasonable efforts to warn the person about the chuck-holes in the road.

Now, however, your relationship with your spouse is changing, whether you like it or not. Even if you love each other (as do many people going through a divorce), the relationship is still going to change. You must move from having a relationship based on intimacy to a relationship based on good-faith, arm's-length transactions. The alternative is to risk being badly hurt.

Getting Yours

What is negotiation? For our purposes, we can say that negotiation is the process of trying to persuade others to give us what we want. Even though your divorce is a legal matter, negotiating a settlement involves a great deal more than law. In your divorce settlement, the law plays somewhat the same role as the out-of-bounds line of the football field. It is very important, but most of the game is played elsewhere on the field. In negotiating a settlement in your divorce case, it is helpful to think in terms other than law. The harsh reality is that bargaining over your divorce case is more like horse trading or playing poker than anything else. The hand that you are dealt or the horse that you own is going to play a big part in the game. Nonetheless, the way you play makes a big difference in the outcome.

The poker game analogy is most helpful in thinking about dividing assets with your spouse. This is because of the uncertainty of the poker game. Both sides have some idea of what the court is going to do, but only a fool would pretend to know for sure. It is risky business.

To avoid this risk, both sides offer to give away some chips. If the other side isn't offering you any chips, then you don't have anything to lose by going to trial. If you are being offered only a small stack of chips, you still have relatively less to lose. Finally, the contrary is true. If you are offered a large number of chips, you run a substantial risk of getting less than this amount if you refuse them and instead choose to go to court.

Since I have told you that negotiating or bargaining your case has more to do with psychology, horse-trading, and poker playing than it does with law, you may be thinking that you can negotiate your case as well as your lawyer. You may be right. You may be able to negotiate better than your lawyer; or your attempt at negotiation may be a complete disaster that destroys your lawyer's chances for helping you.

The question of how and by whom negotiations should be conducted is a serious matter that merits attention from both you and your lawyer. It should not be decided on the spur of the moment. Nor should it be based on your ego-needs, either to play lawyer or to get the best of your spouse, unless you value these needs more than you do your children or property.

Perhaps you have been the dominant personality in the marriage and know more than your spouse about the community property. Perhaps your spouse is represented by an obstreperous lawyer who won't talk with your lawyer. Then, obviously, you may be the one best able to make some progress on your negotiations.

The contrary is also true. If your spouse has always been dominant or knows more about the community business and has employed a lawyer whom your lawyer judges to be willing to negotiate in good faith, then it is probably a mistake to negotiate for yourself. These obvious and extreme examples demonstrate how your lawyer will help you to decide how much of your own negotiation you should attempt. Your lawyer will not encourage you to undertake your own bargaining unless he or she thinks you are capable.

You may be tempted to try to negotiate your contested case first without a lawyer, thinking that if worse comes to worst, you can then hire a lawyer to straighten things out. Don't. At best, this is like going to a sword fight without a sword just to see whether you need one. You might be allowed to go home and get one. At worst, it is like negotiating with Hitler without having an army. He won't let you go home and get one.

Remember: Almost all of your bargaining power is built around the fact that you don't have to settle. If you go to the negotiation party without a lawyer, you are defeating yourself. Perhaps the only words more American than "Remember the Alamo" are "I'm going to get a lawyer and sue you." In our society these words carry power. If you really want to get a job done in negotiations, you won't settle for cheap talk about what you are going to do if your spouse doesn't agree. Just hire the lawyer. Don't say a word about what you're going to do. They'll get the picture. It's the difference between shouting "wolf" and taking the wolf and setting it outside their door. It will save you money in the long run, and it may save your case.

Remember: Negotiations often set the table for litigation, and you may inadvertently set a table that no lawyer can help you serve. There is no clear-cut line between negotiation and litigation. Every experienced lawyer knows that there are many places besides the courtroom where trials and mini-trials take place.

Cases are tried by the parties before they even move out of the house, in the lawyer's office, in the other lawyer's office, at negotiation sessions, in the social worker's office, in the coffee shop, and so forth. More often than not, these informal trials decide the outcome of the case before it gets to court so that even if a courtroom hearing takes place, the outcome, for all practical purposes, is already predetermined.

Br'er Rabbit – The Father of Modern Negotiations

Now that I've given you some background about negotiations, let's get into some do's and don'ts. The credit goes to some big names in the field of negotiations. They have laid the groundwork for the techniques you will be using to persuade your spouse to give you what you want.

Some would say Machiavelli's Prince is the founder of modern negotiations. This simply is false. Modern sophistication, brought on by the advent of television, travel, and education for the masses, has outdated the crude brute force, deception, and sleight-of-hand tricks proposed in *The Prince.*

The true father of modern bargaining, few people realize, is no less than the great Br'er Rabbit, who, by sheer persuasion, used the little bargaining power he possessed to convince Br'er Fox and Br'er Bear not to make him into rabbit soup. This was a significant accomplishment.

But, before we get into the methods developed by Br'er Rabbit, we need to consider some basic concepts developed by Br'er Rabbit's great teacher, Tar Baby. Tar Baby, as you recall, was sitting by the road when Br'er Rabbit came along. The rabbit became angered because Tar Baby would not return the cheerful greeting he offered. Finally, the rabbit started hitting and kicking Tar Baby. With each blow, he became more caught in the sticky tar.

Now, that's when Tar Baby set out the foremost rule of negotiation, which Uncle Remus tells us when he says, "Tar Baby, he don't say nothin'!" This statement is repeated over and over. The more Br'er Rabbit struggled, squirmed, screamed, threatened, hit, and kicked, the more Tar Baby refused to talk. Hence, the words, "Tar Baby, he don't say nothin'," have been written as the immortal ground rules in bargaining. If you wake up in the middle of a bargaining session feeling lost, hurt, wronged, confused, sick, unsure, overpowered, or anemic, you can, with some safety, harken back to the famous words, "Tar Baby, he don't say nothin'."

In other words, "negotiating" does not mean calling your lawyer and your spouse every day just to keep up conversation. Nor does it mean calling your spouse's mother and telling her what you have always suspected about her kinship with other species. If you call your spouse when you're depressed, you may end up telling him or her that you value the new sleeper sofa, which he or she so selfishly refuses to let you have, more than all your other household furnishings combined. This will virtually ensure that your new rented apartment will be furnished with a sleeper sofa and nothing else.

Well, enough about Tar Baby. Except: If you ever find yourself in a negotiation session where you are doing all the talking—stop. Feel to make sure you still have your wallet. Then consider that the other team may have studied at the feet of Tar Baby. It is important to your health that the other side utter such words as "yes," at least occasionally. If they don't, bid them good day and leave. This is what Tar Baby would do under similar circumstances.

And now we return to the rabbit. Shortly after Br'er Rabbit became totally stuck in Tar Baby, Br'er Bear and Br'er Fox came out of the bushes where they were hiding. After they finished laughing themselves almost senseless about Br'er Rabbit's predicament, they discussed what to do with their captured game. At first, the conversation centered around simply making rabbit soup. The rabbit's response to this was that rabbit soup was fine, "but whatever you do, don't fling me in that brier patch." Whereupon the bear and the fox decided that soup wasn't good enough, or bad enough, depending on how you look at it. They then discussed a number of other possibilities, ranging from cutting the rabbit into small chunks right down to letting ants eat him in the hot sun. But whatever they suggested, the rabbit always responded by saying that particular suggestion would be all right, "but whatever you do, don't fling me in that brier patch!"

Well, the bear and the fox became so intrigued with the idea, that they did, in fact, throw Br'er Rabbit in the brier patch. And since Br'er Rabbit liked the brier patch and lived there, the fox and the bear had to suffer the humiliation of hearing him laughing and singing somewhere out in the briers where they couldn't catch him.

Now, what can we learn from all of this?

Rabbit Rule #1: Your Position Is Never Too Weak for Bargaining

Whenever you feel sorry for yourself and start to give up without even trying to bargain, remember the rabbit. There he was with his hands and feet bound and the water already heating for soup. Had he stopped to ponder the unfairness of life, it would have become even more unfair, from his point of view. Power is relative. There is no such thing as absolute power or absolute weakness.

Ironically, your strengths will usually be your weaknesses and vice versa. This is also true of your spouse. If your spouse has always been the dominant personality in the marriage, controls all of the money, is loved by all of your mutual friends, and is by profession a labor negotiator, then you might consider your position worse than that of Br'er Rabbit.

But consider the power that you might gain by deciding to have your way just once. It might be the surprise of your spouse's life. It may be difficult for him or her to maintain the nice-guy image when you are making it plain that he or she will not be able to talk you into giving up this time. The nice-guy image is an asset in bargaining since everybody wants the nice guy to win. But, it is also a liability, since, if the behavior is not nice, the image could be lost. If your spouse is a bully, the same rules apply. You must realize that your spouse's intimidation is of very limited use. Sure, if you continue to let him or her talk with you privately in the kitchen, you will continue to be bullied. But, if you insist that you will talk only in the presence of your lawyer, friends, a tape recorder, or a videotape machine, chances are the bully is going to have some difficulty pulling off the intimidation act, all of which brings us to the second rule.

Rabbit Rule #2: Be Flexible and Adaptable

If you think the rabbit rescued himself because he was the nice guy, you misunderstand the point of this story about human nature. The rabbit was nice and talked in a gentle voice because that is what worked from his position in the soup pot. It makes me feel better to think that he preferred to be nice when he could. But don't kid yourself. Had the shoe been on the other foot, with the rabbit in the position of strength, he would not have held a tea party to soothe the bear's and the fox's hurt feelings. He would have yelled, screamed, kicked, bitten, or done whatever was necessary to rescue himself.

It would seem unnecessary to say that the same things won't always work twice. Nonetheless, we see examples over and over again of how difficult it is for some people to be flexible. If yelling and screaming prove to be ineffective, as the rabbit found out, many people simply add more yelling and screaming. You can imagine what this would have gotten the rabbit. Others who have tried being "nice" for years cannot give up the habit. If being nice has gotten them abused, misused, and taken advantage of, what do they do? They try being nicer. Well, don't.

If what you're doing isn't working after a reasonable period of time, try something different. Better yet, try to start out doing the right thing. If your husband is a middle linebacker for a pro football team, don't agree to arm wrestle for one single item of community property. If your wife deals blackjack in Las Vegas during her summer vacation, don't agree to play cards to decide who gets the house.

Being flexible means choosing your ground, the place where you have the advantage.

Rabbit Rule #3: Be Realistic

A good settlement is a realistic settlement. You must be realistic about what you can expect to get, not what you want. Sometimes, happily, the two coincide. More often, they do not. You may want the moon. That does not mean that you can get it either in court or by settlement.

The rabbit was in the same position. What he really wanted was bear and fox soup. Fortunately, he had sense enough not to make this the central theme of his negotiation.

This is not to say that you are to ask only for what you think you can get or even for what you want. Often, it is desirable to ask for the moon. As is said among lawyers: If you don't ask for it, you won't get it. Sometimes the other side needs you to make some outrageous demand so that they will be able to achieve a victory by talking you out of it.

But, at all times, you should have a realistic understanding of what is acceptable as a settlement.

Rabbit Rule #4: When Necessary, Cut Your Losses

It is safe to assume that, even though the rabbit lived in the brier patch, he did not exactly enjoy being thrown there by his ears. But, given a choice of being thrown by his ears or being cooked in soup, he correctly opted for that which was less damaging. This is what you should do.

Going to court is not all "winning." Frequently, it becomes obvious that a loss is likely. When this is the case, the issue becomes how to cut the losses. This is especially important when you know more about the weaknesses in your case than the other side does. If, for example, the issue in your divorce is the amount of child support you are to be paid, and you know ahead of time that this judge is notorious for setting low child support, you need to try to settle for something above what the judge is likely to give, even if it is not a fair amount. This is doubly true if, by some miracle, your spouse's lawyer does not yet know of the judge's notoriety on this matter. Get what you can get! Don't wait to be completely trounced. The world already has enough martyrs.

Rabbit Rule #5: Don't Tell the Other Side What You Want – Find Out What the Other Side Wants

This may sound peculiar, since it is obvious that sometimes you must say what you want. But don't be too quick to give out this information. Remember, the rabbit got what he wanted by concentrating on the mental processes of the other side. Had he used his time for discussion with the enemy as a therapy session, discussing his own feelings, dreams, hopes, and fears, he would have been soup.

Suppose you and your spouse own considerable community property, which includes two cars of approximately equal value. Now, if you make a point of telling your spouse that you can't stand the blue car, but you just love the red one, it doesn't take a genius to figure out that your spouse will appear at the next negotiation session arguing that the red one should be included in the inventory at a considerably higher price than the blue car.

Another example: You tell your spouse that you have decided to leave the country after the divorce, so you don't want to keep any interest in the mom-and-pop business you started together. What do you think is going to happen to the price of the business? Naturally, your spouse will begin to think that it is worth less than he or she thought when you had a possibility of laying claim to the business.

The converse is also true. If you state that you must have the mom-and-pop store and you are willing to pay cash for your spouse's share, the price is likely to increase.

Rabbit Rule #6: Use Short Sentences

After the rabbit got his act together, he really only used one sentence. In response to whatever the fox and bear suggested, he simply said: "That will be all right, but whatever you do, please, oh please don't fling me in the brier patch." He seemed to be saying a lot. He really wasn't saying anything. He gave away no information.

Compound and complex sentences are some of the most wonderful things in life. People who care about each other should share feelings, hopes, angers, fears, and dreams. The trouble is that many people get it backwards. They won't talk to the people they care about, but then when they talk with the enemy, they "really give them a piece of their mind." Well, save it for the ones you love, and the ones who love you. Your spouse is now in a position adverse to yours. What you say can and usually will be used against you.

If you cannot resist the urge to use long sentences, or if you need to make conversation just to keep the negotiations going, be sure to talk only about the weather, foreign policy, nuclear physics, or some other topic wholly unrelated to your divorce or personal life.

Rabbit Rule #7: Let the Other Side Have Their Victories

A part of being human is the deep-seated desire to look good. The Chinese call it saving face. To some extent we all want to be the hero. The rabbit might have been chosen to show the bear and the fox what a silver-tongued devil he was. He could have used his quick wit to expose their pedestrian mentalities. Instead, he chose to eat humble pie. The rabbit literally saved his neck by being the "goat." He was willing to suffer a loss of face to save a very real part of his anatomy.

In the breaking-up process, egos typically are bent and stretched. This means that you and your spouse are likely to be fighting over some things that are pure ego battles. If you can let your spouse win all of these imaginary battles in exchange for your being allowed to win the battles of property division, child custody, and child support, you will be the real winner. There is plenty of time to be a hero later. Will Rogers said, "Being a hero is the shortest-lived occupation in the world." This is especially true if you become a hero by winning the imaginary points that really don't change the scoreboard.

Rabbit Rule #8: "Shock Treatment" Is of Very Limited Use in Negotiation

You recall that the rabbit began his negotiations by screaming at the top of his lungs. Were the rabbit a lesser figure in the field of negotiations, it might be said that this method simply didn't work. Well, bite your tongue for such thoughts.

I prefer to think that the rabbit intentionally used the screaming act to set the stage for his shift to the low-key approach that was, finally, so successful. Either way, the point is that the screaming, in and of itself, got the rabbit nowhere.

Intimidation is not the main tool of negotiation. Although screaming, wild gyrations, threats, and intimidations are not to be overlooked, their overuse renders them not only useless, but dangerously counterproductive.

For example, if you habitually have allowed your spouse to take advantage of you, there is a good chance that you can stop this by the use of some shock therapy. When your spouse calls, let him or her have a strong dose of your anger. Say that you will not stand to be abused. Threaten to call the police or get a restraining order. This will probably work this one time.

Or, if the time to go to court is near and your reasonable offers have not caused your spouse to move toward a fair settlement, say that you are tired of negotiating and that you have instructed your lawyer to prepare for trial. Again it may work, and if it doesn't, you really haven't lost anything. On the other hand, if you call your spouse every day with some new threat or if you attempt to play the big shot at every negotiation session, your shocking conduct will lose all of its power.

Stated another way: You must respect the other side. Stories of intimidation sell very well in men's locker rooms. Some have even written whole books on intimidation as a negotiation technique. The truth is this game works two ways. If you pick up a stick, you ought not to be surprised when the other team picks up an even bigger one! This is not to say that you should never use a stick. It is to say that you must understand the limits and risks involved in doing so. A very good trial lawyer told me early in my career, "The greatest advantage that a lawyer can have in trial is to be underestimated by the other side." The belief that winning can be accomplished totally through intimidation fails to recognize that the other side also has power. Some of the most powerful figures in history have been vanquished by failure to have proper respect for the enemy. Apparently, the rabbit either heard about them or read about them. We should learn from the rabbit.

Rabbit Rule #9: Don't Crow until the End

This is a spin-off of the previous rule. Be sure you have actually reached the end before letting out a hoot of derision. Remember: Your spouse can still appeal or move for the court to set aside the judgment up to thirty days after rendition of the judgment. And judgment is not always rendered on the day you actually appear in court.

Also, if you have yet to get all of your property from your spouse or if you own property in common with your spouse, you had better gag back your jeers a little longer. And if you have children, face the fact that you are going to need the best possible relationship with your ex-spouse until your children are grown.

Although these are all of the rules handed down by Br'er Rabbit, there is more to bargaining than this. So in honor of the great negotiator, I'll continue to call these additions "Rabbit Rules."

Rabbit Rule #10: Test the Water

You may find yourself in the same position as the rabbit and have no choice about whether to negotiate. This sometimes happens when negotiation is being conducted immediately before the trial. The choice is either to negotiate a settlement or go to trial. More often than not, however, you will have a choice of negotiating or waiting until a later date to discuss the matter. This is very important to understand because people's moods vary greatly from day to day. An offer that is wholly unacceptable to your spouse on one day may be very acceptable on another. But, this probably won't be true if you let him or her say "no" on the first occasion.

Therefore, whenever possible, test the water. If your spouse is in a negative mood, you have everything to lose and nothing to gain by continuing the session. As gracefully and tactfully as possible, make some excuse and leave.

If you can't leave, try to change the subject. Talk about the weather or Aunt Geraldine or Uncle Leroy. If you can't change the subject, tell your spouse that you are not ready to get down to specifics and just want to exchange general information and ideas about a settlement. Then be general and vague. The point is: Don't force the issue. Don't create a confrontational situation at a bad time when you don't have to.

Rabbit Rule #11: Don't Give Your Negotiator Authority to Settle without Consultation

Many lawyers intentionally don't get authority from their clients to settle a case until after negotiations are complete. This is an excellent practice. It puts the negotiator in the position of saying, "I like what you're offering, but I don't have authority from my client to settle the case." Or, perhaps even better, "I like your offer, but I'm afraid you'll have to do better or my client won't accept it." It gives the negotiator the ability to sympathize with the other side, thereby establishing rapport, without giving in. This is often immensely helpful in reaching a settlement.

This technique works so well that many good negotiators, who really have full authority, develop phantom or imaginary authority elsewhere. They pretend not to have authority. Since you obviously have authority to settle your own case, this is the method that you must use when you are the negotiator, if you are to keep from having all of your authority present. You can do this by letting your lawyer be the heavy. When your spouse is pressing you for agreement, tell him or her that you can't give an answer because you must consult your lawyer. Say that your lawyer made you promise not to enter into any settlement agreement without his or her consent.

If necessary, you can go further and say that if you don't abide by this agreement, you're afraid that your lawyer will quit your case. Though you would almost be glad to get rid of the lawyer, since he or she is so mean, you can't afford to do so because you already paid substantial money for legal fees, and you can't afford another lawyer.

If it will make you feel better, go ahead and actually enter into such an agreement with your lawyer. Agree that you will not make any agreements about your case without first consulting with him or her. The important thing is to put yourself in a position that will keep you from being stampeded into an imprudent agreement.

The oldest, and cheapest, sales trick in the world is what might be termed the "once-in-a-lifetime-deal" or "the last of its kind at this price" trick. More people have been sold more junk at ridiculously high prices by this method than by any other method known to mankind.

So, if your spouse is offering you "such a good deal" that he or she can't allow you a few hours or a few days to talk with your lawyer and think it over, then by all means tell your spouse with a touch of sarcasm that the offer is just so good that you can't accept it. People who make legitimate offers can afford to give a reasonable period of time for consideration.

This does not mean that you should always delay or stall in negotiations. If you and your lawyer are convinced that the offer is a fair offer and that you can't do any better or that maybe it really is the deal of a lifetime, then by all means strike while the iron is hot—settle.

The point is, you can't know if it is a good deal until you have had an opportunity to (1) be sure of the facts, (2) know what the law says you're entitled to, and (3) have some idea of what a judge or jury is likely to decide if the case is tried. These things take time—even for a lawyer. If your spouse doesn't have sense enough to recognize this, then you must.

Rabbit Rule #12: Think Ahead or Leave the Back Door Open

The fastest way to lose credibility in negotiations is to make statements that you can't back up. This is true on two fronts.

First, if you make statements that are untrue, then all the other side has to do is check them out to discover that you are wrong. If they do, at best they will think you are sloppy. At worst they will think you're dishonest. Either way, you lose.

Second, if you make threats that you can't keep (bluff), you must consider what the consequences will be if your hand is called. There is an important twist on this consider-the-consequences-of-your-threat-rule. Understand that there are numerous items that make good threats, but are quite lackluster when carried out. An example is the threat to bring up the spouse's adultery. Sometimes, this threat is enough to produce great fear and anxiety in a spouse. The truth is, however, when it is actually brought up in court, on deposition or in pleadings, nine times out of ten it has the effect of a whipping with a wet noodle. The adulterer usually is relieved that the revelation is over, and everyone else shrugs and says, "So what?" So don't push too hard on such threats. Sometimes merely hinting at what you might say gets the job done and leaves the back door open, whereas pushing too hard with wild threats merely gets you so far out on thin ice that you can't get back to shore.

Rabbit Rule #13: Watch Out for Mutt and Jeff

The "Mutt and Jeff" technique is a method used by police to interrogate prisoners. One police officer pretends to be unreasonable and mean and at least verges on being abusive. The other officer pretends to be sympathetic to the prisoner's plight, acting as his protector against the abusive personality, until the prisoner tells all to the sympathetic cop.

Lawyers sometimes use sophisticated variations of this technique in bargaining. If the client is outspoken and demanding, the lawyer pretends to be sympathetic to the other side, but at the same time points out how tough and inflexible the client is. The plea to the other side is for them to give a little more, so that the lawyer can placate this unreasonable client. Or, if the client is rather like Milquetoast, the lawyer will play the heavy to build in some bargaining power.

It is unlikely that a party to a divorce will be sucked in the same way a prisoner is and come to believe that someone on the other team is actually a protector. The real danger is that your attention will be diverted by the drama of the "Mutt and Jeff" act from the real issue of who gets what. Keep your eye on the settlement. That's what's important.

Chapter 14

Getting the Flavor of Mediation

It's easier to tell them to go to hell than it is to send them there.

—Anonymous

In divorce, there are only two people who have the power to give you what you want: the judge or your spouse. If child custody is an issue, then we must hasten to add that a jury may also grant your wishes. Divorce is not a game of solitaire. The very nature of the beast is having to deal, actively and intensely, with someone whom you want out of your life and/or who wants you out of his or her life. When people who were long ago ready to be rid of each other are forced to continue dealing with each other to decide the terms of their separation, little wonder that this produces huge emotional reactions, deadlock, and frustration. If you are sick to death of your spouse, tired of being lied to, betrayed, deceived, used, abused, and manipulated, the natural, human response is to just say, "I don't want to talk about it anymore; I'll just see you in court." Of course, this is what keeps us lawyers in business.

But, to think that you can avoid dealing with your spouse by simply saying, "see you in court," is a misunderstanding of your current reality. Yes, you no longer have to sleep with him or her or see your former beloved every day. On the other hand, you have not been elected "Lord of the Realm" and are not entitled to have your every wish come true. Let me explain.

True, if you choose to have a judge or a jury draw the boundaries that govern your future relationship with your spouse, except for a deposition or two you won't have to see your "old buddy" face-to-face until you get to court; on the other hand, I can virtually guarantee that you will be "dealing" with him or her in ways that you may not have imagined.

Even if a judge or jury decides to grant your wishes, neither can do so until *after* you go to court. This means, you get to spend your time, money, energy, and anxiety getting ready for trial. Not to mention the risk. What if a judge or jury doesn't see the case like you do? This, my dear, whether you like it or not, is called "having to deal with your spouse." For most normal people it is downright miserable. Some find the tension, worry, and cost associated with the trial preparation process virtually intolerable. And then there are those awful moments of stunned disbelief that you see in people when a judge or jury rules against them. Imagine what it will feel like to lose everything in court while knowing in your heart-of-hearts that you turned down a settlement offer that would have provided you with much of what you wanted. Or, that you lost your case before even investigating what you could obtain by settlement.

The point is: Going through a trial when your spouse gives you no choice is one thing; needlessly going through a trial when there is a viable alternative is quite another. When surgery is required, it's the vital, sensible, appropriate route to take. When it is not needed or can reasonably be avoided, it becomes a bizarre, senseless risk of life and limb that verges on the criminal. That's why you must never ignore even the possibility of avoiding a trial. And that is just what mediation is: a possibility of resolving your case without a trial.

The Technical Definition of Mediation

"Mediation is a forum in which an impartial person, the mediator, facilitates communications between parties to promote reconciliation, settlement, or understanding among them." That's the Texas statute. Other definitions refer to the mediator as a "neutral" person. Most dictionaries point out that mediation comes from the Latin word "*medius*," which means "middle" or "to divide in the middle."

Who is this mediator, this impartial person? To begin with, Texas law says, "A mediator may not impose his own judgment on the issues for that of the parties." The law goes on to say that a mediator "shall encourage and assist the parties to enter into a settlement of their dispute but may not compel or coerce the parties to enter into a settlement agreement." In other words, unlike a judge, the mediator can't make anybody do anything. The only power the mediator has is the power to persuade.

The Most Widely Available Tool

So, why make such a big deal about not passing up an opportunity to mediate? The answer is simple. Because, in Texas, mediation is usually the best opportunity to settle a difficult case without a trial. It is not the only method. Often it may not even be the best method. But, in the Texas court system, it has become the settlement coin-of-the-realm, widely accepted and expected by lawyers and judges. Often, with many judges, it is not only accepted, it is virtually demanded.

Mediation has become such a routine ritual in the Texas court system that, in and of itself, it carries power and weight that can benefit or harm a litigant. It is now the way that "we" in this State handle our business. It's written into law. More importantly, mediation is such an integral part of the court system that its use is almost "unconscious." In other words, it's like the carpenter's hammer. It has been used long enough that the carpenter no longer thinks about its shape, the philosophy of using it, or where it came from. He just picks the hammer up and drives the nail. That's what you've got to do with mediation, if you get the chance.

If You Are Ordered to Mediate, Can You Object?

Yes, you can object if you do so within ten days of the time you receive the order referring the case to mediation. If you have a good reason, many courts will allow you to skip mediation. Other courts are inclined to require mediation even if the parties don't want it. A court has considerable discretion to require a party to participate in mediation. There is a split of authority on whether the order can include a requirement that the party mediate "in good faith." All of this is probably academic for parties who are truly not willing to discuss settlement of their cases. The bottom line is that courts don't have the authority to make someone settle. This, of course, goes back to the old adage about being able to lead a horse to water but not being able to make him drink.

As with most portions of the Family Code, there is a family violence exception. If a court finds that there has been family violence, the court is not allowed to order the parties to mediate. Even if the court rejects an objection to mediation based on family violence, the court is to order that the mediation parties will have no face-to-face contact.

Should All Cases Be Mediated?

Absolutely not. Mediation is not always appropriate. There are many divorce cases in which the parties and their attorneys can do perfectly well in working out a settlement. Contrary to popular belief, significant percentages of divorcing couples are very capable and willing to work out their differences in a reasonable manner.

Likewise, there are those cases that are so deadlocked that it is obvious to all involved that settlement discussions are a total waste of time and money. Additionally, there are litigants who know that mediation is not going to resolve anything, but use the mediation process as a tactic to delay the case, demoralize their opponent, or as a discovery tool.

Confidentiality

In some other states, if the parties don't settle, mediators are allowed to make recommendations to the court. Not so in Texas. In Texas the court is not even allowed to know what went on in the mediation. The confidentiality of mediation includes not just what the parties say, but also how they behaved. The law says, "Unless the parties agree otherwise, all matters, including the conduct and demeanor of the parties and their counsel during the settlement process, are confidential and may never be disclosed to anyone including the court." The mediator may not be subpoenaed, and any communication made by a participant in the mediation "may not be used in evidence against the participant in any judicial or administrative proceeding."

The one exception to this rule of confidentiality is the statutory requirement that knowledge or evidence of child abuse be reported to the proper authorities.

This requirement of confidentiality in mediation is an attempt to keep lawyers and litigants from turning mediation into just another discovery tool. If the mediation process were not confidential, sensible people would be afraid to speak because their statements would be used against them in court.

Mediation Essentials – Opportunity to Tell Your Side of the Story

One of the beauties of mediation is its flexibility. There are no rules of evidence or rules of procedure. The rules that are emphasized are basic human civility and politeness. You will be encouraged to express anger, for example, but there is a low tolerance for name-calling or profanity.

A virtually universal rule in mediation is that no one is to be interrupted while speaking and the participants are not to "talk over" each other. Most mediators handle this by making it clear that each participant will be given time to tell his or her version of the story, if necessary, until the cows come home.

Giving each party the opportunity to tell his or her story fully is a method for attacking a dispute on two different levels. On an analytical, intellectual level, forcing the parties to listen to each other provides an opportunity to clarify and "sort out" their concrete, factual differences. On an emotional, psychological level, being allowed to tell your side of the story often changes perspectives in a variety of ways. For example, the feeling that you are finally being heard can dramatically empower and release someone frozen-in-place by a sense of helplessness, allowing that person to feel that they can now make decisions without feeling victimized. Another example: Sometimes when a domineering, controlling spouse observes others, sincerely listening and reacting to his or her spouse's legitimate, moving complaints, it can be a terrifying experience. What if a judge or a jury reacts the same way to his or her spouse's story? Maybe it's time to stop "stonewalling" and discuss a settlement, before a court hears this story and reacts the same way. Of course, not all emotional reactions are positive. Hearing a spouse's angry story can be like throwing gasoline on a fire. Mediation, for all of its positive results, can sometimes worsen a dispute or reinforce the conviction that settlement is not possible.

We are all familiar with the analytical, intellectual nature of disputes. From childhood, it's the way we think of our disagreements. If you and I are dividing two pieces of pie and two pieces of cake, you may be unhappy and offended that I have chosen the biggest piece of pie for myself. Of course, I will admit to having a thing for pie, but I will quickly point out that you previously selected the larger piece of cake for yourself. You will then certainly remind me that you selected that piece of cake only after I had previously taken the cake with the most icing. And so goes the dispute resolution process, with each side factually, analytically discussing merits, values, fairness, and, no doubt, the rules of the road for cake and pie dividing. Resolving disputes over bank accounts, apartment buildings, oil wells, child support, and time to be spent with children is infinitely more complex than two children dividing a seemingly limited supply of pie and cake. But the methodology is the same. It's strictly an intellectual and analytical process. Or is it?

In fact, disputes are seldom all intellectual and analytical. In human life, little outside of nuclear physics or mathematics is purely analytical. And if you listen to some of the disputes among mathematicians and physicists, you have to wonder whether even those lofty areas are exempt from emotions.

To be fair, many divorces are resolved by spouses who refuse to be controlled by hurt feelings and anger and who decide, intellectually and deliberately, who will get what. Believe it or not, there are even those divorces in which, out of respect for a marriage that has been an important part of their lives, both spouses are willing to give the other party more than a court would require. Of course, since these cases with *two* civilized, sensible, practical divorcing spouses don't make much noise or create much of a show, few people even notice.

But in difficult divorces, typically the emotional aspects play a significant role. Emotional reversal is at the heart of the divorce process. Marriage, by its very nature, entails huge emotional commitments. I don't just mean the religious or formal vows that we usually think of as the marriage commitment. I also mean the "accidental" or *de facto* commitments. Marriage usually means sleeping and eating together, sharing bathrooms and owning the same furniture, dreaming the same dreams and having the same house key, not to mention the nine-hundred-pound gorilla of all emotional ties, having the same children. Divorce, of course, is an abrupt attempt to draw boundaries through what has become a way of life. In short, most marriages are like an iceberg. We see the children, the house, the furniture, the car, the bank accounts, and debts that must be divided. What is not "visible" is the largest part—the emotional ties, both positive and negative, that come with two people utterly mixing their lives together over several years. Most difficult divorces are about this emotional nine-tenths of the "iceberg" that is under water.

You might imagine that when mediation provides a forum for an emotionally charged divorcing spouse to tell his or her story, the result would be more akin to a therapy session than a legal proceeding. To some extent this is true. But it resembles "therapy" more in result than in form. At least occasionally, a spouse's attitude is completely transformed after "getting it all off the chest" by speaking his or her piece. But mediation does not resemble a session with a psychologist in the sense of dragging on for hours, days, or years.

It is surprising, given the fact that this right-to-tell-your-story is such a central part of the mediation process, how little time it usually takes for participants to each have his or her say. This part of the mediation is usually over in a few minutes. This is because the participants, including even those most intent on speaking, know that, at bottom, the stated purpose of mediation is to settle the case and not just to make speeches. Since participants are not allowed to argue, but merely respond with their own opinions about what someone else may have said, this also shortens the process by interrupting the "ritual fighting" that the couple may have engaged in over the years. Often a party participant to mediation won't speak at all, simply allowing his or her attorney's summarization to stand as his or her position. Although lawyers may sometimes encourage their clients to speak freely at mediation, on other occasions, an attorney may instruct a client just to listen and not say much or not to speak at all. A final reason for the brevity of party statements is the very limited time that the typical mediation format provides face-to-face contact.

Listening Can Pay Big Dividends

As you probably surmised, this right-to-tell-your-side-of-the-story philosophy assumes that someone will be listening. If you are wise, that someone will be you. And, although listening is something that most of us human beings don't do very well, in mediation you can often be well paid for listening. It is amazing how feeling that one has been heard can soften a party's bitter determination to take a case all the way to a trial. This softening of your opponent can save you money. People who are less bitter or edgy are usually more inclined to settle without making their opponents pay in blood.

So, if your lawyer is urging that you go to the mediation and just listen without saying anything, there may be good reasons for doing so. This idea of listening might even be a useful concept for life outside of mediation.

The Typical Mediation Format

As we have already discussed, the mediation format is flexible. There are no hard-and-fast rules of procedure and no rules of evidence. But, most mediators stick to a formula that is used by almost every mediator across the State. In the days or weeks before the mediation is to take place, many mediators request that the attorneys write a brief summary of the case and describe what they believe to be the issues in dispute. The attorneys may or may not comply with this request.

Typically, the mediation begins with both parties and each of their lawyers in a conference room with the mediator. This session, in which everyone is present, is sometimes called the general session. The mediator begins by giving a general description of the mediation process. Thereafter comes the time when both sides tell their stories. Each side's attorney briefly summarizes or outlines his or her client's view of the case. Usually these outlines focus on the issues that his or her client believes are in dispute. Both of the parties are encouraged to speak, but speaking is not required. This is not a test. If you don't want to speak, you are absolutely free to remain silent. When it appears that the parties and their attorneys have finished stating their positions, the mediator may ask questions about the case, about the parties, whether there have been prior settlement discussions or anything that might have a bearing on settlement.

After the general session is completed, the parties and their attorneys separate into private rooms. From here on, the mediator becomes sort of a roving ambassador, going first to one room to talk with one party and his or her attorney, then to the other room for discussions with the other party and attorney. During these separate meetings, the proceedings are confidential from the other side. The mediator has an obligation not to repeat discussions that he has with one party with the other side. This gives each party and his or her attorney the opportunity to say things to the mediator that he or she is unwilling to say in the presence of the opponent. Of course, the mediator may request permission to tell the other side something that has been said if the mediator believes it will help persuade an opponent to settle.

In these separate meetings, the mediator will ask one of the parties to make a specific offer of settlement and to give the mediator authority to transmit the offer to the other side. Once that offer is communicated to the opponent, the mediator will then request that the offer either be accepted or that a specific counteroffer be made. As long as the parties are willing, counteroffers go back and forth between their separate rooms until settlement is reached. If the parties reach an impasse, this means that the mediation has failed to produce a settlement, and the mediation session is adjourned without settlement. This does not mean that the parties can't reopen negotiations at a later date. Mediation proceedings that appear to have failed sometimes result in a settlement days or weeks later.

If the parties reach an agreement, the mediator and the lawyers draft a written document that will reflect the agreement. Sometimes the parties come back together in a general session to discuss final details of the agreement. Just as often, however, the parties are left in separate rooms during the drafting process. After the drafting is completed, the parties and their attorneys sign the document. The mediator then signs the document to signify his or her consent to the agreement. At this point, as is discussed in more detail in this chapter on page 223, the agreement is, in all probability, absolutely binding.

Most good mediators are far more interested in ensuring that parties are comfortable with the mediation than they are in rigidly enforcing a format. For example, if one of the parties has a legitimate reason for not wanting to meet the opponent face-to-face, most mediators are willing to accommodate by skipping the "general session." Sessions are greatly flexible as to comfort breaks, scheduling, and creature comforts including snacks and drinks. If the session continues for more than half of a day, most mediators arrange for lunch to be delivered so that the session can continue without the participants having to scatter to restaurants.

How Soon Should the Case Be Mediated?

How soon you mediate depends on the kind of case you have. The ideal approach would be to mediate your case and get it resolved before spending money on attorney fees for formal discovery and preparation for trial. This usually only works in those cases that are not too complicated and in which the spouses are not too angry or bitter with each other.

The decision about if and when to mediate may be somewhat like the story of "The Three Bears." If your case is like the "Baby Bear" in that you and your spouse are mature, communicate well, and will be able to work out your differences, you probably won't need to mediate at all. You can probably, either directly with each other or indirectly through your lawyers, work out your differences with a minimum of fuss, anxiety, and expense.

If your case is like the "Mama Bear" in that you have moderate differences with your spouse, but the two of you can be somewhat rational with each other, can identify your differences, and are willing to exchange information necessary to make fair and reasonable decisions, you probably should move to mediation as soon as possible *before* spending a lot of money getting ready for a trial.

But, if your case is like the "Daddy Bear" in that everyone involved is completely bent out of shape, you can't even agree what the issues are, or your spouse is hiding the books and records necessary for decision making, you probably need to save mediation for later, if at all.

In other words, there are two reasons to wait on mediation. First, if you don't have information such as inventories of community property, tax returns, income streams, you can't reasonably be expected to make any decision about settlement. In many difficult divorce cases, getting financial information is a central part of the problem. In child custody cases, the information that is lacking may be information about what an expert witness will say.

A second common reason to delay mediation is that psychology changes as the case progresses. Lawsuits are like war. Both lawsuits and wars are usually more popular in the beginning than after time has passed and the real cost and uncertainty become more apparent. Many who begin lawsuits solely interested in kicking butt and taking names mellow somewhat after receiving multiple bills and legal fees, giving depositions, and experiencing other joys of litigation.

How Long Will It Take?

It is unusual for a mediation session to last more than a day. Usually, if a case is not settled by the end of the day, the mediators and the parties agree that settlement is not likely. Sometimes, participants agree to stay in touch by letter or phone in the coming days or weeks. Many less complicated mediation sessions are scheduled for and completed in a half day.

How Much Will It Cost?

It depends. If you have a difficult case with significant property or issues involving children, you're probably going to need a "real" mediator—that is someone who really knows what he or she is doing. The fees that mediators charge vary from rural areas to the cities. In metropolitan areas most good mediators are going to want a fee beginning in the range of $1,000.00 to $1,500.00 for a day-long session, meaning $500.00 to $750.00 for each party. There are, of course, mediators who have fees of $4,000.00 or $5,000.00 or more a day.

The other extreme of the financial spectrum are the Dispute Resolutions Centers scattered around the State in virtually every metropolitan area. The addresses and phone numbers for these centers can be found quickly by typing in "Texas Dispute Resolution Centers" or "Texas DRC" into a search engine. Most of these centers provide unpaid volunteer mediators. The centers usually charge a small mediation fee of perhaps $50.00 for each side. The mediators at these centers run the gamut of the good, the bad, and the really ugly. Unless you are on a poverty-level budget, you don't have much property at stake, and you don't have any child-related issues, this DRC approach has limited appeal for me.

There is one time that I would use the Dispute Resolution Center. That is when you know mediation is a waste of time, but you are "going through the motions" to keep the judge happy. If mediation is a waste of time, you might as well not waste any more money than you have to. If your opponent wants to take a chance on a volunteer mediator, it may mean that he or she believes either that the case won't settle or that there is not much at stake.

In doing your mental computation of the cost of mediation, you must include your own attorney fees. By the time you get to mediation, you will have hired your lawyer, agreed to the amount of fees, and perhaps paid a bill or two or more. So, you can compute to fees that will result from a day of mediation plus some preparation time. Rarely, I suspect, will your own lawyer's fees be less than what you are paying the mediator. So, contrary to the advertisements posted by the mediation-is-the-cure-for-everything folks, mediation is not cheap. It is true, however, that it is usually, though not always, cheaper than trying your case.

Choosing a Mediator – What You're Looking For

The choice of the mediator is primarily your lawyer's responsibility. But most lawyers consult with the client on the selection in an effort to dovetail the capabilities of the mediator with the facts of the case and the personalities of the parties.

The mediator is the only person who will be present when your opponent and his or her lawyer are considering settlement. Your top priority must be to select a mediator whom your spouse will respect and listen to. This requires the mediator to be knowledgeable about the subject matter of your case. If it is a child custody case, the mediator may need to be someone altogether different from a mediator who would be excellent at valuing the assets of a business. As strange as it may sound, the best way to select someone most likely to persuade your spouse may be to accept a mediator chosen by your opponent.

Picking a mediator with whom the opponent can identify can be of critical importance in avoiding needless litigation. Most trial lawyers have witnessed the "right" mediator "working miracles" in cases in which settlements were thought to be virtually impossible. I once watched a bitter five-year-old corporate lawsuit settled by a mediator in less than an hour. One of the corporate executives who was very angry about the case and had spent tens of thousands of dollars to keep it going was introduced to the mediator as being someone who had fought on the front lines in Korea. The mediator asked him the name and location of his unit. Being told that information, the mediator explained that he had fought with another nearby unit. Instantly a bond was formed between the mediator and this powerful executive who had previously blocked all attempts to settle. The executive, who had before been exceedingly agitated at the very mention of the lawsuit, became calm, listened intently to everything the mediator had to say, and shortly agreed to the very terms of settlement that he had consistently rejected for years. This example is unusual only in its drama and intensity. We humans are commonly willing to take advice from those we feel we can trust.

The mediator also needs to be someone who can add to your education about your own case. As a lawyer, I like mediators who talk directly to my client rather than to me. If, for example, the mediator is another lawyer who has tried similar cases, you will, in essence, get a second opinion about your case. I like it when my client gets a different perspective on the case from a knowledgeable person who has just come from a conversation with the opponent and his or her attorney. Sometimes my client may not agree with the mediator. On other occasions, what the mediator says may cause my client to change his or her mind. And this is what decision making is all about. The client should have every available resource to make decisions about settlement. The lawyer is meant to advise, but if other advice is available, that too should be used.

Additionally, a good mediator can educate your own lawyer. This may sound strange, given the fact that you are paying your lawyer enough that he or she should already be educated. But, keep in mind, preparing your case for trial puts your lawyer at risk of schizophrenia. First, the lawyer, as your advocate, must focus on presenting the positive aspects of your case and minimizing its flaws. Simultaneously, your lawyer is obligated to provide "objective" advice about the merits of your case for your use in evaluating whether to settle. Needless to say, this is a lot to ask—even of a schizophrenic. Being a good advocate may cloud a lawyer's objectivity. Likewise, being coldly objective may hinder a passionate presentation of the client's position. This balancing is required of all trial lawyers. I, for one, welcome the perspective of a mediator who does not have the same attachment to my client that I do. Even if I disagree, which I often do, the mediator's view usually provides me with information that can be used to advise and advocate better for my client.

Choosing a Mediator – Weeding Out the Clueless

But calling yourself a "mediator" doesn't make it so. For some reason, everybody and their dog seems to think that they would be a gifted mediator. In Texas, you don't need a law degree, an accounting degree, or any other formal training. Anyone is allowed to hold himself or herself out as a mediator after taking about the same number of "classroom hours" that would be needed to get through a one-semester course in basket weaving. To mediate child custody issues, one would need "an additional 24 hours of training in the fields of family dynamics, child development, and family law." This "training" attracts the retired, those who have lost their jobs or gone broke in business, and numberless other combinations of people with no experience in the legal system—all of which would be fine, were it not for the fact that the very essence of the mediator function is advising people as to whether they should settle their *lawsuit.*

If your divorce involves significant property or any child custody, child support, or child-related issue, you should think long and hard before you agree to use a mediator without several years of experience in the court system. That's the part that the mediation-as-the-solution-to-everything people don't get. Mediation is not just about moments of endearment and discussing peace on earth. Mediation is about helping real people make decisions about their lawsuits.

Mediation Is Not the Place or the Time for Drama or Surprises

Mediation is not the place for *Perry Mason* or *L.A. Law* stuff. The other side is not going to be impressed with big-time posturing or sleight of hand tricks. You are not going to intimidate anyone into a settlement in a mediation. This does not mean that you need to pull your punches or soft-pedal legitimate facts. It just means that those facts need to be presented in a firm, but matter-of-fact, business-like way. If you want your lawyer to do jury arguments, you should go to trial.

Likewise, big surprises that have obviously been held back for effect usually shut mediation sessions down. A surprise used at mediation signals to the other side that you did not come to mediate in good faith. If you have secret ammo, either send it to them before the mediation or hold it back just in case you have to try your case.

Unintended Consequences – Mediation Sometimes Is Just a Discovery Tool

The fact that the mediation process is confidential does not mean that it is not used as a discovery tool. Think about it. What is *said* in mediation can be protected to the extent that it can't be repeated or the participants can't be called to testify about it. On the other hand, there is no way to take back what someone learns.

Suppose, for example, that in the course of a mediation, your spouse admits for the first time that he or she is a secret owner of a company being operated by a friend. The fact that this was disclosed in mediation will not offer your spouse much protection. True, he or she can't be forced in court to admit that he or she made that statement during the mediation. But, now that you know where to look, there is absolutely nothing to keep you from gathering other evidence to prove that your spouse owns this company. You can subpoena the friend who operates the business to testify. You can get the corporation's books and records. Your lawyer can even put your spouse on the witness stand and ask if it isn't true that he or she is the real owner of the company.

As you may imagine, even in mediation, people usually don't admit that they are hiding assets or committing crimes. But, if a party is negotiating in good faith—really trying to settle the case—it is difficult not to reveal at least some of what will be presented at trial. The very nature of the mediation is such that after it is over, the parties usually have a better understanding of each other's case. Lawyers will see that a particular person is going to be a good witness and that another is likely to make a bad impression. Your spouse's lawyer may see and understand for the first time something that is embarrassing to his or her client. This gives your spouse's lawyer a chance to explain the embarrassing detail in advance to the judge or jury, before your lawyer has an opportunity to pull it out of the bag. This may take the sting out of your evidence. These are examples of the kind of things that are learned in mediation that can be the difference between winning and losing a case.

So it would seem fair that both of the parties learn more about each other's case; then, if they don't settle, both sides know a little bit more when they finally get to trial. But, that's not what we're talking about here.

Mediation has spun off a cottage industry of those who use it only for discovery. Here's how it works. If, for whatever reason, you don't intend to settle your lawsuit at mediation, you agree to mediate and attend the session anyway. When you arrive, because you don't intend to settle anyway, you don't need to say much. You just sit and listen. Maybe you even ask a few provocative questions intended to cause your opponent to really "tell you off." You can even ask the mediator to make inquiries about subjects that may interest you. Then, when the session ends, you simply express your regrets that the mediation was unsuccessful and go on your way with your newly gained information.

Now, you say, this is unfair. You're right. But you only have one defense to this kind of conduct. You and your lawyer must be smart enough to recognize what is happening. As was said above in the "Rabbit Rules," if the other side is not doing some of the talking, perhaps you should feel for your wallet, make sure it's still there, and bid them good day.

Before you completely condemn using mediation for discovery, keep in mind that you may have to do the same thing yourself. You may find yourself in a jurisdiction in which the judge believes that mediation is God's answer to all problems. If you do, you may need to mediate with your hopelessly stubborn and stupid spouse when you know there isn't one chance in a million of reaching a settlement. What are you going to do? That's easy: You're going to go to mediation, keep your mouth shut, and see what you can learn. Now, *that* seems fair, doesn't it?

The Mediation Process Is Not a Substitute for the Trial Process

There is some sloppy thinking about mediation that surfaces occasionally. Even some lawyers and judges have been heard to say things like, "Well, if you don't want to try your case, just work it out in mediation." This is much like telling a nation facing a hostile enemy, "Don't worry about getting ready for war, just work it out through diplomacy." Were this approach a viable alternative, most peace-loving democracies probably wouldn't have standing armies. Few countries can do without military protection. Mediation usually will not work without the trial process being an available alternative.

Lawyers who routinely do mediation are familiar with the symptoms that occur when the other side senses that there is no threat of trial. You go into a mediation hopeful that a fair and reasonable settlement can be reached. The other side listens politely and intently to what you have to say. When the parties go into their separate rooms to begin the negotiation process, you soon learn that the other side has little interest in a fair settlement. You receive only ridiculous offers that don't leave you with anything close to your fair share. The mediator ultimately tells you that this is all the other party and his or her lawyer are willing to offer, because they don't see much risk in going on to court. Your only choice at this point is either to accept an unfair settlement or to leave and begin preparation for trial.

Likewise, lawyers familiar with mediation have attended mediation sessions in which the other side does not have much of a case or is unwilling or unable to prosecute the case. Put yourself in the position of that lawyer who has the obligation to represent his or her own client. When the other side poses little or no threat, it is difficult to justify advising your own client to sacrifice hard-earned money or give up rights to his or her child when there is no reason to do so.

Just as diplomacy is built on the ability of a nation to protect itself, mediation is nothing more than a settlement process that depends on each of the parties having bargaining power that is derived from an ability to prosecute the case in court.

Understanding the Mediator's Bias

Mediators present themselves and are presented by others as "impartial" or neutral. This is usually true as to the parties. Most mediators work hard not to favor one party to the lawsuit over the other. But, mediators have a strong bias toward settlement. This is how they keep score. Most mediators keep up with the percentage of their cases that they settle. Some few even have a sort of notches-on-the-gun attitude about their settlement percentages.

This attitude among mediators is encouraged by many judges who seem to be committed to the idea that all cases should be settled. We lawyers are not exempt from this desire to see cases settled. That's why we encourage our clients to mediate.

A bad settlement may be good for the mediator, but it's not good for you. Likewise, a bad settlement is not good for your lawyer. No decent lawyer wants his or her client to enter into a bad settlement just to get the case over with.

In fairness, there is a significant percentage of mediators who may at least try to discuss the subject with a party who is obviously making a bad settlement. But I worry that you may have a mediator who will only point out the reasons for settlement. This may be acceptable as long as you understand that this kind of mediator is there for only one reason—to get the case settled regardless of whether it's fair or not. In other words, heed the mediator's advice if it makes senses, but don't let yourself believe that he or she is on your side. The mediator is on the side of settlement, whether it's good for you or not.

Can You Mediate without a Mediator?

Yes, you can negotiate settlement of your case without a mediator. In fact, this is how it was done before the advent of the mediation process as we know it today. In former days, lawyers carried on the same process that is now called mediation on "the steps of the courthouse." When a case was set for trial, the parties and their lawyer would go to court and announce to the court that "we need a little more time before the case is called for trial because the parties are discussing settlement." Then, while the court tried other cases, the parties and their attorneys would go into the hallways and jury rooms and carry on a settlement process similar to the process used by mediators today. Many lawyers, especially older lawyers who have not matured in the present culture of mediation, still routinely negotiate without mediators present.

So, why can't we all just skip the mediators and do it like it was done in the old days? Well, this can be done, but the culture and procedures have now changed in such a way that you may need the mediation order to make your case work mechanically without spending a fortune. Let me explain.

Today, the use of mediators and the mediation process is, I believe, driven more by judicial attitudes than by anything else. Settling cases "on the courthouse steps" worked well because courts and lawyers had a very relaxed attitude about allowing opponents the opportunity to prepare for trial. In those days, it was not necessary to spend massive amounts of money and time on trial preparation for a case that was likely to settle. When lawyers knew a case was likely to settle, the parties could often go to the courthouse on the first trial setting with little or no preparation, knowing that if the case did not settle, the court would continue the case to a later date to give opportunity for the "real" trial preparation.

This routine courthouse-steps-settlement process began to crumble a couple of decades ago. A Chief Justice of the United States (who probably never handled a trial docket) began to lament the "overcrowded dockets" in the nation's courts. His concerns trickled down to Texas, and we started keeping statistics on the number of pending cases. Judges, to their horror, began to find that political opponents ran for office against them citing these statistics of "clogged dockets." Hence, judicial attitudes changed. Courts now want the case off the docket. When a case is set for trial, it is likely that it will be forced to trial even if one of the parties is not ready.

As you might imagine, this policy has changed the way we lawyers do business. Now, when a case comes through the door, most lawyers immediately begin filing motions, doing discovery, and taking other steps to get ready for trial. Naturally, the clients must pay for this, even if the case will never go to trial.

Mediation slows down this fast-track, statistics-driven "railroad," which tends to require that clients pay for trial preparation in every case. True, the statistics still show a case pending. But, now the judge has a reason that it is pending—it's being mediated. This works for the lawyers and client because they can show up to mediation without having to spend all of the time and money that are required for trial preparation. If the case doesn't settle, then there is still time for trial preparation.

In other words, the courthouse-steps settlement process is still at work. The name has just been changed to "mediation," and you may need a mediation order and a mediator to invoke a procedure to protect you from spending a lot of money for trial preparation before you explore settlement.

Can You Mediate without a Lawyer Present?

Yes, legally you don't have to have a lawyer present at mediation. But not having a lawyer is usually not a good idea. If you are my client,

I'm probably going to do everything in my power to keep you from attending a mediation without a lawyer present. Reading the following section on the non-revocable nature of mediated settlement agreements should convince you.

In many areas, the courts and Dispute Resolution Centers have worked out procedures whereby most divorce couples attend mediation sessions without having their attorneys present. When my clients mediate at a Dispute Resolution Center, I routinely veto this practice.

There is one instance in which I might make an exception to this rule and send my client to mediation with neither side having a lawyer present. That would be in a divorce in which my client is and always has been the dominant and controlling partner throughout the entire relationship. Even then, I would want specific procedures in place for the mediated settlement agreement to be examined, prior to execution, by a lawyer who already has extensive knowledge of the facts of the case.

Mediated Settlement Agreements Are for Keeps

When you sign this puppy, you've almost certainly "bought the farm." The Texas legislature has apparently lost its sense of humor about people who try to back out of settlements after mediation. The "mediated settlement agreement" is binding on the parties, if it:

1. Provides, in a prominently displayed statement that is in boldfaced type or capital letters or underlined, that the agreement is not subject to revocation.
2. Is signed by each party to the agreement.
3. Is signed by the party's attorney, if any, who is present at the time the agreement is signed.

This is a quote from the Texas Family Code in two separate but identical statutes. This is serious business. Notice: There are no exceptions. There are no "ifs," "ands," or "buts."

It probably means that if you make a really bad deal, it can't be undone. Likewise, if by all rights, you should be the custodian of your children because you have been raising them single-handedly for the past five years, and you agree that your spouse can, without any restriction, establish the primary residence of the children, you might want to check into the bulk purchase of airline tickets to Seattle in case you want to see your children. Or you could find yourself continuing to take care of your children with no child support because Managing Conservators aren't required to pay child support to possessory conservators.

If the mediated settlement agreement gives your spouse all of the millions that you inherited, even though he or she was not entitled to a single penny of it by any theory of law, there's a high probability that he or she will get to keep the money.

How else can I say it? Baby, this deal's for keeps. Don't sign it unless you know what you're doing. Especially don't sign it without your lawyer "sprinkling holy water" on all of its pages. If you don't have a lawyer and can't afford one for your divorce, go hire one for the one hour or less that it will take to look at this agreement. If you have been mentally abused by your spouse, you probably also need to get the mediated settlement agreement blessed by your psychologist, just to make sure that it's not a continuation of the old habits. This is no joke.

The Dark Side of Mediation

Mediation may be your last opportunity to exert control over the outcome of your divorce case. Although many cases are settled after mediation has failed or even after a trial has started, there is never any guarantee that a particular settlement opportunity will remain open; hence my somewhat lengthy introduction to this chapter urging you not to pass up mediation lightly.

But there is a negative side to mediation. Because mediation is such a powerful tool, it can also be very dangerous. Strong medicines, without exception, always have the potential for "side effects," adverse reactions, and unintended consequences. Mediation is no exception; some of its outcomes are not good. For this reason, I want you to think about some of the things we have already discussed and some of the things and attitudes you are likely to encounter while participating in mediation.

Mediation is billed, advertised, and promoted as a "non-adversarial process." Participants are told that mediation is, unlike the courtroom, a place in which we all strive to work together for the same goal of getting the case settled.

It is true that the format or general appearance of mediation is more like a conversation in your living room than it is a courtroom fight. There is no cross-examination. The parties are not allowed to argue. There are no rules of evidence or procedure. Formality gives way to informality. All in all, the parties are encouraged to relax. In fact, this is the best way of settling disputes. We agree to talk civilly to each other.

But, there is another side to the mediation. Notice that the description of the mediation process that I have just given, although accurate, is just a description of the "form" of the mediation. I have said nothing about its "content" or its "substance." In other words, the foregoing description tells you nothing about "what is really going on." What is going on is that, at bottom, the mediation process really is adversarial. In all probability, there is someone in the room who is trying to take away your property, your power and control over your children, or deprive you of other rights and benefits. And, unless you have a strong lawyer by your side, there is no one in the room trying to help you protect yourself. The kind and seemingly trustworthy mediator is not on your side. In fact, the law says that he or she can't be on your side. Although he or she is acting like your friend, the law says that he or she can't be your friend. That would make him or her biased or partial.

In other words, everybody from the legislature to the judge and the mediator, all of whom have great authority, are using the "form" of this proceeding to tell you that it's okay to relax and settle your case. Well, maybe so. But, you should not let the cozy atmosphere, the comfortable surroundings, and warm "personal" relationships make the decision for you.

"Politeness can be just another method of waging war." Yes, it's mediation. Stay and have lunch. Be polite and enjoy the fact that everyone else is cordial. But tighten your belt, make sure you have a strong lawyer, keep him or her close by, and for God's sake make your own decisions using your own brain and what makes sense to you. It's mediation. It's not a picnic even if lunch is served.

Chapter 15

Collaborative Law

Experience has two things to teach: The first is that we must correct a great deal; the second is that we must not correct too much.

— Eugene Delacroix

Experience is a good teacher, but she sends terrific bills.

— Minna Antrim

SETTLEMENT & DISPUTE

Collaborative law is one of the "alternative dispute resolution" mechanisms available for use by divorcing parties in Texas. Formal "collaborative law" is the "new kid on the block," having come into existence by a statute in 2001. Because it is so new, in many ways it is still an unknown. It has not yet been interpreted by courts in written opinions. Lawyers have, at most, two to three years' experience with this method.

The Statutory Definition of Collaborative Law

> "Collaborative law is a procedure in which the parties and their counsel agree in writing to use their best efforts and make a good faith attempt to resolve *their dissolution of marriage dispute* [or] *the suit affecting the parent-child relationship* on an agreed basis without resorting to the judicial intervention except to have the court approve the settlement agreement, make the legal pronouncements, and sign the orders required by law to effectuate the agreement of the parties as the court determines appropriate. The parties' counsel may not serve as litigation counsel except to approve the settlement agreement."

(Actually, the collaborative law definition is contained in two almost identical statutes that vary only in the italicized language separated by "[or]" in the above quote. For convenience here, it is quoted only once.)

The Nature of the Beast – It's a Contract

By its very definition, collaborative law is a contract. It's called a "written agreement." But whether you call it a "contract" or an "agreement," you need to think in these terms: If I make this agreement with my spouse:

1. Can I enforce it against him or her and, if so, how will that enforcement help me?
2. Will this agreement be enforced against me and, if so, what harm might it cause me?

In other words, before you sign on the bottom line, you need to consider that you are entering a legal commitment that can come back to bite you. Typically, contracts "bite" people in two ways. First, you may be disappointed when the person with whom you are contracting fails or refuses to honor the contract or attempts to misuse or misconstrue it. Second, you may be shocked or surprised to learn that the person with whom you contracted is insisting that you perform on obligations or requirements that you did not fully understand when you signed the agreement.

What Is in the Collaborative Law Contract?

This is a part of the problem. Apparently, a collaborative law contract may contain any number of provisions and might be worded in many different ways. Since it is a contract, this could produce a huge difference in its effect.

Although the law does not prescribe or limit its terms, a collaborative law agreement in Texas must include provisions for:

1. Full and candid exchange of information between the parties and their attorneys as necessary to make a proper evaluation of the case
2. Suspending court intervention in the dispute while the parties are using collaborative law procedures

3. Hiring experts, as jointly agreed, to be used in the procedure
4. Withdrawal of all counsel involved in the collaborative law procedure if the collaborative law procedure does not result in settlement of the dispute
5. Other provisions as agreed to by the parties consistent with a good faith effort to settle the matter collaboratively

Waiver of the Attorney Client Privilege

Right off the bat, we need to examine who the parties to this collaborative law contract are. It's not just you and your spouse. Now, you're entering into a contract with your spouse and his or her attorney. And your spouse is also entering into a contract with you and your attorney.

It may be unprecedented in our legal system for opposing parties to have contracts with each others' lawyers. At this point in the development of this new process it's probably not possible to know or understand all of the possible ramifications this has for a divorce case.

But the law is absolutely clear on one thing. The collaborative law agreement must include a "full and candid exchange of information between the parties and their attorneys as necessary to make a proper evaluation of the case." In other words, you are waiving your attorney client privilege and are instructing your lawyer to tell your spouse and his attorney everything that you tell your lawyer that may have bearing on your divorce case. Wow!

So, you say, "Doesn't this mean that my spouse's lawyer must now tell me and my lawyer everything they know about the case"? Yes, in theory, that's what the agreement says. But what if they don't? What are you going to do? Obviously, if you're lucky enough to learn that you're being deceived, you'll go back to court and use all of the remedies that you had before you entered into the agreement. The difference now may be that you will do so with your spouse knowing all of your secrets that you told your lawyer.

Admittedly, your direct statements and those of your lawyer in the collaborative law process should not be used in evidence in a subsequent trial because the statements were made during negotiations.

However, as has been stated in Chapter 14 on mediation, this does not keep your spouse from locating another source for the newly learned information and using that source as evidence in trial.

So, unless you have absolutely no secrets from your spouse and are sure that you will have none in the foreseeable future, the collaborative law process presents considerable risk that those secrets will be revealed.

Disqualification of Your Lawyer

One of the central concepts of the collaborative law process is that, if the process does not work and the case is not settled, the lawyers who have represented the parties in the collaborative law process will withdraw. This means that each of the parties will be required to obtain a new attorney for the trial of the case.

From the first day you hire a lawyer, you are making an investment in educating that lawyer about your case. Every time you meet with the lawyer, you are getting him or her "up to speed" on your case. When your lawyer meets with your spouse, accountants, psychologist, or other witnesses who know about your marriage, your children, and your business, he or she is learning information necessary to try your lawsuit. In fact, this lengthy process of educating your lawyer about you and your case is one of the more costly parts of preparing your case for trial. And by the time trial arrives, clients have usually made a large investment in their lawyers.

Now, right at the time the collaborative law process breaks down, you must discard your investment in your lawyer and start again educating a new lawyer. This can be done. All it takes is time and money. After a year or more of negotiation in a collaborative law process, both time and money may be in short supply. And, even if that's not the case, does it make sense to have to pay double to educate two lawyers instead of one? You need to weigh this question before you sign a collaborative law agreement.

Finally, firing all of the lawyers if the collaborative law process fails to reach a settlement may cause your lawyer to have a strong bias toward settlement. There is nothing wrong with settling a case when possible. No good lawyer wants to try a case that could be settled. Likewise, good lawyers don't push their clients toward settlements that appear unfair or lopsided against the client.

But, if some lawyers begin holding themselves out as collaborative law specialist, will they start viewing cases that don't settle as failures? Will they, as some mediators do, tout their success in percentages of settlements? Only time will tell. But you must think about this possibility now, before you sign a collaborative law agreement.

Do You Need This Agreement?

Maybe. But the answer to this question should require some soul-searching. Surely, by the time we're adults, we all should understand that contracts are not to be entered into lightly. A collaborative law agreement is no different. It should be taken very seriously.

A collaborative law agreement will not be your first contract with your spouse. Remember: You already have a "marriage contract" with your spouse. Presumably, the reason you are now contemplating divorce is because there has been a "breaking" of that marriage contract. So, in answer to our problems with the marriage contract, which is already in existence, we now propose to enter an additional contract creating yet another layer of obligations? The first contract fails, so the answer is to enter yet another contract? Perhaps so. But you need to be asking yourself questions like: Why am I doing this? and How is the second contract going to solve the problems with the first contract?

A collaborative law agreement, if it succeeds, will not be your last agreement with your spouse. *The collaborative law agreement doesn't settle your divorce; it only sets out the procedure you will use in attempting to reach an agreement.* It determines the proverbial "shape of the bargaining table" and who will sit where at that table. Issues of how the property will be divided or who will have custody of the children will be discussed later, after we get past what the collaborative law agreement will look like.

If you and your spouse are on friendly terms, the signing of a collaborative law agreement may not change anything. For decades before collaborative law was even conceived, the great majority of divorcing couples, directly or through their lawyers, worked out their own divorce settlement agreements. These settlement agreements were routinely approved by courts with little or no fanfare. In other words, historically the majority of divorce cases have been settled in exactly the way that is contemplated by collaborative law without there being any need for a "side agreement" blessed by the court or legislature.

At the opposite extreme, if you and your spouse are extremely hostile toward each other, at least a part of that hostility probably arises from a lack of trust. If you don't trust each other, how is entering into yet another agreement going to help? In fact, common wisdom will tell you that the last person with whom you should enter a contract is someone you don't trust.

The bottom line is, *it can be argued that collaborative law works only in those cases that will settle anyway.* If your case will probably settle because there is already mutual good faith between you and your spouse, the use of collaborative law will probably only add to the cost of your divorce and create additional unnecessary risk.

When to Consider the Use of Collaborative Law

Some judges pride themselves on the use of a "rocket docket." They pride themselves on getting cases off their dockets in a hurry. Apparently, this impresses voters who have already been convinced that the world will end shortly because court dockets are "clogged." What no one thinks to tell the voters is that there are cases on the docket that neither side wants tried, and these cases are nothing more than names on a list. It's the cases in which the parties want a trial now that courts should be worrying about. But judges who have decided to focus on having bragging rights about their rocket docket have found that the list can be shortened before the next election by insisting that all cases be forced to trial, even those cases in which the parties have a legitimate reasons for waiting.

Collaborative law provides a solution for spouses who need more time to settle, but are being pushed by a court with a form-over-substance mentality about case disposition. The statute establishing collaborative law provides that when a collaborative law agreement is signed and the court is notified of that fact at least thirty days before the trial date, the court cannot set a hearing or trial, impose discovery deadlines, require compliance with scheduling orders, or dismiss the case. This will give the spouses time to negotiate a settlement without pressure from the court.

Lawyers are also advising clients to use collaborative law when it appears that the client has little to lose by trying this approach. For example, often a lawyer knows in advance the likely division of community property that a particular judge will make. If the client is reluctant to accept that division, the lawyer may suggest that there is little or nothing to lose by entering into a collaborative law agreement and attempting to negotiate a somewhat better arrangement.

Some divorces become "lawyer-driven." In these cases, while the parties have mixed emotions, the positive feeling would probably overcome the anger that has arisen before the divorce, except that one of the spouses is represented by a lawyer whose primary interest is "churning" the case for all it's worth or creating wars where none exist. Since this lawyer's client seems susceptible to this Rambo advice, the case is needlessly boiling over. Naturally, expenses are needlessly increasing, and the case is being prolonged. This may be the perfect case in which to suggest the use of collaborative law. At the very least, use of the process may neutralize the "Rambo lawyer" and give the parties an opportunity to discuss settlement sensibly. If the collaborative law process fails, the offending lawyer will be disqualified from trying the case.

A Settlement That Arises Out of a Collaborative Law Process Is Binding

Make no mistake: a collaborative law settlement agreement is binding. The judge is required to enter judgment on such an agreement if it:

- Provides, in a prominently displayed statement that is boldfaced, capitalized, or underlined, that the agreement is not subject to revocation; and
- Is signed by each party to the agreement and the attorney of each party.

How Long Does the Collaborative Law Process Last?

Apparently, most of these agreements are "at will" agreements that either party can withdraw from at any time, thereby ending the collaborative law process and returning to regular trial procedure. If, however, the process does not result in a settlement or one of the parties does not withdraw from the process, collaborative law can continue for at least a couple of years. The law says if there is no settlement "on or before the second anniversary of the date that the suit was filed, the court may: (1) set the suit for trial on the regular docket; or (2) dismiss the suit without prejudice."

During this two-year period, the parties must provide the court with a status report after the first 180 days after the date of the written agreement to use collaborative law and again on the one-year anniversary of that agreement.

How Much Does the Collaborative Law Process Cost?

It's not cheap. Most lawyers charge the same hourly rates for collaborative law that they charge for all other legal work. Prices for a collaborative law settlement are comparable to prices for "uncontested divorces." But, of course, as with any legal service this is usually going to depend on the amount of time it takes.

As was stated at the beginning of this chapter, the collaborative law process requires the drafting of an additional contract. No doubt many lawyers use "standard forms" for this agreement. If such a standard form is used, the charge for drafting this agreement should be minimal. However, given the seriousness of entering into a collaborative law agreement, you and your lawyer probably should spend significant time discussing the agreement, and the agreement should be tailor-made to fit your particular circumstances. This, of course, will be an additional charge that will be unnecessary if you settle your case without the use of this agreement.

Chapter 16

Arbitration: Easy Solution or Risky Gamble?

Don't ever take a fence down until you know why it was put up.

—Robert Frost

Texas law now provides that the spouses may agree to have their divorce case disposed of through arbitration. This means that you can sign an agreement with your spouse, and, if the judge agrees, your case will be sent to arbitration.

There are two kinds of arbitration: binding and non-binding. There's a huge difference between the two. In binding arbitration, whatever the arbitrator decides is "for keeps." In non-binding arbitration, the arbitrator's decision is just an advisory opinion to give you and your spouse an idea of what a third party thinks about your case.

Depending on the arbitration agreement, a case may be decided by one or more arbitrators. Often parties agree to one arbitrator. If they don't, cases are usually decided by the majority vote of a panel of three arbitrators. The number of arbitrators is one of many details that can be controlled by the agreement.

What the Family Code Says

As to divorce in general, the Family Code says:

a. On written agreement of the parties, the court may refer a suit for dissolution of a marriage to arbitration. The agreement must state whether the arbitration is binding or non-binding.
b. If the parties agree to binding arbitration, the court shall render an order reflecting the arbitrator's award.

As to child custody issues, the Family Code says:

a. On written agreement of the parties, the court may refer a suit affecting the parent-child relationship to arbitration. The agreement must state whether the arbitration is binding or non-binding.
b. If the parties agree to binding arbitration, the court shall render an order reflecting the arbitrator's award unless the court determines at a non-jury hearing that the award is not in the best interest of the child. The burden of proof at a hearing under this subsection is on the party seeking to avoid rendition of an order based on the arbitrator's award.

The Effect of Binding Arbitration

Just reading that a "court *shall* render an order reflecting the arbitrator's award" takes my breath away, and I'm not even contemplating signing such an agreement. An agreement for binding arbitration gives a third party, virtually, the absolute right to make all decisions about your property and your children. If the thought of signing such an agreement doesn't make you a little nervous, either you don't understand what's being said or you're the kind of person who enjoys jumping out of airplanes with a parachute that's been packed by your worst enemy.

Does this mean that I would never advise a client to enter a binding arbitration agreement? No, there are times when binding arbitration may be prudent. But such agreements must not be entered lightly.

An Arbitrator May Have More Power Than a Judge

When you select an arbitrator, you are, in essence, appointing that person as the judge in your case. But the arbitrator may have more discretion or latitude in deciding the issues in your divorce or child custody case than would a judge hearing the same case.

Many decisions made by judges are controlled by rules that dictate what a judge must do. For example, the law says that a judge cannot award one spouse's separate property to the other spouse. A judge has very limited authority to set child support outside of the "guidelines" established by the legislature for child support. A judge cannot deprive a decent parent of the right to have access to a child. These are just three examples of decisions in which a judge will be reversed by the appellate courts if he or she does not follow the law.

Judges have many other decisions in which they have "discretion" to decide either way. For example, judges have broad discretion in deciding about the division of community property between the spouses. But even in making these "discretionary decisions" there are limits on what a judge can do, and the judge must provide reasons to justify the decision. If a judge "abuses his or her discretion," an appellate court will reverse the decision. "Abuse of discretion" is defined as rendering an arbitrary or unreasonable decision or making a decision without reference to any guiding rules or principles. Moreover, appellate courts will weigh the evidence to make certain that a trial judge had admissible evidence to support a decision. If there is not evidence to support the judge's decision, it will be reversed.

Contrast this with the authority given an arbitrator. Here's what the law says about grading an arbitrator's decision:

> Because the courts favor arbitration awards as a means of disposing of disputes, the courts indulge every reasonable presumption in favor of upholding the awards. A mere mistake of fact or law alone is insufficient to set aside an arbitration award. An arbitration award is to be given the same weight as a trial court's judgment, and the reviewing court may not substitute its judgment for the arbitrator's merely because it would have reached a different decision.

The portion of this quote that says "a mere mistake of fact or law alone is insufficient to set aside an arbitration award" should give you pause. This statement means that arbitrators may have more power than judges in deciding cases before them. Since judges are hugely powerful, the very thought of turning your life over to someone even more powerful should make you uncomfortable.

The Rules You Play By

Courts have a bad reputation for hyper-technical rules. Almost every step of the process of having a dispute resolved in the courthouse is controlled by a complex set of rules. These rules are discussed throughout several of the chapters of this book. Politicians, journalists, and radio talk show hosts are among those who love to rant about the seemingly overly complex nature of these rules. Comedians are attracted to the easy target provided by the complex nature of legal proceedings. Even lawyers and judges tire of the bureaucratic nature of this intricate and confusing process. The public becomes suspicious that these rules were created just to create work for lawyers.

You may be tempted to "blow off" all of these courthouse rules as a nonsensical quagmire that you want to avoid. Before you do, you may want to consider that these rules were put in place to protect people just like you and me. Every one of "the rules" and "the exceptions to the rule" and "the exceptions to the exception" was created because of fairness. In a complex world, simple rules can sometimes lead to horrible injustices. In a society controlled by a king or a dictator, the rules can be very simple: All doubts are resolved in favor of the king or the dictator or the favored group. In democratic societies in which many people have the power, rule makers are forced to balance equities and fairness. This naturally means that there are "exceptions" and "exceptions to the exceptions."

So what does all of this philosophical discussion have to do with arbitration? When you enter arbitration, you leave the "rules of court" behind. The arbitrator may or may not use court procedures. If the rules of evidence apply at all, they will apply loosely. In fact, in the arbitration agreement you may choose which rules you want to apply and which you don't. Of course, most persons entering arbitration don't take time to set out all of these rules, so the rules of the American Arbitration Association or the Texas law covering general arbitration provide a broad outline of the arbitration rules to be used. Mostly, however, it will be up to the arbitrator to decide what the rules will be. And, as we discussed above, the arbitrator has very broad discretion.

Sometimes the only thing worse than a huge set of hyper-technical bureaucratic rules is no rules or no bureaucracy. It's called "no man's land." In recent times, "Exhibit A" for the result of no rules or uncertain rules are countries in which government has collapsed, such as those in Eastern Europe, the former Soviet Union, and Iraq. A part of arbitration is deciding in advance just which rules you are going to be governed by. This may require even a smarter lawyer than would be required to try your case in the courthouse.

The Cost of Arbitration

Arbitration has been sold by its proponents as a means of cutting litigation costs and saving money for consumers with small claims. This has not always been the result. The cost of arbitration must include the cost of paying the arbitrators, and the arbitration fees for the organizations that sponsor arbitration are usually higher than the filing fees that you have already paid at the courthouse. Add to this the fact that in more complex arbitration cases both sides are going to need lawyers, and the cost may even exceed that of trying your case in court.

SECTION V

Children in Divorce

In this section:

Chapter 17

How to Tell Your Children about the Divorce

True love in this differs from gold and clay,
That to divide is not to take away.

—Percy Bysshe Shelly

For many, the single most difficult thing about getting a divorce is telling their children about it. Worry about a child's reaction to a divorce is normal. The problem is much easier to deal with, however, if we think through some things that you and your child already instinctively know.

To begin with, let's get your fears out in the open. There is a myth around that divorce ruins children. Someplace deep in your brain there is probably the feeling that you might destroy your child's life by divorcing his father or mother. These fears can even take such extreme forms as fear that the child will be so "destroyed" by divorce that she will take up a life of bank robbery.

To all of this, I say *baloney!* Children's lives are *not* ruined by divorce. Children's lives *are* ruined by a lack of love. The idea that a divorce, standing alone, decides whether or not a child will get this necessary love is pretty farfetched. The truth is that there are many children who live with married parents in the finest homes and who are devastated by the deprivation of affection. The truth is that many parents are better parents and give their children more love after a divorce than they would have had they stayed married. True, you may have to make special efforts, spend extra money, reserve extra time, or drive to another city to express your love for your child after a divorce. But these things can, in and of themselves, become special opportunities for expressing your feelings to your child.

It is undoubtedly true that there are many parents who forget or ignore their children during and after divorce. I suspect that these parents would have treated these children in the same way had they stayed married. The only difference is that their shabby treatment of their children is a little more evident when a divorce has taken place.

A spin-off of the fear that divorce will ruin children is the idea that we *should* stay married *"for the children."* Staying married for the children has a way of placing responsibility of an unhappy marriage on a child's shoulders. Growing up is tough enough without this. It is difficult enough for a child to handle the responsibility for his own life and happiness without having to take responsibility for Mommy and Daddy. Deal with these issues yourself. Don't subconsciously put the responsibility for either the marriage or the divorce on your child.

Another statement that is often made is, "Divorce is harder on children than on anyone else." Or in another variation, "The children are the ones who really suffer." While statements like this offer melodramatic appeal, I seriously doubt that children generally suffer as much or more than adults do in a divorce. True, if you and your spouse use the child as a go-between, or if one of you tells the child that because of the divorce the world is coming to an end, you are probably going to create some serious problems for the child. Likewise, when Grandma talks to the child in the same tone that she would use if Mommy and Daddy were being sent off to the gas chamber, the child is going to be afraid.

I am not denying that children suffer in a divorce. Divorce is usually painful for everyone involved. I am merely trying to get your worries about the child's feelings into perspective.

If, in the midst of your divorce, when you are hurting desperately, you automatically assume that your child is hurting more, this is not going to help you deal with the very real problems that *do* exist for you and the child. This overreaction to the child's problems can cause you to give him pity when he really needs love. If you offer pity, it probably will mean that the child will come to pity himself. If, on the other hand, you can keep the child's pain in perspective, you can avoid wasting your energy on worry or pity, which will only hurt the child. Instead, use your energy to give the extra love that really is needed at a tough time in life.

The Age of the Child

Another factor that is of the utmost importance in talking to your children about divorce is the age of the child. Obviously, you usually can be more explicit and frank with an older child who knows more about life and understands more about what has been going on between you and your spouse. By saying this, I do not mean that divorce is necessarily easier for older children. To the contrary, some older children suffer immensely from their parents' divorce. I also have known younger children who were hardly affected by it at all. The fact is, children, like adults, are individuals who respond differently to different circumstances in their lives. Still, you probably can talk in detail with your eighteen-year-old about the divorce, whereas your five-year-old would consider the same conversation gobbledygook.

The Objective Is Clear

In one sense, talking to your child can be one of the simplest and most straightforward aspects of dealing with your divorce. Why? Because your objective is very narrow. All you care about here is your child's well-being, his or her mental health. You are trying to aid the child in handling this important aspect of his or her life. Accordingly, you can, for the most part, write off concerns about everyone else involved. Ignore what the judge thinks! In dealing with the child, you really can afford to disregard all of the extraneous confusion that has to do with lawyers, your spouse, your mother-in-law, creditors, or parents. In these brief moments when you talk with your child, you can make him or her understand that nothing is more important to you than letting him or her know how you feel about them.

Honesty Is the Only Policy

How do you do this? This is a class where you get very high marks for simple straightforward *honesty*. Here honesty goes such a long way because you are dealing with an intimate, close relationship between you and your child. Anything short of honesty will damage the trust that is at the core of this intimacy. In addition, and at the risk of sounding trite, you can't lie to a child. If you don't tell your child the truth, he will sense it. Remember: Your child already knows much intuitively about you and your spouse's relationship. In reality, your conversation will only serve to confirm much of what the child already knows or suspects. The child may even have thought things were worse than they really are.

Honesty does not mean that you must go into all of the gory details. This will only confuse the child and may make him or her feel like he or she ought to understand more. Face the fact that there is much that the child is not going to understand about the divorce. Think of all that you don't understand about it. Nor does honesty mean that you are to force facts or conversation about the divorce on the child. After you have initially told the child about the divorce (in simple terms: Mommy and Daddy won't live together anymore, etc.) don't initiate conversations unless something happens to make a particular aspect of the divorce relevant. Of course, this will happen over and over. This allows you to keep the discussion of these aspects short, if not sweet. Otherwise, only respond to the child's questions in a short but straightforward manner. Being honest does not mean dragging the child into the middle of a soap opera.

Reaffirm the Relationship

Reassure the child. Tell him or her that this does not change your feelings toward him or her. Also reassure the child that your spouse also will continue to love him or her and that he or she will still see and be with both of you. The child needs to know that *nobody* is divorcing *him* or *her*. It is especially important for you to tell and show the child this. This is all the more important because the child probably already has heard discussions of the divorce that took place in hushed tones, or, just as bad, noticed a lack of conversation about family problems that are obvious even to a child. Your *overt* reassurances will do much to offset the uncertainties created by all of this.

Assume Responsibility

Take responsibility from the child. Assure him or her that he or she had nothing to do with the divorce. It is between Mommy and Daddy. There is nothing that the child did or could have done that would have prevented its happening. The reason it is happening is because of feelings that Mommy and Daddy have about each other, not their feelings about the child. Mommy and Daddy decided it on their own without any help from him or her.

Do Not Say Bad Things about Your Spouse

There are no exceptions to this rule. There seems to be the irresistible urge on the part of many people to use children to strike back at a former spouse. Just as bad are those who use their children to vent their own hostility at the former spouse. You don't have to be a genius to know this is doing much damage to the child and none to the former spouse. Remember: Children get their own feelings of self-worth in large part from their parents. If you tell a child that his father is no good, it is likely that he or she will come to think that he or she is no good as well.

This specifically means that you are not to initiate conversation about your spouse's shortcomings. This does not mean that you cannot tell your child that you and your spouse cannot get along or that you have disagreements. Nor does it mean that you are not to respond to allegations that the child says your spouse made against you.

Answering the Child's Questions

Now, we have covered the easy part; that is, what to say when you're explaining the divorce to the child. The hard part is what to say when you're being cross-examined by your child. Make no mistake about it: Many children are very good at cross-examination. Children have an openness, mixed with honesty and curiosity, that lends them the ability to zap in with key questions that would make a trial lawyer envious.

Moreover, children are not always completely innocent. A child may have his or her own motives and desires, which he or she wants to steer you toward with his or her question. For example, a child may not want you to move out of the house. The idea of Mommy and Daddy living apart is a threat to the child's security since, up to this point, the child has only experienced Mommy and Daddy living together. This leads to such questions as, "Why can't Daddy live here anymore?" and "Why don't you and Mommy just stay married?"

Many people want to answer these questions in the same way that they would make an argument to the jury, to say things like, "Because your father chases wild women," or "Because your mother is a religious nut." *Don't do that.* Save these remarks for patient friends *when your child is not around.*

Instead of giving a blow-by-blow description, talk to the child in *general terms.* Not only will the child understand better, but the general answer is more likely to be accurate and honest. For example, if the child asks why you are getting a divorce, try something like this:

"Mommy and Daddy can't get along. When we are around each other, we just end up hurting each other. Because of this it is better that we live apart."

Or, if the child says that he or she doesn't want you to get a divorce, try this:

> "I know you don't want us to get a divorce. If there were any other way to do it, we would not divorce. But the divorce is not what's ending the marriage between your father and me. When we are around each other, we are not happy. If we stayed together pretending to be happily married, it would just be a lie, and things would get worse. As painful as the divorce is, staying together would be worse."

Probably the most difficult type of questioning from a child results when the child is repeating what your spouse has said about you. Unfortunately there is a strong possibility that your spouse won't have the good sense and restraint that you are going to exhibit in talking with your child. This makes it very difficult to control your anger when you are talking with your child because: (1) you know that what your spouse says is hurting your child; (2) it is probably untrue or at least unfairly stated; (3) it is none of your spouse's business anymore; and (4) it proves that your spouse is more of a louse, slob, pervert, etc., than even you thought. Nevertheless, *you must control your response.* For the sake of your child, you *must not* tell him what a low-life his other parent is, even though it is obvious. *Instead, take careful aim at what is being done or said.* Point out to the child that his mother or father is putting unfair responsibility on him. Tell the child that you do not approve of your spouse's actions in *using* him.

All of this is much easier said than done when you consider the incredible nature of what children are told. For example: "Mommy says that you wrecked our home." "Daddy says you don't love Billy and me at all or you wouldn't have broken our home." "Mommy says that you're crazy and ought to be in a mental hospital." "Daddy says that you sleep with a different man every night." In most cases, you and your children won't have to endure anything this severe. If you do, just be confident that a studied, careful response aimed at *what* is being said and *not at the child's other parent* is not only best calculated to help your child, but is most likely to gain his or her respect. Consider this sample response:

> "John, I am shocked that your father would say those things to you. Even though he is hurt and angry, it is unfair for him to burden you with the fight between him and me. I hope that you won't let it get you down. You are having to learn at a very young age that your parents are human beings just like everyone else, with faults, anger, hatreds, fears. I hope he won't continue to say these things to you."

If your spouse has offered the child an opinion such as, "He says you ruined our family," you might add: "John, that's your father's opinion. I assure you that it is much more complicated than that. We both had our faults. All you need to understand is that we could not and do not get along. We both love you and both of us need your love."

If your spouse has told the child something that is untrue, such as, "Your mother sleeps with a different man every night," without making a big production out of it you might gently add:

> "If it will give you comfort, I can tell you that what your dad said is simply untrue."

If your spouse is telling the child things that are true, for example, "Your Mom goes to honky-tonks every weekend," you might respond by saying:

> "It is unfortunate that your father does not spend his time living his own life. I must live my own life as I see fit. It is none of your father's business. Because I am an adult and have had more experience with life than you have, I cannot let you make my decisions for me either. I can tell you this: I do these things because they are good for me, just like we do things that are good for you. Sometimes adults need things that children may not understand."

Response to the Long-Term Problem

Keep in mind that this discussion of talking with your children about the divorce is focused on the period of time surrounding the divorce. If you are one of those people who are involved in what might be called a "marathon divorce," then these rules obviously will need modification. By marathon divorce, I mean one that does not end the open hostility and combat between the parties. In some of these divorces, one of the parties continues for years after the divorce blaming all of the normal pain and difficulties of life on the former spouse. The former spouse becomes an excuse for everything that is wrong in life. Unfortunately, this type of person usually begins passing this same hostility along to the children. This type will tell the children that he or she still "loves" you, and that the two of you will be getting back together some day, or that he or she lost a job because of something that you did. Of course, all of the problems with visitation or with your children's extracurricular activities or school or economic problems affecting your children will be blamed squarely on you by this kind of person.

If, over the years, you continue to use the gentle language I have urged when discussing this parent with the children, your conversation is likely to take on *Alice in Wonderland* characteristics. When this other parent conducts himself or herself in this sort of irresponsible manner over a long period of time, the child is going to know about it. The only question then becomes whether your conversations with the child will be honest enough to acknowledge what is happening. If you aren't honest with a child about the fact that his or her other parent really is doing these things, then the child either will question his or her own perceptions or think that you are some Pollyanna who has just drifted in on a cabbage leaf—in which case, he or she would have *two* crazy parents.

Parents Are People Too

Children are usually sensitive to their parents' feelings. When something is wrong with the parent, a child can become very upset. Sensing this, most parents work very hard to control their feelings in front of their children during difficult times. Also, if a parent loses control in front of a child, the parent feels guilty about worrying the child over adult problems.

I certainly do not disagree with minimizing the melodrama—the anger and pain of a divorce—that children are exposed to. I doubt that large doses of parents' gnashing teeth ever helped any child.

On the other hand, it is equally absurd to try to keep all of your pain and hurt from your child. Trying to shield your child from the fact that you are human and that you hurt too is like trying to shield him or her from the knowledge of death. These things are realities of life that we must all learn to live and deal with.

The difference between your understanding of pain and that of your child's is that, as an adult, you know you can endure the hurt and that it will pass. Children don't always know this.

So when you become aware that your child is worried about you, don't deny it or run from it. Tell him or her: (1) I am all right; (2) this is just a part of being alive; (3) it will pass, and I will be over it and be my old self; (4) it is not your fault or responsibility; and (5) you are helping me a whole bunch by just caring about me and loving me.

Give Up Your Role – Not Your Child

In Chapter 2, "Coping after Separation," I discussed the role changes that occur at the time of separation. If you are about to give up the day-to-day custody of your children, you are about to undergo one of the biggest role changes of your life. Instead of seeing and being with your children daily, you may only see them weekly, biweekly, or even monthly. In some instances, if either you or your spouse move, you may see them even less frequently.

No one can deny the tremendous pain that many people feel in separating from their children. The feelings a parent has for a young child often are so strong that separation from the child becomes the most agonizing experience of the parent's life and dwarfs all other problems in the divorce. The loss of a child in a courtroom custody battle often carries the emotional wallop of being sent to prison. The voluntary relinquishment of a child to the other parent, for the benefit of the child, often approaches the heroic. Few understand the courage required.

Without denying the reality of this loss, let's take a close look at what happens when you separate from your child.

It may be that separation from your child on a day-to-day basis is not so much the loss of your child as it is the loss of your role as parent. Often this role entails the idea of moment-by-moment supervision and instruction, as if the child is so dumb that he can only learn about life with Mommy and Daddy standing right there to point out every piece of the puzzle.

No doubt *young* children do need constant attention and supervision. By taking custody, your spouse is taking a larger role in this aspect of your child's life than you are. This direct moment-by-moment supervision as the child gets older will be assumed more and more by baby-sitters, teachers, coaches, scout leaders, and others. At times, though perhaps not as often as you would like, you will be the supervisor.

If your view of the traditional parent is that of a schoolmarm or guard dog, there probably are going to be some problems. About the time you get started marming or guarding, it will be time for the child to return home. You can discipline, and you can supervise, but you cannot make discipline and supervision the theme of your relationship with your child in these limited moments that you have with him or her.

As it turns out, this may be a lucky break for you and the kid. Children need a lot more than discipline and supervision. Many people who grew up with plenty of these things have very low self-esteem.

Children need friends, not just other children, but big friends who know a lot about life and living and who want to talk with them about ordinary day-to-day things. Children need loyal supporters, a cheering section that lets them know how important they are. Children need people who, at least occasionally, think it's worth going to lots of trouble just to be there for a few moments at the ball game, the recital, or the cookout without saying anything except "You did really well," or "I had a great time."

Children may need moral lectures occasionally, but they always need somebody to talk to—to listen to not-too-funny jokes and laugh, to hear what is fair and not fair at school, to listen to the discussion of why so-and-so is a creep and who is really the best quarterback.

Children also need examples. Not examples of people who smother them every minute or who are present every moment. Not necessarily examples of people who make lots of money or succeed as community leaders. But people who have the courage to live their own lives even when the going gets tough, as in divorce. People who know how to laugh and cry, work and play, and share the good times and the bad. It especially helps when these good examples can be their very own parent—somebody to identify with, even if that person is not around all the time.

But more than all of this, children need to know that they can make it on their own. A parent can give a child no greater gift than the ability to get along without the parent. The best way for a parent to do this is to have confidence in the child.

Letting children go younger and sooner than you expected is tough business. It is never easy. But some parents never let their children go. Then the parent is sixty and the child is forty, and the parent still acts like a parent. Usually they don't ever get to be friends. By letting your child go early, you may get a friend sooner than you thought.

Chapter 18

Reconciling Divorce and Parenting: Your Mission, Should You Choose to Accept It, Is to Be the Adult

He that has no children brings them up well.

—Proverb

Facing Our Fears

We Americans are fond of saying how much we love our children. It is nearly impossible to find a parent who does not profess undying love for his or her child. And no doubt, most of us do passionately care for our children. But, apparently, "love" is not enough. We have this problem. Johnny still can't read. Too many kids quit school. Our teenagers have massive drug and alcohol problems. Many kids are depressed. Young kids get pregnant and have more kids. Our prisons are full of young people who have just finished failed childhoods. The list goes on.

Almost no one on either side of the political battles or religious wars will dispute that many of our children are in crisis. Likewise, there is general agreement that the crisis affecting our children is closely associated with the "breakdown of the family." And for many "breakdown of the family" has the same meaning as "divorce."

In our collective consciousness, "divorce" is closely linked to childhood maladies. Phrases like "juvenile delinquency" and "teenage drug use" regularly appear in the same conversations that are linked to "divorce." The word "divorce" usually implies that the children are in jeopardy.

Now, because you are considering divorce, it comes to your attention that your child is involved. He soon may be a "child of divorce." She will be said to be from a "broken home." Just the implications—and that is mostly what this is about—are enough to terrify any loving parent. Only a fool or a psychopath could divorce without having some concern about its impact on his or her child.

So, you may say to yourself, if a divorce will cause all these destructive things to happen to my child, I just won't do it. I'll just keep my child's "family" together at all cost. And this approach will probably work out well for you if you're one of the well-known moral lecturers giving general theoretical advice to the public.

But, if your spouse is physically or emotionally abusive, violent, hateful, mean, addicted to drugs, an alcoholic, or any of a thousand other possibilities, staying together to save a "home" that's already been shattered may be absurd or counterproductive. When your child sees one parent throwing dishes, or invectives, or maybe even just the hateful looks at the other you may begin to wonder whether this is good for the child. In fact, if you're one of the many parents who simply must divorce to protect your child from harmful events happening in your "home," the idea of saving your child by staying together may appear laughably stupid.

So, where's the disconnect? Why is it that, on the one hand, you are clear that you must get yourself and your child out of this poisonous environment, and on the other hand, you are being bombarded by the guilty feeling that this divorce may ruin your child?

The Phony Solutions: Slogans and One-Size-Fits-All Answers

What's wrong with this picture? A parent attempting to rescue a child from an emotionally damaging environment by filing for a divorce is accused of ruining the child's life by breaking up the "home." A parent facing an inevitable divorce feels guilty about accepting the inevitable and moving on with the business of raising her children, because of the fear that giving up a dead marriage will ruin her child's life. Could it be that this kind of contradiction arises out of some really fuzzy thinking—not just in the mind of these individual parents faced with this issue, but widespread fuzzy thinking throughout society? Could it be that this "breakdown of the family" thing has complicated and confusing roots and is not susceptible to simple solutions or easy answers?

Unfortunately, with large numbers of people distressed to no end about the "breakdown of the family," there is no shortage of simple "solutions" offered by a variety of politicians, TV evangelists, radio talk show hosts, newspaper commentators, and other self-appointed "authorities" on the subject. Even more unfortunately, by the very nature of these sources, their "solutions" must not only be simple—they must be capable of being reduced to slogans, sound bites, and one-size-fits-all answers that seemingly apply to everyone. These "solutions" are appealing because they *sound* so obvious and correct. They appeal to our hopes and longings. *Stay married if you can. Divorce is bad. Love your children. Don't be self-centered. Two devoted loving parents are better than one. The hand that rocks the cradle rules the world. Families are the foundation of our society.* These are only examples.

And who could disagree? And who would even question these great truths? Unless, of course, you're the wife who has to deal with a violent, drunken husband in the middle of the night, while trying not to wake up the kids who will certainly be upset yet again. Or unless you're the husband who is trying to explain to the children why their mother is gone again for the fortieth time. Or, you might even think to question the absolutely positive meaning given to the word "family" by all politicians, if you're one of those "lucky" spouses with a "good marriage" who lives on edge waiting for the next vicious verbal attack and hoping it won't be in front of the children. Where is that TV psychologist when you really need her?

News Flash: Parent's Clear Thinking Saves Child

The essence of the one-size-fits-all "solutions" to child rearing and of simply lamenting the "breakdown of the family" is that it takes away the need to think. If every difficult decision is susceptible to being solved by a slogan or sound bite, then all that remains is to recite the slogan and follow it. If every question can be answered by a broad-brush answer, then, simply plug in the one-size-fits-all solution and, like magic, the problem is solved—if you're not the one having to live with it.

The devastating result of this kind of "thinking" is not that it stops divorces from happening. The gory realities of life will eventually win out over all but the most extreme delusional "thinking." Rather, people are harmed because, by focusing on these stereotypical generalities, they prolong suffering and delay asking the real question: *Given the realities of my life, what must I do to keep my body, mind, and soul together so that I can take care of my children?*

Let's look at how this one-size-fits-all approach to divorce decision making may be hindering your clear judgment about your children and your marriage.

First, consider that many of these slogans and seemingly simple "solutions" are meaningless under real-life conditions. Let's examine the proposition that "divorce is bad." Oh, really? As compared to what? Which is worse, a divorce or a wife being regularly beaten by her husband? How "bad" is it for her to divorce, if she's just occasionally beaten? What if she's just threatened and lives in fear? What if it's her child who is being beaten? Is divorce bad then? What of a wife who spends all of the grocery money on drugs—and refuses treatment? Should her husband forego divorce because it is bad? Compared to these things, divorce would seem to be relatively "good."

Second, the one-size-fits-all approach to decision making is often dishonest. Most of the public figures who portray themselves as defenders of children, the family, the American way of life, etc., have a list of acceptable reasons to divorce. Typically, these reasons might include adultery, alcoholism, drug addition, physical violence, child molestation, and their own select *moral* violations. Everything else, according to these "experts," doesn't reach the threshold required to justify breaking up the sacred institution of marriage. The use of the list keeps it simple. Your marriage is either on the list or it's not.

The problem with this "list" is that it overlooks the fact that spouses may subject their partners and their children to subtle, sophisticated, and manipulative treatment that may be more destructive than the conduct on the "list." Take child abuse, for example. You don't have to spend much time on this planet to figure out that most child abuse is emotional rather than physical. So, again by this one-size-fits-all approach to divorce, a parent who lives with a mentally ill spouse inflicting constant, intense, vicious verbal abuse on a child would be precluded from seeking a divorce as a means of protecting the child. Rather, this spouse is apparently supposed to stay married and thereby proclaim to the world that the family is intact, when, in fact, for the abused child, this so-called *family* is a torture chamber. By most definitions, calling a torture chamber a family is a lie. Not a small lie but rather the kind that can lead to childhood suicide, psychotic breaks, or life-long emotional problems. But the people with the list want you to believe that these little lies are okay, regardless of the cost.

Your Divorce Is Not the Cause – It's the Result

Divorces don't come out of vacuums. Most children of couples who are divorcing were not living in a perfect little "Ozzie and Harriet" world before the divorce. The same forces that propel children into drug abuse, alcoholism, childhood pregnancy, dropping out of school, and prisons are often the same forces that require spouses to seek the protection of the divorce court. It's often the divorce that rescues a child—not the pretense that the family is still intact.

Now turn the issue around. Ask yourself a couple of questions that none of the politicians or moral lecturers on the subject of divorce are willing to ask.

First, how many children have been saved by divorce? I mean saved from the "broken family" syndrome, because one parent had the courage to file for divorce and move the child out of an unstable "home" into a stable environment where the child grew into a healthy, productive adult? Yes, raising a child as a single parent really is difficult. It should be avoided, if possible. But to say that it's to be avoided at all costs is to ignore reality. The reality is that many parents who stay in marriages are, for all practical purposes, single-handedly, without any help from their spouse, raising their child. In many marriages, this solo parenting must be done while the other spouse is engaging in conduct harmful to the child. Is it better to raise a child by yourself while you or the child or both are being abused, threatened, subjected to a drunk or a drug addict, always waiting for the other shoe to drop? Have you ever lived in a house in which the dominant spouse was just plain mean? Perhaps the commentators who uniformly condemn "divorce" should hang out in some of these "homes" or spend a little time with some of these "families." Were they to do so, it might require them to rearrange their intellectual furniture. No longer would "family" or "home" always fit into the "good" category. If these paragons-of-everybody-else's-virtue were required to stay and raise children in some of these "homes," the word "divorce" might take on a whole new meaning. "Divorce" might be seen as a way of saving children.

Second, why is it necessary to see marriage, any marriage no matter how bad, as more valuable and sacred than the people being harmed by staying in that marriage? Words like "divorce," "marriage," "family," and "home" should reflect the reality of life. When absolute, rigid meanings are ascribed to these words, the words stop reflecting reality and become a defining "label" that often obscures reality. Assigning a word like "marriage" an absolute meaning implies that the institution represented by this word is more sacred than the people who are supposed to benefit from it. This puts us in the position of "worshiping," if not a word, then at least an institution represented by a word. This would seem to violate the prohibition against worshiping graven images. It is also known as idolatry.

So, if you truly love your child and you want to live an honest and authentic life, you must look at the facts and not the labels. You must separate causes from effects. Your job is to figure out what is best for the human beings. Your child. Yourself. And, yes, if possible, your spouse. This means that you can't hide behind labels that imply that you don't have to make hard decisions. When you hear the preacher using the words "marriage," "family," and "divorce" in poetic and lyrical ways, do not go all misty eyed. Even if a congregation of thousands is swooning at the very idea that the mere use of the word "family" means that every kid will have a life just like Beaver Cleaver's, your sacred obligation is to ask yourself what this word "family" means in your house and to your child.

First, Don't Make It Worse

So, what can you do?

If we were writing a rule book for divorcing parents, perhaps Rule 1 should be: *Don't make things worse than they already are.* This sounds pretty easy. I fear that it's more difficult than it appears, because, by the time the divorce arrives on the scene, things are often already very bad. And very bad situations are the easiest to make worse. Many divorces come about as a result of lives and families that are already in trouble. Things were not good before the divorce or the divorce would never have happened. If this is true in your life, then you are already under a lot of stress. You won't have to look very far in the world of divorce to see that many divorcing parents pass this stress right along to their children. Divorce is a time when it is very easy to become hysterical, or depressed, or helpless, or overbearing, or resentful, or vengeful, or cynical, or paranoid, or irresponsible, or any of about a thousand other negative things. (Paradoxically, these same things often cause divorces.) If you indulge yourself in any of these negative opportunities, then it is not just your sleazy spouse or your horrible marriage that is harming your child. You, personally, are adding to the burden your child is carrying. However dysfunctional your spouse is; no matter how poor you are; regardless of the bad neighborhood you live in; as bad as all of these things are, if you subject your child to any of the numberless negative emotions you feel at the time, it is not just your spouse who is making your child's life worse. It is also you.

The whole thing boils down to this: *If you don't want to make things worse for your child, you have to start by not becoming crazy yourself.* You have lived long enough to know that, on some days and in some situations, "avoiding being crazy" is a pretty tall order. If your life is anything like mine, there are many days when the world closely resembles an insane asylum. When these full-blown-crazy-times are underway in my life, if I am not careful, I find myself shouting at the other inmates. Someone looking in from the outside might think that my medications are overdue. And I'm not even getting a divorce.

If you're the parent who is worried sick about how your divorce will affect your child, this frail statement—*you must remain sane and not make things worse for your child*—probably appears to be but a slender reed in a raging sea. You may be tempted to reject this whole idea of self-control in favor of a quick fix or a guaranteed formula. But, I think, it is the most important initial decision you can make. Remember, this statement is not a solution. It is only a place to begin and a place to return to when you lose your way. It is a way of being honest with yourself and your child. You cannot make your child's world perfect. In fact, insisting that your child's world must be perfect is just another form of insanity, guaranteed to produce bad results for the child. If, in your worst moments, you can remember not to lose your head, or your temper, or your patience, you will avoid making your child's life worse. If you are the steady, sane voice of reason in moments of crisis, it is virtually certain that your child's world will be much better.

The One Sane Parent Pledge

Your child may be lucky. Your divorce may be one in which you and your spouse are both mature healthy adults who are working out your differences in sane, sensible ways, designed to protect your child and minimize the pain and damage that you cause each other. If this is the case, and it often is, the divorce will still be painful for all concerned, including your child. But, your child will be truly blessed to continue to have two good, loyal parents who will share at least one common goal—to provide him or her with all of the love and support necessary for the development of a healthy and happy adult.

On the other hand, many divorces are a direct result of one of the spouses "acting out" destructive, antisocial, and sometimes deadly conduct. Sometimes this antisocial behavior is targeted at the child. More often, the negative effect on the child is a byproduct of that spouse's malicious or immature behavior. If your divorce fits into this category, your child probably already has one parent who's doing crazy things: depriving the child of safety or stability, failing to show up when promised, being oblivious to the child's basic needs, being unable to relate to the child, indulging in emotional blackmail, saying negative things about the child's other parent, or dozens of the other destructive possibilities afforded truly misguided or malicious parents. If this describes your spouse, then *your child is already short one sane, adult parent.* This leaves only one issue up for grabs: *Is your child going to have one sane parent or none?*

Here's where you come galloping on stage on your white horse. It's time for you to decide whether you're going to play games or get real. You write the script. It's a dramatic moment. The possibilities are limitless. You can lie to yourself about magic wands, castles in the sky, and how your child was born a prince or princess. Here, choosing badly has the added attraction of decades of drama in which, using your right to free speech, you can constantly proclaim that your child's life was ruined because his other parent would not or could not play the role that you had scripted and that God, of course, had ordained. This is not the script for a healthy, sane parent!

On the other hand, you can cut the Greek tragedy and write the script honestly. *You can clearly, deliberately decide that you will commit yourself to being the sane parent in your child's life, regardless of how his or her other parent behaves.* You cannot promise more. Your spouse will have to decide whether your child will be lucky enough to have two sane parents. Thinking you can control your child's other parent's behavior is just another form of insanity—leaving your child no sane parent.

Yes, you're right. My urging you to promise yourself that you will be sane is trite, simplistic, and obvious. It's also vital. You have heard other versions of it. Psychologists often point out that, in an emergency, the airlines tell you to place the oxygen mask on yourself first, then place it on your child. A teacher on marriage and family that I knew many years ago had as his mantra: If the tree is to provide shade for others, it must first take the nutrients, water, and sunshine necessary to keep itself alive and healthy. Student pilots are told over and over that in an emergency, the pilot's first job is to fly the airplane. All of these, and dozens of other metaphors, tell us that the crazier and wackier the stuff is that is thrown at us, the more important it is to remain calm and collected—especially if we are the sole parent available to care for a child or children. Remember: When you signed on for this mission of being a parent, the voice on the tape said, "Your mission, should you choose to accept it, is to be the adult."

And, yes, you're right again, this determination to strive toward responsible adulthood—promising yourself to be sane as a gift to your children—is nothing more than a philosophical or theological *commitment* to use every ounce of your strength to join those who want to be a part of the solution rather than a part of the problem. Again, these words are used so often that we hear them as a cliché. But words like "commitment" and "sanity" demand that we look past our own belly button to understand that our own sanity is not just about ourselves but about our connections to others, and in this case, our connections with the most important people on earth—our children—the people who will run the planet after we are gone.

In my view, promising yourself that your child will have at least one sane parent is a pledge you should make secretly to yourself alone. It is not to be shared with anyone else. To share it is to use this pledge for your own aggrandizement or as a means of gaining advantage over your spouse. If you are really serious about being the good parent in bad times, the only way the rest of the world will ever find out is by watching how you treat your child.

Being the Sane Parent under Combat Conditions

So, what does it mean to be a sane parent in a divorce? Be a strict disciplinarian? No, be more tolerant? Get custody at all cost? No, don't fight over custody? The airways, bookshelves, newspapers, and coffee shops are filled with all kinds of formulas about how to be a good parent. Only that vital issue of how to lose weight can compete with the space absorbed by advice on parenting. Contrary to popular belief, there is no simple answer or a formula that works in all situations. But being a good parent during divorce and hard times is not a state secret.

Make no mistake: I am not talking about being the sane parent when life is perfect. Being sane when life is smooth and everything is fine is a non-issue. When Mom, Dad, and the children are healthy and happy, the rent is paid, the family is scrubbed and sitting together in church, and the sky is blue, to even speak of sanity seems silly.

On the other hand, how to be a sane parent in "Real Life 101" is an extremely difficult question when the landlord is calling and Dad has just left with the paycheck, or Mom is a schizophrenic who hears voices giving instructions that could be harmful to the children, or one spouse is bipolar, paranoid, alcoholic, addicted to drugs, depressed, chronically criminal, violent, hateful, mean, under arrest, psychopathic, or just plain indifferent because he is the best brain surgeon ever discovered on the planet, or she is completely emotionally unavailable because she is solving the Middle East Crisis. The variety of ways that spouses, children, and families can have their lives wrecked is limitless.

I hope the varieties of dysfunction described above are more extreme than you now face. But, as you probably know since you're reading a book about divorce, it is not always possible to gauge how and when life moves from the serenity of sanity to the absurdity of insanity. Sometimes it takes years. Sometimes it happens in a nanosecond. But, no matter how it happens, the very nature of losing one's "sanity" or "bearings" or "clear thinking," the experience of having one's life turned upside down has a subtle, fuzzy, confusing, bizarre, ambiguous quality to it. No matter how clear and blunt a slap in the face is, the person being slapped may not always understand all of the implications of how, in a heartbeat, we went from civil discourse to the flashing of canine teeth. In the breakup of marriages, the one doing the "slapping" also does not always clearly understand how or why the change has occurred. It takes time to answer the questions. What happened? How could my life have turned out this way? How could I have married someone whom I now see so clearly is a sociopath, alcoholic, manipulator, etc.? Can we get back together? How could she have betrayed me? Should I give him another chance?

Yes, traumatic events in the life of even a normal, very mentally healthy person can drive you crazy—not to mention those among us who are not "very mentally healthy." None of us, I dare say, has been "sane" at every moment in our lives. Those who think they are immune to losing their sanity if things get bad enough probably haven't experienced much life yet. They probably also haven't read the books about grown men in the midst of combat, breaking down and literally, like babies, crying for their mothers, or the percentages of combat troops who, over a period of time, have psychotic breaks. The point is, the kind of trauma visited on many people in divorces, at the very least, creates mental confusion. Often, people divorcing function with far less than their usual mental or emotional resources. This is normal. It is absolutely human. Time is needed to adjust and get back to "normal."

When the traumatized spouse is also the parent who has primary or, perhaps, sole responsibility for a child, life gets more complicated. Children, especially very young children, can't wait. Their need to have parental attention, guidance, love, and support is constant. While you're sorting things out mentally and emotionally, they still have to have you as their parent. Believe it or not, the mental and emotional sorting out can be done at the same time the parenting is taking place. It has been done over and over by many people. If the truth be known, it has been done by most parents at one time or another.

The point is, sanity gets judged from the point of view of the child. It's not whether a doctor or a psychologist would recommend hospitalization, pills, psychotherapy, a visit to a spa, or whatever. It's whether you pick the kid up from day care, or get him a bowl of soup for supper, or if you can't heat the soup, get him a peanut butter and jelly sandwich. He'll like that better anyway. You can do the healthy stuff later when you are technically, medically, and certifiably sane.

Under this system, being sane is getting the diaper changed and getting the other kid in the bathtub. You get high marks for sanity if you attend your kid's school play when you really want to stay home under the covers in a fetal position sucking your thumb. (If you show up, you still get the points for sanity, even if you missed the last play because you did stay home in the fetal position.) I assure you that you are extremely sane if you continue your weekend visits with your children, even when your spouse is telling you that your children would be better off without you. You get triple points for sanity if, at every opportunity, you read bedtime stories with grace and aplomb, even when your heart is breaking because your spouse is trying to move your children to another city, you can't pay the rent, you have lost your job, or any of the other thousands of reasons that we humans have broken hearts. If you are the parent with responsibilities for daily care of your children, you may multiply your sanity points by four every time you are able to send the children off *happily* for a weekend with your soon-to-be ex-spouse or your parents or his parents. Allowing other people to help you mess up your children's lives demonstrates real sanity. Only the truly insane want to totally dominate their children's future discussions with their psychiatrists.

You get the drift. You don't need a thousand examples from me. If you're a divorcing parent, you're still allowed to have a broken heart. You're allowed confusion and disorientation and anger and intense sadness and, probably, at least some of the symptoms from the *DSM-IV*. But you're not allowed to focus totally on your own belly button, to the exclusion of your child. You've got to focus some of your attention on your child, the most important person in your life. As I have said, your child is the person who's going to be running the world after we're all gone. Or maybe even before.

The Divorcing Parent – Engaged in Opposites at the Same Time

Describing divorce as a betrayal of children confuses cause and effect. Some divorces are filed to protect children. Some parents are better parents after divorce. As I continue to say, keeping your child in a home with another parent who is mean, cruel, or abusive may be the real betrayal of your child. So, even after we become intellectually clear that divorce is not a crime against our children, why does it create so much emotional anxiety for parents?

I think that divorce is so emotionally threatening to parents and children alike, because, in some ways, divorce is the opposite of the parent-child bond. Being a divorcing parent forces you to do two exactly opposite things at the same time. The divorcing parent must cast away and keep at the same time.

Divorce is about establishing boundaries. In divorce, lines are being draw in the sand. Someone, and sometimes everyone, is saying stay away from me. The separation is not just legal. It is also emotional, financial, personal, spatial, and intellectual. A separate identity is being established for each spouse.

The very nature of the bond between a parent and a child, particularly a young child, is that there are no boundaries. The young child is totally helpless and needs continual reassurance that the parent will always be there. Good parents have an overwhelming awareness of the child's weakness, vulnerability, and need for assurance. Boundaries between the parent and child eventually do form, but only naturally, slowly, and largely unnoticed, over the course of the childhood and even into adult life.

Divorce displays the conditional nature of human relationships. It focuses on accountability for broken conditions or perceived broken conditions. To the extent that the couple's affairs can't be separated, divorce establishes conditions for the future conduct of those inseparable matters.

The parent-child bond, on the other hand, is centered on unconditional love. Conditions are imposed gradually, as a part of the child's learning process. No matter how many times you spill the milk, and no matter how upsetting it is to your parents, you get another glass of milk along with instructions on how not to spill it this time. It is only in the teenage years, after much spilt milk and fights over hygiene and homework, that childhood conditions even begin seriously to approach an adult level.

In short, divorce says things about the nature of relationships that neither parent nor child wants to hear. Divorce reminds us that, as good as the parent-child bond feels, all of life can't be about coming together. Young children sometimes feel threatened when a parent steps out of the house for even a moment. The child's very survival depends on staying connected to the parent. When the parent, in the midst of this overwhelming bonding with the child, is forced to deal with divorce, separation, and drawing lines in the sand, it is no wonder this conflicted parent experiences emotional confusion.

The pain inherent in separation tempts us to search for simplistic intellectual shortcuts. Just like the child, there is a part of us that wants to believe that we can live in a world that is all sunshine, where there is no separation, parting, or conflict. It is a nice dream, but it is a dishonest assessment of real life. As much as we may want it to be, our relationship with our spouse is not always the same as the inseparable bond we have with our child. This is why adult experience, rather than the child's wishes, must be used in making these decisions. Adult experience? You know, that stuff that you spent all of your childhood and part of your adult life learning: *You've got to call 'em as you see 'em and not as you want 'em to be.*

The wisdom of an ancient writer may shine some light. "For everything there is a season, and a time for every matter under heaven…a time to break down, and a time to build up…a time to embrace, and a time to refrain from embracing; a time to seek, and a time to lose; a time to keep, and a time to cast away; a time to rend, and a time to sew…a time to love, and a time to hate; a time for war, and a time for peace." The ancient author fails to mention that the divorcing parent must both keep and cast away at the same time.

As sacred as the parent-child bond is, not all of life can be defined by or built upon the premise that all relationships will always be the pure "togetherness" experienced between parent and child. To say that, no matter what happens, you will respond to your spouse as if one of you were the child and the other the parent, is to deny reality. Yes, there is intimacy. And that is good. But there also always must be boundaries. And that too is good. It's the way the world is. Parent-child love is a big part of all of this. So too is protecting oneself and one's children, when necessary, with divorce. To deny either is to deny reality. Some say that the denial of reality is insanity. Some say it's sacrilege.

Chapter 19

Texas Child Custody Law: The Rules of the Road

When a parent files for divorce in Texas, the filing triggers a comprehensive set of child custody rules. These rules are *available* to govern each parent's relationship with the child from that day forth. But, the word "available" means that, to the extent that the divorcing parents agree on custody issues, they can make their own mutual decisions without reference to the custody rules.

In contentious divorces, custody rules are immediately used to determine who will have custody during the pendency of the divorce, and those rules may, daily, continue to affect the child's relationship with the parents until the child is eighteen years of age. Likewise, if one of the parents is concerned about the child's safety, a temporary restraining order may be entered, even before a hearing, to protect the child from the other parent.

In divorces in which the parents have less intense differences about custody issues, the child custody laws may not be invoked until the final divorce is granted. And after the divorce is granted, these parents with less intense differences often use the custody rules as a flexible guideline for sharing access to children. Visitation guidelines are invoked only in rare moments of disagreement.

A few divorced parents, sharing very similar views on their children, virtually ignore the child custody rules. Although the visitation guidelines appear in all divorce decrees, these parents have their own mutual ideas about how the children should go back and forth and who should do what, so that court orders and visitation guidelines play no role in their lives. All children should be so lucky!

But in every case, the Texas custody laws will shape the nature of each parent's relationship with the child in the days and years following the divorce. If you are a parent who loves your child, you must become familiar with these rules. If you and your spouse have strong disagreements over custody issues, you probably will need a more in-depth, detailed, and intimate knowledge of this body of law.

A Quick Study, Not a Detailed Anatomy of the Beast

The Texas Family Code is detailed and complex. Portions are straightforward and clear. Other aspects rely on unspoken cultural "understandings" and subtle nuances related to other areas of law and legal tradition. In addition to the Family Code, child custody cases also require a thorough understanding of the evidence, the rules used to conduct civil trials, and the procedures used to operate the court system. There are many comprehensive technical books for lawyers on this subject. This is not one of them.

This chapter is written for the divorcing parent. It is designed to give you the basic information necessary to get your head in the game, to cause you to think about your relationship to your child and what that relationship will be after the divorce. Reading this chapter will not make you a lawyer or prepare you to handle your own custody case. It is a quick study. By its "down and dirty" nature, it necessarily glosses over complex issues. Most importantly, it is an *aid* to use in working with your lawyer. It is not a substitute for a lawyer.

Finally, besides being comprehensive and complex, Texas child custody law is a moving target. The Texas legislature has made significant changes to the Family Code in *virtually every session over the past thirty years*. Why is this important to you? It tells you that society is paying detailed attention to this aspect of our lives. This is an important message for parents who care about their children. You are not alone.

It's Between the Parents

Parents have superior rights to their children. Courts refer to this as the *parental presumption.* It means that, in a contest between a parent and a non-parent, barring exceptional circumstances, the law strongly sides with the parent. In a divorce case there is a presumption that the parents are the ones who will be granted custody. In other words, in a dispute between a parent and a non-parent over custody of a child, it does not matter that the non-parent would be a better custodian of the child; if one or both of the parents are even marginally "fit," a parent will still be given custody. There are, of course, exceptions.

Parents can lose their superior rights to have custody of their children. Although the law says that parents are presumed to be the best custodians, it is a rebuttable presumption. This means that, if evidence is presented demonstrating that granting the parent custody "would significantly impair the child's physical health or emotional development," the court may decide to give custody to someone else. If it is proved that a parent has left the child in the care of another for a year or engaged in a pattern of family violence, then the presumption that the parent is the one entitled to custody vanishes, and the parent is on equal footing with a non-parent in a struggle over custody. Needless to say, any showing of physical or sexual abuse of a child would certainly cause a court to refuse to give a parent custody and open the door for a non-parent who is seeking custody.

The parental presumption can be lost yet one more way. Custody litigation that attempts to modify prior custody orders carries no parental presumption. In other words, the parental presumption is for the *first* custody case only. Thereafter, a parent already awarded custody is not entitled to the presumption if it is being properly alleged that the prior custody award is not in the child's best interest.

Beginning Assumptions

Fifty years ago, when a couple was contemplating divorce, the assumption was that the mother would get custody of the children. Back then, when clients asked lawyers about child custody, they were uniformly told "mothers usually get custody." The concept was so well entrenched that few divorcing men bothered to ask for custody. Unless the man had extraordinary facts, he simply would not get custody. In short, before the case even started, everybody knew what the result would be, unless the mother had huge problems.

This short history lesson is related solely to illustrate that we must always have *a starting place*. There are always *beginning assumptions*. Human decision making begins every inquiry with assumptions. Often we, individually and collectively, are not aware of what those beginning assumptions are or that we are using them and being controlled by them.

Today, if a couple is contemplating divorce, the assumptions about child custody are very different. A client asking a lawyer about child custody will be told that custody and visitation are controlled by a *Standard Possession Order*. The Standard Possession Order is today's *starting place for thinking about child custody*. It is the *beginning assumption* about how divorce custody arrangements will come out.

So, in ordinary language, what does all of this talk about Standard Possession Order mean? It simply means that one, and only one, of the parents is given primary custody (power to decide where the child lives), and the court enters written orders specifying exactly when and for how long the other parent is to have possession of the child.

Should you decide to tell the judge that you want to skip the Standard Possession Order altogether, your request will probably be viewed with suspicion, and you'd better be armed with very good reasons. Otherwise, your request will probably be ignored.

Why is all of this important? Because, by not understanding "the thought process" used by everyone else in the case, you lose your ability to influence the outcome. The "standard" stuff may or may not fit your case. You may be in a position requiring you to insist that your case be treated differently, or understanding the "standard" approach may allow you to relax because it is exactly what you need.

Interpreting the Standard Possession Order – The Shorthand Version

So, what is this "Standard Possession Order"? The really short answer is that it's the system of dividing weekends and holidays between divorced parents. For those of you who like to begin by going off the high board at the deep end of the pool (or who are already familiar with the system), the entire Standard Possession Order, as it appears in most Texas divorce decrees, appears at the end of this chapter. The rest of us can begin with this simplified version as follows:

Basic Concept 1. The parent with primary custody "has" the child or children except for specifically described periods when the other parent (the visiting parent) is allowed "possession" for weekend, holiday, and summertime visits. The "*right to designate the child's primary residence*" is the legal and official terminology for the parent with primary custody.

Basic Concept 2. The visiting parent's weekend visits are the *first, third, and fifth weekends* of every month beginning at 6:00 P.M. on Friday and ending at 6:00 P.M. Sunday. Anytime there is a *School Holiday* on the *Friday before* or the *Monday after* a visiting weekend, the visitation period is extended to include that day. If the visiting parent elects, at the time of the divorce, the decree may provide that this period be extended to begin at the time school is regularly dismissed on Friday and end when school resumes on Monday.

Basic Concept 3. The visiting parent also gets *Thursday nights* from six to eight during the regular school year. If the visiting parent elects, at the time of divorce, this period can be extended to begin at the time school is out on Thursday and end when it resumes Friday morning. If the visiting parent lives more than 100 miles away, there is no Thursday visitation.

Basic Concept 4. Holidays are split between the parents. This is accomplished by an odd-year, even-year split. For example, Mom gets the entire Thanksgiving holiday in even years; Dad gets it in odd years. The same kind of odd-year, even-year system is used for Spring Break, unless the visiting parent lives more than 100 miles from the child, in which case the visiting parent gets Spring Break every year.

In even years, the visiting parent gets the child when school is dismissed for the Christmas Holidays and brings the child home at noon on December 26th. In odd-numbered years the visiting parent gets the child beginning at noon on December 26th and returns the child home at 6 P.M. on the day before school resumes after the vacation. *Holidays trump weekends if there is a conflict.*

Basic Concept 5. The visiting parent gets a thirty-day visit in the summer. But if the visiting parent resides more than 100 miles away, summer visitation is expanded to forty-two days. There are extensive rules about when the summer visit occurs and how the period can be altered by each parent giving notice by ceratin dates in the Spring.

Basic Concept 6. *If both parents agree, all of the foregoing rules can be disregarded*, and the times for visitations can be reshuffled any way the parents see fit.

Basic Concept 7. I have broken a major rule by using the terms "visiting parent" and "custodial parent." In Texas legal terminology, great effort is made to indicate that there is no "custodial parent" and no "visiting parent." Officially, these terms have been replaced with *Managing Conservator* and *Possessory Conservator*. But it's really hard to stay sane and discuss Texas custody law without occasionally using the terms "custody" and "visitation" unless you are a law professor or really good at chess.

The Right to Designate Residency – The Fundamental Custody Issue

The concept of the *Standard Possession Order* is premised on one parent having the right to designate the child's primary residence (custody). If one parent didn't have the right to designate the primary residence, why would the other parent need a *Standard Possession Order* to protect his or her right to have access to the child? Whether the parent with custody is called the "Managing Conservator," the "Primary Joint Managing Conservator," or is just the parent who is given the right to designate the child's primary residence, the result is the same. One parent has custody, and the other has visitation or "specific rights to access."

This is the very nature of the child custody beast. As is indicated by the story of King Solomon deciding a custody dispute, children cannot be divided in two. They cannot live in two places at once. Neither does it make much sense for a child to alternate days or weeks living at one parent's house for one period and then switching to the other's house for the next period.

I am merely trying to describe the system. I am not complaining about the concept that one parent has the right to designate the child's residency. Children cannot be split in two. I do not have a better idea. The Texas legislature has advanced light years in the past three decades of its attempt to abolish the winner-take-all approach to child custody. Replacing the term "all rights to custody and control over the child" with "right to designate the primary residency" is about as far as changing a single phrase can go in making the statement that the child has not lost either parent.

Compare and Contrast Time Division under a Standard Possession Order

Before you start a war over who will be granted custody of the child, it may make sense to examine the actual time that each parent has with the child under the Standard Possession Order. The typical *Standard Visitation Order* calendar, included on the next page, is designed to give you a graphic view of the time that each of the parents will have with the child under a Standard Possession Order in which the non-custodial parent elects the maximum extensions of the weekend and Thursday visits.

Agreements between Divorcing Parents Settle Most Cases

Fortunately, most parents are able to settle the question of who will have custody between themselves. Usually, one or the other of the parents was the primary caregiver and hands-on Mom or Mr. Mom before the divorce, and, therefore, it makes sense to have that person carry on that day-to-day role after the divorce. Sometimes there is a bond between a child and the parent of the same sex, so the two of them really

Standard Visitation Order calendar

Child Access Periods for a Typical Year*

JANUARY

				1	2	3
4	5	6	7	8	9	10
11	12	13	14	15	16	17
18	19	20	21	22	23	24
25	26	27	28	29	30	31

FEBRUARY

1	2	3	4	5	6	7
8	9	10	11	12	13	14
15	16	17	18	19	20	21
22	23	24	25	26	27	28
29						

MARCH

	1	2	3	4	5	6
7	8	9	10	11	12	13
14	15	16	17	18	19	20
21	22	23	24	25	26	27
28	29	30	31			

APRIL

				1	2	3
4	5	6	7	8	9	10
11	12	13	14	15	16	17
18	19	20	21	22	23	24
25	26	27	28	29	30	

MAY

						1
2	3	4	5	6	7	8
9	10	11	12	13	14	15
16	17	18	19	20	21	22
23	24	25	26	27	28	29
30	31					

JUNE

		1	2	3	4	5
6	7	8	9	10	11	12
13	14	15	16	17	18	19
20	21	22	23	24	25	26
27	28	29	30			

JULY

				1	2	3
4	5	6	7	8	9	10
11	12	13	14	15	16	17
18	19	20	21	22	23	24
25	26	27	28	29	30	31

AUGUST

1	2	3	4	5	6	7
8	9	10	11	12	13	14
15	16	17	18	19	20	21
22	23	24	25	26	27	28
29	30	31				

SEPTEMBER

			1	2	3	4
5	6	7	8	9	10	11
12	13	14	15	16	17	18
19	20	21	22	23	24	25
26	27	28	29	30		

OCTOBER

					1	2
3	4	5	6	7	8	9
10	11	12	13	14	15	16
17	18	19	20	21	22	23
24	25	26	27	28	29	30
31						

NOVEMBER

	1	2	3	4	5	6
7	8	9	10	11	12	13
14	15	16	17	18	19	20
21	22	23	24	25	26	27
28	29	30				

DECEMBER

			1	2	3	4
5	6	7	8	9	10	11
12	13	14	15	16	17	18
19	20	21	22	23	24	25
26	27	28	29	30	31	

*This calendar assumes that parents live within 100 miles of each other. This calendar also portrays access periods for an even-numbered year. In an odd-numbered year, the parent without the right to designate the child's primary residence would have access to the child during Thanksgiving Break rather than Spring Break, and during the last half of the Christmas Break rather than the first. Summer access may be affected by advance written notice from either parent.

It is important to note, when viewing this graphic depiction of access periods, that a disproportionate amount of the child's time with the parent who has the right to designate his or her primary residence is spent in school. Thus, in terms of actual hours spent in the parent's presence, the time is even more equally divided than it appears to be in this calendar.

prefer living with each other. Frequently, one of the parents has a work schedule that makes day-to-day care of a child difficult or impossible. Tragically, there is often no real choice because one of the parents is emotionally, mentally, or physically incapable of caring for the child. The reasons for agreement about who will be the primary custodian are limitless. But, for whatever reason, the vast majority of divorcing parents work it out between themselves.

Two Divorced Parents Who Agree, Trump All of the Rules

Just in case you missed what was just said, let me repeat it. If you and your spouse agree about custody and possession of your child, then you can disregard all of the rules of child custody and all of the orders that are contained in your divorce decree about terms of possession. Buried somewhere in your divorce decree you will find words that say something to this effect: "the parties may have possession of the child at times mutually agreed to in advance by the parties...." This is the law in Texas. Both the legislature and courts of this State have made it clear that they have no interest in being involved in the decisions of parents who agree on how to raise their children. The custody laws and court system are to be used *only* when the parents don't agree.

So, you may ask, if everything can be solved by the parents just agreeing with each other, why all of the heavy artillery? Why all of these custody laws and pages and pages included in divorce decrees describing to the minute who has the right to possession of the child?

The short answer is "experience." The Texas "child custody system" is willing to grant you and your ex-spouse the absolute right to solve all of your problems by agreement. On the other hand, those responsible for resolving child custody disputes in this State have decided that they will not take it on faith that you and your ex-spouse will always be able to solve all of your problems by agreement. Decades of dealing with divorced parents has taught us that, often, the parents cannot agree about custody issues. Therefore, instead of waiting for the dispute to arise, the decision has been made to tell the parties in advance what the rules are, if they, as parents, do not agree about possession of and control over their child.

You should learn from this. Yes, you and your spouse may always be able to agree on everything so that all of this stuff about child custody never will make any difference. Ideally, this will be the case. *But you don't know this. You don't know for sure how your spouse will behave after you are divorced.* Before you tell your lawyer or the court that there is no need to worry about what the divorce decree will say, because you and your spouse will always be able to agree, think again. What if you are wrong? *You are betting the security, health, safety, and well-being of your child on what you think you know about the future.* If you are so good at predicting the future, why did your marriage fail? Why haven't you gotten rich from predicting the stock market? The lesson of history is that none of us can predict the future, and, therefore, we must learn from each other's experience. Get the rules in place, just in case.

Finally, there is an additional reason for having the rules set out ahead of time. Just knowing what the rules are often prevents disputes. Your ex-spouse may agree to be flexible about deciding the child's schedule from week-to-week, just because he or she knows that, if push comes to shove, you can insist on the rigid schedule set out by the court in the divorce decree. In other words, often, those who would otherwise jerk you around are willing to "work with you" when they know you have the power to fight back. Take my advice. Get it in writing, signed by a judge. Then, perhaps, you'll never need to use it; that's the goal.

Changing the Labels – "Transformation" by Terminology

The Texas legislature, beginning in the 1970s, has attempted to do away with the terms "custody" and "visitation." The legislature undertook this effort because it feared that these terms left the impression that a divorce automatically destroyed the children's relationship with one of the parents. Before that time, in all divorces, one parent was awarded "custody" of the children, and the other parent was left with only the right to "visit." The legislature correctly perceived that this system was not conducive to encouraging the continuation of the child's relationship with the "visiting" parent. It also created a "winner-takes-all" system of child custody.

The law was changed to label each divorcing parent as a "conservator." The person who had previously been the "custodian" of the children is now the "*Managing Conservator.*" The "visiting parent" is now referred to as the "*Possessory Conservator.*" This re-labeling was an attempt to discourage the "winner-take-all" mentality that pervades child custody issues in many divorces. Of course, it was also an attempt to emphasize the child's need to continue a relationship with *both* parents.

These were and are admirable goals. But, by and large, merely changing labels did not stop custody battles. And changing the labels did not keep one of the parents from being disenfranchised. To paraphrase a famous writer, "A rose is still a rose by any other name." In short, the labels changed, but the law did not. For many years the Texas statute on the subject read:

> "A parent who is appointed Managing Conservator of the child, retains all of the rights, privileges, duties, and powers of a parent, to the exclusion of the other parent...."

The same statute essentially awarded the Possessory Conservator the right to visit. As you might imagine, divorcing parents and the lawyers who represented them soon recognized that, although the labels had changed, not much else was different. Custody fights in Texas came to mean a fight over who was going to be the Managing Conservator.

The Texas legislature, with some success, has continued its efforts to rid the child custody system of its winner-take-all approach and to keep kids connected to both parents after divorce. The quoted language above is no longer the language used in the Texas statutes defining conservatorship. But, at least in the exceptional cases in which there is a Sole Managing Conservator, the current Texas law on the subject still contains the residual concept that, to some extent, one of the parents can still "win custody." A portion of the current statute reads:

> "Unless limited by court order, a parent appointed as *sole* managing conservator of a child has ...the following exclusive rights:
>
> (1) the right to designate the primary residence of the child...." (emphasis added)

The current Texas law also gives the Sole Managing Conservator exclusive rights to determine the child's medical treatment, legal actions, educational choices, and various other matters. Just reading this current law reveals why many divorcing couples still, to this day, battle over who will have the label Sole Managing Conservator. If you are a parent contemplating divorce, it also tells you why you must pay intense, detailed attention to this issue in your divorce. The right to decide where and with whom your child will live, where your child will go to school, and who will decide about your child's medical treatment is pretty much the lifeblood of the parent-child relationship.

The Texas Version of Joint Custody – Joint Managing Conservators

The Texas policy preference is to appoint both parents *Joint Managing Conservators*. This is not always possible, and even when the Joint Conservatorship is used, it still leaves many loose ends and complicated issues to be resolved.

A reasonable observer with no axe to grind (presumably having just flown in from the planet Mars!) might assume that the easy way to prevent child custody fights and to keep the child in contact with both parents would be simply to make both parents joint custodians. Such are the observations of first-time sailors eyeing a calm sea. The fair weather may be a sign of things to come, or it may be the calm just before the hurricane. Texas has been experimenting with joint custody for over twenty years. The lesson is: A *Joint Managing Conservatorship* can be a wonderful solution for everyone, or, with the wrong parties, it can make a bad situation worse. (To risk a Yogi Berra-ism: Two parents are better than one, except when they're not.)

When possible, joint custody is the solution of choice. If you are lucky enough to have a spouse with the maturity to put your child's interest ahead of his or her self-interest, a *Joint Managing Conservatorship* is probably the best solution for you and your child. In this context, "maturity" must mean that your spouse (1) will not use your child as a means of getting back at you, and (2) is willing to assume his or her share of the day-to-day responsibility for care and nurture of the child.

Of course, these are big "ifs." If, on the other hand, your spouse does not fit this description, at best, a *Joint Managing Conservatorship* will just be a label that disguises the fact that you are your child's only parent. At worst, it will give your "immature" spouse another tool to use in interfering with your efforts to nurture and protect your child.

The first problem with the term "*Joint Managing Conservator*" is trying to decide what it means. The term itself carries a powerful message. It indicates, in a very positive way, that both parents are still equally connected to the child. But this implication can be misleading since the term "*Joint Managing Conservator*" itself does not describe either parent's specific rights to have control over or access to the child. Hence, the use of the joint custody terminology alone leads us right back to never-never land: Joint custody works well only in circumstances where both parents can agree or work out their differences without outside help. As was stated before, Texas courts are reluctant to grant a divorce based on the idealistic assumption that the parents will be able to solve their own problems. Divorce decrees must contain language that describes what will happen if the parties can't agree.

The central problem with any attempt to *force* the use of joint custody is that it begs the question: Who will have the right to determine the child's primary residence? As used by Texas courts over the past twenty years, the term "*Joint Managing Conservatorship*" is, in many respects, just a label. This is not to say that it is not an important concept or that it has not been helpful. But, in the final analysis, under *Joint Managing Conservatorship*, courts have usually awarded one parent ("the *Primary Joint Managing Conservator*") the right to designate the child's residence. The other *Joint Managing Conservator* is then awarded access to the child under a Standard Possession Order. Substantively, this is the exact result that would have been reached by naming one of the parties as *Managing Conservator* and the other *Possessory Conservator*. In essence, the *Possessory Conservator* becomes "*Joint Managing Conservator*" in name only.

As you can see, joint custody works well when: (1) there is no controversy between the divorced parents over the child's residence; (2) the parents are not too geographically separated; (3) both parents are willing to work together; and (4) both are authentically and legitimately involved in child rearing. Actually, there are many divorced families that fit into this category.

Joint Managing Conservatorship – What It's Not

Having both parents appointed as *Joint Managing Conservators* does not require the court to award each parent equal or nearly equal periods of physical possession and access to the child.

Being appointed as *Joint Managing Conservator* is not a way to escape paying child support. The court still has the absolute right to have one *Joint Managing Conservator* pay child support to the other *Joint Managing Conservator.* Child support will usually be paid to the parent who has the right to designate the primary residence of the child.

The Continued Decline of the Winner-Take-All Approach to Child Custody

In fairness, the Texas legislature has made great progress both in reducing the winner-take-all approach to child custody issues and in strengthening the child's connection to both parents after the divorce. To do this, the legislature has developed four tools:

- The Standard Possession Order
- Limitations on changing the child's primary residence
- The explicit sharing of various rights of parents
- The Joint Managing Conservatorship
- The enforcement of access.

These items are discussed throughout this chapter and play a central role in Texas child custody. It can be reasonably argued that Texas has succeeded in its effort to equalize child custody to the point that it is no longer accurate to speak in terms of the "non-custodial parent" or the "visiting parent." Some have argued that the more accurate term would now be "lesser-custodial parent." I'll leave such refined distinctions to you as you read on and consider your own circumstances.

The Standard Possession Order – Why It Was Developed

The *Standard Possession Order* is probably the best single defensive tool ever developed for the "visiting parent" or Possessory Conservator. It can also be great comfort and assistance to the "custodial parent" or Managing Conservator. Before its development and use, most divorce decrees contained only language stating that the Possessory Conservator was entitled to "reasonable visitation." This worked well only in those cases in which the divorced parties got along and could be reasonable with each other. In other words, it worked well only in the cases in which it was not needed at all, since it provided no identifiable time when the non-custodial parent had a right to possession of the child.

In the cases where one or both of the divorce parties were crazy, belligerent, or unreasonable, a divorce decree that stated that the visiting parent was to have "reasonable visitation" didn't work at all. In the context of two angry parents fighting over visitation, the term "reasonable visitation" was meaningless. Therefore, in these chronically difficult cases, where the fighting continued after the divorce, the parties had to return to court and ask the judge just what "reasonable visitation" meant. The judge would then issue a new order describing, in detail, which party would have the child. The order usually included specific times for the pickup and return of the child. In short, after the divorce was supposedly concluded, there was a second trial over the custody of the child. This not only took a lot of court time, but it was also frustrating for the party who already had the vacation planned or thought he or she had an agreement with the former spouse about how the Christmas holiday was to be handled.

The *Standard Possession Order* changed all of this. Now, virtually all Texas divorce decrees contain explicit language describing the rights of the parties in the event of a disagreement about what is or is not reasonable possession of the children. It is this explicit language included in the divorce decree that is referred to as "*The Standard Possession Order.*" Therefore, as long as they can agree, the divorced couple can decide the questions of who is to have the children and when and where possession will take place. When they can't agree, the feuding former lovers can whip out the divorce decree and read exactly what the judge has ordered concerning who has the kids and the times, dates, and places that the hostages (children) are to be exchanged.

Why the Standard Possession Order Is "Standard"

Finally, to understand the nature of the child custody process, we must examine why the Standard Possession Order is *standard.* That is, the exact same order is being used in virtually every divorce decree across the State of Texas. This may seem strange to you, since you, of course, have experienced your life and your children as the special, unique, mysterious, one-of-a-kind creation of the Almighty. Having experienced all of this uniqueness reserved only for us Americans, born as we are under a special ray of light, you may be tempted to rebel against this cookie-cutter, one-size-fits-all disposition of your custody problems. In fact, you may have compelling reasons for such resistance, but, before you begin acting out your rebellion, you need to understand this problem from the point of view of those who have responsibility for the day-to-day operations of the courts.

A more flexible approach to specific visitation has actually been tried. In about 1983, when everybody was fed up with the vagaries of "reasonable visitation," courts were, for the first time, required to include specific terms of visitation in divorce decrees. However, each individual judge could fashion his or her own specific terms of visitation. Now, as you may imagine, if you were a judge faced with hundreds or, perhaps even thousands of divorce cases, the prospect of trying to fashion tailor-made custody orders for each case could be quite daunting. There are just not that many King Solomon types available to decide these cases. So, what happened? The vast majority of judges used their own standard orders, not unlike today's *Standard Possession Order.* A minority of judges used abbreviated orders that short-changed the non-custodial parent. This experience led to the development of today's *Standard Possession Order.* It was thought, and probably correctly so, that the uniformity and predictability of a statewide system outweighed the supposed benefits of leaving the decision to each judge. Viewed from the position of those who are trying to make the system work, it makes very good sense. Viewed from the point of view of one whom the standard order does not fit, it causes headaches.

Problems with the Standard Possession Order

The *Standard Possession Order* does not solve all problems. Although mandating a minimum level of contact between the child and the visiting parent is a positive influence in most cases, like most human creations, this "standard" approach, when misused, can have undesirable and unintended consequences.

The first problem with the Standard Possession Order is just that. It is *standard.* This is its greatest strength. It sets a minimum standard for keeping parents and children together; in essence, it uses a formula to keep children from being separated from their parents. The fact that it is a formula is also its greatest weakness. Cookie-cutter solutions do not always work for human beings and human circumstances. Efforts to force all problems through an overly simplistic one-size-fits-all system are not only dehumanizing, they have great potential for making the original problem worse.

Let us be clear here. We are not talking about a defect in the "law" that created the *Standard Possession Order.* The law gives the court ample authority to change the terms of the standard possession, if there are legitimate reasons for doing so.

The problem with the use of the *Standard Possession Order* arises from human nature. Because it is presumed to be the correct answer, and especially because it really does work so well in the vast majority of cases, it becomes the knee-jerk, easy-answer, "perfect solution" in *every* case, even in the cases where it probably should not be used. Beginning assumptions have a way of becoming self-fulfilling prophecies, and those trying to resist this standard approach to custody may find themselves swimming up stream.

An easy example of a situation in which a parent should not receive standard and usual contact with his or her child is the child abuse case. Of course, courts will quickly agree to limit access when the parent has physically or sexually abused a child, but the real problem arises when the abuse is more subtle. I suspect that the vast majority of child abuse is psychological or emotional rather than physical, but the evidence of emotional abuse is not as dramatic and requires a great deal more effort and insight to understand. Hence, the path of least resistence for the court is often to ignore the evidence of subtle abuse and simply follow the normal habit of granting standard access. This judicial inclination can lead to costly litigation requiring the use of paid experts.

I'm not saying that courts ignore all problems and uniformly grant all parents standard access to their children. A few trips to busy courtrooms around Texas would reveal that this is not true. It is easy to find cases in which judges limit or totally restrict a parent's access to a child. What I am saying is that, if you have a situation that the *Standard Possession Order* does not fit, but neither is there the standard child abuse, family violence, or other overt and obvious abuse, then you must be extremely aware that you are likely to be swept along with the "business-as-usual" nature of the court system, unless you take strong action to demonstrate that subtle abuse is occurring. This is not easy.

Modifications to the Standard Possession Order

Courts are usually willing to modify the *Standard Possession Order* to fit particular circumstances. Often, the other spouse will agree that the *Standard Possession Order* needs to be modified because of non-standard circumstances. If you are a fireman, a policeman, emergency room nurse, or anyone else who works odd hours, it is likely that, if your spouse will not agree, the court will be willing to make reasonable modifications to the standard order to fit your schedule more realistically. Virtually every lawyer who does divorce law in Texas will be able to provide patterns that are used for parents who have unusual work schedules. This doesn't mean that the established pattern orders will fit your situation, but looking at them might stimulate your thinking.

The Child under Three – An Exception to the Standard Possession Order

The *Standard Possession Order* does not apply to children under three. The legislature has left this issue in the hands of individual judges. The access given non-custodial parents varies widely across the state and sometimes from one courtroom to another in the same courthouse. Some judges give the "visiting" parent very little access to the young child, whereas others go ahead and apply the terms of the Standard Possession Order or something very close to it.

Among psychologists, social workers, and other child development experts, this limitation on visitation with the child under three is hugely controversial. Of course, it's usually the father who is in the non-custodial position with very young children. Those on both sides of the argument have ample material. Fathers, as you may have guessed, range from teenagers with no clue about how to care for a child and perhaps little desire to learn, to other men who often have as much or more experience caring for young children as do the mothers who just gave birth. Here again, we are fighting the stereotype. As with all generalizations, it contains a core of truth that can be absolutely wrong in a specific case. If you find yourself on the wrong side of the stereotype, find out if you are before an open-minded judge and, if not, prepare for an uphill battle.

Where the Child Will Live – Geographical Limitations

In many custody cases, the question of who will control the geographic location of the child's residence is by far the most important question to be resolved. As many parents who have been left behind can tell you, more attention should be paid to the question of who will control the child's domicile. More recently, parents who want to move but cannot do so without leaving their children behind have discovered this critical issue.

For many years, the parent who was appointed *Managing Conservator* could take the children and move to Montana without getting the consent of the parent who was the *Possessory Conservator*. As you might imagine, it was shocking and painful to discover that your children had been moved out of town. It quickly became apparent to the visiting parents who experienced such moves that court orders regarding access and visitation, without control over where the children would live, were nothing but cruel hoaxes. The right to visit on weekends is pretty meaningless if your child is living in New England and you live and work in Houston.

Now Texas has addressed this problem. Although divorce decrees almost always give one parent the right to establish the child's primary residence, the court has the power to include a provision that limits the movement of the child's primary residence to a particular geographic area, even including, perhaps, a subdivision. Typically, the parent designating the primary residence will be limited to a particular county, or in metropolitan areas that cover multiple counties, the child's residence may be limited to the counties that make up the metropolitan area. For example, in the Dallas area, a divorce decree may provide that a *Managing Conservator* may establish the child's primary residence anywhere in Dallas, Collin, or Tarrant Counties.

Courts are given discretion either to include or not include geographic limitations on the child's primary residence. Because it is discretionary, customs vary from one part of the state to another and from one judge to another as to whether such limitation will be included in the typical divorce decree. Typically, in the large metropolitan areas, unless strong reasons are provided or the parties agree otherwise, geographical limitations will almost automatically be required in most divorce decrees. In many rural areas, the opposite is true. Unless one of the parties is extremely persuasive about the need for geographical limitations, the typical divorce decree in these areas will not contain such limitations.

As you might imagine, in many divorces, the primary contested issue is whether there will be geographical limits on the child's primary residences, and if so, what those limitations will be. You can see why. The very essence of parenting is the day-to-day contact with the child. Contact with a child over long distances is a matter of both physics and economics. If the child and parent are separated by great distances, it takes an enormous amount of time and money for them to be together. Likewise, in the mobile world that is the reality in most of our lives, parents can have compelling reasons to relocate for vocational or educational reasons, not to mention emotional, financial, and logistical support from an extended family. Then, of course, there's the remarriage issue that occurs when the spouse who has the right to establish the child's primary residence becomes connected to someone who lives somewhere else. Finally, we cannot completely discount those cases in which a primary custodian desires to move the child somewhere else to get away from his or her former spouse or to punish a former spouse by taking the child away.

If your divorce is one in which you and your spouse have strong connections and commitments to the same place, then the issue of who will have the right to establish the child's primary residence probably won't be much of a problem. In all likelihood the two of you will not only agree to have the child's residency limited to one area, you will also probably both live a short distance from each other. If you are both good parents and determined not to use the child in your dispute with each other, your geographical proximity will allow your child the full experience of having two parents.

If, on the other hand, you and your soon-to-be-ex have strong desires or imperatives to be in different and distant places, your child has a very different experience in store. Like it or not, the physical distance alone, and probably the economics, means that the child is going to be separated from one of you. This fact alone changes the divorce experience for all concerned—the child and both of the parents. Between parents who are mature and can agree, it leads to much soul-searching and painful decisions about what is going to be sacrificed and who will make those sacrifices. Between parents who cannot agree, or who are perhaps caught on an absolute collision course, this struggle over geography almost certainly leads to a contested fight over this issue.

The Dark Side of Geographic Limitation on the Child's Residency

It is admirable that Texas is now attempting to protect the child's geographic proximity to both parents, but make no mistake, this is not an easy issue of bad-parent-takes-child-and-leaves-good-parent-behind. The concept of geographic limitations on the child's primary residence has great potential for misuse. It can be a wonderful weapon for the parent whose primary interest is in obstructing the other parent's efforts to care for and raise the child.

For example, a divorced parent whose primary objective is to use the child to make his or her ex's life miserable, will see the ex's need to relocate as the opportunity of a lifetime. The fact that the child's other parent is trying to "take his or her child away" can be fodder for the propaganda campaign against the other parent and the authority that parent needs for control and care of the child. The "real parent," the one providing emotional support and taking all of the responsibility for the day-to-day care of the child, frequently has a compelling reason to relocate. This may be a better paying job, an opportunity to continue education, or to be closer to extended family members who can actually share the burden of child nurturing and care. In short, being a single parent with all of the real responsibility for the child's well-being is an overwhelming responsibility. Having a "co-parent" who uses his or her "rights" as a means to interfere with child rearing, adds immeasurably to the burden of single parenting. Handing the stealthily destructive parent the right to veto the real parent's opportunity to move the child to better conditions can be devastating. In those circumstances, we can only hope for judges and juries with the wisdom to "see" what is really going on.

Please be clear about this. As I lament the misuse of the geographical limitation by misguided or malicious non-custodial parents, I am not advocating a change in this law. Malicious parents also come in the variety of those who have been given the right to designate the child's primary residence and would, if allowed, move the child completely across the country for no other reason than to deprive their ex-spouses of contact with their child. This issue is right where it needs to be—in the courthouse where everyone can be heard on the subject.

"Move" Is a Four-Letter Word

As we have established, we live in a society obsessed with the notion that children are ruined by divorce. Everyone is aware that divorce hurts children. What is often overlooked is that a parent moving to another city or children moving away from one of their parents often has a bigger impact on the children than does the divorce. After the divorce, parents who live nearby each other can attend school functions, pick the kids up from school, take turns attending Little League, or help with homework. A move to a different city changes all of this, and individual parents, as well as the community as a whole, need a raised level of consciousness on the impact moving has on children of divorce. Having a parent move or moving away from a parent can be the biggest single event in childhood.

When you married your spouse, you didn't think about marrying a geographical area. But when you had children together, you definitely created a geographical link to each other. Unlike some self-appointed authorities on the subject, I don't have any simple, easy answers. Sometimes it's either move and make a good living or stay and work for minimum wage or, perhaps, even be unemployed. I am not one to say that you and your children should do without money. Poverty certainly does not help with child rearing. Dozens of other factors, including remarriage, housing, extended family, health considerations, educational opportunities, and age of the children, just to name a few, can play a huge and legitimate role in a parent's decision to move or stay put. Whether you're the "mover" or the one being left behind, this issue deserves a lot more thought than it usually gets.

If You Move after the Divorce, You Might Have to Pay Extra

The Texas legislature has weighed in on divorced parents moving and thereby affecting access to the children. If a parent changes residence and that change results in increased expense for one of the parents, the court may "allocate those increased expenses on a fair and equitable basis, taking into account the cause of the increased expenses and the best interest of the child." This statute goes on to say that payment of the increased expenses by the one whose residence is moved, "is rebuttably presumed to be in the best interest of the child."

So what does this mean, besides the fact that the legislature is apparently really interested in who is moving when a child is involved. I suspect that it doesn't mean much if you're moving up the street or maybe even across town. It might mean a lot if you're thinking of making a move across the state. It might also make a difference if you are moving because you must, rather than just to get even with your ex.

Child Custody – Items That Have Been Removed from the War Zone

There was a time in Texas when a lawyer would receive a call from some poor soul who simply wanted to see his child's report card or talk to a teacher, but was not allowed to do so because the other parent had been "awarded custody." And, of course, by having been awarded "custody," the parent knew that she was, somehow, Queen of the Nile, and her spouse, who positively had not been awarded "custody," was to spend the remainder of his days in perdition and should never be favored with the sacred information contained on his kid's report card. Nor was he to receive any of the child's medical or educational information of any kind, and sometimes he was not even to receive knowledge of the child's whereabouts. Such was the application in those days of Lord Acton's famous statement that, "Power tends to corrupt and absolute power tends to corrupt absolutely."

Of course, even in those unenlightened times, everybody, including the Queen of the Nile, knew that this was unmitigated poppycock. Usually, the poor soul's lawyer would call the Queen of the Nile's lawyer to suggest that not even the Queen would fare well in the courthouse on such a ridiculous issue. After an appropriate period of begging, the poor soul would at least get to see the kid's report card. Then he would get tired of fighting over such issues. When you have to fight the Queen on this level for everything, most people don't have the resources to stay in the poker game.

Then one bright shining glorious day in Austin (I don't know exactly when), the Texas legislature decided to shut down this portion of the game. No longer could parents fight over who had a right to the report card, the doctor's report, the dental records, and so forth, because, in Texas, it was written on the wall in bold print that, barring very special circumstance, both parents would always have a right to this kind of information. Let me repeat, *no matter who wins the right to designate the primary residence, both parents get this information*. If a spouse attempts to deprive the child's other parent of this information, it is likely that he or she will be punished.

Both parents have the right:

- To information concerning the child's health, education, and welfare
- Of access to the child's medical, dental, psychological, and educational records
- To consult with the child's physician, dentist, or psychologist
- To consult with school officials concerning the child's welfare and educational status, including school activities
- To be designated on the child's records as a person to be notified in case of an emergency
- To consent to medical, dental, and surgical treatment during an emergency involving an immediate danger to the health and safety of the child
- To manage the estate of the child to the extent the estate has been created by the parent or the parent's family

These rights of each parent will be included in the divorce decree. Moreover, the divorce decree will include an order that each of the parents provide this kind of information to the other parent.

Unlike those days of yesteryear when information about the child could be used as just another way to jerk the non-custodial parent around, today any parent playing this game of hide-the-ball on the child's information could easily find himself or herself in contempt of court.

So, if you're thinking of allowing your spouse to have the day-to-day care of your child, you don't have to worry about being cut off from any part of the child's school life, medical care, or any other aspect of the child's life that has to do with his or her welfare. If, on the other hand, you will be the one with day-to-day access to these matters, you will need to make this information available to your spouse.

If you believe that sharing this kind of information with your spouse creates a danger for your child, it can be restricted, but you will need some very good reasons.

Standard Possession Order

The Court finds that the following provisions of this Standard Possession Order are intended to and do comply with the requirements of Texas Family Code sections 153.311 through 153.317. *It is ordered* that each conservator shall comply with all terms and conditions of this Standard Possession Order. *It is ordered* that this Standard Possession Order is effective immediately and applies to all periods of possession occurring on and after the date the Court signs this Standard Possession Order. *It is, therefore, ordered*:

(a) **Definitions**

1. In this Standard Possession Order "school" means the primary or secondary school in which the child is enrolled or, if the child is not enrolled in a primary or secondary school, the public school district in which the child primarily resides.

2. In this Standard Possession Order "child" includes each child, whether one or more, who is a subject of this suit while that child is under the age of eighteen years and not otherwise emancipated.

(b) **Mutual Agreement or Specified Terms for Possession**

It is ordered that the conservators shall have possession of the child at times mutually agreed to in advance by the parties, and, in the absence of mutual agreement, it is *ordered* that the conservators shall have possession of the child under the specified terms set out in this Standard Possession Order.

(c) **Parents Who Reside 100 Miles or Less Apart**

Except as otherwise explicitly provided in this Standard Possession Order, when Possessory Conservator resides 100 miles or less from the primary residence of the child, Possessory Conservator shall have the right to possession of the child as follows:

1. Weekends—On weekends, beginning at the time the child's school is regularly dismissed, on the first, third, and fifth Friday of each month and ending at the time the child's school resumes after the weekend.

2. Weekend Possession Extended by a Holiday—Except as otherwise explicitly provided in this Standard Possession Order, if a weekend period of possession by Possessory Conservator begins on a Friday that is a school holiday during the regular school term or a federal, state, or local holiday during the summer months when school is not in session, or if the period ends on or is immediately followed by a Monday that is such a holiday, that weekend period of possession shall begin at the time the child's school is regularly dismissed on the Thursday immediately preceding the Friday holiday or school holiday or end after a Monday holiday at the time school resumes after that school holiday, as applicable.

3. Thursdays—On Thursday of each week during the regular school term, beginning at the time the child's school is regularly dismissed and ending at the time the child's school resumes on Friday.

4. Spring Break in Even-Numbered Years—In even-numbered years, beginning at the time the child's school is regularly dismissed on the day the child is dismissed from school for the school's spring vacation and ending at the time school resumes after that vacation.

5. Extended Summer Possession by Possessory Conservator—

With Written Notice by April 1—If Possessory Conservator gives Sole Managing Conservator written notice by April 1 of a year specifying an extended period or periods of summer possession for that year, Possessory Conservator shall have possession of the child for thirty days beginning no earlier than the day after the child's school is dismissed for the summer vacation and ending no later than seven days before school resumes at the end of the summer vacation in that year, to be exercised in no more than two separate periods of at least seven consecutive days each, as specified in the written notice [include if applicable: , provided that the period or periods of extended summer possession do not interfere with Father's Day Weekend]. These periods of possession shall begin and end at 6:00 P.M.

Without Written Notice by April 1—If Possessory Conservator does not give Sole Managing Conservator written notice by April 1 of a year specifying an extended period or periods of summer possession for that year, Possessory Conservator shall have possession of the child for thirty consecutive days in that year beginning at 6:00 P.M. on July 1 and ending at 6:00 P.M. on July 31.

Notwithstanding the weekend and Thursday periods of possession *ordered* for Possessory Conservator, it is explicitly *ordered* that Sole Managing Conservator shall have a superior right of possession of the child as follows:

1. Spring Break in Odd-Numbered Years—In odd-numbered years, beginning at 6:00 P.M. on the day the child is dismissed from school for the school's spring vacation and ending at 6:00 P.M. on the day before school resumes after that vacation.

2. Summer Weekend Possession by Sole Managing Conservator—If Sole Managing Conservator gives Possessory Conservator written notice by April 15 of a year, Sole Managing Conservator shall have possession of the child on any one weekend beginning at 6:00 P.M. on Friday and ending at 6:00 P.M. on the following Sunday during any one period of the extended summer possession by Possessory Conservator in that year, provided that Sole Managing Conservator picks up the child from Possessory Conservator and returns the child to that same place [include if applicable: and that the weekend so designated does not interfere with Father's Day Weekend].

3. Extended Summer Possession by Sole Managing Conservator—If Sole Managing Conservator gives Possessory Conservator written notice by April 15 of a year or gives Possessory Conservator fourteen days' written notice on or after April 16 of a year, Sole Managing Conservator may designate one weekend beginning no earlier than the day after the child's school is dismissed for the summer vacation and ending no later than seven days before school resumes at the end of the summer vacation, during which an otherwise scheduled weekend period of possession by Possessory Conservator shall not take place in that year, provided that the weekend so designated does not interfere with Possessory Conservator's period or periods of extended summer possession [include if applicable: or with Father's Day Weekend].

(d) Parents Who Reside More Than 100 Miles Apart

Except as otherwise explicitly provided in this Standard Possession Order, when Possessory Conservator resides more than 100 miles from the residence of the child, Possessory Conservator shall have the right to possession of the child as follows:

1. Weekends—Unless Possessory Conservator elects the alternative period of weekend possession described in the next paragraph, Possessory Conservator shall have the right to possession of the child on weekends, beginning at the time the child's school is regularly dismissed, on the first, third, and fifth Friday of each month and ending at the time the child's school resumes after the weekend. Except as otherwise explicitly provided in this Standard Possession Order, if such a weekend period of possession by Possessory Conservator begins on a Friday that is a school holiday during the regular school term or a federal, state, or local holiday during the summer months when school is not in session, or if the period ends on or is immediately followed by a Monday that is such a holiday, that weekend period of possession shall begin at the time the child's school is regularly dismissed on the Thursday immediately preceding the Friday holiday or school holiday or end after a Monday holiday or school holiday at the time school regularly resumes after that school holiday, as applicable.

Alternate Weekend Possession—In lieu of the weekend possession described in the foregoing paragraph, Possessory Conservator shall have the right to possession of the child not more than one weekend per month of Possessory Conservator's choice beginning at the time the child's school is regularly dismissed on the day

CHILDREN IN DIVORCE

school recesses for the weekend and ending at the time the child's school resumes after the weekend. Except as otherwise explicitly provided in this Standard Possession Order, if such a weekend period of possession by Possessory Conservator begins on a Friday that is a school holiday during the regular school term or a federal, state, or local holiday during the summer months when school is not in session, or if the period ends on or is immediately followed by a Monday that is such a holiday, that weekend period of possession shall begin at the time the child's school is regularly dismissed on the Thursday immediately preceding the Friday holiday or school holiday or end at the time school resumes after that school holiday, as applicable. Possessory Conservator may elect an option for this alternative period of weekend possession by giving written notice to Sole Managing Conservator within ninety days after the parties begin to reside more than 100 miles apart. If Possessory Conservator makes this election, Possessory Conservator shall give Managing Conservator fourteen days' written or telephonic notice preceding a designated weekend. The weekends chosen shall not conflict with the provisions regarding Christmas, Thanksgiving, the child's birthday, and [Father's/Mother's] Day Weekend below.

1. Weekends—On weekends, beginning at the time the child's school is regularly dismissed on the first, third, and fifth Friday of each month, and ending at the time the child's school resumes after the weekend. Except as otherwise explicitly provided in this Standard Possession Order, if a weekend period of possession by Possessory Conservator begins on a Friday that is a school holiday during the regular school term or a federal, state, or local holiday during the summer months when school is not in session, or if the period ends on or is immediately followed by a Monday that is such a holiday, that weekend period of possession shall begin at the time the child's school is regularly dismissed on the Thursday immediately preceding the Friday holiday or school holiday or end at the time school resumes after that school holiday, as applicable.

1. Weekend—One weekend per month, of Possessory Conservator's choice, beginning at the time the child's school is regularly dismissed on the day school recesses for the weekend and ending at the time the child's school resumes after the weekend, provided that Possessory Conservator gives Sole Managing Conservator fourteen days' written or telephonic notice preceding a designated weekend. The weekends chosen shall not conflict with the provisions regarding Christmas, Thanksgiving, the child's birthday, and [Father's/Mother's] Day Weekend below.

2. Spring Break in All Years—Every year, beginning at the time the child's school is regularly dismissed on the day the child is dismissed from school for the school's spring vacation and ending at the time school resumes after that vacation.

3. Extended Summer Possession by Possessory Conservator

With Written Notice by April 1—If Possessory Conservator gives Sole Managing Conservator written notice by April 1 of a year specifying an extended period or periods of summer possession for that year, Possessory Conservator shall have possession of the child for forty-two days beginning no earlier than the day after the child's school is dismissed for the summer vacation and ending no later than seven days before school resumes at the end of the summer vacation in that year, to be exercised in no more than two separate periods of at least seven consecutive days each, as specified in the written notice [include if applicable: , provided that the period or periods of extended summer possession do not interfere with Father's Day Weekend]. These periods of possession shall begin and end at 6:00 P.M.

Without Written Notice by April 1—If Possessory Conservator does not give Sole Managing Conservator written notice by April 1 of a year specifying an extended period or periods of summer possession for that year, Possessory Conservator shall have possession of the child for forty-two consecutive days beginning at 6:00 P.M. on June 15 and ending at 6:00 P.M. on July 27 of that year.

Notwithstanding the weekend periods of possession *ordered* for Possessory Conservator, it is explicitly *ordered* that Sole Managing Conservator shall have a superior right of possession of the child as follows:

1. Summer Weekend Possession by Sole Managing Conservator—If Sole Managing Conservator gives Possessory Conservator written notice by April 15 of a year, Sole Managing Conservator shall have possession of the child on any one weekend beginning at 6:00 P.M. on Friday and ending at 6:00 P.M. on the following Sunday during any one period of possession by Possessory Conservator during Possessory Conservator's extended summer possession in that year, provided that if a period of possession by Possessory Conservator in that year exceeds thirty days, Sole Managing Conservator may have possession of the child under the terms of this provision on any two non-consecutive weekends during that period and provided that Sole Managing Conservator picks up the child from Possessory Conservator and returns the child to that same place [include if applicable: and that the weekend so designated does not interfere with Father's Day Weekend].

2. Extended Summer Possession by Sole Managing Conservator—If Sole Managing Conservator gives Possessory Conservator written notice by April 15 of a year, Sole Managing Conservator may designate twenty-one days beginning no earlier than the day after the child's school is dismissed for the summer vacation and ending no later than seven days before school resumes at the end of the summer vacation in that year, to be exercised in no more than two separate periods of at least seven consecutive days each, during which Possessory Conservator shall not have possession of the child, provided that the period or periods so designated do not interfere with Possessory Conservator's period or periods of extended summer possession [include if applicable: or with Father's Day Weekend].

(e) **Holidays Unaffected by Distance**

Notwithstanding the weekend and Wednesday periods of possession of Possessory Conservator, Sole Managing Conservator and Possessory Conservator shall have the right to possession of the child as follows:

1. Christmas Holidays in Even-Numbered Years—In even-numbered years, Possessory Conservator shall have the right to possession of the child beginning at the time the child's school is regularly dismissed on the day the child is dismissed from school for the Christmas school vacation and ending at noon on December 26, and Sole Managing Conservator shall have the right to possession of the child beginning at noon on December 26 and ending at 6:00 P.M. on the day before school resumes after that Christmas school vacation.

2. Christmas Holidays in Odd-Numbered Years—In odd-numbered years, Sole Managing Conservator shall have the right to possession of the child beginning at 6:00 P.M. on the day the child is dismissed from school for the Christmas school vacation and ending at noon on December 26, and Possessory Conservator shall have the right to possession of the child beginning at noon on December 26 and ending at the time the child's school resumes after that Christmas school vacation.

3. Thanksgiving in Odd-Numbered Years—In odd-numbered years, Possessory Conservator shall have the right to possession of the child beginning at the time the child's school is regularly dismissed on the day the child is dismissed from school for the Thanksgiving holiday and ending at the time the child's school resumes after that Thanksgiving holiday.

4. Thanksgiving in Even-Numbered Years—In even-numbered years, Sole Managing Conservator shall have the right to possession of the child beginning at 6:00 P.M. on the day the child is dismissed from school for the Thanksgiving holiday and ending at 6:00 P.M. on the Sunday following Thanksgiving.

5. Child's Birthday—If a conservator is not otherwise entitled under this Standard Possession Order to present possession of a child on the child's birthday, that conservator shall have possession of the child and the child's siblings beginning at 6:00 P.M. and ending at 8:00 P.M. on that day, provided that conservator picks up the children from the other conservator's residence and returns the children to that same place.

6. Father's Day Weekend—Father shall have the right to possession of the child each year, beginning at 6:00 P.M. on the Friday preceding Father's Day and ending at 6:00 P.M. on Father's Day, provided that if Father is not otherwise

entitled under this Standard Possession Order to present possession of the child, he shall pick up the child from the other conservator's residence and return the child to that same place.

7. Mother's Day Weekend—Mother shall have the right to possession of the child each year, beginning at 6:00 P.M. on the Friday preceding Mother's Day and ending at 6:00 P.M. on Mother's Day, provided that if Mother is not otherwise entitled under this Standard Possession Order to present possession of the child, she shall pick up the child from the other conservator's residence and return the child to that same place.

(f) Undesignated Periods of Possession

Sole Managing Conservator shall have the right of possession of the child at all other times not specifically designated in this Standard Possession Order for Possessory Conservator.

(g) General Terms and Conditions

Except as otherwise explicitly provided in this Standard Possession Order, the terms and conditions of possession of the child that apply regardless of the distance between the residence of a parent and the child are as follows:

1. Surrender of Child by Sole Managing Conservator—Sole Managing Conservator is *ordered* to surrender the child to Possessory Conservator at the beginning of each period of Possessory Conservator's possession at the residence of Sole Managing Conservator.

If a period of possession by Possessory Conservator begins at the time the child's school is regularly dismissed, Sole Managing Conservator is *ordered* to surrender the child to Possessory Conservator at the beginning of each such period of possession at the school in which the child is enrolled. If the child is not in school, Possessory Conservator shall pick up the child at the residence of Sole Managing Conservator at [time], and Sole Managing Conservator is *ordered* to surrender the child to Possessory Conservator at the residence of Sole Managing Conservator at [time] under these circumstances.

2. Surrender of Child by Possessory Conservator—Possessory Conservator is *ordered* to surrender the child to Sole Managing Conservator at the residence of Possessory Conservator at the end of each period of possession.

3. Return of Child by Possessory Conservator—Possessory Conservator is *ordered* to return the child to the residence of Sole Managing Conservator at the end of each period of possession. However, it is *ordered* that, if Sole Managing Conservator and Possessory Conservator live in the same county at the time of rendition of this order, Possessory Conservator's county of residence remains the same after rendition of this order, and Sole Managing Conservator's county of residence changes, effective on the date of the change of residence by Sole Managing Conservator, Possessory Conservator shall surrender the child to Sole Managing Conservator at the residence of Possessory Conservator at the end of each period of possession.

If a period of possession by Possessory Conservator ends at the time the child's school resumes, Possessory Conservator is *ordered* to surrender the child to Sole Managing Conservator at the end of each such period of possession at the school in which the child is enrolled or, if the child is not in school, at the residence of Sole Managing Conservator at the time school would normally resume.

4. Surrender of Child by Possessory Conservator—Possessory Conservator is *ordered* to surrender the child to Sole Managing Conservator, if the child is in Possessory Conservator's possession or subject to Possessory Conservator's control, at the beginning of each period of Sole Managing Conservator's exclusive periods of possession, at the place designated in this Standard Possession Order.

5. Return of Child by Sole Managing Conservator—Sole Managing Conservator is *ordered* to return the child to Possessory Conservator, if Possessory Conservator is entitled to possession of the child, at the end of each of Sole Managing Conservator's exclusive periods of possession, at the place designated in this Standard Possession Order.

6. Personal Effects—Each conservator is *ordered* to return with the child the personal effects that the child brought at the beginning of the period of possession.

7. Designation of Competent Adult—Each conservator may designate any competent adult

to pick up and return the child, as applicable. *It is ordered* that a conservator or a designated competent adult be present when the child is picked up or returned.

8. Inability to Exercise Possession—Each conservator is *ordered* to give notice to the person in possession of the child on each occasion that the conservator will be unable to exercise that conservator's right of possession for any specified period.

9. Written Notice—Written notice shall be deemed to have been timely made if received or postmarked before or at the time that notice is due.

10. Notice to School and Sole Managing Conservator—If Possessory Conservator's time of possession of the child ends at the time school resumes and for any reason the child is not or will not be returned to school, Possessory Conservator shall immediately notify the school and Sole Managing Conservator that the child will not be or has not been returned to school.

This concludes the Standard Possession Order.

Chapter 20

Enforcement: Your Decisions at Divorce Determine Which Rules Will Be Enforced For and Against You

Do not mistake a child for his symptom.

—Erik Erikson

A divorcing parent sometimes thinks it unnecessary to pay much attention to the details of custody arrangements. Right now, during the divorce, it doesn't seem to be much of a problem. Either I'm too busy to worry much about the children who are living with my spouse, or the opposite is true: My spouse never comes around, so I can't imagine it's going to be a problem. Or my spouse has always treated me fairly with regard to the child. Or, perhaps, my spouse is causing so many problems with the divorce that I'm just willing to overlook problems with the child custody provisions. For whatever reason, the attitude is: "*Whatever custody order gets entered will have to be all right; I'll deal with it later.*"

Big, big, big mistake! If you choose to ignore what child custody orders are being entered in your divorce, please mark this page so that you can find the place where "I told you so." Unless you are extremely lucky, you will live to regret it.

Here's why. Courts enforce all of their orders, even the unfair ones, the ridiculous ones, and the ones that don't fit. Courts don't care whether you showed up during the divorce when the order was being entered. And just because you didn't show up to explain why the order was ridiculous at the time of the divorce does not mean that the Court will be even slightly interested in your explanation now that the rule is being enforced. The point is, when custody orders are being entered in a divorce, the court assumes you're "playing for keeps." Although there are methods for modifying the custody provisions in a divorce decree, those provisions are limited, and it's expensive to go back to court to undo what should have been done right in the process. So, if a divorce decree is about to be entered that does not reflect the realities of your and your spouse's relationships with the children and with each other, now is the time to step forward.

A Culture of Compliance – Courts Enforce Custody Arrangements

Sometimes social and cultural attitudes affect conduct more than the laws on the books. An easy example of this is racial discrimination. Passing laws prohibiting discrimination was a helpful and absolutely necessary step, but racial discrimination only stops when the whole society "gets a bellyful" and decides that such conduct will no longer be tolerated.

In the "good old days" of winner-take-all child custody, the non-custodial parent's biggest problem was a lack of enforcement. In many parts of the State, the non-custodial parent's right to have access to his children was often not taken seriously. Even with an order for specific access in hand, going to court to get visitation was a maybe-or-maybe-not proposition. As often as not, the strongest thing a visiting parent could get out of a judge was, "Now, Mabel, you really ought to let him see them kids."

Times have changed, and so have attitudes toward enforcement. Courts are now aware that, without compliance and enforcement, the *Standard Possession Order* is worthless. Moreover, there is a different attitude about a non-custodial parent's relationship with his or her children. Courts now reflect the public attitude that divorce should not cut children off from either parent. The lines between divorced parents have now blurred to the point that the only significant difference is something called the "right to designate the child's primary residence."

This willingness of the court system as a whole to insist that everyone abide by court orders has played a huge role in the decline of the winner-take-all world of child custody. It puts everyone on a level playing field in the sense that both sides *know* with some certainty that the court system will be an honest broker.

This willingness to play by the rules indicates a maturing of the Texas child custody system. It signals that society has ceased treating divorce as a "no-man's-land" where a certain amount of lawlessness was tolerated simply because, it was thought, anyone who would go there "deserved it." There is less and less reluctance to intervene when a divorced parent refuses to play by the rules.

Sadly, courts are just beginning to police the more subtle versions of parental attempts to break the bonds between the child and the other parent. Some courts are becoming aware of parental alienation and other methods commonly used to encourage the child not to continue a relationship with the other parent. Subtle undermining of the other parent's relationship with the child will end only when courts realize that subtle violations of trust are just as damaging and more contemptible than outright, open defiance.

How Courts Enforce Possession and Access to Children

Enforcement of visitation privileges is carried out by Contempt of Court. In other words, if one of the parents refuses to abide by the terms of possession set out in the divorce decree, the court may hold him or her in contempt and punish the offender for the disobedient conduct. This usually is done by the threat of jail and, finally, the actual jailing of the person committing the contempt. The judge's contempt powers are largely at his or her discretion, and he or she may choose how severely to punish someone who has disobeyed court orders. This discretion is limited. Courts are required to enforce their orders. At some point, an appellate court will require a judge to take appropriate steps to enforce a prior order. Most family law judges in Texas are now keenly aware that the whole *Standard Possession Order* system in this state depends on courts enforcing those orders.

When your divorce decree uses language to the effect, "*It is hereby ordered...*," it means just what it says, so you should pay attention. If these guys decide to, they have the power to play for keeps.

Chapter 21

How Courts Decide Who Gets Custody

There is no duty we so much underrate as the duty of being happy.

—Robert Louis Stevenson

If you and your spouse cannot agree who will have custody, then you must prepare for a contested custody battle. While you are preparing for that custody battle, you will probably be looking for ways to compromise with your spouse. The choice about whether to fight for custody and the alternatives to that custody battle are the subjects of huge portions of this book. So, if this decision is your current struggle, keep reading.

Family Violence – A Disqualification

There was a time, not that long ago, when the courthouse and police accepted family violence as something inevitable. That is no longer the case. Women's groups and children's advocates spent decades calling attention to the awful statistics and begging for help with this issue. Society has now taken due notice. Texas courts are prohibited from appointing a parent who has engaged in a pattern of family violence as *Managing Conservator* of his or her child. Note the use of the word "pattern." In other words, one incident of the police being called or one conviction presumably won't disqualify a parent. But common sense tells us this is a little bit like trying to convince the minister of your church, who finds you in a bar completely soused, that you are not an alcoholic. To get the job done, you'll probably need to be in church every Sunday from now on.

The Facts of a Custody Case Are Fluid

The facts of a custody case are made and re-made on a daily basis. In a collision between two cars, the facts are made on the day the collision occurs. Assuming both sides do their homework, those facts will remain the same whether the case is tried today or a year from now. In a child custody case, on the other hand, the facts change on a daily basis. The facts of a custody case involve the track record of the parents in taking care of the children. Hence, you have an opportunity to harm or improve that record every day. If you become enmeshed in a custody case, it will be necessary for you to discuss your activities with your lawyer and to regulate your conduct so that it will not offend local community standards.

Because custody cases are fact-driven, you should not expect results in the courtroom that don't reflect the realities of your life. For example, if your spouse takes care of the baby, changes all of the diapers, prepares and serves all of the meals, and stays home with the child every evening while you're in the laboratory all day discovering a cure for cancer and out on the town every night, don't expect the judge or jury to turn the kid over to you just because you have a higher IQ and a better sense of humor. In other words, as the kids say, "Get real."

Temporary Custody While the Divorce Is Pending

Remember: The divorce court has power to enter orders making one of the parents *Temporary Managing Conservator* during the pendency of the divorce.

Do you need temporary orders granting you custody while the divorce is pending? Let's look at some possibilities.

Many couples get through the divorce just fine with no temporary orders ever being entered. For example, if your spouse readily agrees that you should have custody of the child, the child is already with you while the divorce is pending, your spouse is paying child support, and you trust your spouse not to stop paying support or to take the child, then going to the trouble and expense of obtaining a temporary order granting you custody of the child while you are waiting for the divorce would seem to be a waste of time and money.

If, on the other hand, you have been the one who has had the primary responsibility for and daily care of your child, and, now, while the case is pending, your spouse is insisting that he or she have the child and take over the day-to-day care, then you probably need to *run* to your lawyer's office to get a *Motion for Temporary Orders* started as soon as possible.

Obtaining the "*Temporary Managing Conservatorship*" is used to maintain the status quo, or, if the status quo is not good, it is a way of protecting and stabilizing the child's environment. This serves two purposes. First, it protects the child and allows the person most able to care for the child the opportunity to do so. Second, it allows the parent with custody the opportunity to establish a track record. This can be extremely important in a final custody battle. If you are the one who has successfully cared for the child in the year or two years when the divorce was pending, a judge or jury may be reluctant to change that arrangement. In other words, the parent who persuades the court to grant him or her temporary custody and care for the child every day usually has a tremendous advantage on custody issues at the final divorce.

Who Makes the Decision about Which Parent Will Have Custody?

When divorcing parents can't agree about who is to have custody, someone has to make the decision about who will be awarded custody. If neither party asks for a jury trial, then the judge decides all issues of custody.

If, on the other hand, either party to the divorce action asks for a trial by jury, then the jury has the absolute right to make the decision regarding who is to have custody. What this means is that the jury can decide:

- Whether there will be a single Sole Managing Conservator or both parents will be named Joint Managing Conservators
- Which parent will be named Sole Managing Conservator

- Which of the Joint Managing Conservators will have authority to designate the primary residence of the child
- Whether there will be geographical limitations on the primary residence of the child, and, if so, what those restrictions will be

Unlike other states, Texas does not have the jury acting in a mere advisory capacity on child custody decisions. In Texas, the judge is not allowed to contravene a jury's verdict as to custody of a child. The judge does, however, retain the power to decide other issues, such as the specific terms of visitation or other limitations on the powers of a Conservator. But, if the judge does limit such powers, he or she must make written findings that explain and justify the ruling.

If you have a contested child custody case, turn to Chapter 12 on "The Trial of Your Contested Divorce Case" and read the sections on judges and juries. Jury trials actually decide few Texas child custody matters. This does not mean that you should completely discount the possibility of asking for a jury trial. But, the possibility of a jury trial probably affects settlement of a significant number of custody cases. If your case is before a judge whom you suspect is unsympathetic to your position on custody, electing to have your case heard by a jury can be critical. On the other hand, if your spouse believes that the judge lacks sensitivity toward his or her position, you may be facing a jury trial based on an election made by the other side.

Associate Judges

Unless your child custody case is being heard in a rural county, there is a good chance that at least a portion of the case will be heard by an Associate Judge. A Statewide system of Associate Judges aids the regularly elected judiciary with its caseload. Under certain circumstances, a judge is allowed to appoint an Associate Judge to work with him or her in hearing the court's caseload. Sometimes an Associate Judge is appointed by a group of judges and hears certain kinds of cases for all of them. For example, the Associate Judge may hear most or all of the "temporary hearings," asking that a *Temporary Managing Conservator* be appointed and child support be establish for the period during which the divorce is pending.

An Associate Judge's ruling affects your case in much the same way that a ruling by a District Judge does. Therefore, just because your case is not being heard by the District Judge, or in some counties by a County Court at Law Judge, that does not mean that you can relax.

Yes, there are rules allowing the Associate Judge's ruling to be appealed to the "regular" judge. But you must give notice within three days of the time the Associate Judge signs the order. Having only three days to appeal is frightening enough, but you must remember that just because you appeal, this does not mean the regular judge is going to reverse what "his" or "her" Associate Judge did.

The system of Associate Judges is an additional layer of tactical decisions that must be considered by your lawyer. In some cases, your lawyer may prefer the Associate Judge over the Regular Judge. In other cases, the Associate Judge may present a problem.

Associate Judges can be disqualified if the election to disqualify is filed within ten days of the time that the case is assigned. Because some Associate Judges are assigned whole categories of cases by blanket appointment, this may mean that any disqualification will necessarily need to be in your initial pleading. This is a decision for your lawyer.

The Best Interest of the Child

"The best interest of the child shall always be the primary consideration of the court in determining the issue of conservatorship and possession of and access to the child." That's what the Texas law says. The best interest of the child is the bedrock of Texas child custody law. There is no definition of what this term means, but it is cited and quoted to support all manner of things. So, within some limits, it means whatever a judge or jury says it means.

How Much Discretion or Leeway Does a Judge or Jury Have in Deciding Which Parent Should Have Custody of a Child?

The answer is: virtually absolute discretion. The issue of custody of a child is considered by Texas courts a "pure fact" question. It is difficult to conceive a set of circumstances where an appellate court would overturn a trial court's decision concerning the custody of a child, once a judge or jury has determined that the best interest of the child would be served by being in the custody of a particular parent. This is unlike many of the decisions made by courts. For example, neither a judge nor jury would be allowed to give one spouse's separate property to the other spouse. Neither has the discretion to make that decision. Other decisions, such as the division of community property or the amount of child support, must be decided within very narrowly defined bounds. In the matter of custody, once again, there are almost no bounds. But keep in mind, losing a battle for Managing Conservator or the parent with the right to designate the child's primary residence does not deprive you of access to and possession of your child. There is no winner-take-all deal anymore.

Does a Parent Have an Absolute Right to Possession of the Child?

Almost. Texas law states that the only way a judge can deny possession of or access to a child by a parent is if the court finds that such access or possession is not in the best interest of the child *and* would endanger the physical and emotional welfare of the child.

In other words, the people of this state have made a strong statement that they intend for both parents to have the right to see their children. This statement is made all the stronger by the fact that the burden of proof is on the person urging the court to deny visitation. That person must *prove* that it would endanger the physical or emotional welfare of the child.

Moreover, the law states that it is presumed that the time set out in the *Standard Possession Order* is the minimum time that a non-custodial parent should have with the child. This is a rebuttable presumption, but if the court restricts the parent's possession or access, it is the least restriction required to protect the child.

May the Child Choose the Custodian?

The child is never given the absolute right to make a decision about his or her custody. There is, however, a statute that says that at age twelve the child may, by "writing filed" with the court, name the person whom the child prefers to have the exclusive right to designate his or her primary residence, *subject to the approval of the court.* In other words, the judge still retains the final say. A judge or jury may consider the opinion of a child under the age of twelve. In a non-jury trial, the judge has a right to interview children in chambers to find out the child's wishes regarding his or her custody.

Obviously, the older and more emotionally and mentally mature the child is, the more likely the judge is to consider the child's preference on custody. It is safe to say that, if the child is at least twelve years old, the judge will always consider the child's wishes, along with other factors. With a younger child, most judges are likely to rely more on other factors and less on what the child says is his or her preference. It would seem that most jurors would have a similar view.

Most judges are acutely aware of the potential for subtle parental influence and pressure on the child. This is why many judges are reluctant to meet in chambers with a child, even though the law allows such meetings.

When children are sixteen or seventeen, judges realize that courts and parents usually have limited ability to override a teenager's strong desires. Therefore, barring unusual circumstances, most judges will not argue with a child this age regarding who should have custody.

May the Child Testify?

No sane parent would look forward to having his or her child testify in a contested custody case. Forcing the child to take sides and choose between his or her parents arguably verges on child abuse. The very essence of childhood is to be protected from the politics of adulthood. Putting the child on the witness stand somehow reverses the proper order of responsibility and makes the child responsible for the parents and, particularly, the parents' feelings. Parents who don't understand all of this are probably, at least unconsciously, guilty of emotionally abusing their children.

Yet, in the most devastatingly difficult cases children must sometimes be called as witnesses. Although a sane parent will always regret having to call a child and try to find ways to avoid it, no loving parent can categorically say that he or she would never call his or her child under any circumstances. The child's testimony may be absolutely necessary for the child's own protection.

Calling a child, particularly a young child, as a witness carries great risk for the parent. Judges and juries respect the child's right to love both parents and not to have to take sides. If the parent calling the child as a witness is perceived as the one forcing the child to choose sides, the judge or jury may punish that parent. In other words, if a child is to be called, it needs to be obvious that there is no other choice.

So, yes, a child can testify, provided that he or she is old enough or mentally mature enough to understand the meaning of what he or she is doing. The judge makes that decision. Obviously, the more mature the child is perceived to be by the judge or the jury, the greater the weight that will be given to the testimony.

There is also a special rule that a parent may be able to use to keep a child from being forced to testify in open court in front of both parents. The court may, on the motion of either party, order that the child's testimony be taken outside the courtroom and be recorded for showing in the courtroom. The parents are present at the live testimony only through their attorneys so that the child does not have to face them while testifying. If this method is used, the child cannot be forced to testify in open court.

In child abuse cases, the court may allow videotaped interviews with the child into evidence or allow the child to give testimony by a live television transmission.

If the child custody trial is before the court without a jury, there is another alternative to calling the child to testify. The judge may interview the child in chambers. A parent has a right to require the judge to interview the child in chambers, if the child is twelve or older and the *Managing Conservatorship* is being contested. The fact that a judge interviews a child in chambers does not take away any of the judge's discretion to decide the case as he or she chooses.

The judge may choose to allow the lawyers for the parents to be present for the interview, or the lawyers may be excluded. A parent may require that the interview be recorded by the court reporter, or the judge may elect to have a court reporter present.

In non-jury trials, the in-chambers interview is a good way to avoid calling a child to testify in open court in the presence of the parents. Such an interview does not prevent a parent from calling a child as a witness in open court, but it usually makes open court testimony impractical or meaningless. If the judge has already heard what the child had to say in chambers, it is probably not going to change the court's opinion if the child says something different in the presence of a parent.

Does the Mother Have More Rights to Custody Than the Father?

This question must be answered on both a theoretical and a practical level. Theoretically, the answer is no. The law in Texas provides for both parents to have equal rights to the children. This means that in a custody case, the law says that the judge or jury is to consider the parents on matters other than their sex. The issue is, who is better able to give the child the care and nurture that the child needs.

The practical answer to this question is somewhat different. Among most jurors and judges, there is a cultural bias in favor of the mother as custodian of minor children. Of course, this bias comes from the fact that in former days the woman was the primary parent responsible for child rearing and, for many jurors and judges, was the parent who reared the children to maturity. Since custody is a "fact question" to be decided by the judge or jury, this means the woman has an advantage if everything else is equal.

A Custody Decision Is Difficult to Change without Agreement

That portion of your final divorce decree controlling *Conservatorship* and the right to designate your child's primary residence should be regarded as a *permanent* decision. There is much talk among quarreling divorced parties about going back to court and *changing custody.* Although there are provisions in the law for changing the custody or *Conservatorship* of children, the law does not look favorably upon such changes. In the original divorce hearing, both parents are equally entitled to be considered for *Managing Conservator* or as the parent who will have the right to designate the child's primary residence. The law leaves these questions to the discretion of the judge or jury, instructing only that the decision is made based on what is in the best interest of the child or children.

In a hearing to change the *Managing Conservator* or person with power to designate the primary residence (Motion to Modify), the law does not play this neutral role. The judge or jury is instructed that the conservatorship or person with power to designate the child's primary residence will not be changed unless it is in the child's best interest and (1) there is a material change of circumstance; (2) the child is at least twelve years of age and has filed a written preference for the person to have the exclusive right to designate his or her primary residence; or (3) the person who has the exclusive right to designate the primary residence of the child has voluntarily relinquished the primary care and possession of the child to another person for at least six months. If the evidence is not strong enough to establish these requirements, then the fact-finder is not allowed to change custody.

In short, you need to take the original custody fight or agreement seriously, because it may be difficult to change later.

Child custody orders can be changed only by court order. In other words, if your former spouse, who is the *Managing Conservator* of your child, brings the baby to you in a basket, along with a note in her handwriting on the back of an envelope saying that he or she is giving you custody, this does not automatically make you the new Managing Conservator or give you the right to designate the child's primary residence. Courts do not look fondly on handing children around like watermelons. If your former spouse returns later to claim the child, the court might very well support him or her since he or she is the legal *Managing Conservator*.

Of course, the note written on the envelope, along with the fact that you were given the baby, is evidence that can and should be used in court to get the judge to change the *Managing Conservatorship* or give you power to designate the child's primary residence.

The point is that you should insist that any *agreed* change of custody be made legally and officially by having the judge enter a new order. When both parties agree, this can be done very simply and relatively inexpensively. Seldom will a judge disagree when both of the parties have worked it out.

Guardian *Ad Litem*

In a contested child custody case, the judge may appoint a guardian *ad litem* to represent the child. This is an attorney who owes no allegiance to anyone except the child. This attorney sits at a counsel table, participates in selecting the jury, and makes closing arguments. In short, the child becomes a full participant in the trial through this attorney.

In some cases, such as ones terminating parental rights, guardian *ad litems* are required. The use of a guardian ad litem in custody cases between parents is fairly rare. Few judges use guardian *ad litems* routinely in ordinary custody cases. Most do so seldom or not at all.

When a guardian ad litem is appointed, this usually becomes a major factor in a child custody case. Your attorney will develop a specific strategy involving the guardian *ad litem*.

The Social Study

In a contested child custody case, the judge may order a social study of the background of the parties and the child. Some judges do this routinely in every divorce case in which custody is in dispute. Some judges do not use social studies. A social study can have substantial impact on a child custody case.

Though it can vary widely, there is a typical pattern that is followed when a social study is done:

1. You and your spouse will be contacted and interviewed by a social worker, psychologist, or other mental health provider.
2. At least one "home visit" will be made to interview you and your spouse in your respective homes.
3. At least one interview with each of the parents will take place with the child present.

4. Usually you will know in advance of the visits and interviews.
5. You and your spouse will be asked for references—friends, relatives, neighbors, babysitters, etc.—who know you and the child. Each of these references will be interviewed by the mental health professional; some of these interviews may be by phone.
6. The mental health professional may want time alone with the child; the time spent with the child could vary from one session to several sessions.
7. A written report is made by the mental health professional and filed with the court. Your lawyer is allowed to copy the report from the court's file.
8. In many cases, the mental health professional remains neutral, simply reporting facts and stating that both parents are good parents and could care for the child if granted custody. Sometimes, however, the mental health professional recommends one parent over the other.

In a case that is being heard by the judge without a jury, the social study can be read by the judge, since it is a part of the record in the case. In a jury trial, however, the social study itself cannot be introduced into evidence since it is hearsay. (Some case law says it is an exception to the hearsay rule; most judges won't agree.) In jury trials, the social worker who made the report is called as a witness to testify to the content of the social study.

The social study should be taken seriously. The social worker can be a strong witness for or against you. You should approach the social study as sort of a mini-trial. Be on your best behavior. Be polite, but also be your own advocate. Tell the worker what is wrong with your spouse and why you would make a better parent. Your spouse will do you the same favor. Do not deny or cover up your shortcomings, but do not dwell on them. In the interview with your child present, *be patient with the child, let the worker see you holding, touching, and loving the child.* If the child interrupts the interview, try to strike a balance between attending to the child and talking with the social worker. If the child chooses this moment to misbehave, use your judgment, but do what you have to—don't just be a bump on a log in such a crisis. A word of caution: Most social workers have a strong bias against corporal punishment. This might be a good time to demonstrate your use of "time-outs" or other behavior modification techniques.

Do not say bad things about your spouse in front of the child, even if invited to do so by the social worker. Having a good interview is not worth harming your child. If you can't work it out for the child to go play in the other room, tell the worker that you would like another interview or that you will complete the interview by a phone call or by another visit. Ideally, the social worker will not schedule the only visit with you while the child is present. And ideally, the social worker will have good sense about what is really going on. Unfortunately, this is not always the case.

Psychologists and Other Experts

Will you need a psychologist, psychiatrist, or social worker as an expert in your child custody case? No one can answer that question for you without knowing and understanding the facts of your case in detail. The decision to employ an expert witness should be based on your lawyer's recommendations, but you need insight into why you may need the assistance of a psychological expert. Ironically, to gain this insight, we won't focus on psychologists, their training, or their methods. Rather, we will focus on the child custody case from the point of view of the judge or jury and what they need to know to make a decision.

The same things that cause divorce are often psychologically harmful to the children of the marriage. This is why "divorce courts" are magnets for less than admirable parental behavior. Often, it is concern for the children that causes a spouse to file for divorce. In many situations, the easy part is getting the divorce. The truly difficult task is trying to save the children from the other spouse. This quest to protect the children is complicated by the "bad guy's" utter refusal to wear a label that says "bad parent." The bad parent is often the one protesting loudest that he or she is, in fact, the savior of the child. Finally, a desperate parent, bringing these "life-and-death" issues to the courthouse will discover to his or her horror that this critically important case is to be dumped in the hopper with hundreds or, in some counties, thousands of other cases. It will be treated as just another routine matter to be handled along with all the rest. Then onto the scene of this confusion comes the judge and the jury. Suppose you're this "good" parent trying to protect your child. What are you going to tell the judge and jury? What are you going to show them? How are you going to do it?

In child custody cases many of the facts that the judge or jury will need to make a decision are self-evident. The jury needs to know who takes care of the child: Who changes the diapers, puts meals on the table, does the cleaning and bathing, talks, laughs, and cries with the child, reads stories, takes the child to the doctor, and helps with homework? We all understand that these and many other obvious matters must be attended to if the average kid is going to grow into a healthy, happy, and productive adult.

Unfortunately, many custody cases don't provide positive choices for the judge or jury. Rather, the choice must be of the lesser of two evils. In many tragic cases, the struggle is to determine which parent is least immature or whether the child would be better off with the heavy drinker or with the borderline psychotic. Child custody often boils down to who is the least worst parent.

This is not to minimize the difficulty of deciding the run-of-the-mill custody case. It is often not easy to determine who is telling the truth. Does the father really do all of the child care and housekeeping as he swears? Or, is the mother correct when she testifies that this is all a big show he puts on in the presence of others, while paying little or no attention to his child when the family is alone? Who is telling the truth about how much the father drinks or how often the mother is gone in the evenings? These kinds of issues are standard fare for those making decisions in courtrooms. I wish that I could report the existence of special tools or methodologies that these fact-finders use in making their decisions. Unfortunately, special truth detectors don't exist. Judges and juries must use the same methods that you and I use when we are trying to determine which politician, preacher, or used car salesman is telling us the truth. Frightening, isn't it!

Those deciding custody cases face other problems that are at least as difficult as deciding who is telling the truth. The untrained judge or juror may not see or understand the damage inflicted on a child by the parent's emotional pathology. Some of the things most damaging to children are subtle, hard to detect, and not susceptible to scientific measurement or easy proof in the courtroom. For every parent who physically or sexually abuses a child, there are dozens of parents who emotionally abuse their children. Many parents, often quite unintentionally, emotionally sabotage their children. An example might be the different responses of two fathers who attend their respective sons' Little League baseball games. One father may use the attendance as an opportunity to reinforce his son's confidence and feelings about himself. The other father, at the very same ball game, may let his son know in a thousand ways that he is no good, that he just does not measure up and probably never will. One mother changing a diaper may let her baby know that she is the most precious and wonderful baby ever to arrive on the planet. Another mother changing the diaper may communicate to the baby that nobody really wants her, that she is obviously unworthy and, merely by being born, has created a hardship for everyone around her. A jury being told that the father attends all of the son's Little League games or that the mother changes all of the diapers can see only the quantity of care. They cannot always understand the quality of that care or the subtle, but very different, messages being communicated by two parents carrying out essentially the same functions.

By identifying, describing, and calling attention to these more subtle aspects of the case that might otherwise go unnoticed, a psychologist may change the way a judge or jury views the situation. A qualified psychologist or social worker will have training in childhood development, the parameters of normal behavior, the symptoms of abnormal behavior, and the effects of covert and subtle mistreatment on children. As you might imagine, if you had the responsibility of deciding a difficult case, this is just the kind of information that you would want. When properly used, a psychologist or other health-care provider can change the outcome of the case.

However, psychologists and health-care providers cannot work in vacuums. For a mental health professional to give credible testimony, he or she must spend time with the child, the parents, and other people who interact with the parents and children. This means that the expert must be planned for in advance. The expert will usually need weeks, if not months, for the interviews necessary to give him or her a solid and realistic understanding of the case.

Mental health professionals are expensive. Interviewing the family is usually not just a one-time event. Usually, several sessions with the child and parents are necessary. Sometimes, dozens of other people must also be interviewed. Courts often require the expert to provide a written report. Since many mental health professionals have hourly rates that approach those of the legal or accounting profession, all of this can add up to significant cost. This, of course, is a factor that you must weigh when deciding whether to hire such an expert.

The cost creates another problem. Since the judge or jury will know that you are paying the psychologist to testify, this fact alone can hurt his or her credibility. The jury or judge may see your expert as just another "hired gun" who will say whatever you are paying him to say. For this reason, it is often desirable to use a mental health professional who is already seeing you or your child for legitimate counseling unconnected with the child custody trial. If you can show the judge or jury that your expert is primarily working with you and your child as a mental health counselor you have employed to improve your child's life and health, this can help establish the counselor's credibility.

Your spouse may have already hired an expert or may be planning to do so in the near future. In this case, you may have no choice. If you are faced with a mental health professional who is going to tell everyone how bad you are, you probably will need your own expert to contradict some of these assertions. No matter how honest you and your expert are, if your spouse looks hard enough, he or she will probably find an "expert" who will have all manner of harsh things to say about you. Yes, there really are hired guns who will say virtually anything.

This is not to say that the experts will not have to be "qualified." In the past few years courts have imposed strict standards on expert witnesses. Before an expert is allowed to testify, he or she must show the court that he or she is qualified in his or her field and that the testimony to be given is based on a methodology that is accepted by his or her peers in the profession.

Chapter 22

Parental Alienation Syndrome

A hero is the one who does what he can.
The others do not.

—Romain Rolland

Imagine your spouse disappearing with your child. After months or years of searching, you finally locate them. You file a lawsuit and obtain a court order instructing that you have access to your child. Upon being reunited with your child, you are horrified to learn that the child has changed. This child, who loved you so much and was so attached to you, now passionately and intensely hates you. The child sees you as the villain who abandoned him or her and his or her other parent. Rather than referring to you as his or her father or mother, the child now refers to you by your first name. He or she seems to have total amnesia about the good times and close relationship the two of you had before he or she was taken away.

You, of course, present strong facts to disprove everything the child is saying. But facts don't seem to matter, except that your child sees everything you say as more evidence that you are untrustworthy. After weeks of continued attempts to re-establish communication, you hire a psychologist and obtain a court order requiring that the child meet with the psychologist, all to no avail. It becomes apparent that your child is now an active and intense participant in this effort to keep you away. He or she has no mixed emotions or ambiguity about his or her relationship with you. He or she sees the world in black and white with no gray. In his or her eyes, you are definitely "the bad guy." His or her other parent is, in his or her view, definitely the good, loving parent who is being unjustly and unfairly harassed by you, your lawyer, "your" psychologist, and the judge who continues to interfere in his or her other parent's life.

Unless you have witnessed at close hand a child "brainwashing," this description may be difficult for you to believe. At least you don't believe it could ever happen to you, because of your close bond with your child. The fact that it is so difficult for good parents to believe their own child could turn against them is what produces the shock, horror, and disbelief when it happens. Of course, the shock and horror soon turn to absolute rage.

Although the example used above does not begin to describe the varied methods employed, it is not unusual for one parent to use his or her influence over a child to convince the child that the other parent is "the bad guy." In fact, it is so common that it has been given a name. It is called "Parental Alienation Syndrome." The term "syndrome," which means "a set of symptoms," fits these cases because they all share common elements. The most frightening, ever-present central feature is the active participation of the child against a parent who is innocent of misconduct.

Parental Alienation Syndrome is a term that was first used by Richard Gardner in 1985. Gardner is a child psychiatrist who noticed a pattern of children being totally committed to one parent while persistently and obsessively denigrating the other parent. Gardner's research revealed a systematic "programing" of the child by one parent. The focus of the "programing" is to cause the child to form an all-encompassing relationship with that parent to the complete exclusion of the other parent.

Gardner has continued to write on the subject. His books are well known by mental health professionals and lawyers working in the child custody area. Gardner has now been joined by other commentators on this subject, so there is a considerable body of literature describing an experience fairly common in divorce.

Parental Alienation Syndrome is a controversial "theory." Although it is difficult to argue that parental alienation does not exist, its meaning, interpretation, and application are highly disputed by and among many mental health professionals. In child custody cases in which this issue is raised, it is not uncommon to see mental health experts testifying for both sides reaching exactly opposite conclusions based on the same facts.

A part of the problem with Parental Alienation Syndrome is that it is just one of various types of parental alienation. If you have raised teenagers, or been a teenager, you know from experience that it is perfectly normal for children to be "alienated" from a parent. When a child reacts negatively against parental discipline, this usually is "normal parental alienation." Moreover, if a parent is habitually drunk, abusive, or has abandoned or neglected the child, it is normal for the child to be "justifiably alienated." We marvel at children who are *not* offended by these types of conduct in their parents. So, as with other things in life, it's not always easy for a layperson to tell whether a child has been programed by one parent to hate the other. Professionals, on the other hand, have developed fairly sophisticated guidelines to be used in making judgments on these issues.

Divorce is a fertile field for Parental Alienation Syndrome. The separation of the parents often means that the child is separated from one of the parents. When the child's attachment to the parent who leaves is particularly strong, the child may experience the sudden absence of that loved parent as a betrayal or abandonment by one he or she thought totally trustworthy. After separation, the child may be spending more time with the parent who remains behind. If that parent feels angry, betrayed, and insecure, this is the perfect opportunity for the angry parent to use the child's feelings as a weapon against the now-absent parent.

Another variety of Parental Alienation Syndrome arises when, throughout the marriage, a child has longed for a relationship with a parent who has been more or less emotionally absent. Now, when the couple separates, this immature parent senses that the child is his or her last grip on the "family" and the other spouse. This emotionally immature spouse now uses each and every moment with the child to discuss how he or she wants to keep the family together and how the other parent is the evil person destroying the "family." This approach also takes advantage of the fact that few children are happy about their parents being separated. In these cases, a spouse who may have tolerated years of emotional abuse before deciding to leave, will now be indirectly abused through a child who finally has the attention of the longed-for parent.

Make no mistake: The programing of a child against another parent is child abuse. The fact that it is emotional rather than physical abuse keeps parents who do it from being prosecuted. Because it is not commonly understood by the community at large, many parents "get away with it." Friends may not notice much when Marge talks in front of the child about how Leroy just doesn't care about his kid, how lazy he is, what a skinflint he is, or how dishonest he is. Or friends may ignore Leroy's talk in front of the child about Marge being a slut and about her many other flaws. What is virtually guaranteed is that the child does hear what is being said, and, if this propaganda works as intended to cause the child to become alienated, the damage to the child can be as great as physical abuse. The child loses one of the greatest assets on earth, a parent. Additionally, someday, the child may come to identify with the targeted parent. The child's thinking will be, to the effect, "If my parent is no good, then I'm probably not either."

Being the target of the other parent's propaganda campaign sends most parents into a rage. If the other parent's programing efforts are successful, causing the child to become the "active participant" that defines the Parental Alienation Syndrome, the rage turns to an outrageous desire for the other parent's blood. Since murder is not allowed, the great temptation is to strike back in kind, to even the score by telling the child a few things about his or her other parent's black and villainous heart. *Don't do this!* All you are going to do is compound the damage being done to your child. Your child is not qualified or trained to run a mental hospital. If we were going to put children in that role, we would equip them with thorazine and electroshock equipment.

After getting the rage sort of under control, many parents respond to the negative attacks from their child and former spouse by becoming depressed. No doubt, having the child you love more than anything or anyone else on earth turn on you is among the most painful things on the planet. But, a pity party never got anybody anything. And you have a job to do. You've got to rescue someone who is already on the way to being brainwashed. You've got to rescue your own child.

If you are the victim of full-blown Parent Alienation Syndrome, three things will help.

First, admit that you have lost your child's mind for the time being and start thinking about the long run. You've got to rebuild your relationship with your child, and you've got to let actions rather than words speak for you. Short-term manipulative tactics won't work. You've got to get busy being the long-term, rock-solid, what-you-see-is-what-you-get kind of parent. We're talking Biblical faith here. If you focus on what your child is saying now or just this weekend, you've already lost. Remember: Your child already has one manipulative, phony parent. You're the real parent. And your child doesn't know it now, but he or she is watching how you are behaving in a combat zone, under fire, with megatons of emotional bombs being dropped on you. What better opportunity to show your child what you are really made of? Perhaps the child will understand the heroics involved in being a real parent under difficult conditions when he or she is about forty. That's not too late, when you're figuring out that your parent was the real thing and that he or she loved you.

Second, you absolutely must remember that your child does not mean what he or she is saying, and, if he or she does, it doesn't make any difference because you're still the parent offering unconditional love. When your child says that he or she hates you and there is no uncertainty, no equivocation, and seemingly no doubt, you are hearing one of the elements of Parental Alienation Syndrome. Normal people have ambiguous feelings about other people. Normal relationships are built on positive and negative feeling. So, when your child professes to have no mixed feelings about you, a mental health professional will hear this as a sign of the "disease." You should too. Deep down, your child still cares about you and the relationship between the two of you. Never, never forget this or stop believing it. It's your job description as a parent.

Third, when you do use words on the subject of your child's other parent, use extremely short sentences. And I do mean "extremely." As your relationship with your child begins to repair, there may be openings or maybe even questions that will allow you to expound on your own virtues and gingerly "explain" some of the moral ambiguity that surrounds your relationship with his or her other parent. In some of these situations, you must say something or have the child think that you are a complete idiot. When this happens, you are like a politician at a news conference. If you can't say it in a "sound bite," don't say it. A sound bite won't win the election, but it may help your cause. A lengthy statement will take you backward. A diatribe will convince your kid that your ex-spouse is right about everything. Keeping it short is difficult for ex-spouses. The very nature of marriage is that you learn volumes about your spouse. In a bad marriage, one usually learns libraries of bad information, and that information is linked to an urge to disseminate it to all who will listen. It's a big mistake to tell your child any of this stuff until he or she is over thirty-five.

As with other aspects of divorce and child custody, Parental Alienation Syndrome is extremely complex. The subject is capable of permanently crossing the eyes of six or seven very wise rabbis. Obviously, comprehensive coverage is far beyond the scope of this book. If you have this issue in your divorce, your lawyer or mental health professional can provide insight and resources. Gardner's books are widely available. A search on the Internet will provide many additional resources.

Chapter 23

Common Sense, Common Decency, and Visitation

Nothing so saps the profound resources of life as finding life too easy.

—Jose Ortega y Gasset

Unfortunately, the granting of the divorce does not always end the friction between parents. Even with elaborate language in the divorce decree setting out the specific periods of possession, some parents continue the battle of the divorce for years by fighting over and through the children. This is one of the most regrettable things that I know about human beings. The greatest loss is to the children who are caught in the middle, but there is also a tremendous loss of time, energy, and creativity on the part of the parents caught up in this struggle.

If you are a parent who is having your relationship with your child hindered by a spouse or ex-spouse, I have very few words of encouragement. All you can really hope for is that your spouse or ex-spouse will act directly and overtly. The outright denial of visitation directly in violation of a court order is relatively easy to stop. Courts will now enforce violations of the Standard Visitation Order or other terms of access with contempt of court carrying penalties that include fines and jail, if necessary.

If your ex-spouse is of the more intelligent, subtle variety, such as the kind that sponsors the child's event-of-the-year or the trip to

Disneyland on your weekends or mentally manipulates your child, your task will be more complex.

Society in general and the courts in particular are becoming more aware of this subtle and sophisticated kind of conduct. Even at the risk of sounding too hopeful, some courts may view this kind of subtle or manipulative interference as grounds for changing custody.

If you are a parent who has custody, but your ex-spouse uses visitation to propagandize against you, manipulate or play games with your child's mind, or otherwise "set you up," again, I have few words of encouragement. To fight back in the same terms will be devastating to your child. To go to court and attempt to withdraw visitation means that you will be depriving the child of his or her other parent. This, of course, assumes that the court will agree to allow such withdrawal. Some, faced with these circumstances, move the children to another community. Others stay and endure the problems. In the cases I am familiar with, the children usually grow to adulthood and discover, on their own, that the crazy parent really is crazy just as everyone had suspected. But not always. Sometimes the crazy parent is successful at brainwashing and convinces the kid that he or she is the only sane person on earth.

We have now established that there is not a lot you can do about your child's other parent. What you can do is make sure that you are not a part of the problem. To help you avoid being a part of the problem, I will set out some ideas. Consider these in light of your love for your child and your knowledge that your child needs both parents for a healthy emotional maturity.

"The Child Doesn't Want to Visit" Syndrome

"The child doesn't want to visit his father. What can I do?" Judges hear this line of reasoning all of the time. The best answer to this question comes from a judge I know. When someone appears in court saying that visitation was not granted or should not be granted because the child doesn't want to go, this judge says:

> "Who is in charge here? What would you say if your child announced that he wasn't going to school because he didn't want

to? Why, you wouldn't stand for that for a moment! He would be on the way to school so fast it would make his little head spin. Now, we've got the same problem here. The child needs to know his other parent just like he needs to go to school. True, the parent isn't perfect, but this is no excuse for his not seeing him. The school is not perfect. That is no excuse for his non-attendance. I trust that you will not return to my court on this matter again."

This does not mean that you must turn your child over to a child molester, to someone who will physically harm the child, or to someone who is drunk and on drugs. Nor does it mean that you can't petition the court for protection from someone who does bizarre things like scaring the child or awakening the child to read the divorce decree in the middle of the night.

Young Children

Babies and young children need constant attention and care. They cannot wait for meals. They need special clothing. In short, they cannot be handled incidentally to everything else. If you cannot provide these things, because of lack of time, money, or facilities, consider an abbreviated visit until you can make other arrangements.

Older Children

When children reach the teenage years, they often have very full lives of their own. Both parents need to allow for this. Insisting on visitation over a very special activity or social event may not be what the child wants or needs.

Don't Enlist Your Child in the CIA

Next to cleaning sewers or chicken houses, spying is one of the dirtiest businesses there is. This is especially true if it must be done on neighbors, friends, or former lovers. Sometimes in war, politics, or divorce cases it must be done. If you must do it, do not involve your children. You will ruin their minds and corrupt their souls, and they will end up manipulating you to boot. Perhaps you are so mature that you could be dropped behind enemy lines, live with the people, eat their food, drink their wine, make love to them, be loved by them, and then use all of this against them without having it drive you crazy. At least not any crazier than you already are! Your child cannot do this. Your child thinks that love is for real and that he shouldn't bite the hand that feeds him. He also thinks that betraying either Mommy or Daddy is wrong. Your child is right!

Killer Ideas

Very few children have ever been killed by exposure to ideas that their parents didn't agree with. Of course, parents are sure that any ideas that do not agree with their own are harmful. And sometimes wars are fought to keep these awful ideas from the children. Naturally, some of the children are killed in these wars.

You and your ex-spouse probably have different ideas. These different ideas about politics, religion, or sex may have caused your divorce. Now, you must have enough faith in your children and your ideas to avoid starting a war over those beliefs.

Be On Time for Your Visits

Your ex-spouse and your children should not have to spend long hours waiting for you. More importantly, your children are likely to worry if you do not appear when you are expected.

Be Flexible

Do not expect your ex-spouse to be exactly on time. It is not as if this is a weekly TV show that must be broadcast beginning at the exact second. Your ex-spouse may need to drive for several hours to visit or may have a demanding work schedule. If you schedule an activity for yourself that begins at the exact moment your children are scheduled to leave, you may be setting everyone up for a crisis.

Put Up or Shut Up

Don't tell your child that you will soon be gaining custody and that he or she will be coming to live with you. This is a cruel hoax that produces all kinds of problems. If nothing else, have enough respect for yourself to put up or shut up. Hire a lawyer and file a Motion to Modify or be quiet.

Include Your Ex-Spouse in Your Child's Schedule

Do not schedule activities during your ex-spouse's visitation period. The child's time with the other parent is a high priority. Do you work as hard to schedule this time as you do the child's other activities?

Real Life vs. Show Biz

If you are the visiting parent, schedule some "ordinary" time. Not all of life is movies, restaurants, and show time. Your ex-spouse may not be able to compete with this show biz approach. If you are the parent with custody, you must remember that since the visiting parent has a much shorter time with the child, the intensity of the visit may lead to some special frills for the child. This may not be that your ex-spouse is showing off as much as it is a heartfelt and desperate need to make the most of a very limited time period.

Having a Parent Leave Is Not Business as Usual

Woody Allen says that eighty percent of success is just showing up. That may not be true for putting a satellite in orbit or running a marathon, but showing up is probably the most important thing you can do for your children. If you are the parent who has "left" the child's home, you have a special responsibility to assure your children that you are not leaving them. Just saying so won't get it done. Although you may tell your children that you only left the other parent and not them, to the children it looks a lot like you left them too. Only your actions are going to count. Change your priority list. Move the periods of access, school events, and other child activities up about ten notches on the list. Be in that minority of parents who make time to visit the school and actually get to know the teacher's name.

Don't Get Married to the Standard Possession Order

If you can agree with your former spouse to use common sense and decency in the place of the Standard Possession Order, by all means do so. Many parents are able to let the children come and go pretty much as they please. The access periods can be worked around special events. There are still two parents to cover school activities, get the kid to the dentist or the doctor, or take care of the child when the other parent has to work late. If your spouse will be fair about these kinds of arrangements, this is far superior to making the calendar lord of all scheduling decisions. Even if you can't work with your spouse totally by agreement, try to find a little flexibility in your soul when it comes to accommodating your children and former spouse. (I know. If the situation were reversed, your ex certainly wouldn't let the children attend your family reunion on his or her weekend; why should you accommodate your ex now that it's his or her family reunion and it's your weekend? No doubt, these can be tough questions.)

Child Support and Visitation Aren't Linked

If a former spouse is failing to make child support payments, can visitation be refused until payments are made? No. Child support and visitation are not linked. Two wrongs don't make a right. You should use all of the remedies available for collecting support, but don't allow your anger to interfere with your children's relationship with their other parent. Besides, if you deny visitation, you could be the one in trouble with the court.

Don't Make Your Child Choose

Have you ever watched the For-Public-Display Parent or the Control-Freak Parent at a community gathering, school event, or church function? If so, you are aware that it is preordained by God that the Chosen Parent's child *must* sit with or next to the Chosen Parent. As the child leaves the stage or finishes the piano solo, there occurs that dramatic moment when the child's return to the beloved parent's side will be displayed for all to see. When attending these events, you may also have noticed that some divorced parents, who often don't sit together at these events, are *both* chosen by God as the one with whom the poor child is supposed to sit. Watching a child attempt to honor these conflicting divine decrees is a painful sight.

For the sake of all that is decent, don't put your child in this position. If reasonably possible, sit together with your ex or soon-to-be ex. If this is not possible because your former true love is a smoldering volcano or, perhaps, his or her new spouse is totally uncivil, then assure your child that sitting with the other parent is just fine. Let the child know that where he or she sits does not rise to the level of even mild concern, much less the international crisis implied by his or her other parent. Let the child know that you are there. There will be ample time to communicate how proud you are and how special the event was for you. Anyway, hugs, affection, smiles, tears of joy, special pats on the head, and the wonder of a parent and child sharing life together are primarily not designed for public display. The real thing is private and only incidentally occurs in public. If it *must* be done in public, then it's only show biz.

Chapter 24

Grandparent Rights to Access or Custody

Children need love, especially when they do not deserve it.

—Harold S. Hubert

Grandparents play a huge role in the lives of many children. Sometimes this role is only that of the traditional extended family. Increasingly, for many children, the grandparent is the rescuer who steps in when the parent is overwhelmed. The grandparent is the person who drops the kids off or picks them up from school, fixes meals, gets a child to a dentist or doctor, buys school clothes, provides lunch money, or any of the hundreds of other must-happen things that can save a child from embarrassment, deprivation, or loneliness. Very often, the grandparents' home is a place of refuge. If Dad is already "gone" and now no one knows where Mom is or when she will be home, or she is mentally ill, immature, an alcoholic, on drugs, or just plain unreliable, grandparents can become the *de facto* "parents." It is not altogether unusual for the grandparents' home to become the default "child's primary residence."

Grandparents can also find themselves in the role of a disaster relief agency. They are sometimes called in after a family disaster to pick up the pieces and rescue grandchildren whom they hardly know, grandchildren who live in distant cities or who have been kept away by a hostile parent.

As with everything else in child custody, the grandparents don't always play a positive role. Grandparents have been known to interfere in the parent-child relationship, based on their disapproval of the parents' lifestyle or disagreements over the religious training being provided for their grandchildren. It is not unheard of for a grandparent to be the one with "mental problems," and sometimes the grandparent's mental problems are manifested in interference with a child's family life. Grandparents are notorious for being unhappy with the spouse chosen by their own child. And since, as it works out, the "inferior" spouse will end up as a parent of the grandchildren, there is already a conflict over how the grandchild should be raised, even before the child is born.

So, how does all of this work? What is the grandparents' legal relationship to their grandchildren? How do children sometimes end up in the care and custody of their grandparents?

We begin with our earlier discussion of the *parental presumption. The parent has superior rights to the child*, unless exceptionally strong facts indicate parental misbehavior or mistreatment of the child. This means that in a contest between a parent and any non-parent, including a grandparent, the parent wins, unless the parent has really fumbled the ball.

The parent's superior rights to the child sometimes make headlines. In the widely publicized United States Supreme Court case of *Troxel v. Granville,* a Washington State Court's holding that granted grandparents visitation rights was struck down. The Supreme Court said that granting grandparent visitation violated the parents' constitutional right to raise their children as they see fit.

At first blush, this ruling might strike fear into the hearts of all grandparents, but it should not. The Washington statute that was struck down was extremely broad. In essence, the Washington law said that a court, in its discretion, had power to order that *anyone* who applied to the court could be given visitation rights with a child against the parent's wishes. The Supreme Court thought this law gave judges too much power over parents who hadn't done anything wrong.

This is also pretty much where the Texas law comes down. As long as the biological family made up of mommy, daddy and the kids is together, grandparents have no right to intervene or impose any control over the grandchildren, except with the consent of a child's parent. It is when the family becomes "broken" that grandparents have a right to "step in." Whether the family is "broken" is something that is clearly defined by the courts and not by the grandparents. Moreover, the grandparents' rights must be divided between the right to access (visitation) and the right to *Managing Conservatorship* (custody).

Grandparent Visitation

Grandparents may realistically request a court to grant access or visitation when the family is broken by:

- The death, incarceration, mental incompetency, or termination of parental rights of the parent who is the grandparents' child
- The child's parents filing for divorce or living apart for three months
- The child having been abused or neglected by a parent
- The child having been adjudicated to be a child in need of supervision or delinquent
- The child having resided with the grandparent requesting access for at least six months of the twenty-four months before the request is made

Should any of these events occur and the grandparents request a court to grant access to the grandchild, the court "shall" order reasonable access, provided that such access is "in the best interest of the child." What this means is that, as usual, the court has discretion to do as it sees fit, since, as we said earlier, "the best interest of the child" is pretty much in the eye of the beholder.

Of course, all of this grandparent access is based on the idea that, at the time of the request to the court, there is at least one biological parent whose parental rights have not been terminated. This requirement is designed to keep a grandparent of a child who is being adopted from interfering. This makes sense. If you're going to rescue your grandchild, better not wait around until the rest of the world has decided that there's no other choice but adoption.

Grandparent Custody

To understand how grandparents become the *Managing Conservators* (get custody) of grandchildren, it is necessary to think back to the earlier discussion in this chapter regarding the parents' superior right to children. Remember: The presumption that the parent will be the *Managing Conservator* can be lost if it is shown that having the parent as custodian would not be in the child's best interest because it "would significantly impair the child's physical health or emotional development." Therefore, if there is a likelihood that the parents' retention of control over the children will "significantly impair the child's physical health or emotional development," the court is going to be looking for someone to step into the parents' shoes. That grandparents are selected for the substitute parent role is no accident. Frequently, it is the grandparents who intervened in the divorce case or other proceeding, provided the proof of the parents' unfitness, and show that they are the logical ones to care for the child. Of course, sometimes both parents agree that the child will be better off with a grandparent.

Abandonment or leaving the child for a lengthy period may destroy the presumption that the parent should be made *Managing Conservator*. Grandparents, and anyone else for that matter, have the right to ask to be made *Managing Conservator* of any child who resides with them for at least one year. Even having a child left with someone for six months gives the non-parent care provider the standing (i.e., the right to be heard by the court) to ask to be made *Managing Conservator*.

Also, remember the noted exception to this rule is that in a subsequent case, after a parent already has custody and that custody is being modified, the appointment of the parent is not presumed to be in the child's best interest. In other words, when custody is being modified, parents and grandparents are on more of a level playing field.

Chapter 25

Preventing Child Snatching

Don't limit a child to your own learning, for he was born in another time.

—Rabbinical saying

Having your child stolen by your spouse is one experience even more traumatic than a fight for the custody of your child. Although very few divorces involve this problem, when it does happen its consequences can be emotionally devastating.

Let's be clear about what is meant by "child snatching." The term means to steal away a child with the intent to deprive the other parent of contact with the child for a long period of time—or forever. Merely taking the child somewhere and holding the child while a lawsuit is being filed, papers are being served, or until a temporary hearing can be held, is not child snatching. Sometimes such actions are necessary to protect the child from being taken by the other spouse or to protect the child and you from physical violence. Sometimes it is also necessary to get the child out of the way to avoid exposing him or her to a melodrama when the divorce is announced or the papers are served.

Even in such circumstances, the spouse who is being deprived of contact with the child should be given as much information as is *safe.* He or she should be told, for example, "The children are still here in town and are safe. You will be allowed to see them after the temporary hearing on Friday." Since such conversations usually must take place by telephone or through a third person, a good amount of information concerning the well-being of the children usually can be given without revealing their whereabouts or jeopardizing their safety.

What we're really talking about is kidnaping, except that other criminal laws besides the kidnaping laws apply to parents who take children. Without going into the emotional problems that motivate someone arbitrarily to deprive a child of the right to know the other parent, it is an act that is seldom justifiable.

Throughout this book you have been told you have plenty of time, that there is no need to push in making decisions about your marriage. If, however, you have a spouse who is likely to snatch your child or children, you do not have the luxury of weighing your affections and pondering the future of your marriage. Even if the likelihood is fairly low that your spouse will go through with the threats, the consequences could be devastating. Accordingly, you must act calmly, deliberately, and immediately.

In determining whether there is risk that your spouse will take your child, consider the following questions:

1. Are your children under age ten?
2. Has your spouse made threatening statements about running off with the children?
3. Is your spouse inclined to disregard the law when it suits his or her convenience?
4. Does your spouse lack ties to the community you live in, such as family, friends, job, or other circumstances that would make it difficult to leave town at a whim?
5. Is your spouse insecure or unstable about himself or herself?
6. Has your spouse attempted in the past to manipulate or use the children against you?
7. Has your marriage been mobile? That is, have you and your spouse frequently moved from one place to another?
8. Does your spouse's family live in another state or nation or did your spouse grow up in another state or nation?

9. Does your spouse think of the children as property instead of as persons with certain rights, feelings, and wishes?
10. Would your spouse prefer to see something destroyed rather than be taken from him or her?
11. Perhaps most importantly, does your spouse feel desperate and helpless? Does he or she believe that he or she must resort to physical acts rather than persuade with words?

Although answers to these questions do not guarantee any set response, several "yes" answers should give you pause. And should you decide that you have a potential child snatching problem in your divorce, you should heed the following guidelines:

Avoid Threatening Words

Don't make any threatening statements about keeping the child away from your spouse, depriving him or her of visitation, or running away with the child. This kind of talk may scare your spouse into grabbing the child and running first.

Respond Correctly to Threats

Respond to your spouse's threats to take the child by saying you believe that depriving the child of the right to know both of his or her parents would hurt the child more than anything else. Say that, for the sake of the child, you would never think of depriving your spouse of contact with the child.

Don't Make False Starts

This is like grabbing the rope on the wild horse before you are prepared to tug—you'll scare him, and he'll drag you to death. If your spouse threatens to take the kids every time you talk about divorce, then don't talk about it anymore—ever. You will have to decide about your marriage by yourself or by talking to someone else. Don't grab for the child until you can stay gone and keep the child out of your spouse's reach until a lawsuit is filed and restraining orders are granted. Making fast unplanned moves in front of a potential child snatcher is like waving a red blanket in front of a bull.

Go See a Lawyer

Preferably, as far in advance of your divorce as possible. Dealing with a potential child snatcher deserves thought and planning.

If Your Spouse Lives or Works in a Distant Place, Do Not Wait to File Your Divorce

Your residence and domicile might be where you live, and your spouse might have an equally valid claim to residence in another county or domicile in another state. When this is the case, the spouse who files first usually retains jurisdiction to the determent of the other. Your spouse may claim residence or domicile somewhere else, with a relative or friend or where he or she has been working. In such cases, early filings are easier to prove than residency or domicile is to disprove. In a custody fight, *where* the battle takes place can be crucial.

Consider Filing Your Divorce Even If Your Spouse Cannot Establish Domicile Elsewhere

Texas has a criminal statute that is invoked if a parent takes a child out of the state for more than seven days while knowing that a divorce suit is pending. Also, if you have a divorce filed and your spouse has been served, you have numerous remedies not available otherwise. You can request restraining orders, temporary custody orders, writs of attachment (ordering any sheriff in the state to pick up the child), contempt orders, and writs of *habeas corpus* (ordering that the child be brought before the court). In short, if you get your spouse in court, he or she still might run with the child, but you won't have to go looking for him or her by yourself. You will have the power of the law to help you in the search. It will be much more difficult for your spouse to hide from all of organized society than from you alone.

Chapter 26

Child Support

We think in generalities, but we live in details.

—Alfred North Whitehead

The best brought up children are those
who have seen their parents as they are.
Hypocrisy is not the parent's first duty.

—George Bernard Shaw

Child support is nothing new. In common law, the parents had a duty to support their children. That duty has, of course, been brought forward to the present.

In a divorce case, this duty to support is handled by having the Possessory Conservator (non-custodial parent) pay money to the Managing Conservator (custodial parent). Usually these payments are made on a weekly, biweekly, or monthly basis. However, courts are not limited to ordering periodic payments. Parents can be ordered to make large lump-sum payments, to purchase an annuity, to set aside property to be administered for the support of the child, or any combination of all available methods.

The money paid for support is, typically, paid to the Texas "state disbursement unit" or the "state disbursement unit of another state," and that organization then forwards it to the receiving parent after having made a record of the payment for the court. (In prior times, payment was made to the local district clerk who then forwarded it to the receiving parent. Some older divorce decrees may still be controlled by this procedure.)

The parent receiving the money, although generally obligated to care for the child, may spend the money in any way he or she sees fit. The court requires no accounting for these monies after they are received.

In Texas, *in addition* to a dollar amount, the term "child support" also means providing the child with health insurance.

This Is Not Your Father's Oldsmobile

Whether you're the spouse paying child support or the one entitled to receive it, this whole concept of "child support" bears a second look. If you're the one paying, you may be tempted to see it as just another obligation you owe. Or, if you're the one receiving support, you may view it as just some additional income.

A child support obligation is not just another debt. Nor is it the same as your boss increasing your income by giving you a pay increase for the same amount.

A $500.00 per month wage increase is not equal to receiving $500.00 in child support from your ex-spouse. A pay increase is subject to income tax being withheld at the applicable rate, as well as withholdings for social security and medicare. So, a $500.00 per month raise means taking home, at best, $400.00 of that money, and, if you are in a higher tax bracket, perhaps closer to $300.00. If, on the other hand, you are paid $500.00 in child support, you get to keep it all. Your ex-spouse has already paid the tax, and social security and medicare have been withheld. It comes to you tax free.

Likewise, child support obligation is not the same as money owed on a credit card or for a car payment. If a credit card is not paid, it will be canceled. If car payments are not made, creditors will take the car away. If child support is not paid, someone may go to jail or have a driver's license canceled in addition to all of the other bad things that can happen when debts are not paid. As will be seen in this chapter, a child support obligation is a debt on steroids.

Who Decides about Child Support?

Decisions about child support are made by the judge. Unlike the decision about child custody, which can be made by a jury if one of the parties so elects, the question of who will pay and how much are exclusively within the judge's realm of decision making.

In making these child support decisions, the judge has limited discretion and must largely be guided by rules and guidelines that prescribe the terms of support.

Of course, the divorcing parents may enter into agreements regarding the amounts and terms of paying support. However, even these agreements are subject to review by the judge who must determine whether such agreements are "in the child's best interest."

Setting Child Support by Agreement

Child support also can be set by agreement between the divorcing spouses, although such agreements are subject to approval by the judge who must determine whether such agreements are "in the child's best interest." Judges usually like to encourage agreed amounts of child support, since it helps settle cases, thereby lightening the court's workload. Most judges are also aware that people usually honor something they have agreed to better than something that they are ordered to do. Of course, such agreements are entered as court orders and can be enforced just like any other child support order.

Child support agreements are subject to "public policy" limitations. This is not just a contract between two people. The State will always have an interest in looking out for the best interest of the child. No agreement is allowed to fix child support permanently. If and when the court thinks it needs to step in to revise the agreement, it will always have the power to do so.

Who Pays?

Child support is an obligation of the parents. Only parents can be ordered to pay. Even if grandparents, step-parents, or others intervene in the divorce, are awarded custody, or end up taking care of the child, they cannot be ordered to pay child support.

In divorce, the idea is that the parent who is actually taking care of the child will receive child support from the parent who is not as involved in the child's care. So, traditionally, the Possessory Conservator (the non-custodial parent) was ordered to pay support to the Managing Conservator (the custodial parent). Historically, it was the man who paid the woman. This was because the woman was the one who stayed home and cared for the child, and the man didn't have time to take care of the child because he worked and made all the money. Sometimes things still work out this way.

But often they don't. To begin with, the law now says that it is presumed to be in the child's best interest for both parents to be named as Joint Managing Conservators. This means that frequently, at least in name, we are all custodial parents. Then the addition of the Standard Possession Order gives literal meaning to this everybody-has-custody ideal. Using a Standard Possession Order to count the days on a calender quickly reveals that the division of actual time the child spends with each parent is very close to being equal. So, in a world of equals, who should pay and who should receive child support? Never fear! The system always has easy answers that are satisfactory to everyone except those who have actually thought about it or have to live with those answers.

Of course, one of the Joint Managing Conservators will be given the right to designate the child's primary residence. And this is where judges, law professors, and others who are charged with providing answers every day of the year, find their way back to telling us who pays and who receives child support. Even though we say that everyone is equal in the world of Joint Managing Conservators, it turns out that some are more equal than others. For purposes of setting child support, the parent who has the right to designate the child's primary residency is treated as the custodial parent and is presumed to be the appropriate one to receive child support. Likewise, the parent who does not have the right to designate the child's primary residency will be treated as the non-custodial parent and is presumed to be the appropriate one to pay child support.

In summary, child support is just one more item deserving of consideration when it is decided who is to be Sole Managing CSonservator or the Joint Managing Conservator with the right to designate the child's primary residence.

How Long?

Child support must be paid until the child reaches 18 years of age or graduates from high school, whichever occurs later. If, after reaching age 18, the child remains enrolled in a public or private accredited secondary school and meets the minimum attendance requirements, child support will continue until graduation, which must occur before the child reaches age 21.

If a child dies, is emancipated by marriage or through removal of disabilities of minority by court order or other operation of law, then child support ends before age 18.

Finally, if a child is disabled, support can be ordered to continue indefinitely into adulthood.

Child Support Guidelines

Texas has adopted uniform, statewide guidelines for judges to use in setting the amount of child support to be paid. These guidelines are based on a percentage of the "Net Resources" of the *person who is paying the support* (sometimes called the "obligor"). The term "Net Resources" roughly means the total income minus income taxes, social security and medicare contributions, union dues, and amounts spent on health insurance for the children of the person paying support. Additionally, the guidelines "are specifically designed to apply to situations in which the paying parent's (obligor's) monthly net resources are $6,000.00 or less."

The guidelines are as follows:

- 1 child 20% of Paying Parent's Net Resources
- 2 children 25% of Paying Parent's Net Resources
- 3 children 30% of Paying Parent's Net Resources
- 4 children 35% of Paying Parent's Net Resources
- 5 children 40% of Paying Parent's Net Resources
- 6+ children Not less than the amount for 5 children

When one of the children receiving support reaches age 18 or otherwise has support terminated, then the support reverts to the level of support for the remaining child or children. For example, if support is being paid for two children at the level of 25% of net resources, when child support for one is terminated, the support reverts to the 20% level required for the remaining child.

Applying the Guidelines to More Than One Household

What if the person paying support has the legal obligation to support more than one set of children? If ex-spouse one has two children and ex-spouse two has another child, who gets paid what?

The law provides a formula that modifies the guidelines to take into account the fact that the paying spouse has other children that he or she is *legally* obligated to support. This formula is rather lengthy and involved. Usually judges, lawyers, and others in the family law system use an alternate set of percentage guidelines that are set out in chart form in the statute on this subject, which follows:

Multiple Family Adjusted Guidelines

Percent of Net Resources

The numbers across the top represent the number of children before the court.
Numbers down the left side represent the number of *other* children
for whom the obligor has a duty of support.

	1	2	3	4	5	6	7
0	20.00%	25.00%	30.00%	35.00%	40.00%	40.00%	40.00%
1	17.50%	22.50%	27.38%	32.20%	37.33%	37.71%	38.00%
2	16.00%	20.63%	25.20%	30.33%	35.43%	36.00%	36.44%
3	14.75%	19.00%	24.00%	29.00%	34.00%	34.67%	35.20%
4	13.60%	18.33%	23.14%	28.00%	32.89%	33.60%	34.18%
5	13.33%	17.86%	22.50%	27.22%	32.00%	32.73%	33.33%
6	13.14%	17.50%	22.00%	26.60%	31.27%	32.00%	32.62%
7	13.00%	17.22%	21.60%	26.09%	30.67%	31.38%	32.00%

Parent with Net Income above $6,000.00

If the income of a parent paying support is high enough so that he or she has net resources that exceed $6,000.00 per month, in computing child support the court will apply the percentage guidelines to the first $6,000.00 of net resources. Any additional child support, after the amount that is computed using the $6,000.00 as net resources, must then be based on the "proven needs of the child." In other words, the parent asking that higher child support be paid will be required to demonstrate for the court that the child has needs over and above the amount of child support that is required by the guidelines being applied to the $6,000.00 amount. If the child is shown to have additional needs, then the court will allocate the responsibility for meeting the child's additional needs between the parents based on their circumstances.

How Are "Net Resources" Computed?

The court's decision about the amount of child support necessarily begins with a determination of the amount of the total resources available to the paying parent. Here's how the computation is made.

Resources Include:

- 100 percent of all wage and salary income and other compensation for personal services (including commissions, overtime pay, tips, and bonuses)
- Interest, dividends, and royalty income
- Self-employment income
- Net rental income (defined as rent after deducting operating expenses and mortgage payments, but not including non-cash items such as depreciation)
- All other income actually being received, including severance pay, retirement benefits, pensions, trust income, annuities, capital gains, social security benefits, unemployment benefits, disability and workers' compensation benefits, interest income from notes regardless of the source, gifts and prizes, spousal maintenance, and alimony

Resources Do Not Include:

- Return of interest or capital
- Accounts receivable
- Benefits paid in accordance with aid for families with dependent children

The Court Then Deducts the Following Items to Determine "Net Resources":

- Social security tax
- Federal income tax based on the tax rate for a single person claiming one personal exemption and the standard deduction
- State income tax
- Union dues
- Expenses for health insurance coverage for the paying parent's child

The bottom line from this computation is the "net resources" that the judge is to use to multiply times the guideline percentage (e.g., times 20%, if there is one child).

"Whenever feasible, *gross income should be computed on an annual basis* and then should be recalculated to determine average monthly gross income." (*emphasis added*).

As you can see, the "guidelines" process leaves the judge very little "wiggle room" or discretion.

Office of Attorney General Tax Charts

Actually, judges, lawyers, and others working in the family law system seldom do the actual computations described above to determine net resources. Each year the Texas Attorney General is required by law to publish a "tax chart," which can be used to convert the paying parent's "gross wages" or "monthly net earnings" from self-employment into "net monthly income." When federal tax law changes during the year, there are times when the Attorney General revises the tax chart more than one time per year. Since the charts change every year, a copy of that chart is not published with this book. Copies of the current Attorney General tax charts for both employed and self-employed persons can be found at: http://www.oag.state.tx.us/AG_Publications/pdfs/2003taxcharts.pdf.

Must the Judge Always Follow the Guidelines?

No, not always. But almost always. The amount of child support computed by using the guideline process is *presumed* to be the correct amount. If the judge goes above or below this amount, he or she must specifically give reasons that were used in making the decision to "depart" from the guidelines. In other words, the judge's decision *not* to follow the guidelines is subject to very close examination by an appellate court.

What are some of the reasons (factors) a judge may legitimately use to "rebut the presumption" and order an amount of child support that is above or below the guideline amount? Here are a few reasons that may be used:

- The age and needs of the child
- The ability of the parents to contribute support
- Any financial resources available for the support of the child
- The amount of time of possession and access to the child
- The amount of the person-receiving-support's (obligee's) net resources, including the earnings potential of the obligee if the actual income of the obligee is significantly less than what the obligee could earn because the obligee is intentionally unemployed or underemployed and including an increase or decrease in the income of the obligee or income that may be attributed to the property and assets of the obligee
- Child care expenses incurred by either party in order to maintain gainful employment
- Whether either party has the Managing Conservatorship or actual physical custody of another child
- The amount of alimony or spousal maintenance actually and currently being paid or received by a party

- The expense for a son or daughter for education beyond secondary school
- Whether the paying parent (obligor) or receiving parent (obligee) has an automobile, housing, or other benefits furnished by his or her employer, another person, or a business entity
- The amount of other deductions from the wage or salary income and from other compensation for personal services of the parties
- Provision for health-care insurance and payment of uninsured medical expenses
- Special or extraordinary educational, health-care, or other expenses of the parties or of the child
- The cost of travel in order to exercise possession of the child
- Positive or negative cash flow from any real and personal property and assets, including a business and investments
- Debts or debt service assumed by either party
- Any other reason consistent with the best interest of the child, taking into consideration the circumstances of the parents

Accounting Is a Required Course

It is clear that judges must have financial records and accounting in order to make accurate decisions about "net resources" as well as other child support issues. The Texas legislature has clearly said that courts are to "require" a party to "furnish information sufficient to accurately identify that party's net resources and ability to pay child support." This specifically, at the very least, must include copies of income tax returns for the past two years, a financial statement, and current pay stubs.

The New Spouse

The new spouse's net resources cannot be added to the net resources of the paying spouse to calculate the child support to be ordered. Likewise, the fact that a person receiving support has married a rich spouse is not supposed to affect the amount of child support he or she is being paid.

By the same token, the judge is not allowed to subtract the needs of the new spouse and his or her children from the net resources of the spouse paying support. Nor should the needs of the new spouse of a parent receiving support and the needs of his or her children be considered as a reason for an increase in support.

Income Withholding

Virtually every person who is employed in the United States has part of his or her income withheld by his or her employer to pay income taxes, social security, and medicare. Essentially the same system is used by the State of Texas to withhold money that has been ordered paid as child support.

When a divorce decree is entered, a separate court order is also entered ordering the paying parent's employer to withhold the child support from the paying parent's wages and forward it to the person or office named in the withholding order. Texas courts have no discretion *not* to enter a withholding order. The court is allowed only slight "wiggle room" in that it may, "for good cause shown or on agreement of the parties," provide that the withholding order not be issued or delivered to the employer unless and until a violation of the child support order occurs or the paying parent is behind more than thirty days. There is no doubt about the legislature's seriousness on this subject. Even child support orders that fail to include the provision for withholding "must be construed to contain a withholding provision."

Further evidence of the seriousness of income withholding is the fact that the employer is liable to the receiving parent for all amounts not properly withheld, along with interest thereon. Additionally, an employer may be fined for non-compliance.

Intentional Unemployment or Underemployment

If the paying parent is intentionally unemployed or underemployed, the judge has authority to determine the paying parent's "earning potential" and apply the child support guidelines to that amount instead of the amount that is actually being earned.

"Buried Treasure"

If the paying parent has assets that have value but are not producing income, the court may assign a reasonable amount of "deemed income" to that property. Also, the court can decide whether non-income producing property "can be liquidated without an unreasonable financial sacrifice because of cyclical or other market conditions."

What about those cases in which the parent who has an obligation to pay child support has decided to "sell" or "give" Cousin Charlie the apartment building that brings in rent every month or the oil well that regularly pays a royalty check? This way, the paying spouse figures, the judge won't be able to use the income from the apartment rents or the oil income in calculating his or her net resources. Wrong! Unfortunately, this kind of "creative" income planning is not new to courts. So, the law says that the judge can include the income that the paying parent would have received from income-producing assets that he or she "has voluntarily transferred or on which earnings have intentionally been reduced."

Minimum Wage Presumption

Finally, even if the judge setting child support has no evidence of how much income the parent paying child support earns, the court is still entitled to presume that the paying parent has wages or salary equal to the federal minimum wage for a forty-hour week. This presumption is so strong, even when there is no evidence to the contrary, that a trial court's ruling to this effect was sustained on appeal even when the paying party was in jail.

Health Insurance Is a Part of Child Support

The parent being required to pay child support is, with rare exception, also required to provide or pay for health insurance for the child *in addition to the child support mandated under the guidelines.* Texas has mandated that judges follow prescribed guidelines ("priorities") to provide health insurance to children as an additional part of child support. Judges can vary from this mandated process only if "a party shows good cause why a particular order would not be in the best interest of the child."

This mandatory system of priorities is built around a concept of "reasonable cost." In other words, insurance coverage for the child will be provided by the most preferred manner (paying parent's employer), if insurance can be purchased in that manner at a "reasonable cost." If it cannot be purchased at a "reasonable cost," then the court resorts to the second most preferred method (support receiving parent's employer). Then the third, fourth, and fifth methods, until, hopefully the child can be provided health care at a "reasonable cost."

The key to this priority system is the definition of "reasonable cost." "Reasonable cost" is defined as "a health insurance premium that does not exceed 10 percent of the responsible parent's net income in a month."

Judges are to order that health insurance coverage be provided to the child in the following order of priority *if it is available at "reasonable cost"*:

> *First,* through the paying parent's employment, union, trade association, or other organization, and if that won't work, then;
>
> *Second,* through the support receiving parent's (obligee's) employment, union, trade association or other organization, and if that won't work, then;
>
> *Third,* through any other source, and if that won't work, then;
>
> *Fourth,* the parents are ordered to apply on behalf of the child for participation in a medical assistance program under Chapter 32, Human Resources Code, or under Chapter 62, Health and Safety Code, and the parent paying child support is to pay for participation in one of these plans by having additional child support withheld from his or her wages, and if that won't work, then;
>
> *Fifth,* the parent paying child support is ordered to pay an additional amount of support over and above the guideline amount that will be withheld from wages and referred to as "medical support."

In other words, in a world in which health insurance coverage can be hard to come by for many people, the Texas legislature is committed to the idea that at least children of divorcing parents are going to have that coverage.

Child Support Obligations – Debt on Steroids

Except for child support, only the Federal Government in all of its majesty is allowed to require that money be withheld from a payroll check. Payroll checks are so sacred in Texas that no other creditor can touch them. Federal withholding and child support are exceptions to this sacrosanct status. This says a lot about the priority that society gives to seeing that child support obligations are paid.

Child support orders can be enforced in a number of different ways:

- *Failure to pay support can result in the defaulting spouse going to jail.* The party receiving the support may file a Motion for Contempt asking that the person who has failed to pay the support be held in contempt of court for disobeying the court's order to pay. The court then issues a show cause order, ordering the person who allegedly has not paid to appear and show cause why he or she should not be held in contempt of court. Upon hearing, the court will be interested in only two defenses: (1) I really did pay, and here is proof that I did; and (2) I could not pay, and here is strong proof that I could not. Courts are not at all impressed with evidence that it was inconvenient to pay, or that you couldn't pay because of payments on the color TV or the new car.

  Often a judge will give someone who is behind in child support at least one chance to purge himself or herself of the contempt. The court will order that the arrearage be paid within certain time periods on certain terms. Often attorney's fees are awarded against someone held in contempt.
- *Child support can be enforced by having it reduced to a money judgment.* There is a provision in Texas law that allows this to be done by giving the person who has failed to pay the support ten (10) days' notice, after which time a hearing is held, and the judge enters the money judgment for the amount of the support. After the judgment becomes final in thirty days, the sheriff can be sent to execute on any non-exempt property owned by the nonpaying spouse.

- *Failure to pay child support can result in the loss of a license.* This means that any license issued by the State of Texas can be taken away. The most obvious is the driver's license. But there is a long list of activities that require a license issued by the State of Texas before that activity is legal. Some examples of people who can lose their license for failure to pay child support are: bartenders, appraisers, architects, barbers, chiropractors, CPAs, cosmologists, court reporters, dentists, dietitians, funeral directors, social workers, psychologists, nurses, optometrists, pharmacists, plumbers, security guards, realtors, lawyers, vets, doctors, insurance agents, and engineers. There are others, not to mention that you can lose your license to hunt or fish.

  To lose a license for nonpayment of child support, the amount overdue must be equal to or greater than the total support due for three months, and the delinquent paying parent must have been given an opportunity to pay and have failed to comply with a repayment schedule. Of course, to get this done there must be a petition to the court, notice to the individual who is delinquent, and a hearing or opportunity for a hearing.
- *Child support obligations easily cross state lines.* When a person owing an ordinary debt moves to another state, it can be difficult to follow the debtor to the new state to collect the delinquent debt. Not so with child support. There are a variety of laws that aid a parent who is owed support by an ex-spouse who has left Texas. Employers in other states can be required to honor Texas withholding orders. Sometimes Texas courts retain power over nonpaying ex-spouses and can bring them back for contempt of court proceedings. Texas has enacted the Uniform Interstate Family Support Act. This means that other states have agreed and are required to cooperate with Texas in collecting child support from Texas residents who have moved to other states.
- *Child support obligations are not barred by a statute of limitations.* Other debts or claims, of course, require that actions for collection be brought within a reasonable period or the right to collect is forfeited. Usually this period is two years, four years, or some similar period. Not child support. It is not lost by any statute of limitations.

- *Child support obligations cannot be discharged in bankruptcy.* Unlike other debt, which is discharged (written off) when an individual takes bankruptcy, child support obligations continue past bankruptcy and, if unpaid, will follow the delinquent spouse to the grave.

SECTION VI

Divorce Property Division

In this section:

Chapter 27

Marital Property: Basic Concepts

Money is the seed of money, and the first franc is sometimes more difficult to acquire than the second million.

—Jean Jacques Rousseau

To get a divorce you don't need to be an expert on the law of community property. You do need an overview of some basic concepts so that you can know what you are getting or giving up in a settlement offer and whether you should settle or try your case.

This chapter is designed for such an overview and may not encompass all of the details and ramifications that affect your case. It is important that you rely on a lawyer to help you make decisions about your individual case. Laws change and are sometimes applied somewhat differently from court to court.

Although there is a short discussion of premarital and post-marital agreements in a subsequent chapter, *the discussion in this chapter assumes there is no premarital or post-marital agreement between the spouses.* Naturally, a valid premarital or post-marital agreement can change all or a portion of the rules discussed in this chapter.

Caution: Although there are several states that are community property states, the laws vary somewhat from state to state. It is dangerous to assume that the laws are the same. In making decisions about your Texas property division, do not rely on materials from other states or on law school materials that are prepared to teach students about community property in general. Also, do not rely on this chapter as an accurate statement of the law in any other community property state.

The World's Shortest History Lesson

Virtually the whole legal system in most of the United States, including Texas, is patterned after the common law system used in England. This is *not* true, however, of the Texas law that governs the property rights of married couples. Texas is commonly referred to as a community property state. Rather than coming from the English common law system, community property comes from the civil law developed by the Romans and used in Europe. Our community system came to us from Spain by way of Mexico.

When Texas won its independence from Mexico, a law was passed kicking out the Mexican civil law and adopting the English common law system. That same law retained the community property aspect of the Mexican law.

Well, that's enough history.

A Short Interpretation of the World's Shortest History Lesson

Throughout history women had very few rights. Mostly, women were treated as the slaves or property of men. The concept of community property broke with this tradition of women as property. Community property laws gave women an *ownership interest* in the property acquired during the marriage. The philosophy of community property is that the marriage partners are a team or a "community." The idea is that whatever one spouse earns the other has an *ownership interest* in, because of his or her supportive role in helping the partner who actually earned or acquired the property.

What All of This Has to Do with Your Marriage

Instead of forgetting about all of this ancient history, modern law has decided to hang onto it. It is hard to overstate how seriously the state of Texas takes the community effort or teamwork concept. If you are married, the state assumes the existence of a community.

If, while you are married, you discover the cure for the common cold and become a billionaire overnight, your spouse has an interest in your billions. This is true even if your spouse has spent the last ten years (while you were doing your research) in the Texas penitentiary making license plates by day and reading trash movie magazines by night—and hasn't sent you a postcard the whole time. Your spouse still has an ownership claim in the billion-dollar community.

Similarly, if your spouse writes the great American novel and makes millions, while you spend all your time on skid row and make nothing, you still have an ownership interest in the community property.

What Is Community Property?

If you were taking an exam on community property, there is one rule you would need to memorize to pass the test:

> *Community property is* all *property acquired* after *the marriage,* except *property that* one *spouse is* given, inherits, *or* recovers for personal injuries.

That's the main rule.

The day before you married, your wages were your *separate property.* The wages you earn the day *after* you are married are *community property.* The day you are married, the *interest* from your savings account and dividends from your stocks starts being community property. Just like the rule says: *everything* you acquire after you are married, except gifts, inheritance, or recovery for injuries, is community property.

Now, don't read over the definition of community property thinking it is just an ordinary definition. It is heavily weighted in favor of community property. It is one of those trick definitions that's more than it appears to be at first glance. It's like the contracts the white man made with the Indians: "You guys take these glass beads, the shiny mirrors, this knife, and this hatchet, and we take *everything else*" (emphasis added, since such things are written in fine print). It is written in what lawyers refer to as catch-all language.

I do not point out this tilting of the playing field in favor of community to show disapproval. This weighing of things in favor of the community probably accurately reflects our society's values. I merely want you to understand that the law is written heavily in favor of community property.

What Is Separate Property?

Separate property is property owned by a married person in which the spouse has no *ownership interest.*

As you see, separate is the missing part of the pie in the community property definition; I will repeat it again.

Separate property is only:

1. Property acquired before marriage
2. Gifts
3. Inheritance
4. Recovery for personal injuries

Not all recoveries of monies in a personal injury lawsuit are separate. For example, recovery for loss of earnings is *community property.*

Income from Separate Property

Unlike some other states, Texas considers that the income from a spouse's separate property is community income. If your spouse rents her apartment house that she inherited, the rental income is community property.

What If the Marriage Occurs during the Transaction? Is the Property Community or Separate?

Now that we are clear that property owned before marriage is separate and that property acquired afterward (with a few exceptions) is community, we must consider what "acquired" means. If you go down to the store, hand the clerk $1,000, and take delivery on a new dining table, it is obvious that you bought or acquired the table on that date. But many transactions cannot be handled like this. Purchases of real estate, companies, inventories, and so on, usually are completed over weeks and sometimes even months. Texas is referred to as an *inception of title* state. This means that when the first act that is legally binding on the parties to the contract is carried out, that is the time when title is acquired for community property purposes. So, if someone is married in the middle of such a transaction, is the property separate or community? For example, what if the wife entered into a contract to purchase a house before she married, but did not receive the deed to the property? In Texas, it is separate property because the initial contract was binding.

The *inception of title* rule also applies to credit contracts. For example, if the wife paid only $5,000 down on a house when she purchased it *one week* before the marriage and over the next ten years the couple paid $50,000 on the mortgage, the house is still separate property. Of course, the community will be entitled to recover for its economic contribution of the principal paid by the couple.

What Difference Does It Make Whether Property Is Characterized as "Community" or "Separate"?

A big difference! *Generally,* since community property is owned by both spouses, it will be *divided* between them. It is not unusual for a judge to attempt to divide the community property equally—one-half to each side. However, it is important to understand that the court is not *required* to divide the community property *equally.*

On the other hand, since separate property is owned by only one spouse, the judge is not free to give it to the other spouse or to divide it between spouses. The judge *must* award separate property to the spouse who owns it. The judge is free, however, to "administer" separate property for the benefit of minor children of the marriage. And, as is discussed below, the court can attach a lien to separate property to make certain that the community property or the other spouse's separate property is paid back for any "economic contribution" made to the separate property.

Living Apart Does Not Change the Law

What effect does separation or living apart have on the community property laws in Texas? None! Whoever it was that told you separation makes a difference was thinking about the laws of some other state.

This does not mean a particular judge may not consider the separation in dividing the community. It does mean that all salary, interest, dividends, winnings from gambling, and other income are still community property. Any property you are acquiring while separated, from any source, is still presumed to be community.

Living in Another State during the Marriage May Affect the Division of Property in a Texas Divorce

When a couple moves to Texas from another state, the property they bring with them enters Texas with the same ownership characteristics that it had when it left the other state. For example, property earned by the husband in a *common law* state, which would be community property had the couple lived in Texas, may be considered separate property in the other state. Texas has a statute that treats such property as community property. It is often referred to as *quasi-community* property. Likewise, Texas law treats as separate property, property acquired while living in another state that would have been separate had it been acquired in Texas.

The Name on the Property

With a few exceptions the name in which property is held has no significance in deciding whether it is community or separate property. Remember, it is the *source* of the property that decides whether it fits into the community or a separate category. Even if property is held in your name, your spouse's name, or both of your names, once *ownership* is established *during* the marriage, it still is presumed to be community property. Changing the name or label will not erase the presumption of community.

There are a couple of exceptions:

Exception One

If one spouse transfers property from his or her name of control into the other spouse's name, there is a presumption that a gift was intended. For example, if the husband owns land that he deeds to his wife, it is presumed that he intended to make a gift of all the land to her. If he deeded his separate property land to himself and his wife, it is presumed that he intended to give her a one-half undivided interest in the land as her separate property. If the husband were to deed the wife land that they both owned as community property, it is presumed that he intended to give her his community interest to hold as her separate property. All of these examples would still be true if it were the wife deeding property to the husband.

Exception Two

If the husband participated in a transaction in which property was placed in the wife's name, it is presumed to be her separate property. For example, if the husband purchased land with funds under his control and has the deed name his wife as owner, it is presumed to be her separate property. Given the Texas equal rights amendment, it may be that the reverse would be true when the wife purchases property in her husband's name.

Also, if the husband makes such a purchase and has the deed made to his wife as "her sole and separate property," it is likely that the rules of evidence will prevent him from presenting evidence to the contrary in court. In this case, the name would be conclusively controlling to place the title in the wife's name as her separate property.

Although the name on the property does not usually determine whether the property is community or separate, it definitely does play a big role in deciding who has control of the property. This will be discussed in a subsequent section.

If Separate Property Is Placed in a Trust for One Spouse, Is Income Therefrom Community Property?

Maybe yes, maybe no. If funds are actually paid to the beneficiary spouse from trust income, those funds are community property.

Some trust instruments *require* trust income to be paid on an annual basis. Other trust instruments allow the beneficiary spouse to demand payment of trust income. If a trust contains such a provision, the trust income is probably community property even if the beneficiary spouse elects to have it retained in the trust.

If, on the other hand, the trustee has the sole discretion to determine whether the beneficiary spouse is to be paid the income, and no income is paid, then any income the trust may have earned but retained in the trust is not community property.

If a spouse is the "settlor" or the person who set up the trust, there is a likelihood that any income from the trust is community property. This is doubly true if the spouse retains any right to revoke or other powers over the trust. Such trusts are said to be "illusory."

Many trusts are established for estate planning purposes. Because the Internal Revenue Code requires that gift recipients have a "present interest" in gifted property and estate tax rules relating to the ownership and taxability of insurance policies, many trusts that appear on the surface to be exempt from community property claims may, in fact, contain community property subject to division on divorce.

Other topics in this chapter discuss "alter ego" and "fraudulent transfers." It is important to remember that a trust is subject to these concepts.

A spouse will not be allowed to thwart the community property laws by making transfers into a trust.

These are but examples of the complexity of this subject. If you are facing a divorce and your spouse is the beneficiary of one or more trusts, the trust documents should be closely and thoroughly examined by an attorney familiar with financial matters.

Credit Is Presumed to Be Community Property

After the marriage, the credit of the parties, individually and jointly, is presumed to be community property. The use of community credit can keep a transaction from being merely a change in form of separate property and cause it to be community in character. For example, suppose the wife owns a farm at the time of the marriage (separate property), which she decides to trade for another farm. If she trades even, or if she sells the first farm and uses the un-commingled funds to buy the second farm, then it is still separate property, since we can *trace* the funds from one farm to another and find that it was only a change in *form* (mutation). If, on the other hand, she sells the first farm for $200,000, and buys another for $250,000, by using the $200,000 in separate funds *and* borrowing an additional $50,000, then the second farm is community property because the community credit has been used in its purchase. This is true even if her husband did not sign the note for the loan. Of course, on divorce she could *trace* the $200,000 in separate funds, and her separate estate would be entitled to a claim for economic contribution.

Texas courts, however, do recognize separate credit. In the foregoing example, if the wife had an agreement from the bank that loaned her the $50,000 that the bank would look only to her separate property for payment of the loan, then the credit would be separate credit, and hence, the farm would be separate property. Also, if she only temporarily borrowed the $50,000, intending to pay it back with other separate property, it is likely that the court could still find that the farm was her separate property.

Increase in Value (Appreciation)

The increase in value of separate property is separate. The increase in value of community property is community. In times of high inflation, this factor is critical.

For example, assume that one week before the marriage in 1994 the husband purchased a $60,000 house by making a $5,000 down payment and borrowing $55,000. In 2004, when the house was worth $150,000, the couple divorced. The court will probably rule that the house is the husband's separate property and that the community is entitled only to a claim for economic contribution for payments on principal, amounting to less than $6,000. The house payments made by the community were several hundred dollars per month; however, most of these payments went for taxes, insurance, and interest, which the court would not allow as a part of the claim for economic contribution.

Now, let's assume that the husband bought the house one week after marriage, using the very same $5,000 of his separate monies to make the down payment and borrowing the same $55,000. On divorce in 2004, the judge would have found the house to be community property and that the husband was entitled to have a claim for economic contribution for the $5,000 separate property down payment. The remainder of the value on the date of divorce ($150,000) might be divided equally after subtracting the cost of sale (assuming the judge decided to divide equally). The wife nets $72,500 less one-half of the remaining mortgage and cost of sale, instead of $3,000 for her one-half of the reduction in principal described in the first example. Obviously, the question of who gets the appreciation can be very important.

Professional Degrees

It is not uncommon in young marriages for one spouse to work to earn the money to send the other spouse to school. Many communities (couples) invest large amounts of income in enabling one of the spouses to obtain a medical, dental, law, or some other kind of professional degree. If, after this big investment, there is a divorce, the spouse with the degree, of course, takes a disproportionately large part of the community resources out of the marriage. The problem is compounded by the fact that these couples often have very little community property with which the court can equalize the situation upon divorce.

This often leads to an attempt by one of the spouses to claim that the professional degree, acquired during the marriage, should be considered community property. This would allow the non-degreed spouse to be repaid for the contribution made to the cost of the degree.

In Texas, this is not the law. A professional degree is not community property.

Good Will

A successful business creates *good will* on the part of the public. This *good will* causes customers to continue spending money with the business. For this reason, *good will* is a property right apart from the real estate, fixtures, or inventory of a business. It can be bought or sold. *Good will* may be community property.

Since a professional degree is not community property subject to division, spouses have been quick to look to the professional's *good will.* Like other businesses, a doctor, lawyer, dentist, or veterinarian has *good will* that is property. Some courts have been able to distinguish between the personality of the professional spouse or his or her degree on the one hand and his or her business *good will* on the other. Such a distinction is not always possible. It is easier to separate the two if the professional is working in a corporation or in a group that has good will apart from that of the individual professional.

If a court can determine that such separate *good will* exists, it will take this property interest into consideration in dividing the property on divorce.

Sometimes professional corporations or partnerships deny compensation for *good will* to their individual professional partners by requiring all members of the group to sign buy-sell agreements that exclude the value of *good will.* In these instances, there is no *good will* to divide since the spouse partner does not have any interest except by continuing to practice his or her profession as a member of the firm.

A Short Lesson in Oil and Gas Law

Assume that your spouse signs an oil and gas lease for his or her inherited West Texas ranch, which is separate property, leasing it to the Big Oil Company. The lease gives Big Oil the right to drill on the property and to produce the oil and gas found there. Your spouse reserves a one-eighth undivided royalty in any oil or gas that might be produced. Big Oil strikes oil. When the royalty checks begin to arrive, your spouse informs you that his "royalty income" is his or her separate property. Well, the very idea!

Don't waste your hard-earned money (from waiting tables, no doubt) to consult a lawyer on this question. This one time your spouse is right. Make a note of it.

The royalty payment is not "acquired" during the marriage. It is payment for a one-eighth interest in the oil pumped to the surface. Your spouse never sold this oil until now, since it was reserved in the lease. In Texas, oil, gas, or other minerals are considered to be a part of the land. When the oil is sold, it is like selling a part of the land, rather than receiving income from the land. "Bonus" payments, which your spouse may also have received by virtue of the lease, are considered advance royalties.

On the other hand, the oil and gas lease may have required Big Oil to pay your spouse rental payments or "delay rentals." If so, these items are considered, like any other rental income, community property. Should your spouse participate in the operation of the oil and gas properties and thereby be compensated for efforts or risk that are not associated with his royalty interest, income from such activity is community property.

Separate Maintenance: The Texas Version of Alimony

Historically, other states have used the concept of "alimony" to balance unfair or unequal divorce property divisions. Texas has long been famous (some would say notorious) as the only state in which a court could not order post-divorce alimony. This changed in the mid-1990s when the legislature enacted a system of post-divorce spousal maintenance. As you will see, for the most part Texas post-divorce spousal maintenance is "alimony" in name only. (Please forgive this small play on words since the legislature went to great lengths *not* to call it "alimony.")

The reason I say it is "alimony" in name only is because, with rare exception, this law provides for welfare-level subsistence compensation to a spouse who must be completely destitute to qualify.

Basically, the spouse seeking alimony must have been married for at least ten years and must be totally unable to be self-supporting. Even then alimony payments are limited to three years, and the highest total monthly payment cannot exceed $2,500.00 or 20% of the supporting spouse's income, whichever is less.

There are exceptions. If a spouse is convicted of or receives deferred adjudication for family violence, the ten-year marriage requirement is waived. So, at least theoretically, a spouse married only one week but convicted of beating the other spouse could be required to pay alimony. Also the three-year limitation on the length of alimony payments does not apply to a spouse who is incapable of self-support because of "an incapacitating physical or mental disability," in which case support can be ordered for an indefinite period as long as the disability continues.

Alimony terminates on the death of either former spouse or the remarriage of the person receiving alimony. Alimony is to be terminated if the court finds that the ex-spouse receiving support "cohabits with another person in a permanent place of abode or on a continuing conjugal basis."

Payment of alimony can be enforced in much the same way that payment of child support is enforced, and those procedures are discussed in some detail in Chapter 26 on child support in this book. Alimony can be enforced by contempt of court, entry of a money judgment, or withholding of income from salary for current or back alimony.

Court-ordered alimony should not be confused with agreed, contractual, post-divorce payments to a spouse. Texas has always allowed divorcing spouses to enter into agreements whereby one spouse would make periodic payments to the other as part of the divorce property settlement agreement. That practice continues with spouses settling divorces by one spouse agreeing to make payments to the other spouse as a part of the divorce property settlement.

Chapter 28

Premarital and Post-Marital Agreements

A married couple are well suited when both partners usually feel the need for a quarrel at the same time.

—Jean Rostand

The vast majority of married couples have never entered into any agreement concerning the ownership or control of their property. Texas law does provide, however, that married couples may, either before marriage or after, enter into an agreement that will change the rules governing both their separate property and community property. If such an agreement exists in your marriage, naturally you will need to look to that document to discover the rules that will be used in dividing your marital property.

If you are contemplating entering into such an agreement, you should seek your own, individual, legal counsel to advise you on these matters. These agreements are taken very seriously by Texas courts and can have far reaching and sometimes unintended consequences that can gravely affect your future economic life.

Premarital Agreements

Couples contemplating marriage may contract between themselves to change the Texas marital property laws in virtually any way they desire. For example, they can agree that all property will be kept separate. Or, they can convert all of their property into community property.

They can change not only the ownership and control of property now in existence, but also property that will be acquired in the future, such as future wages or income from property. The law is broad enough so that, from a property point of view, it is only a slight exaggeration to say a couple could, literally, make one spouse the master and the other the slave. Except for a prospective spouse's own brain and the willingness of the other prospective spouse to be fair, there are few limitations. One limitation, however, is that these agreements may not adversely affect child support.

There are sometimes valid reasons for a premarital agreement. Both prospective spouses may be independently wealthy and wish to avoid mixing their assets. One spouse may be extremely wealthy and fear that the marriage is simply a method of obtaining access to wealth. Texas law attempts to force the couple to work through the "valid reasons." To be enforceable, the agreement must be in writing and signed by both parties. It must also be signed voluntarily and "a fair and reasonable disclosure of the property or financial obligations of the other party" must be provided giving the other party "adequate knowledge" of that information.

If the other party is provided with adequate knowledge of a prospective spouse's financial condition, a court will not be allowed to disregard or set aside a premarital agreement no matter how unfair. The complaining party will not have a right to a jury trial on the issue of whether the premarital agreement is unfair or "unconscionable."

Post-marital agreements

Married couples "may partition or exchange between themselves all or part of their community property, then existing or to be acquired as the spouses may desire." When so partitioned it becomes separate property and, unless the agreement provides otherwise, future earnings and income from the property will be separate. Spouses "may agree that income or property arising from separate property that is owned by one of them, or that may be thereafter acquired, shall be the separate property of the owner."

To be enforceable, a post-marital partition agreement must be in writing, signed by the spouses, and make the same disclosures about property and financial obligations that are described above for premarital agreements. Like the premarital agreement, if done properly, these partition agreements between married couples are very enforceable.

Post-marital partition agreements cannot be used to cheat or defraud existing creditors. In other words, a spouse who owes a debt can't keep the property away from that creditor by transferring it to his or her spouse.

Converting Seperate Property to Community Property

Married couples "may agree that all or part of the separate property owned by either or both spouses is converted to community property." There is a difference from the premarital agreement and the post-marital partition agreements described above. Married couples can agree only to convert existing property to community property. Married couples cannot agree to convert gifts or inheritances that may be received in the future into community property.

Agreements between married couples converting separate property to community property are widely used for estate planning purposes. The Internal Revenue Code allows tax benefits (e.g., a "step up" in the basis) for community property assets on the death of one of the spouses. Individuals with larger estates can, in some circumstances, also receive a doubling of the tax-free amount allowed for estate taxes. The problem that arises is that the conversion to community property gives the other spouse a community interest in property that was formerly separate and could not be divided by a divorce court. For this reason, to be enforceable, an agreement to convert separate property to community must: be in writing, be voluntarily signed by both of the spouses, identify the property being converted, and include a fair disclosure of the legal effect of converting the property to community property. The legislature has suggested a lengthy disclosure that is placed in most of these agreements in bold print.

Chapter 29

How Courts Divide Community Property

You can be as romantic as you please about love, Hector; but you mustn't be romantic about money.

—George Bernard Shaw

The Judge Decides Who Gets What

In Texas, only a judge can divide community property. A jury is not allowed to make the decision about how community property is to be divided. Juries may play a role in property division because they are allowed to decide whether property is community or separate and juries may decide the values of different pieces of community property. Decisions on these issues can greatly impact the judge's division of community property because, as you will recall, judges are not allowed to deprive a spouse of his or her separate property.

The Reasoning Judges Use in Dividing Community Property

The Texas law regarding division of community property says in part:

> "...the court shall order a division of the estate of the parties in a manner that the court deems just and right, having due regard for the rights of each party and any children of the marriage."

There it is! The court may divide the property in any way "the court deems just and right." Without coming right out and saying it, the legislature has said that the judge may do whatever he or she wants to do about dividing community property. In essence, it is a *value* judgment. It is very subjective. Decisions vary greatly from judge to judge. Even with the same judge, decisions can vary greatly as some judges are consistent and some are not.

The judge may divide the community property in kind or by awarding one spouse one asset and the other spouse something else. One spouse may be awarded all the real estate while the other is awarded cash. The judge may choose virtually any combination.

Because of the subjective nature of community property division, it is impossible for you or your lawyer to know exactly what a particular judge will do. Your lawyer will know something about the judge's prior decisions or track record. By comparing the judge's track record to the probable facts of your case, your lawyer can make an educated guess about what this judge might do in your cause. All of this is a little bit like crystal-ball gazing.

There are some good reasons for a judge to want to divide community property equally:

1. Equal division is in keeping with the spirit of community property—both parties really own the property.
2. It is easier.
3. It is unreasonable to expect that a judge hearing a case for a short period of time can know the subtle facts that really make one party more deserving, needy, or at fault than the other. Equal division avoids having to search out such distinctions.
4. Equal division is uniform. Lawyers and parties know what to expect, and this encourages everyone to simply make the equal division out of court.

There are some bad reasons for making equal division. The most obvious is that it is a failure of the judge to do the job that he or she is responsible for doing. The legislature had the wisdom to realize that an equal division is not always fair. The law putting the decision in the hands of the judge contemplates that the judge will take a hard look at the facts of the case and not take the easy way out.

Take this example: Suppose the husband makes a very high salary, is healthy, and has substantial separate property. The wife is paraplegic, has heart disease, and has a modest disability income. She has no separate property. The couple have been married twenty-five years and have a very modest community estate consisting of a small home, furniture, and a small savings account. Texas law allows very limited alimony in very limited cases. The judge is not allowed to take the husband's separate estate. The only choice the judge has is deciding how to divide the community property.

If you were the judge, would you divide the community equally? If you answer "yes," the rest of us can hope you aren't a District Judge.

All of which is to say that there are some very good reasons for having the community property divided unequally. Even though I covered some of these reasons in my prior example, I will set them out here. The following factors are some examples that might justify an unequal division of community property:

1. The fault of one spouse in breaking up the marriage
2. The disparity of income or earning capacities of the parties
3. Capacities and abilities of the parties
4. Benefits that the party not at fault would have received from continuation of the marriage
5. Business opportunities
6. Education
7. Relative physical condition
8. Relative financial condition and obligations
9. Disparity of age
10. Size of separate estates
11. Nature of the property
12. Fraud committed on the community
13. Failure to obey temporary orders
14. Children or a disabled adult child

The above are examples that courts have given. It is safe to say that there are many additional reasons.

Be aware, however, that the judge *may* consider one or more of these matters in dividing property. He or she *may* also ignore any or all of such elements. Trying to reverse a judge's decision on this sort of thing is very difficult, often impossible.

Typically, judges stay near the middle of the pie. If a judge moves toward one side or the other, very good reasons are usually given as to why the unequal split was made.

You can see why a trial judge with good sense and a social conscience might have difficulty on some days enjoying his or her work. You might also understand why lawyers, trying to second-guess judges on such things, get headaches and talk about why they want their children to be engineers, dentists, and such.

I cannot overemphasize the fact that these are *general* guidelines given merely to illustrate how the *process* works. Ideally, they will help you to understand better what your lawyer is up against in a contested case. *Do not* get hung up on these general rules when it comes to your specific contested case. Your judge is an individual who has a very individual interpretation of the general rules. There are judges who divide the property down the middle, even if you prove that your spouse has just inherited a million dollars, that you are a penniless cripple, and that the only community asset is your wheelchair.

Listen to your lawyer, or, if need be, pay for a second or third opinion from other lawyers. But face the fact that community property division is a subjective area that rests largely on the values and personality of the *particular* judge you have. You must make many decisions with an understanding of this fact.

Fighting over Whether Property Is Community or Separate – A Rigged Game

If you and your spouse end up fighting over whether a piece of property is separate or community in nature, you might think that both of you would be on equal footing—that it would be just a matter of who could come up with the best proof. *Not so!* Once again, the public policy of the state has weighted the game in favor of community property.

The outcome of a lawsuit doesn't always turn on what you *know* to be true. In court, it doesn't go on the scoreboard unless you can *prove* it. *Proof* is the name of the game. Our forefathers, being keenly aware of this fact, established a *presumption* in favor of community property. It is *presumed* that all of the property during the marriage or at the time of divorce is community property. This means that if neither side presents *any* evidence regarding the nature of the property, the court will treat it as community property. The burden of proof is *always* on the party contending that the property is his or her separate property.

Moreover, it takes more than ordinary proof to overcome the "community presumption." Unlike most other matters in a divorce case that need only to be proved by a preponderance of the evidence, to establish that property is separate property, the evidence must be "clear and convincing evidence."

But, don't overestimate this presumption. This is the kind of presumption that is referred to as a *rebuttable* presumption. As soon as satisfactory evidence is presented that a particular piece of property is separate, the presumption that the property is community is rebutted. At this point the wind shifts. The party who is contending that the property is community in nature must present evidence to support that contention or give it up.

Interspousal Lawsuits

In ancient times, after marriage, the law considered the husband and wife to be one person. This made it impossible for the spouses to sue each other because to do so would be to sue yourself. An exception was made for divorce.

Later, when the legal fiction of the spouses' oneness was discarded, there remained a prohibition against suits between husband and wife on the grounds that such suits would destroy the peace and tranquility of the family. This view prevailed for a long time.

Recently, common sense has overcome this approach. Texas courts now allow suits for such torts as assault, conversion, and for negligence.

This is based on the theory that the wrong that has occurred, for which the suit is being brought, has already destroyed the peace and tranquility of the family. So, if a spouse has physically injured the other spouse, either intentionally or unintentionally, or intentionally inflicted emotional distress on the other spouse, it is possible to bring a claim for those causes of action right in the divorce case. Likewise, it may be possible to sue a spouse for wrongful acts committed against separate property such as conversion (theft) of or negligent damage to separate property.

Texas courts strictly prohibit use of tort theories to redistribute community property. In other words, if a spouse commits fraud by secretly transferring community property to someone else as a means of hiding that property, no separate fraud lawsuit can be brought for that act. However, division of community property remains in the discretion of the trial judge. In making the property division, the court can take the fraudulent act into consideration. This means that, in theory, the court can still award the larger share to the innocent spouse and thereby punish the wrongdoer for a fraudulent act against community property.

Loans

If the court finds that a loan has been made between the couple, be it from one separate estate to the other, from separate to community or vice versa, it will be treated under laws that apply to loans. For example, unlike *claims for economic contribution or reimbursement,* a loan *might* draw interest. Or, a loan might go unpaid because there might not be anything with which to pay it.

Court-Ordered Attorney's Fees

The court may order one spouse to pay the other's attorney's fees. Possibly no other single fact has so much potential for creating anger and controversy in your divorce. If you have an uncontested case and want to keep it that way, be careful about asking that your spouse be ordered to pay your lawyer.

You must also be aware that asking for attorney's fees does not mean that you will get them. The judge must be given some reason for ordering your spouse to pay your fees. You must show that your spouse is more able to pay than you are, that your spouse has committed substantial wrongs against you, that your spouse has refused to cooperate in handing over information, or some other good reason. If all things are equal between the two of you, there is a good chance that the judge will not order your spouse to pay your legal fees.

In the proper case, however, attorney's fees can be the great equalizer. Court-ordered attorney's fees allow a spouse with few resources to fight back against a spouse with money and property.

If your divorce case involves the division of large amounts of property or is a child custody case in which one side or the other is well financed, the attorney's fees will be substantial. Therefore, either obtaining such fees or keeping the other side's fee to a minimum can make a big difference in the amount of money you take home after the divorce.

In 1983, Texas passed a law allowing the court to award interim attorney's fees. This allows the court to order one side to pay the other side's fees in advance. Although there is some potential for abuse in this law, it is an absolute necessity in a society that has as one of its stated values the idea that everyone is entitled to a fair trial. There can be no fair trial where one side is well financed and the other penniless.

Unlike attorney's fees that are awarded as a part of the final judgment and property division, interim fees can be enforced by contempt of court.

Also, after the divorce decree has been entered, you may collect attorney's fees if your spouse refuses to comply with the court's order concerning the division of property, child support, or child custody and visitation. Needless to say, the judges are not reluctant to award attorney's fees against someone who has failed to comply with their orders.

A Special Note on Your Spouse's Legal Fees

Two things about your divorce are highly probable: (1) Your spouse's lawyer will require all or a large portion of his fees in advance of the divorce; and (2) The fee will be paid out of community property.

In addition, if your case is contested over either custody or property, this fee may reach into the thousands of dollars.

The following questions should be asked:

1. Are your spouse's attorney's fees significantly greater than yours?
2. Were your spouse's attorney's fees paid out of community property while yours were not?
3. Were your spouse's attorney's fees paid before divorce whereas your fees are to be paid afterward?

If any of the three questions above is answered affirmatively, then your spouse's attorney's fees should be treated as a community asset that your spouse is receiving in the division of property. It is a credit that has been paid in advance by the community.

If you paid an approximately equal amount to your attorney out of community funds in advance of divorce, then all of this is probably academic since it will balance anyway.

This should encourage you to pay your attorney's fees out of divisible funds before the dividing starts.

Community Property Not Considered or Disposed of by the Court

Parties to divorce suits sometimes think that they are doing themselves a big favor by hiding (or at least failing to mention) property at the time of divorce. The folks who wrote the law (whoever they were) already thought of this. The rule is: Any property of the parties not disposed of by the divorce court, which is later shown to be community property, is held as tenants-in-common (one-half undivided ownership) and may be partitioned. In a new lawsuit to partition the property or to have the title declared, the same presumption of community ownership applies as would have applied back in the divorce court.

So, if you're thinking of hiding a big piece of property, it will make lawyers happy. It might mean two lawsuits instead of one.

Chapter 30

Accounting Problems: Separating Different Kinds of Property

Capital accounting in its formally most rational shape...presupposes the battle of man with man.

—Max Weber

When Community and Separate Property Get Mixed Together

Mixing community and separate property together is called *commingling* the property. For example, a couple has a checking account that contains $8,000 of the husband's salary from his job (community property) and $50,000 the wife inherited from her father (separate property). Since the funds are in the same account, they are said to be commingled.

Initially, there is the presumption that all property owned during the marriage is community. If no evidence is presented concerning whether the property is community or separate in character, all $58,000 in the account will be found to be community. If, on the other hand, the wife comes forward with evidence that the *source* of the $50,000 was from her father's estate, she would be *tracing* her separate property. Once she has traced her separate funds by presenting a canceled check, or deposit slip, or even her own testimony showing the source from her father's estate, the court is required to find that the $50,000 is her separate property.

In cases like the one described above, tracing is a fairly simple process. In real life, however, it is not always this simple. In bank accounts, monies are usually deposited and withdrawn in such a random and sporadic manner that it is impossible to prove *exactly* how much of the money is separate property. In such instances, the presumption that property is community becomes of paramount importance. Neither side can *prove* how much is community and how much is separate, so the court presumes that it is *all* community.

Courts have adopted accounting rules that sometimes aid in tracing funds. If, as in the example used above, community funds are mixed with separate funds and some of the money is withdrawn, there is a "community first-out" presumption that may aid in tracing separate funds. Likewise, if identical sums are deposited and withdrawn, the party attempting to trace may be able to show that there is a link or a pattern that will identify the funds being withdrawn. If the amount of the account never drops below the amount of separate property funds originally contained in the account, this may allow those funds to be identified in the account. And, in some cases, a *pro rata* method can be used to apportion the funds between two estates.

Preventing Commingling

A spouse is often able to prevent commingling of separate funds with community funds by keeping the separate funds in different accounts and *systematically* removing interest or dividend income, which is community property. This can be done easily in stock brokerage accounts by instructing brokerage firms to pay dividends rather than reinvesting them in the account. Banks and savings and loan associations typically allow owners of certificates of deposit to elect to be paid interest income, rather than having it accumulate. Even if interest accumulates on a savings account, if the exact amount of interest is withdrawn by an instrument labeled as such, there is a high probability that this will be adequate to prevent commingling from occurring. *Records* and *documentation* of such transfers are necessary to make such a program work.

Of course, if the couple is able to agree, they can enter into an agreement as described above, agreeing that income from separate property will remain separate property.

Repaying Economic Contributions to One Estate by Another

The rules of tracing work relatively well to separate money in a bank account. Tracing is also a workable method for dividing wheat in an elevator or the value of inventory. But, how do you separate, for example, community funds that have been used to pay off debt on a separate property house? Since the house is not divisible in the same way that a bank account is, it is necessary to have different rules. When funds from different marital estates become mixed in a specific asset, Texas allows the one estate to make a "claim for economic contribution" against the estate receiving the benefit of the other estate's contribution.

Assume, for example, that on the date of marriage the husband already owns a house worth $100,000. Obviously, since he owned it before the marriage, it is his separate property. Immediately after the marriage, the couple decided to remodel the house and spent $50,000 of the wife's money that she had before marriage (her separate property) to build this addition. Now, several years later, the couple is divorcing. Since the husband must be awarded the house, now worth $300,000, as his separate property, the wife wants the judge to award her share of the house represented by the $50,000 she invested in the house. The court will award the wife her share by using a formula. The court will divide the contribution made by the wife ($50,000) by the total contributions of both ($100,000 plus $50,000 = $150,000). This results in showing that the wife contributed one-third of the original value of the property. Hence, the court will award the wife one-third of the $300,000 value of the house at the time of the divorce.

This same formula would be used if, instead of remodeling the house the money had been used to pay off any kind of debt secured by the property on the date of marriage. It would also be used if the contribution (cost of remodeling) had been paid by the community estate, or if the house was community property and the cost of remodeling was paid by the husband. The point is, any estate—the wife's separate property, the husband's separate property, or the community property—is entitled to be repaid for economic contribution it has made for the benefit of property owned by another estate. Needless to say, each estate is subject to being required to pay back any benefit to a particular piece of property it may have received from another estate.

In the examples above, for purposes of simplification, I have assumed that the economic contribution came at the time of the marriage. It is important to understand that the formula for calculating economic contribution does not use values from the time of marriage. Rather, the values that are "plugged into" the formula are the values at the time the first economic contribution is made. In other words, if the remodeling of the house had happened ten years after the marriage, the values that would have been used for the house would be the value at that time rather than the $100,000 that we assumed it was worth on the date of marriage.

Not every payment made by one estate for the benefit of property in another is subject to repayment through a claim for economic contribution. Payments for ordinary maintenance and repair, taxes, interest, insurance, and the contributions by a spouse of time, toil, talent, or effort during the marriage cannot be claimed as economic contribution.

If proven, claims for economic contribution must be awarded in divorce decrees. The court has no discretion *not* to award this claim and must "impose an equitable lien on property of a marital estate to secure a claim for economic contribution ...." In fact, except for a homestead, the court may impose the lien on other property of the estate receiving the benefit and not just the item of property that benefited from the economic contribution.

Finally, the use and enjoyment of the property during marriage for which a claim for economic contribution to the property exist does not create an offsetting benefit against the claim. However, if different estates have valid offsetting claims against each other for economic contributions, the court must offset those claims.

Mixing Separate Property with Community Labor

If your spouse inherits stock in a corporation, that stock is separate property. If the value of that stock goes from $1,000 when it was inherited to several million dollars when it is finally sold, it is still separate property, even though you were married all of the time that the stock was increasing in value. That's fine.

Suppose, however, that the corporation your spouse inherited had, as its only asset, a restaurant of little or no value that was also heavily in debt. During the twenty years of your marriage, while the restaurant was increasing in value, your spouse worked there twelve hours a day, seven days a week. Not only is your spouse a gourmet cook, but she is also an excellent entertainer and has audiences flocking to see her show inside the restaurant. During the years of the marriage, your spouse took only an ordinary cook's salary. She poured the huge amount of money being earned by the restaurant into building a lavish and expensively expanded restaurant building well known to everyone in the metropolitan area because of the vast sums she spent on advertising. Now upon divorce, your spouse claims that the several million dollar value of the inherited corporation is her separate property.

"Just a minute," you say in stark disbelief. "Something is wrong here."

The law agrees with you. Something is wrong here. The fruits produced by a spouse's time, talent, and labor are community property. If your spouse had been working outside of her restaurant, her earnings from being a great manager-chef-entertainer would have been community property, and she would have received a salary many times higher than the ordinary cook's pay.

Courts are clear that the fruits of community time, talent, and labor are community property, even if expended enhancing the value of separate property. The real problem comes in trying to divide the separate portion from that part of the increase in value that comes from the community labor expended.

The Texas Supreme Court has defined the rules by which this division can be made. The court's rules are not exact. Roughly, the community is allowed credit for the increase in value of the separate property caused by the expenditure of a spouse's labor beyond that which would normally be expended to maintain and preserve the separate property. In the example above, an expert witness might testify that a gourmet cook and entertainer of your wife's caliber would have earned a salary many times higher that the ordinary cook's salary she paid herself. Accordingly, the community would be entitled to credit for that portion of the increase in the restaurant corporation that occurred because of the extra labor and talent.

Of course, the community may have already received "adequate compensation" for some of this extra labor in the form of wages or dividends. If so, this will be included in the formula. This is just a rough outline. It is safe to say that courts realize this concept to be highly fact specific. As you can see, questions about the value of labor, what compensation is adequate, the effect of inflation, etc., can turn all of this into a real donnybrook.

Paying Back the Community

In the example given above, the hugely talented and energetic spouse diverts her resources from the community and shelters them in what would otherwise be a relatively valueless separate property corporation. If left unaddressed, this would create a great unfairness in the community property concept. But it is not just community time, talent, and labor that can be drained away. A spouse may bring a heavily indebted business into the marriage. During the marriage, all of the debt may be paid. Upon divorce, this spouse wants to walk away with this now valuable "separate property" business without giving the community any credit for the years of blood, sweat, and tears that it took to pay off this debt.

To combat this unfairness, Texas has developed a concept referred to as "reimbursement." This may sound much like the "claim for economic contribution" described above. But it's different. Economic contribution must be for the reduction of principal on a *secured* debt on a specific asset or for *capital improvements* on a specific piece of property. The example above relating to paying down debt on the separate property business may be simply paying off *unsecured* debt. A claim for economic contribution will not reach payments for these unsecured claims or over uses of community time, toil, and talent. Hence, we must rely on "reimbursement."

Reimbursement differs from a claim for economic contribution in other ways. Unlike the claim for economic contribution, reimbursement is completely discretionary. The trial judge does not have to grant reimbursement. Also, unlike economic contribution, in considering reimbursement a court may offset it with the use benefit and enjoyment of the property. In other words, even if during the marriage the couple paid off a large debt on the husband's business, the court may consider the fact that the business provided the couple with a very nice income during the years of the marriage, thereby compensating the community for its aid in paying off the husband's separate property debt.

There are some claims that a court cannot order reimbursed. These include child support, alimony, spousal maintenance, living expenses for a spouse or a child of a spouse, contributions of property of a nominal value, payment of debts in nominal amounts, and student loans owed by a spouse. The theory is that all of these items are either the kind of things a spouse has an obligation to pay or the kind of things that a spouse should know upon marriage will have to be paid by his or her beloved.

Reimbursement may also sound similar to the tracing of separate property when it is commingled with community property. Although there are similarities, there are also major differences. In tracing, the burden of proof is strict in that the party attempting to trace must prove an *exact* amount and *clearly* identify the specific property to be traced. In reimbursement, the proof does not have to be so exact nor the identification so specific. If property is successfully traced, then the judge has no discretion but to award it to the spouse who has traced it; it has been proven to be separate property. Reimbursement, on the other hand, is discretionary. The judge *may* reimburse all, part, or none, even after the party requesting the reimbursement has proved conclusively that community funds were invested. Reimbursement is referred to as an equitable remedy, which means (roughly) that the judge is to use it to establish fairness and balance to his judgment.

Hiring an Accountant as an Expert Witness

If your divorce involves a dispute over business assets or property that is difficult to identify, value, or locate, it is likely that you will need an accountant to assist your attorney in preparation of your case and to act as an expert witness on your behalf should your case go to trial. If you are the spouse in control of the business assets or other property, it is likely that you will already be working with an accountant in the day-to-day conduct of your business. If, on the other hand, you are the spouse who is unfamiliar with your spouse's business or investment affairs, you may need your own independent accountant to assist you. If you are not familiar with the family financial affairs, you and your lawyer will have to determine how much you can rely on information provided by your spouse and the accountant or accountants whom he or she has hired to help operate the business. Although these "inside" accountants sometimes act as honest brokers and "shoot straight" with the non-business spouse and his or her lawyer, often their loyalty lies with the spouse who is operating the business or handling the investments. They know that this is the person who has been writing them checks over the year and, they believe, will be the one likely to write them checks in the coming years after the divorce is over and forgotten.

If you don't have an accountant loyal to you *and* sophisticated about the kind of business or investments involved in your divorce, you should rely heavily on your attorney to help you choose the appropriate accountant. Most attorneys who have handled business or investment litigation, bankruptcy cases, or divorces involving complex property disputes either already know accountants who understand these issues and will make good witnesses or they know how to look for such accountants. This is particularly true in cases in which the opposing spouse and lawyer have just decided to refuse all cooperation, "stonewall," and deny all access to the critical records. Although much of the work required to deal with these "stonewallers" will be done by the attorney, sophisticated accountants who have dealt with these issues before are critically important because they can usually tell the difference between bogus records that have been produced to lead the opposition down a rabbit trail and the real records needed to determine the value of assets.

The decision to hire an accountant needs to be made early in the case. Unless the case is extremely simple, it is difficult for an accountant to "get up to speed" quickly. Also, if the other side sees that you have adequate expert accounting help, it may discourage stonewalling, discourage a trial, and bring forth better settlement offers.

Chapter 31

The Effect of Divorce on Debt

If only God would give me a sign! Like making a deposit in my name in a Swiss bank account.

— Woody Allen

Am I Legally Responsible for My Spouse's Debts?

This question cannot be answered with a simple yes or no. To have an accurate answer to this question, we must deal with a new concept—something called *Management, Control, and Disposition Powers* over property.

To this point, we have discussed only two kinds of marital property—separate and community. We have not discussed who has *control* over community property. In fact, for some purposes, community property must be divided into three categories:

1. That controlled by the husband
2. That controlled by the wife
3. That controlled by both the spouses

When you marry in Texas, the law says that your wages, interest income, dividends, and winnings at gambling *all* become community property. This does not, however, mean that you lose control of this money. Even though it becomes community property in which your spouse has an ownership interest, you are still the person who has the right to control it, dispose of it, and manage it during the marriage. In short, each spouse has the right to control, manage, and dispose of community property that would have been his or her separate property had he or she remained single. Income, interest, and dividends from their *joint* ventures become property subject to each of the partners having powers of control, management, and disposition.

When the term *Management, Control, and Disposition Powers* is used, it means just what it says: the power to buy, sell, mortgage, lease, give away, trade, tear down, and otherwise alter or change the funds or the capital, subject only to the rights of the spouse that might be exercised during a divorce, upon death, or in a dispute over a homestead.

So now we see that a couple's property may be classified into five categories:

1. Wife's separate property
2. Community property subject to the wife's control, disposition, and management powers
3. Community property subject to joint management, control, and disposition powers
4. Community property subject to the husband's control, disposition, and management powers
5. Husband's separate property

Now, keeping all of this in mind, we can return to the discussion of liability for debts. The rules are really very simple. Obviously, everyone is responsible for his or her own debts. Therefore, a spouse's separate property and community property under his or her management, control, and disposition powers are subject to his or her own debts. This includes property that is under *joint* management, control, and disposition powers.

In addition, the law says that you have a responsibility to support your spouse, if your spouse is unable to do so. Therefore, your separate property as well as community property under your control, management, and disposition powers is subject to debts incurred by your spouse for necessities he or she might be unable to provide alone. This would presumably include such things as food, reasonable amounts of clothing and shelter, and so forth. On the other hand, you are not responsible for debts incurred by your spouse in his or her name. However, community property that you have an interest in, under your spouse's control, management, and disposition powers, may be taken to pay those debts.

Last, but not least, many of the obligations that you and your spouse enter into, such as for the purchase of a home, or real estate, or other large undertakings, will be undertaken by both of you jointly. The bankers and loan companies require that both of you sign in order to get a loan. Obviously, both of you are liable for all of these debts. The lenders can look to whoever has the money to satisfy such debts.

Divorce Does Not Change Debt Obligation to Third Parties

You might go into a divorce with the mistaken idea that if the judge orders your spouse to pay a debt incurred during your marriage that this order will alleviate you from responsibility for the debt. *Nothing could be further from the truth!*

For example, assume that during your marriage you and your spouse borrowed money from High Finance Loan Company. At the divorce, the court orders your spouse to pay the debt. Three months later, *you* receive a call from a High Finance collector who says that your spouse is not paying and insists that you must pay the debt. You quickly point out that the court ordered your spouse to pay the debt or that your spouse agreed to do so as part of the property settlement. The collector then tells you that the divorce decree did not affect the rights of his company since the company was not a party to the lawsuit (divorce). He states further that the court had no jurisdiction or authority to affect a contract between you and a third party (High Finance Loan Company) who was not in court.

Sadly, the collector would be correct. Of course, since the court did affect the rights you have as to the debt between you and your former spouse, you could sue your former spouse for the debt, *after* you pay it, that is, and if your former spouse has the money. In other words, you can't get blood out of a turnip.

So in negotiations to settle your divorce, don't let your spouse trade you promises to pay debts in exchange for valuable property. For example, if your spouse says, "I will pay the $7,000 MasterCharge bill if you will let me have the $7,000 car," don't agree to do this unless your spouse will pay the debt before the divorce is granted. If for some reason you must enter into such an agreement without the debt being paid before divorce, you should know that you will probably have to pay the debt *and* be deprived of the car unless your spouse is as concerned about his or her credit as you are about yours and he or she has the ability to pay the debt.

Are You Liable for Your Spouse's Torts?

No. You are not personally liable for your spouse's wrongful acts. However, all of your community property (every last stick, except for property that is exempt, such as your homestead) could be taken to pay for your spouse's torts.

For this reason you must be certain that both you and your spouse are covered by automobile and other liability insurance until the day after your divorce is final.

Chapter 32

Retirement Benefits

Ultimately poverty affects the soul.

—Bettye White

In many divorces the retirement benefits of one or both of the spouses are the largest assets, often surpassing the value of the couple's home, business, or other investments. Even in cases in which other assets are larger, retirement benefits often account for a significant portion of the couple's net worth.

The General Rule. That portion of a spouse's retirement benefits earned during the marriage is *treated* as community property and is divisible upon divorce. The reason I say that retirement benefits are *treated* as community property is because, over several decades, the Federal Government and the states have disputed the characterization of retirement benefits. Commentators still argue about whether these assets are really community property or whether the United States Congress is just allowing Texas courts to treat them as such. Assuming that you are not reading this book because you are a legal historian, I will spare you this interesting history. Here we are interested only in the bottom line: Retirement benefits, to the extent that they are earned during marriage, are absolutely divisible by Texas courts.

When we say "Retirement Benefits," what are we talking about? Primarily we are talking about *retirement plans* established by private employers. But, the term also includes *retirement plans* established by the Federal Government and state governments for employees and for members of the armed forces. Long ago the Federal Government established a special Railroad Retirement System for railroad employees. Each of these various types of retirement benefits is discussed in more detail under individual topics that follow this general discussion.

What are "Retirement Plans" and why do they exist? Retirement benefits are held in retirement plans. The easiest way to describe retirement plans is to say that they are *trust funds*. A *trust* is, of course, a legal entity in which one person (the trustee) holds and controls money or property for the benefit of another (the beneficiary). But retirement plans are not just ordinary trusts. Retirement plans are trusts on steroids. The Federal Government has imbued retirement plans with huge tax benefits. Equally as important, by the use of *anti-alienation* statutes, Federal law makes it all but impossible for creditors or anyone else to take these retirement benefits away from the employee who earned them.

But there's a catch. To obtain these "super-power" benefits, the Federal Government requires employers and plan administrators to meet certain standards and requirements in order to become a *qualified plan*. For example, in order to be a *qualified plan* and receive the associated benefits, a plan must provide all employees equal opportunity to participate in the plan. This means that in order to obtain the special tax benefits for themselves, company higher-ups must provide the same opportunity for lower-level employees to participate. This, of course, is one of the reasons retirement plans have become so widespread in the past few decades. (Note: It's not technically accurate to say that the military retirement and portions of the railroad retirement are *trusts* because these payments are made directly by Congress from taxes received from the taxpayers.)

Separating the Community Property from the Separate Property

The Texas rules of community property are strictly applied in the division of retirement plans. If a spouse has worked at the employment from which a retirement plan arose longer than he or she has been married, only that portion earned during the marriage is community property. Texas courts are not allowed to divide the portion of retirement benefits that were earned before marriage and are therefore separate property. So, how do courts separate the separate portion of a retirement plan from the community portion?

Often courts will prorate retirement benefits. For example, if retirement plan benefits have been earned over twenty years of employment, but the couple have been married only ten years of that time, the court may divide the ten years of marriage by the twenty years of employment and determine that only half of the retirement benefits are community property and subject to division. In other cases retirement plan account records may identify a specific value of the account on the date of marriage, thereby providing an exact amount that must be set aside as separate property and not subject to division on divorce.

Courts are also careful not to divide a retirement plan in a manner that gives a non-employee spouse benefits earned after divorce. For this reason, court orders dividing retirement must be drawn to reflect values that already exist on the date of divorce.

Spouses Are Protected – If They Are Careful

In establishing retirement plans, Congress has protected the employed person's spouse. The laws that create the various retirement plans have provisions requiring that, if the retirement benefits don't go to the employee because of death, then these benefits must be paid to the employee's spouse (the *alternate payee*). Likewise, the employee's spouse is automatically entitled to *survivor benefits* (discussed more in a moment). There are only two ways that a spouse can lose his or her interest in retirement benefits: (1) sign a document saying that he or she consents to giving them up, or (2) lose his or her status as a spouse through a divorce without taking the proper steps to preserve the retirement benefits.

Congress has provided a way for a divorcing spouse to protect himself or herself from loss of his or her interest in a spouse's retirement plan. Congress did this by granting state divorce courts the power to divide retirement benefits. Hence, Texas courts are free to divide retirement accounts and to award all or a portion to the spouse of the employee. But, for this to happen two things must take place. First, the non-employee spouse must identify the retirement plan and obtain a court ruling dividing the retirement benefits. Second, the divorce court must follow a very precise "recipe" or "road map" in order for a division of retirement benefits to be effective and valid. For example, courts can only divide private retirement plans by the use of a *qualified domestic relations order* (QDRO). Likewise, division of military retirement, federal employee retirement, and railroad retirement can only be accomplish by a different set of strict (hypertechnical) rules. I repeat, none of this is automatic. *If the divorcing non-employee spouse fails to obtain a proper court order dividing retirement benefits, those benefits will be lost.*

There are different kinds of retirement plans.

When someone uses the term "retirement plan," you cannot assume that you know what this means without investigation of that particular plan. The two basic categories for retirement plans are *defined contribution plans* and *defined benefit plans*. These two basic plans are just what their names imply:

- A *defined benefit* plan agrees to pay each employee (plan participant) a specific or defined benefit at retirement. The amount of the payment is usually based on a formula that takes into consideration such items as the years of employment with the employer and the salary.
- A *defined contribution plan* has a separate account for each employee (plan participant). All *contributions* are paid into that separate account. These *contributions* include all payments made into the individual's plan account by the employer and employee, gains and losses on investments made for the account, interest, dividends, etc. Upon retirement, the benefits payable to the employee are based solely on the "account balance." In fact, the benefit payed by defined contribution plans is often a lump sum payment of the "account balance."
- Many plans are mixes and combinations of the *defined benefit* plan and the *defined contribution* plan and have more than one level of benefits, some of which are *defined benefits* while others are *defined contributions.*

Some retirement plans have two, three, or more levels of benefits. For example, a company may establish a retirement plan for its employees that has:

- A *defined contribution* plan into which the company makes payments to guarantee every employee a specific level of benefits based on length of employment with the company and the salary level of the employee.
- A *defined contribution* plan into which the employee may elect to pay a percentage of his or her salary and have his or her contribution matched by a company contribution.
- An *employee stock ownership plan* (an ESOP) by which employees can acquire company stock for a retirement account based on a formula established by the company (technically this is another variety of *defined contribution* plan since the amount of benefit received by an employee is based on the value of the stock at the time it is sold or transferred outright to the employee).
- A *profit sharing plan* which, according to a formula, pays a percentage of company profits into a retirement plan for employees (again, this is a *defined contribution* plan because the amount that the employee will receive will be based on the amount of profits payed into his or her individual account).

Failing to understand that your spouse may have more than one kind of retirement may cause you to overlook your ownership interest in a significant marital property asset.

Retirement Plans – Survivor Benefits

On page 404, we discussed the fact that Congress requires employers and plan administrators to comply with rules in order to be classified as a *qualified plan*. And, remember, if it's not a *qualified* plan, it doesn't receive all of the "super-power" tax benefits and immunities from creditors so desired by employers establishing these plans.

One of the Congressional requirements is that *each* qualified *retirement plan must provide protection for the employee's surviving spouse in the event of the employee's death.* This means that each *qualified* retirement plan has an additional level of *survivor benefits* over and above the *retirement benefits*. Additionally, retirement plans may provide for *survivor benefits* over and above those required by Federal law.

Each retirement plan requires that, unless an employee elects differently and his or her spouse consents, payments made under a retirement plan must be in the form of a "*qualified joint and survivor annuity*" (QJSA). This means that the annuity must be calculated on both the employee's and the employee's spouse's lives, so that if the employee dies before his or her spouse, the spouse will still receive an annuity payment that is at least fifty percent of the amount received by the employee before his or her death. If the death of the spouse occurs before the employed spouse retires, the plan must pay a surviving spouse a *survivor benefit* called a *qualified pre-retirement survivor annuity* (QPSA). (Some defined contributions plans can meet the *survivor benefit* requirements by requiring that the entire balance of the retirement plan be paid to the surviving spouse and thereby be relieved of the QJSA and QPSA requirements.)

Similar *survivor benefit* provisions are included in military retirement, civil service retirement, railroad retirement, teacher retirement, and state employee retirement.

So why am I making such a big deal about describing this *survivor benefit* aspect of retirement plans? It's because after the divorce from your spouse with the retirement plan, you will no longer be the surviving spouse and therefore will not be entitled to these *survivor benefits*—unless you and your lawyer take certain deliberate steps. Federal law allows state courts to include in the divorce decree (QDRO, DRO, or other appropriate order) a provision requiring that the divorced spouse continue to be treated as a surviving spouse. But if those provisions are not included in the terms of your divorce, you lose these benefits. It's something to ask for in negotiations, or if negotiations fail, something to request the court to include in the decree.

Retirement Plans – The Interaction with the Divorce Court

The interaction between divorce courts and retirement plans often confuses divorcing spouses and baffles some lawyers and judges. But the basic concept is pretty simple and takes only a minute or two to understand. Here's the way it works.

When a divorce is filed, the divorce court (usually a district court in Texas) "takes control" over everything to do with the divorce. In legal and technical terms, we say that the divorce court has *jurisdiction* over the case. This means that the divorce court has the final say over everything involved in the couple's marriage—the property, the children, injunctions for the protection of a spouse or property, child support, and dozens of other things that are in some way related or connected to the divorce. If, for example, marital property is wrongfully held by a third party, the divorce court even has *jurisdiction* to make that person a party in the lawsuit and to order him or her to return the wrongfully held marital property. This concept of jurisdiction is accepted as gospel in courts in the United States. It is the bedrock of how lawyers think and the way courts do business.

Then, along comes this "animal" called a *qualified* retirement plan or a retirement account. Doesn't a divorce court dividing a retirement account have authority to enforce its judgment? What if the *plan administrator* or other person in control of the retirement money won't honor the court's order dividing this property? Is the divorce court helpless? The answer is that, unlike other marital property over which the divorce court has direct control, it has no such direct power over a *qualified* plan or the plan's administrator. The divorce court cannot bring the plan or its administrator into court or hold the administrator in contempt.

All *qualified* retirement plans were created by the Federal Government and are "federal animals." The same is true of military retirement, federal civil service, and railroad retirement. In other words, all of these retirement plans are the "creation" of the Federal Government and come under Federal jurisdiction. The United States Constitution contains a "supremacy clause" stating that when Federal law conflicts with state law, Federal law controls. In every one of the laws creating retirement plans, Congress has included language indicating that these plans will be controlled by Federal law except to the extent that Congress specifically grants state courts permission to make decisions. And, for the most part, the only power Congress gives state courts is the power to decide how to divide these retirement plans. The power to *enforce* the division is reserved for the Federal system.

So, the bottom line: Congress has retained exclusive control and jurisdiction over retirement plans and their administrators to the exclusion of state courts. This does not mean that state courts cannot *indirectly* force plan administrators to divide retirement plans. Congress has provided a "road map" for state courts to use in drafting orders for the division of retirement plans. If the state court follows Congress's "road map" for dividing a particular type of retirement plan, plan administrators are not allowed to ignore the state court's division orders. If the plan administrator does not comply with the "road map" drafted by the state court judge, then the order can and will be enforced by a Federal court.

In the following topics on the various types of retirement benefits, there is a discussion of the various "road maps" that Congress has provided state courts and divorcing spouses for the division of retirement benefits.

QDRO's – Qualified Domestic Relation Orders – for Private Plans

We have said, in prior sections, that divorce decrees dividing employee retirement plans must be very exact in dividing retirement plans or they will not be honored. In fact, the people who administer private retirement plans (plan administrators) are instructed *not* to honor a divorce decree dividing retirement plans unless it is a *Qualified Domestic Relations Order*. So the question becomes, how does that portion of a Texas divorce decree that divides a private retirement plan become a *Qualified Domestic Relation Order*? The answer, like magic, is that, if a divorce decree (1) is from a domestic relations court, (2) contains certain things, *and* (3) does not contain others, it is automatically a Qualified Domestic Relations Order (QDRO—pronounced "QUAD-row"). Since there is absolutely no question about the fact that Texas courts that grant divorces are domestic relations courts, we can eliminate that factor from our discussion.

To be a *qualified domestic relations order*, a divorce decree *must contain* the following:

- The name and address of the participant (employee spouse) and the alternate payee (non-employee spouse)
- The name of each retirement plan to which the court order or divorce decree applies
- The dollar amount or percentage (or the method of determining the amount or percentage) of the benefit to be paid to the alternate payee (non-employee spouse)
- The number or payments or the time period to which the order applies

To be a *qualified domestic relations order*, a divorce decree *absolutely must not contain* the following:

- Any requirement for the retirement plan to provide either of the spouses any type or form of benefit or option not otherwise provided under the retirement plan
- Any requirement for the plan to pay increased benefits
- Any requirement for the retirement plan to pay benefits to an alternate payee (non-employee spouse) that, under a previous QDRO, are to be paid to another alternate payee (former spouse, child for child support)
- Any requirement for the retirement plan to pay benefits to an alternate payee (non-employee spouse) in the form of a *qualified joint and survivor annuity* for the lives of the alternate payee (non-employee spouse and his or her subsequent spouse)

These are the simple but hard-to-apply rules. If a divorce decree has the items that it is supposed to have and doesn't have the prohibited items, then a plan administrator must recognize it as a QDRO. In practice, it's usually not that simple.

Although the QDRO is a part of your divorce decree signed by the judge, this and other parts of the decree are usually drafted by one or both of the lawyers. It is common practice for lawyers to draft QDROs as separate documents so that a short document of three or four pages can be sent to the retirement plan administrator, rather that sending the entire divorce decree, which may be thirty or forty pages and contain other items that have no bearing on the division of the retirement plan.

The icing on the cake: every bit of the foregoing discussion focuses on technical nuts and bolts necessary for a QDRO's acceptance by a retirement plan administrator. If you focus only on these technical matters required for QDRO recognition, as many clients and attorneys do, you will be missing the icing on the cake. Just as with the rest of the divorce, primary attention must be paid to understanding the details of a retirement plan so that the QDRO will contain all of the bells and whistles necessary *to get you the maximum benefits available.*

QDROs Don't Fit All Retirement Plans

If you spent time in the military, you certainly know that referring to a rifle as a gun is a near life-threatening mistake. All rational people may know that the darn thing is, in fact, a gun. But all sane people in the military quickly come to understand that the earth will stop turning on its axis if we don't all agree that it really is a rifle. The gods of the retirement plan world, apparently, were trained by a military wordsmith. The term "QDRO" applies only to some retirement plans and not to others. Although the concepts used by all retirement plans are similar, *there are differences in both the label used to identify the court orders transferring retirement benefits and in the technical details that must be included in those orders.*

Qualified Domestic Relations Order (QDRO) is a term used by Congress in the laws governing *private* retirement plans. These laws include the *Employee Retirement Income Security Act* (ERISA) and the *Internal Revenue Code* and relate primarily to private retirement plans established by non-government employers. The term "QDRO" is also used by the State of Texas for the orders necessary to transfer a spouse's interest in Texas *Public Retirement System* benefits. But the Texas *Public*

Retirement System QDRO, although using the same name, differs slight from the ERISA QDRO in the technical detail required.

Although the concepts are the same, use of the term QDRO as well as a failure to modify the form and detail of the QDRO to fit other plans will likely result in "throwing a wrench in the machine." For example, the *Uniformed Services Former Spouses' Protection Act* requires that military retirement benefits be divided by a *Domestic Relations Order* (DRO) rather than a QDRO. DROs must comply with the technical requirements established by Congress and the *Defense Finance and Accounting Service* (DFAS). Likewise, both the *Civil Service Retirement System* and the *Federal Employees' Retirement System* do not recognize the term QDRO and require instead a *Court Order Acceptable for Processing* with the form and detail required by Congress and the *Office of Personnel Management*. Finally, the *Railroad Retirement Act* establishes a similar but specifically distinct methodology that must be used in transferring railroad retirement benefits.

Drafting Your QDRO, DRO, Etc. – The Process Is Important for a Good Result

Although the judge of the divorce court is the person who signs the QDRO, DRO, or other order, it is safe to say that the divorce judge probably will not read the documents controlling a retirement plan being divided in your divorce. This means that unless one of the attorneys in the case brings it to the court's attention, the judge will have no idea about what assets are available to be divided or who will have the right to control whether a non-employee spouse will have *survivor benefits*, *early retirement subsidy benefits*, or the right to make decisions regarding investment of assets held in the retirement funds. If your lawyer explains these benefits and complexities to the divorce judge, chances are he or she will be interested, appreciative, and willing to enter orders that will protect your rights to future benefits. Likewise, especially if you are the employee spouse, there may be terms and conditions of your retirement plan that your lawyer will need to work around, not mention, and avoid including in the QDRO, DRO, or other order entered by the court. The information required for decision making, bargaining, advocacy of your case in court, and, finally, the drafting of the QDRO, DRO, or other order cannot come out of a vacuum. Information must be gathered, studied, discussed, and acted upon.

Information necessary for the drafting of a QDRO, DRO, or other order is gathered by a proper request to the retirement plan administrator or appropriate agency. Federal law requires plan administrators to provide both spouses and/or their attorneys with complete information about the retirement plan. Complete information includes both the terms and conditions the plan has established for all employees and their spouses and the specific amounts of benefits and credits to which an individual employee is entitled.

Many divorce attorneys employ outside experts (usually other attorneys) who specialize in writing QDROs to assist the divorce attorney in drafting the QDRO. Often, this actually saves the client money because most of these "QDRO" specialists have specific and up-to-date knowledge about specific plans and will work for a relatively small flat fee. This means that the client has the benefit of a person who can assist the divorce attorney in maximizing the benefits that can be obtained for a client.

Some retirement plans, as a part of their services to plan participants, provide "model QDRO" that can be used in dividing plan benefits. It is not safe to assume that these model documents will always provide you with the best benefits. Federal law prohibits retirement plans from requiring a specific form for QDROs. It is absolutely necessary for someone, you, your attorney, or the QDRO specialist, to have a thorough knowledge of the retirement plan terms and conditions before deciding whether a model document will work best for you.

Dividing retirement benefits of military or state and federal employees has the advantage of a more standard procedure. Nevertheless, if it applies to you, it is necessary for you to be educated by your attorney on the nature of the benefits available under each of these systems.

Methods for Dividing Retirement Benefits

Let's be clear. As with all other community property, there are two ways of getting a retirement plan divided. First, and most desirable, you and your spouse can agree to the way in which you want the retirement benefits divided, incorporate the terms of the agreement into a written settlement agreement, divorce decree, or separate QDRO, and by the court's signature and court order have your agreed division reduced to a court order acceptable to those in charge of the retirement plan or plans. The second way is to go to court, persuade the judge of the merits of your proposed division, and get the judge to sign and enter a divorce decree or separate QDRO that incorporates those terms.

Now the question becomes, how are we going to suggest, to our spouse or the court, that the retirement benefits be divided? Here are three broad concepts used in dividing retirement benefits:

1. *Don't divide a particular retirement plan.* Use it as a set-off against other assets that are being given to the other spouse. For example, if both spouses are employed and have retirement plans of approximately equal value, if the couple's goal is an equal division of property, it's ridiculous to divide the plans when each spouse can simply keep 100% of his or her own plan.
2. *The separate-interest QDRO.* Some retirement plans are easy to divide, making QDROs easy to draft. For example, if a retirement plan is a defined contribution plan, containing $100,000.00 in stocks and bonds, all of which has been earned during the marriage, it can be divided into two separate $50,000.00 accounts, one for each spouse. This is referred to as the *separate-interest QDRO*, which establishes a wholly separate retirement plan account for the non-employee spouse. This has the advantage of completely separating the benefits so that each former spouse can take the benefits in the most desirable form. In the example above, one former spouse could elect to take benefits as a lump sum without interfering with the other former spouse's desire to have his or her benefits paid in the form of monthly annuity payments for the rest of his or her life. Preretirement survivorship protection may still be necessary if this method is used with some plans.
3. *The shared-payment QDRO.* Rather than attempting to divide the retirement plan or its assets, the payments can be divided as they are made. This method is referred to as the *shared-payment QDRO* and may be the only method available under some plans.

> This is probably the only way to divide some defined benefits plans. In these circumstances, it is necessary to include provisions for pre-retirement and post-retirement surship benefits in the QDRO so that payments will not stop on the death of the employee spouse.

Remember: The foregoing description is just a way of giving you a general understanding of how retirement plans can be divided. Each retirement plan requires specific legal analysis before a determination can be made about the method of division that will benefit you most. Finally, since retirement plans can contain multiple layers of benefits, more than one method may be required to divide a plan to secure the most benefit for you.

Valuing Retirement Benefits

At some point in a divorce, in order to divide property, it is usually necessary to establish the relative values of different community assets. Comparing the value of retirement plans with other assets requires a few extra calculations. Otherwise, you may be comparing apples to oranges without realizing there is a difference.

An easy example is comparing $100,000.00 in stocks and bonds in a defined contribution retirement plan with $100,000.00 owned by the same couple in a savings account. If one simply compares the account statement from the bank with the account statement from the retirement plan, the two appear to be of equal value. But their values are usually not even close. That's because the $100,000.00 in the couple's savings account is probably after-tax dollars. On the other hand, the $100,000.00 in the qualified retirement plan is only tax deferred. As long as the money remains in the retirement plan, no taxes are due on the principal amount or on any interest or earnings from that $100,000.00. However, when money is withdrawn from the retirement account, income tax will have to be paid on those withdrawals. No one knows the exact income tax rates that will be charged several years from now when the retirement money is withdrawn. But past experience indicates that income taxes could absorb thirty cents out of every dollar withdrawn. If you use this single calculation, this could mean that the retirement fund is worth only $70,000.00 as opposed to the $100,000.00

that appears on the retirement plan account statement. And this is not all. If, perchance, we assume that the person who receives the retirement asset must spend it now to pay off debts from the marriage or to re-establish a viable life after the divorce, then there may be an additional income tax penalty of ten percent over and above the regular income tax. This means that, to a spouse in that position and in a thirty percent tax bracket, this retirement account may be worth only $60,000.00 as opposed to the $100,000.00 appearing on the plan statement.

Of course, the above example fails to consider other advantages of having money in a retirement plan. If the $100,000.00 retirement account is awarded to a divorcing spouse who is thirty years old and can wait until age seventy to withdraw the funds, being able to defer taxes on the interest and earnings for forty years or more may make the retirement plan more valuable to that spouse than the $100,000.00 in the couples savings account. It will probably take a professional investment advisor to say whether this is true or not.

The Texas Public Retirement System

The retirement plans of all employees of the State of Texas and its political subdivisions are divisible on divorce, using, with few exceptions, the general rules described above. Most State employees, including those working for local governments, are covered by the *Texas Public Retirement System.*

The *Texas Public Retirement System* includes the following:

- The Employee Retirement System of Texas
- The Judicial Retirement System of Texas Plan One
- The Judicial Retirement System of Texas Plan Two
- The Teacher Retirement System of Texas
- The Texas County and District Retirement System
- The Texas Municipal Retirement System
- Any other continuing, organized program of service retirement, disability retirement, or death benefits for officers or employees of the state or a political subdivision or of any agency or instrumentality

of the state of a political subdivision and includes the optional retirement program governed by Chapter 830

Just as with other retirement accounts, divorce courts are deprived of jurisdiction over the Texas Public Retirement System and don't, directly, have power to enforce a QDRO. However, just as with other retirement accounts, if the divorce court's order is in proper form, the retirement system must recognize and enforce the divorce court's ruling or be subjected to its own administrative appeal process, which concludes with an appeal to the Texas court system.

Benefits paid to a divorced spouse of a retiree of the *Texas Public Retirement System* are usually paid on the same terms, at the same time, and in the same form that benefits are paid to the retiree. Moreover, the divorced spouse's benefits will be paid in the form elected by the retiree. For example, if the retiree has an option to have payments made in either a monthly installment annuity or in a lump sum, the choice made by him or her will control the form of payments made to the former spouse. Generally, the public retirement system itself may make its own choice about the form of payments to divorced spouses. The exception to this rule that former spouses are "locked in" to the choice made by either an ex-spouse or the administrators of the public retirement system are the Teacher Retirement System and the Employee Retirement System of Texas, both of which allow the former spouse choice about the form of the payment.

Federal Retirement

The retirement benefits of all Federal employees who reside in the State of Texas are community property and divisible by divorce courts in roughly the same manner as has previously been described. Federal employees may come under one of two retirement systems, the *Civil Service Retirement System* or the *Federal Employees' Retirement System*. Both of these systems are administered by the *Office of Personnel Management*. Payments from these plans payable to a retiree may instead be paid to a divorced spouse of the retiree to the extent ordered by a Texas divorce court. These systems recognize terms included in divorce decrees providing for survivor annuities up to fifty-five percent of the maximum annuity that the retiree could receive.

The *Federal Employees' Retirement System* has an additional layer of benefits known as the *Thrift Savings Plan*, which is a defined contribution plan divisible in much the same way that other defined contribution plans are divisible. The court order used to divide a *Thrift Savings Plan* is called a *qualifying retirement benefits court order.*

Military Retirement

In 1982, Congress passed the Uniformed Services Former Spouses' Protection Act, which allowed Texas courts to divide military retirement in the same way that other community property is divided. In addition, this Act provided an extra remedy for those spouses married to military employees for more than 10 years. These spouses may require the Federal government to make payments of their share of the military retirement directly to them.

Railroad Retirement

In 1983, Congress amended the Railroad Retirement Act to allow division of benefits, except for certain supplementary payments that are roughly equivalent to Social Security. This non-divisible Social Security-like portion of railroad retirement is commonly referred to as "Tier I.." The "Tier II" portion of railroad retirement that is divisible as community property on divorce is based on the retired worker's railroad earnings.

Social Security Benefits

Social Security benefits are not divisible by the divorce court.

Chapter 33

Valuing Community Property

Lack of money is the root of all evil.

—George Bernard Shaw

Knowing community property law, by itself, is not enough for you to obtain a fair division of marital property. No fair division of items between two people can take place without knowledge of the worth of the individual pieces being divided. Likewise, you can't negotiate or plan the prosecution of your divorce case without understanding the relative worth of the various pieces of community property. If your spouse offers to take the house and give you the retirement plan, you cannot know whether this is a good agreement for you until you know how much each is worth, including how much tax you will have to pay when you withdraw money from the retirement plan. Knowledge and proof of values often are the difference between winning and losing in a divorce trial. If your spouse persuades the court to accept inflated values for property awarded to you and unrealistically low values for property being awarded to him or her, this fact alone will skew the property division against you.

Knowing the value of property is not difficult if it is cash in a bank account, regularly traded stocks, or other documents that represent specific dollar amounts and are readily marketable, or if it is an asset that can usually be divided equally or fairly. These are the kind of assets that make division easy for a divorce court.

On the other hand, some property is very difficult to value. For example, it is sometimes difficult to know the worth of real estate, stock in a small company whose stock has never sold, a hardware store, a farm, an insurance agency, a professional practice, manufacturing equipment, a partnership, a boat, an airplane, a fleet of trucks, or any of a thousand things in which people invest their money. An additional problem with these items is that they often cannot be divided without destroying the asset. It's these hard-to-value, indivisible pieces of property that make for hard decisions in a divorce.

The Nature of Divorce – Why Valuation Is Central to the Process

There is a way to avoid all disputes about the value of indivisible community property. Sell it and divide the net cash proceeds from the sale. Judges have the power to order all community assets sold and to divide the sale's proceeds. And parties to a divorce can certainly enter into an agreement to sell all property, split the cash, and start over separately. In fact, it is not unusual to see a court or a divorcing couple decide to sell a single asset that neither party wants or needs and divide the proceeds.

But, by and large, ending a marriage by selling all of the community assets is usually hugely destructive and hurts both spouses. In a forced sale, many essential items sell at wholesale or fire-sale values and have to be replaced at full retail price. Worse, many of life's necessities have no market value. My toothbrush has no market value, but if it were to be taken away I would need to replace it immediately. The same can be said for most items of clothing, household furnishings, many automobiles, much of the equipment and many tools used in professions or trades, and even some real estate and business assets. The bottom line: It's usually not practical or desirable to liquidate community property as a means of division on divorce.

There is yet another way to avoid disputes over the value of indivisible community property, which is to award each divorcing spouse an undivided interest in the property. This allows the divorce parties to continue as joint owners. Occasionally, couples divorcing but otherwise on good terms agree that they will continue as joint owners in a particular piece of property. For example, it is not unusual for a couple to agree that both will retain their interest in their home so that the spouse rearing the children can keep them in the home until they finish school. Usually such agreements have provisions for the home to be sold or one of the spouse's interest to be bought out after the children leave home.

But in most divorces, leaving the spouses as joint owners of property is tantamount to continuing the war long after the divorce is over. The whole idea of divorce is, to the extent possible, stopping the couple's interaction. If a couple has strong enough negative feelings to cause a divorce, continued joint ownership of property is likely to cause conflict. This is why Texas law requires the divorce court to make a just and right *division* of the community property. For this reason divorce courts must have good reasons for leaving a divorced couple as joint owners of even a single piece of property.

So in dividing community property, the divorce court starts off with considerable practical restraint. In the case of an oriental carpet, for example, assume:

- The carpet cannot be torn in half without destroying or diminishing its value.
- The couple cannot be left as joint owners of the carpet.
- If sold in a forced sale by the court, it would bring a reduced price.

This leaves the divorce court with only one practical alternative: divide the community property "in kind" by awarding individual items of property to each party.

Practically speaking, this means that the divorce court must divide property just as you would do it at home on the kitchen table. That is, the court must, so-to-speak, draw a line down the center of a sheet of paper and place individual items of property in one column for one spouse and in the other column for the other spouse. The husband gets the oriental carpet; the wife gets the painting by the famous artist. The husband is awarded the dining room furniture; the wife will receive the living room furniture. Each party is awarded the car he or she is driving, and so on, until all of the community property is in either the husband's or the wife's column.

While the court is not required to divide the property fifty-fifty, no matter what percentage division the court decides upon, if it is to be done fairly or even with some accuracy, it will be necessary for the judge to have some idea of the value of the property. This is where the rubber hits the road in most divorce cases.

It's human nature. If two people know the court is trying to divide property based on a dollar amount by separating individual items, each party is going to want the items that are placed in his or her column to have the lowest value possible. Likewise, each party is going to want the items placed in the other person's column to be given the highest price tag possible. This will ensure that more items end up in "my" column.

This is why, whether you want to or not, you must pay attention to the price tag that is being placed on your community property during the divorce process. If you don't, you will end up with a very small pile of overpriced items, and your ex-spouse will end up with a large pile that he or she acquired at a ridiculously low price.

How Lucy Is Forced to Fight over the Value of Property—Or Lose It

Charlie married Lucy twenty years ago. Neither had any money. After being married a few years, the couple began making widgets in their garage. The widget business took off. Soon the Browns formed a company called Widget, Inc., which is now the most successful manufacturer of widgets in the state. Although the Browns are financially well off, they have come to dislike each other bitterly. Recently, Lucy filed for divorce.

In his first meeting with his lawyer, Charlie tells a sad story of how he worked his fingers to the bone building Widget, Inc., into a powerhouse in the industry, while Lucy passed her time playing bridge at the local country club. He ends this woeful tale by instructing his lawyer that Lucy is not to have "a penny" from Widget, Inc. Why, Charlie demands, should Lucy share his company when he did all the work?

Reluctantly, the lawyer explains the facts of life to Charlie. The stock in Widget, Inc., is community property. There is no evidence that would give the slightest credibility to an argument suggesting that Widget, Inc., is really Charlie's separate property. Charlie's lawyer continues with the bad news. The judge of the court in which the divorce is pending invariably divides community property "right down the middle." And since virtually all of the couple's wealth is represented by the value of the Widget, Inc., stock, it is highly probably that the unworthy Lucy will end up with a substantial portion of the couple's shares in the company.

Charlie is absolutely distraught at this news from his lawyer. This is not what he expects from lawyers. He was referred to this so-called lawyer by the very good law firm that has "always" represented Widget, Inc. That law firm—unlike the lawyer now before him—really knows what they are doing. They are always able to get Charlie what he wants legally. Surely, a "good" lawyer would know how to protect his shares in *his* company. So, he ask his lawyer, "Isn't there *something* that can be done to protect Widget, Inc., from Lucy?" The lawyer responds by asking him many questions about his company and its financial condition.

Finally, Charlie's lawyer tells him, "Maybe there is a way to keep the divorce court from giving Lucy a portion of Widget, Inc. Or, at least, we can minimize the number of shares Lucy ends up with." The lawyer then shares a few ideas. Because the last three years were Widget, Inc.'s worst ever, a plausible argument can be made that Widget, Inc., is no longer worth the millions of dollars reflected in the couple's last financial statement. The financial statement, given two years ago when they built their dream home, reflected Widget, Inc.'s value before its recent decline in profits. Of course, to prove the lawyer's theory, Charlie will need to hire expert business appraisers to work with Widget, Inc.'s accountants to "normalize" the company's accounting records. Then, these experts will testify at the divorce trial about Widget, Inc.'s decline in fortunes that has resulted in its stock being now virtually worthless. Finally, if the court is persuaded that Widget Inc.'s stock really has been overvalued and the value of the stock should be lowered, this changes the whole landscape of property division. Charlie may be able to persuade the judge that a fair division of the community property could be accomplished by awarding Lucy the couple's home and its lavish furnishings, the retirement plan, her automobile, and the country club membership. Charlie would be given his personal possessions and all of the stock in Widget, Inc. In fact, Charlie's lawyer can argue to the judge that Charlie is really being generous with Lucy, because *on paper the assets that Lucy is receiving are worth substantially more than those that would be awarded to Charlie.*

Lucy is outraged by the audacity of Charlie's manipulative attempts to deprive her of her interest in Widget, Inc. "What about the financial statement?"she asks. "Why, just two years ago the Widget, Inc. shares were listed at two and one-half million dollars. In fact, before the divorce was filed, Charlie had always maintained that Widget, Inc., was worth considerably more than the intentionally low figure that the two of them agreed to use on the financial statement. Has Charlie forgotten that she was the one who came up with the idea for the first widget and that she was the one who designed and built the first model?" Charlie's treacherous behavior is a particularly bitter pill for Lucy because she had reluctantly left her management role in the company fifteen years earlier in an attempt to save their marriage. Finally, she solemnly tells her lawyers that she must have a settlement that reflects the "real" value of Widget, Inc.

Lucy decides not to give in to Charlie's "re-valuation tactics." She employs a business appraiser and two accountants to testify that Widget, Inc., is still a valuable company. Working with these experts, her lawyers develop strong evidence that Widget, Inc.'s decline in profitability was caused by Charlie's bad management, which resulted from his spending too much time with his secretary, who has now also become his constant companion.

For his part, Charlie, his legal team, and his experts are more convinced than ever that Widget, Inc., stock was overvalued and that Lucy was just lucky that she received the benefits of the high-income years when it was a highly productive company. They now see Lucy, her legal team, and her experts as unrealistic outsiders who just don't understand the realities of the industry.

This, ladies and gentlemen, is how the battle takes shape in many divorce cases. Whether you want to or not, you may be forced to fight over the price tag on your community property or face the prospect of having it taken away from you. Here, although there was absolutely no question about Lucy having an ownership interest in the Widget, Inc., shares, without defending the price of those shares, she could not defend her legitimate property from loss. Of course, the asset in dispute is not always shares of stock. Nor are disputes about values focused on a single asset. In most divorces, it is absolutely necessary to pay attention to the price tag being placed on the property.

Chapter 34

Taxes

Nothing can be said to be certain,
except death and taxes.

—Benjamin Franklin

The property settlement that you enter into without taking taxes into consideration may be a complete disaster when you get the bill from the government. In terms of dollar amounts, the tax losses or gains of divorce for an average middle-class spouse who fails to "figure in the tax" can approach the value of the car or the equity in the house. For wealthier persons, the difference may be measured in the hundreds of thousands of dollars. But those who would not think of ignoring the car, the house, or any other large assets or liabilities, waltz right past tax benefits and liabilities without giving a second thought.

If you or your spouse have been running a business that requires tax accounting, consulting an accountant or lawyer familiar with taxes is as necessary as consulting a divorce lawyer. If there is already an accountant familiar with your tax situation, paying that accountant to talk with your lawyer is money well spent. The fact that this is the year of your divorce doesn't make your tax problems any less critical. In fact, the decisions you make now can affect your taxes for years to come.

If you are an ordinary middle-class wage earner, make sure you bring up the subject of taxes with your divorce lawyer. Ask whether he or she is willing and able to give you advice about the tax consequences of your divorce. If not, ask for a referral or go see the accountant you already know. Most divorce lawyers are familiar with the tax ramifications of a divorce. But these lawyers are more likely to focus on these matters if you show them that you are in that minority of clients who will listen to their advice on taxes.

Because Texas is a community property state, the application of Internal Revenue Service laws to Texas residents is somewhat different than in other non-community property states. The information given here about taxes will not be accurate for those states.

Responsibility for Reporting Compared with Liability for Payment

While married, you are technically jointly liable for all of your spouse's taxes as well as your own. You will remember from Chapter 31, "The Effect of Divorce on Debt," that the divorce court can only allocate debts between you and your spouse. In that chapter we established that the divorce court cannot affect the rights of a third-party creditor who is not in court. The Internal Revenue Service is a third-party creditor who is not in court on your divorce. There is nothing that the divorce court can do to change that liability. If the IRS forces you to pay more than your fair share of taxes after divorce, your only remedy is to look to your former spouse for reimbursement. If the IRS can't collect from him or her, you may also have some difficulty in getting your money back.

In the year that you divorce, you are liable only for taxes on that portion of your spouse's income that was earned before the date of the divorce.

While married, if you file a separate return, you should report one-half of your income and one-half of your spouse's income on the tax return. Of course, this assumes that you are on good enough terms to exchange financial information. If this is not the case, your problems are greater. If you don't come under one of the exceptions mentioned in the next topic, you just have to do the best you can with what you've got. Usually what you've got is your own financial information and some documentation that your spouse won't cooperate. My suggestion is that, with the assistance of your tax accountant, you report your own income on the return and then write a note to be attached to the return stating that you cannot get the needed information from your spouse to complete the return correctly.

For the year that you are divorced, you report one-half of your own income and one-half of your spouse's income (just as described above) *for that portion of the year before the divorce.* After the divorce, you report only your own income.

Filing Jointly or Separately

The IRS allows you to file a joint return with your spouse or former spouse only if you are married at the close of the tax year. So for the tax year in which your divorce is granted, there is no decision to be made. Each of you will file separate returns.

The question of whether to file joint returns arises when the couple is separated but the divorce is not final, or when the divorce is granted after the close of the tax year but before the tax return is due. A typical example would be a tax year that closes December 31, with the tax return not due until the next April 15 and the couple's divorce set for between those dates on, say, March 1. In this case you may choose to file separately or jointly. If one of you has little or no income, it probably will mean a tax savings if you file jointly. The crunch comes when you find there will be a savings if you file jointly but you don't want to rely on your former spouse. If you can save money by filing jointly, here's the risk:

You are jointly and individually liable with your spouse for the tax on both of your incomes whether you file jointly or separately. This means that if taxes are owed on money earned by your spouse, the IRS can look to you to pay those taxes. Filing separately may not protect you from this liability. However, if your spouse cannot be relied upon to report income and be honest on deductions, you may be risking penalties by signing the return. There is a relief provision in the law for the "innocent spouse." This provision offers some protection even if you file a joint return. This provision applies in cases where one spouse has no knowledge or receives no benefit from income (e.g., embezzlement attributed to the other spouse) and there is a substantial understatement of taxes due. Do not rely on this provision. The burden of proof is on you.

If your spouse or former spouse is the kind of person who is likely not to report income, don't take a chance. File a separate return.

By filing a separate return, you may be able to avail yourself of additional protection. There is a provision that allows a spouse to avoid liability for taxes on the other spouse's income if:

1. The spouse files a separate return
2. At least one of the spouses has earned community income for the year
3. They live apart for the entire year
4. The "abandoned" spouse did not receive any of the income earned by the other spouse

This provision gives broader protection than that offered by the "innocent spouse" provision mentioned above. The innocent spouse provision protects only against liability for fraud or other gross understatement errors on the part of your spouse. This provision also avoids liability for taxes on income that your spouse may have correctly reported but failed to pay.

Exemptions for Dependents

The IRS currently allows a taxpayer to exempt $1,000 for each dependent child the taxpayer supports. After divorce, the question arises as to who gets to claim the dependency exemption for the minor children on the income tax return.

For divorces granted after 1 January 1985, the rule is:

The parent who has custody of a child for the greater part of the year gets the exemption. The only way that the custodial parent can be deprived of the exemption is for him or her to sign a written declaration that he or she will not claim the exemption and attach it to his and her tax returns. By using the proper language, the court probably can order the custodial parent to sign such declaration every year.

Child Support

If you receive money from your spouse or former spouse for child support, you are not liable for tax on these payments. If you pay money to your spouse or former spouse, then you are not entitled to a deduction for these payments. Translated into bottom-line economics, this means that the one who is paying child support must earn more than the child support just to pay child support. For example, if you pay $500 per month child support and you are in a thirty percent income tax bracket, you must earn $650 in order to pay the child support and the tax on the money you earned to pay child support. Actually, it is closer to $695 because you also had to pay taxes on the taxes ($150 x 30%). In addition, you must pay 7% Social Security tax if the income comes from wages. Without becoming obsessed with the math, all of this mean that a spouse must earn over $700 per month in order to pay $500 in child support.

Alimony

Although Texas law provides for only very limited permanent alimony or spousal support, there are IRS provisions controlling taxation of both alimony and "contractual alimony." Accordingly, the IRS rules concerning tax on alimony can become important in Texas.

The rule is:

Alimony payments are taxable to the person who receives them and deductible by the one who pays them if:

1. They are made pursuant to a decree of divorce ordering support or a separation agreement incident to the divorce.
2. The spouse or former spouses are not members of the same household.
3. The payments are in money as opposed to being the transfer of other kinds of property.
4. The decree or agreement does not designate the payment as not includable in the recipient's gross income.
5. They do not extend beyond the death of the person receiving payment (this point will need to be stated explicitly in the decree or agreement).
6. If more than $15,000 is paid in any calendar year, then certain recapture rules may apply.

7. Payments are not made between spouses who file a joint tax return.

Beware: If it appears that payments are made to offset the receiving spouse's interest in community property, then they may not be taxable and deductible as set out in the rule above.

Beware also: This is a technical area that is safest when it is being crossed by a lawyer or accountant who is looking at the current tax laws. If you are in a high tax bracket and your spouse is in a low one, it might benefit you to agree to pay alimony in lieu of child support. It is conceivable that such an arrangement might save both of you some money.

Temporary Alimony

Since alimony is deductible by the person paying it, doesn't this mean that temporary alimony is also deductible?

Probably not. *Remember:* Temporary alimony is usually being paid out of community income. The rule has been that temporary alimony is deductible only to the extent that it exceeds one-half of the community income. This usually isn't the case. Again, if this becomes a close question, consult an accountant.

Property Division

If payments are made by one spouse to the other to equalize a property settlement, or if such payments are ordered by a judge for this purpose, then the spouse receiving such payment does not incur tax liability. The word sometimes used by lawyers for such equalizing is "owelty." It is important that property settlements be worded so that the IRS cannot escape the conclusion that equalization is what is being done.

Equality in the exchange of property between divorcing spouses is not necessary to avoid tax liability. Congress has instructed the IRS to, for the most part, treat divorce as a non-taxable event. If substantial property is involved, attempts to show equality in division still might be wise, pending any new regulations from the IRS.

Afterword

Thoughts on New Beginnings

Freedom is what you do with
what's been done to you.

—Jean-Paul Sartre

This book begins with the first sentence saying, "This is a book about choices." Of course, that first sentence refers to the choices and decisions you confront when facing divorce. But life after divorce is still a series of choices, no less important than those made during the divorce. Perhaps the first critical post-divorce decision is deciding what meaning you will ascribe to your marriage and divorce. Stated another way, how will you choose to think about the part of your life that culminated in divorce? What does your divorce tell you about you and your life? Will you choose to see that part of your life as "wasted"? Will you choose to see yourself as a victim? If so, by whom were you victimized? Your spouse, your marriage, your own immaturity, your parents, or the divorce court? Will you choose to be bitter? Will you spend the rest of your life focusing on who was at fault in the marriage? Will you assume that all members of the opposite sex are untrustworthy? Will you go out of the way to continue the fight with your ex-spouse through your children? Will your divorce be a central part of all of your conversations for years to come? Perhaps the most devastating question is, will you continue to blame yourself for the failure of your marriage? In short, will you continue to live in the past or will you move on?

The answers to these questions and others like them are critical. Our future choices are largely determined, perhaps unconsciously, by our interpretation and view of past events in our lives. Mental health seems to require a balanced view of our own role on the stage of life. If we see ourselves as blameless victims of a world in which we have no control, this absolves us of all responsibility for our own actions. (Whatever happened was somebody else's fault.) Seeing ourselves as wholly responsible and at fault for all of the problems of humankind is equally delusional. (This is sometimes termed as "being over-responsible.")

Standing on the threshold of life-after-divorce, you definitely won't be able to change many of the realities of your life, at least not in the short run. Most external realities, such as the state of your health, the amount of money in your bank account, your social status, your relationship to your family, decisions made by the divorce court, the kind of job you have or don't have, and a whole list of other things, cannot be changed overnight. You may never be able to change some of these things. The reality of life is that, at least in the short term, you may have limited choices about many external realities.

The one thing in life over which we all have huge control is the way we choose to think about things. You can't always control what happens to you, but you can control your attitude toward those events that do happen. This is not some newly discovered theory being pitched by some self-appointed guru. The individual's power to self-adjust his or her own mental and emotional attitudes is one of the eternal verities of the ages; it is a central theme of all major religions and common wisdom found throughout human literature.

Because failure of a marriage and the resulting divorce is likely to be among the most emotionally and mentally wrenching events in life, events like this don't just vanish from the average person's emotional radar. For this reason it is important to give some careful thought about how you are going to think about your divorce. What is the story you are going to tell yourself about why and how your divorce happened? Here are a few short thoughts that just scratch the surface of a very complex subject.

First, forgiveness of past offenses, wrongs, slights, insults, and trespasses is a necessary part of living life in the present and building a life for the future. Forgiveness does not mean being stupid or forgetting information that you need to protect yourself. If someone has failed to repay a debt, has treated you shabbily, beaten you, or otherwise done you harm, you shouldn't loan that person more money, trust him or her with your body or soul, or otherwise make yourself vulnerable. As we have discussed throughout this book, you must establish boundaries to protect yourself and, when necessary, meticulously maintain those boundaries. (That's why we had to get the divorce.) But, protecting yourself by retaining a clear memory does not include bitterly clinging to past events and living for opportunities to retaliate. All ancient wisdom tells us that such bitter resentment and living-for-revenge has a way of boomeranging and turning back on the person who harbors those feelings. Because life is so short and you are your only constant companion, the cost of bitterness and resentment quickly outweighs the benefits. To use the old cliché, "The best revenge is living well."

Second, don't forget the wake-up call provided by your divorce. Divorce, like almost every crisis in life, causes most of us to perform a "reality check." We reconsider and rethink aspects of our lives that we previously took for granted. This is not bad. Awareness of our own misconceptions, even awareness provoked by ugly and painful events, is a good thing. Taking life on as it really is, is not easy. But, living a life of delusions and illusions is, ultimately, self-destructive. Therefore, commit yourself to Reality with a capital "R." Shakespeare's admonition of "To thine own self be true..." may be the most difficult thing on earth to accomplish. Very few of us are really good at sorting out the realities in our own lives from our self-delusions. This lack of clarity about ourselves is the nature of the human predicament. But, just because it's difficult or perhaps even impossible, does not mean that we can avoid making this quest for self-honesty our goal. Searching for "Reality" and self-honesty really is the only sane game in town. To do otherwise is to choose to give up a part of one's own mind, soul, and life.

Self-honesty begins with humility. It is ironic that so many of today's public purveyors who profess to be "speaking the truth," "telling it like it is," or "dealing in reality" are so absolutely certain about everything.

Absolute certainty is the enemy of human efforts to seek truth and reality because it leaves no room for us to question our own perceptions, our information, or our reasoning. Certainty presumes that we can reduce the risk of our decisions to zero. Certainty presumes that we are making our decisions from the vantage point of the gods, with a clear view of the universe as it is. This is simply not the case. Our human view of life, especially our own lives, is murky, to say the least. Shakespeare's Macbeth, in a moment of despair, says, "Life's…a tale told by an idiot, full of sound and fury, signifying nothing." Although this probably overstates our difficulties in evaluating the world on most days, anyone who lives long enough eventually has those moments that seem to make Macbeth prophetic. No, we should not give up firmly holding opinions and making strong commitments. But we should always leave a little room for doubt, even in those choices and decisions involving friends, families, lovers, and, even our lives and sacred honor. Even if we learn this from divorce or some other harsh experience in life, it's still a good thing to know.

Third, divorce teaches us that not all of our blessings come from the things we want or think we want. Take, for example, that person we thought we "just had to marry." Sometimes the things we "just must have" turn out to be complete disasters. Likewise, some of the things we do not want, resist, or even dread turn out to be the things that make life worth living. An easy example for most of us who enjoy our work might be the experience of being forced to get a job rather than live on the French Riviera. For some who dreaded divorce, the divorce turned out to be the pivotal positive event that allowed them to regain sanity and find happiness.

In a word, we need to learn to be thankful for our past life as it was and not as we think we wanted it to be. Of course, this outrageous idea of being thankful for what has happened means that we would need to be thankful for knowledge and experience gained from our obnoxious ex-spouse. Likewise, it means being thankful for knowledge gained from pain we suffered and even pain we caused. We would have to accept our own past misjudgments and mistakes.

I usually don't talk about being thankful for the bad things that have happened in life to people who are nearby. It's an idea that can provoke anger and physical violence. Being thankful for an imperfect life somehow seems un-American. Weren't we suppose to live the perfect life our parents conceived for us? But it's not to be, and it never was or could be in the world we live in.

It doesn't mean that you and I don't have regrets. I'm always amazed at those people who say that if they had their lives to live over, they would do everything the same way. Not me! If I had known then what I know now, I would have done many things differently. But that's the point; when we were younger and "stupider," we did not know. We could not have possibly known. Unlike Macbeth, we didn't even understand the basic rules of the game that we were about to play.

Yes, we are responsible for our past lives, but responsible in the context of someone who lives as a human and not as a god. All of this circles around to forgiving ourselves for not living the perfect lives we think we would live if we could do it over with what we now know.

But, hold on just a minute! Doesn't this leave out humility? Even if you could live your life again, how do you know that knowing what you know now, you wouldn't botch it up worse than you did the first time? Don't be too certain! Remember how certain you were about some of those decisions the first time? Knowing what you know now, you still have to live the rest of your life as best you can. Living your life from here on out in the best way possible is a pretty tall order and a high calling. Doing a good job of living in the present might not leave much time or energy to second-guess yourself about how you should have lived in the past. So, don't let dwelling on the past steal from you the most precious thing in life: the present moment.

Index